International Arbitration Law Library

VOLUME 44

Editor

Professor Julian D.M. Lew QC has been involved with international arbitration for more than 40 years as counsel, as arbitrator and as an academic. He has held the position of Professor and Head of the School on International Arbitration, Centre for Commercial Law studies, Queen Mary University of London since its creation in 1985. He is now an independent arbitrator at 20 Essex Street, London.

Introduction

Since its first volume published in 1993, this authoritative practitioner-oriented series has published in-depth and analytical works on niche aspects of international arbitration, authored by specialists in the field.

Objective

This authoritative and established series covering in-depth analyses of niche areas appeals to both practitioners and academics.

Frequency

A volume is published whenever an interesting topic presents itself.

The titles published in this series are listed at the end of this volume.

The Notion of Award in International Commercial Arbitration

A Comparative Analysis of French Law, English Law, and the UNCITRAL Model Law

Giacomo Marchisio

Published by:
Kluwer Law International B.V.
PO Box 316
2400 AH Alphen aan den Rijn
The Netherlands
Website: www.wolterskluwerlr.com

Sold and distributed in North, Central and South America by:
Wolters Kluwer Legal & Regulatory U.S.
7201 McKinney Circle
Frederick, MD 21704
United States of America
Email: customer.service@wolterskluwer.com

Sold and distributed in all other countries by:
Quadrant
Rockwood House
Haywards Heath
West Sussex
RH16 3DH
United Kingdom
Email: international-customerservice@wolterskluwer.com

Printed on acid-free paper.

ISBN 978-90-411-8391-0

e-Book: ISBN 978-90-411-8392-7
web-PDF: ISBN 978-90-411-8393-4

© 2017 Kluwer Law International BV, The Netherlands

All rights reserved. No part of this publication may be reproduced, stored in a retrieval system, or transmitted in any form or by any means, electronic, mechanical, photocopying, recording, or otherwise, without written permission from the publisher.

Permission to use this content must be obtained from the copyright owner. Please apply to: Permissions Department, Wolters Kluwer Legal & Regulatory U.S., 76 Ninth Avenue, 7th Floor, New York, NY 10011-5201, USA. Website: www.wolterskluwerlr.com

Printed in the United Kingdom.

About the Author

Giacomo Marchisio is a Research Associate at McGill University's Faculty of Law, where he conducts research in the fields of comparative civil procedure, international arbitration, and contract law. He holds a doctoral degree and an LLM from McGill University, and a law degree from the Università degli studi di Torino. Dr Marchisio is the Academic Coordinator of the Private Justice and the Rule of Law Research Group at McGill University, and the former Editor-in-chief of the McGill Journal of Dispute Resolution. He is a member of the ICC Task Force on emergency arbitration, and of the Canadian Committee of the ICC.

This book is based on a condensed and updated version of a doctoral thesis carried out at McGill University.

Table of Contents

About the Author	v
Foreword	xi
Preface	xiii
Acknowledgements	xv

CHAPTER 1
Introduction 1
§1.01 The Issue: Uncertainties Regarding the Definition of Arbitral Award 1
§1.02 Theory and Methodology 4
§1.03 Scope and Limitations 8
§1.04 Structure and Summary of the Analysis 10

CHAPTER 2
Diverging Understandings of Arbitration 13
§2.01 Introduction 13
§2.02 Overview of the Monodimensional Model: The Arbitrator Resolves a Dispute in a Final Manner 15
§2.03 Overview of the Multidimensional Model: The Arbitrator Renders Justice 17
§2.04 The Silence of the New York Convention 20
§2.05 Conclusion 23

CHAPTER 3
The Influence of Arbitral Institutions on Today's International Commercial Arbitration 25
§3.01 Introduction 25
§3.02 A Theoretical Overview of Institutionalism 26

Table of Contents

§3.03	Arbitration in the Nineteenth Century: A Weak Competitor of State Justice	28
§3.04	Arbitration in the First Half of the Twentieth Century: The Rise after Institutionalization	30
	[A] A Historical Overview of the ICC	31
	[B] The ICC's Impetus in Favour of Arbitration	33
	[C] The ICC's Difficulties Implementing International Commercial Arbitration	35
§3.05	Arbitration in the Second Half of the Twentieth Century: The ICC's Success in Creating an Effective International Regime	38
§3.06	Arbitration at the Beginning of the Twenty-First Century: The Consecration of Institutions	41
	[A] Further Actors Contributing to Institutionalization: An Overview	41
	[B] The Privatization of Justice as an Important Motor of Arbitration's Institutionalization	43
§3.07	The Consequences of the Institutional Roots of International Commercial Arbitration	46
§3.08	Conclusion	49

CHAPTER 4
Contentious Awards 51

§4.01	Introduction	51
§4.02	The Notion of Contentious Judgment in Western Law	52
	[A] Historical Inceptions	52
	[1] Classic Roman Procedure and the Absence of *Ius Dicere*	53
	[2] The *Extra Cognitio* and the Emergence of *Ius Dicere*	55
	[B] Contemporary Epiphanies: The Purpose(s) of Judgments	56
	[C] The Effects of Judgments	59
§4.03	The Notion of Contentious Award in National Arbitration Acts	61
	[A] The Scope of the Enquiry	61
	[B] France	61
	[1] Formal Requirements	62
	[2] The Substantive Requirements	65
	[C] England	70
	[1] Formal Requirements	71
	[2] Substantive Requirements	73
§4.04	The Notion of Contentious Award in Arbitral Practice	82
§4.05	Conclusion	84

CHAPTER 5
Jurisdictional Awards 87

§5.01	Introduction	87
§5.02	A Comparative Overview of the Role of State Courts in the Pre-award Phase	90

		[A]	France	90
		[B]	England	92
		[C]	Allocation of Jurisdiction and Arbitral Practice: The Issue of Bifurcation	94
§5.03	Jurisdictional Decisions Can Take the Form of Awards and Are Thus Enforceable			97
	[A]	The Romano-Canonical and Common Law Traditions on Jurisdictional Rulings		97
		[1]	The Romano-Canonical Perspective	97
		[2]	The Common Law Perspective	98
	[B]	Positive Jurisdictional Rulings Are Enforceable Awards: The Convergence of French and English Law		99
	[C]	Negative Jurisdictional Rulings Can Be Enforced as Awards		101
		[1]	Negative Jurisdictional Rulings Are Not Awards: An Out-dated Conception	102
		[2]	Negative Jurisdictional Rulings Are Enforceable Awards	103
	[D]	The Peculiarities of the Recourse under Article 16(3) of the *Model Law*		105
§5.04	Conclusion			107

CHAPTER 6
Consent Awards 109
§6.01 Introduction 109
§6.02 The Award by Consent in ICC Arbitration 110
§6.03 The Award by Consent and the UNCITRAL *Model Law* on International Commercial Arbitration 114
§6.04 Consent Awards in England 118
 [A] The National Framework 118
 [B] Consent Awards under the *Arbitration Act 1996* 121
  [1] The Role of the Arbitrators 121
  [2] Challenges 122
  [3] Enforcement 127
§6.05 Consent Awards in France 128
 [A] The National Legal Framework 128
  [1] *Contrat de Transaction* 128
  [2] *Jugement sur accord des Parties* 130
 [B] Consent Awards under French Arbitration Law 131
  [1] Only International or Foreign Consent Awards Can Be Enforced in France? 131
  [2] Alternatives in Light of the Lack of Enforcement of Domestic Consent Awards 134
  [3] Challenges to Domestic Consent Awards 137
§6.06 Conclusion 137

Table of Contents

CHAPTER 7
Awards *Ante Causam* 141
§7.01 Introduction 141
§7.02 Provisional Measures in the Romano-Canonical and Common Law Traditions 143
§7.03 Provisional Protection *Ante Causam* and the Interplays Between Courts and Arbitrators 144
    [A] Courts' Jurisdiction on Provisional Measures Before the Constitution of the Tribunal 144
    [B] The Principle of Complementarity in French and English Arbitration Law 145
§7.04 The Emergence of a Provisional Adjudicatory Power *Ante Causam* 151
    [A] The Precursor: The *International Arbitration Rules* of the ICDR 151
    [B] The *Arbitration Rules* of the SCC: A Relief That Is Truly *Ante Causam* 152
    [C] The 2014 *Arbitration Rules* of the LCIA 154
    [D] The *Arbitration Rules* of the International Court of Arbitration (ICC): A Missed Opportunity? 157
        [1] Exclusion of Emergency Arbitration 158
        [2] Emergency Arbitration Application and Proceedings 159
        [3] The Emergency Arbitration Decision 163
        [4] The Effects of the Emergency Arbitration Decision on the Arbitration Proceedings 164
        [5] The Interplays with State Courts 165
§7.05 The Nature and Enforcement of Emergency Decisions: The 2006 Amendments to The UNCITRAL *Model Law* 165
§7.06 Conclusion 173

CHAPTER 8
Conclusion: The Need for a Non-unitary Notion of Award 175

Bibliography 185

Table of Cases 197

International Tribunals and Arbitral Tribunals 201

Conventions 203

Index 205

Foreword

From a sociological perspective, international commercial arbitration may be viewed as a semi-autonomous social field constituted by the practices and understandings of the actors who participate in and influence the private adjudication of international commercial disputes. From a legal perspective, those practices and their interpretation define the field by shaping the key legal notions that distinguish and situate arbitration within the broader universe of law. Notably, the legal notions in question guide and in time determine the important relationship between arbitration and national legal systems and their courts.

There are three closely related legal notions that define the field: arbitration, arbitrator, and arbitral award. This important work of Giacomo Marchisio adopts a McGillian, transnational approach to legal inquiry. Although presented in the English language and clearly influenced by the pragmatism associated with the English legal tradition, his work follows naturally from, and usefully builds upon, the French tradition of fundamental theorizing about arbitration. After the immensely influential work of Charles Jarrosson on the notion of arbitration and the brilliant and encyclopaedic treatment of the notion of arbitrator by Thomas Clay, this book is poised to become an international reference on the notion of arbitral award.

This study comes at a key moment in the development of international arbitration practice. This is because the recent adoption of emergency arbitration provisions by all of the significant commercial arbitration institutions has made the notion of arbitral award and its pivotal role in determining the enforceability of decisions a focus of renewed concern. This has served to highlight the fact that, although the New York Convention and the UNCITRAL *Model Law* give the impression of a near-universal, common understanding of 'award' (after all, their enforcement provisions turn in key respects on that notion), one need only scratch the surface to reveal the absence of such common understanding. This is a serious issue not only in the theoretical terms that define the social field of arbitration, but also in the legal and very practical terms of determining which decisions are enforceable under the relevant international instruments.

Mr Marchisio takes us through the difficulties of defining the arbitral award through a study of three kinds of decision that can be viewed as borderline cases:

xi

decisions on competence, awards by consent, and awards *ante causam* (with emphasis on emergency arbitrator decisions). The comparison of English Law, French Law and the UNCITRAL *Model Law* is enlightening for each of these borderline cases, highlighting for each of them the contrasting models he uses to help show the way forward: a monodimensional model of the award in which the arbitrator resolves a dispute in a final manner, and a multidimensional model of the award in which the arbitrator renders justice. This builds on the first chapter of the book where a persuasive account of the evolution of arbitration from the beginning of the twentieth century to the beginning of the twenty-first century lays the table for what follows. The undeniable institutionalization of arbitration, it is shown, naturally begs for a notion of award that is capable of accommodating the various kinds of decisions actually made by arbitrators who are increasingly expected to render justice by deploying the broad range of tools available to state judges.

The course taken by Mr Marchisio is not an easy one to steer. By broadening the range of decisions that may be characterized as awards, one faces the constant danger of swallowing up – and thus subjecting to judicial review – the countless procedural decisions that make arbitration run smoothly on a day-to-day basis. Having all procedural orders subject to review because they now fall under a broader definition of award would quickly sound the death knell of arbitration. Mr Marchisio, skilfully steers the course toward a tentative notion of arbitral award that guides us, I believe, in the right direction. He does so with a rare combination of theoretical awareness and attention to the requirements and self-understandings of arbitral practice. It is this salutary combination that makes this work an important piece in the ongoing construction of the field that is international commercial arbitration.

Prof. Fabien Gélinas
Sir William C. Macdonald Professor of Law
McGill University, Canada

Preface

Devoting an entire book to the notion of arbitral award may come across as an otiose exercise. Some will wonder – is there anything we don't already know about awards? As a matter of fact, we know very little. Even the most venerated arbitration treatises take dogmatic positions, providing mere overviews of the concept. Such a lack of interest can be regarded as a consequence of scholars' excessive emphasis on the contractual aspects of international commercial arbitration, to the detriment of its procedural components. The neglect of the procedural dimension of international commercial arbitration has somehow survived the numerous developments that have led to an increasingly sophisticated arbitral procedure.

In general, a silent tension can be observed in the field. Since the effectiveness of arbitral decisions depends on their enforceability, there is a tendency to place the label of award on heterogeneous decisions with a view to ensuring their enforcement. This is so because, contrarily to the decisions rendered by state courts, whose enforcement can be guaranteed regardless of the form that they take (be it an order, an injunction, or a final judgment), arbitral decisions will generally be enforced only if they amount to awards. There is more. Not only is the notion of award crucial for practical purposes (i.e., it allows one to predict which arbitral decisions will be enforced by state courts), but also for theoretical ones. By reflecting on arbitral awards, new light can be shed on our understanding of the adjudicative powers of arbitral tribunals. As pointed out below, the notion of award provides a useful reflection of how arbitral justice operates, indicating the extent of its role vis-à-vis public justice.

Acknowledgements

I am immensely grateful to Professor Fabien Gélinas for his precious guidance throughout my doctoral studies. I feel privileged to have had the chance of observing his scholarly finesse and infinite patience. I am also profoundly indebted to Professor Frédéric Bachand, from whom I learned countless things on civil procedure, many of which I thought I already knew. Likewise, I wish to thank the members of my doctoral committee, Professors Andrea Bjorklund and Vincent Forray, for their advice and support.

The drafting of this book would not have been possible without the immense support of my family, and my dearest Éloïse. Every day, I remind myself of how blessed I am to have them in my life.

– *'e il naufragar m'è dolce in questo mare'*.

CHAPTER 1

Introduction

§1.01 THE ISSUE: UNCERTAINTIES REGARDING THE DEFINITION OF ARBITRAL AWARD

The work and research relating to the present book started from a banal observation: international commercial arbitration literature has not been able, so far, to generate a comprehensive and satisfying analysis of the notion of arbitral award.[1] With a few exceptions,[2] there are virtually no contributions on the topic.[3] At the same time, given the controversial nature of the notion of award, some of the most important arbitration treatises merely provide short overviews of the concept. Gary Born, for instance, limits his study to a summary description and classification of awards.[4] Gaillard and Savage's treatise is also instructive on this point.[5] After noting the lack of consensus on this notion, the authors dogmatically conclude that an award is 'a final decision by the arbitrators on all or part of the dispute submitted to them, whether it concerns the merits ..., jurisdiction, or a procedural issue leading them to end proceedings.'[6] Conversely, Redfern and Hunter endorse a stricter definition, according to which 'the

---

1. Alan Redfern et al., *Redfern & Hunter on International Commercial Arbitration*, para. 9.05 (Oxford University Press 2015) ('There is no internationally accepted definition of the term "award". Indeed, no definition is to be found in the main international conventions dealing with arbitration, including the Geneva treaties, the New York Convention, and the *Model Law*').
2. Jean-François Poudret & Sébastien Besson, *Comparative Law of International Arbitration*, 631 (Sweet & Maxwell 2007).
3. Few articles have appeared on the matter. *See*, e.g., Jacques Pellerin, *La sentence arbitrale: incertitudes et propositions* in *Mélanges Mayer* 679 (LGDJ 2015); Jennifer Kirby, *What Is an Award, Anyway?* 31:4 JOIA 475 (2014); Philipp Peters & Christian Koller, *The Award and the Courts – The Notion of Arbitral Award: An Attempt to Overcome a Babylonian Confusion* in Christian Klausegger et al., *Austrian Yearbook on International Arbitration* 137 (Manz'sche Verlags 2010).
4. Gary Born, *International Commercial Arbitration*, 3012 (Kluwer Law 2014).
5. Emmanuel Gaillard & John Savage, *Fouchard Gaillard Goldman on International Commercial Arbitration*, 735 (Kluwer Law 1999).
6. *Ibid.* at 737.

1

term "award" should generally be reserved for decisions that finally determine the substantive issues with which they deal'.[7] This is as far as the most venerated literature is willing to go, showing self-restraint and caution. Most often, in fact, the notion of award is treated incidentally, when matters such as enforcement or annulment proceedings are considered.[8] The neglect of arbitral awards has two distinct explanations.

First, it is a direct consequence of the emphasis placed on arbitration's contractual dimension, which tends to reduce the arbitral process to a contractual phenomenon,[9] allowed and sustained by national legislators (the so-called contractual theory).[10] In this context, the award would merely amount to the performance of the arbitrator's contractual duties and would acquire the status of a judicial-like decision only with its recognition by a national legal order.[11] In recent years, however, the focus on the contractual dimension of arbitration has been greatly tempered by Emmanuel Gaillard's theory of an autonomous arbitral legal order.[12] His work has allowed scholars to look at arbitration as a system of justice and not only as a private (contractual) phenomenon, creepingly surviving under the shadow of the States. At the same time, the flourishing of forum selection clauses in private international law has also made clear that, while the element of consent may be a prerequisite for submitting a claim to a certain jurisdiction, it does not entail that the subsequent proceedings will necessarily have a contractual nature.[13]

---

7. Redfern, *supra* n. 1, at para. 9.08.
8. *See* e.g., Christopher Liebscher, *Article V(1)(e)* in Reinmar Wolff, *The New York Convention* 356 (Hart Publishing 2012); Dirk Otto, *Article IV* in Herbert Kronke et al., *Enforcement of Foreign Arbitral Awards: A Global Commentary on the New York Convention* 150 (Kluwer Law 2010); Christopher Liebscher, *The Healthy Award*, 137 (Kluwer Law 2003).
9. On the non-adjudicative nature of arbitral awards, *see* Daniel Levy, *Les abus de l'arbitrage commercial international*, 174 (L'Harmanattan 2015); Florian Grisel, *L'arbitrage international ou le droit contre l'ordre juridique*, 124 (LGDJ 2011).
10. Redfern, *supra* n. 1, at para. 1.08 ('[The] emphasis on the [principle of] "autonomy of the parties" might suggest that parties and arbitrators inhabit a private universe of their own. But this is not so. In reality, the practice of resolving disputes by the essentially private process of international arbitration works effectively only because it is supported by a complex public system of national laws and international treaties. Even a comparatively simple international arbitration may require reference to at least four different national systems of law, which in turn may be derived from an international treaty or convention – or indeed from the UNCITRAL *Model Law* itself').
11. Sylvain Bollée, *Les méthodes du droit international privé à l'épreuve des sentences arbitrales*, 38 (Economica 2004). *See also* Pierre Mayer & Vincent Heuze, *Droit international privé*, 520 (Montchrestien 2007).
12. Emmanuel Gaillard, *Legal Theory of International Arbitration*, 35 (Martinus Nijhoff 2010) [Gaillard, *Legal Theory*]. Cf. Julian D.M. Lew, *Achieving the Dream: Autonomous Arbitration* in Julian D.M. Lew & Loukas A. Mistelis, *Arbitration Insights* 455, 464–465 (Kluwer Law 2007).
13. *Convention of 30 June 2005 on Choice of Court Agreements*, entered into force on 1 October 2015, 44 ILM 1291 (2005) [*Hague Convention*]. *See* Art. 5(1) ('The court or courts of a Contracting State designated in an exclusive choice of court agreement shall have jurisdiction to decide a dispute to which the agreement applies, unless the agreement is null and void under the law of that State'). For a commentary, *see* Ronald A. Brand & Paul M. Herrup, *The Hague Convention on Choice of Court Agreements* (Cambridge University Press 2008). *See also* Paul Beaumont, *Hague Choice of Court Agreements Convention 2005: Background, Negotiations, Analysis and Current Status*, 5:1 J Priv Int'l L 125 (2009); Andrea Schulz, *The 2005 Hague Convention on Choice of*

Second, the neglect of arbitral awards has been caused by the very literature that aimed to consecrate their importance by emphasizing the adjudicative nature of arbitration (the so-called adjudicative theory). In particular, I am referring to works of Henri Motulsky,[14] Bruno Oppetit,[15] Charles Jarrosson,[16] and Antoine Kassis.[17] According to these scholars, the adjudicative role of an arbitral tribunal is ultimately tied to its power to issue a final decision resolving a dispute between the parties (*mission juridictionnelle*).[18] The arbitrator, in light of the contract that he or she has entered with the parties, performs a duty that transforms him or her into a private judge;[19] as such, arbitral awards should look more or less like the final judgments[20] rendered by judges in fulfilment of their main duty.

The main problem with the above theory is that it relies on an out-dated paradigm of adjudication, which considers the rendering of *contentious* judgments (i.e., decisions resolving disputes in a final manner) to be the sole function of an adjudicator. This understanding obscures important aspects of the exercise of adjudicative functions, which are not limited to the resolution of a dispute between the parties and instead cover a range of ancillary functions that are indispensable to the administration of justice.[21] The above authors, Oppetit, Jarrosson, and Kassis, were relying on the theory of *acte juridictionnel*, which is no longer helpful in defining today's adjudication, especially in light of drastic changes that have affected state justice and the notion of civil litigation.[22] Since the 1970s, with the emergence of the welfare state, the function of adjudicating has expanded beyond the classic notions of *acte juridictionnel*[23] and of *intérêt à agir* (standing). We have witnessed the emergence and increasing use of a plethora of special proceedings, either extending the notion of standing – as in the case of class actions – or eroding those of trial and judgment – as in the case, for example, of pre-trial proceedings, injunctions, or summary judgments. Likewise, international arbitration has greatly changed over the last forty years, becoming an often-chosen mechanism to deal with disputes over complex international transactions involving multiple parties. What remains to be done is to reconsider our conception of arbitration in light of these social changes, which have brought about an expansion of the types of decisions rendered by state courts and, in turn, by arbitrators.

Court Clauses, 12 J Int'l & Comp L 433 (2006); Louise Ellen Teitz, *The Hague Choice of Court Convention: Validating Party Autonomy and Providing an Alternative to Arbitration*, 53:3 Am J Comp L 543 (2005).
14. Henri Motulsky, *Écrits – études et notes sur l'arbitrage*, 6 (Dalloz 1976) ('L'arbitrage est une justice privée, dont l'origine est normalement conventionnelle. ... La mission de l'arbitre est exactement la même que celle du juge').
15. Bruno Oppetit, *Théorie de l'arbitrage*, 217 (Dalloz 1998).
16. Charles Jarrosson, *La notion d'arbitrage*, 101 (LGDJ 1987).
17. Antoine Kassis, *Problèmes de base de l'arbitrage*, 27 (LGDJ 1987).
18. Jean Robert, *L'arbitrage*, 170 (Dalloz 1993).
19. Jarrosson, *supra* n. 16, at 101.
20. Robert, *supra* n. 18, at 170 ('La sentence constitue l'aboutissement de la procédure d'arbitrage').
21. *See* Louis Marquis, *Droit de la prévention et du règlement des différends*, 144 (Les Éditions de la Revue de Droit 2015).
22. Serge Guinchard et al., *Procédure civile*, 717 (Dalloz 2014).
23. *Ibid*.

In light of the above, the present work will take a fresh look at the notion of award, by placing it in a broader context, that of the contemporary evolution of adjudication. To do so, I will employ a sociological and comparative methodology, which offers an analysis of arbitration in terms of an institution administering justice rather than as a purely contractual creature.

§1.02 THEORY AND METHODOLOGY

In recent years, the literature on international commercial arbitration has made increasing use of the term 'judicialization'. In political science, the field from which the term was borrowed, judicialization refers to 'the process by which non-judicial negotiating and decision-making *fora* come to be dominated by quasi-judicial (legalistic) rules and procedures'.[24] In this field, the concept has been used to explain the judicialization of politics and the concurrent expansion of the judicial powers of state (and non-state) litigation *fora*. A major example of judicialization, in this context, can be found in the expansion of constitutional litigation.[25] At the international level, the term has been employed to indicate the significant increase in specialized international adjudicative bodies for the resolution of investment law disputes or the prosecution of human rights violations.[26] Taking a closer look at the process of judicialization in private matters (such as commercial cases and other private law disputes), Alec Stone Sweet has defined judicialization as the construction of legitimacy by a third party in a position of authority vis-à-vis two litigants.[27]

Interestingly, the judicialization of private justice can be contrasted with the process of contractualization of public justice. Contractualization refers to the trend toward leading parties to agree on most of the aspects of a civil trial, so as to implement a cooperative approach favouring a non-adversarial attitude, and encouraging them to enter contractual agreements for the settlement of their disputes.[28] Therefore, it can be noticed that at the same time as, on the one hand, private justice tends to become a

---

24. Neal C. Tale, *Why the Expansion of Judicial Power?* in Neal C. Tale & Torbjörn Vallinder, *The Global Expansion of Judicial Power* 26, 28 (New York University Press 1995).
25. Neal C. Tale & Torbjörn Vallinder, *Judicialization and the Future of Politics and Policy* in Tale & Vallinder, *supra* n. 24, 515, 516 ff.
26. Cesare Romano, *The Shadow Zones of International Adjudication* in Cesare Romano et al., *The Oxford Handbook of International Adjudication* 90, 104 (Oxford University Press 2013). *See also* Karen Alter, *New Terrain of International Law: Courts, Politics, Rights*, 335 (Princeton University Press 2014) ('Judicialization occurs where citizens, organizations, and firms see law as conferring upon them rights, and where politicians conceive of their policy and legislative options as bounded by what is legally allowed. Where judges have jurisdiction and litigation becomes a useful way to reopen political agreements, negotiations among actors become debates about what is legally permissible, and politics takes place in the shadow of courts with the lurking possibility of litigation shaping actor demands and political outcomes').
27. Alec Stone Sweet, *Judicialization and the Construction of Governance* in Martin Shapiro & Alec Stone Sweet, *On Law, Politics, and Judicialization* 55, 71 (Oxford University Press 2002) ('The "judicialization of dispute resolution" is the process through which a [triadic dispute resolution] mechanism appears, stabilizes, and develops authority over the normative structure governing exchange in a given community').
28. Loïc Cadiet, Jacques Normand & Soraya Amrani Mekki, *Théorie générale du procès*, 213 ff. (PUF 2013) [Cadiet et al., *Théorie générale*].

'public' matter, on the other hand, public justice aspires to transform itself into a 'private' matter.

Be that as it may, in international arbitration, the term 'judicialization' has been used in the most disparate ways. Sometimes, it is seen in a group of critiques concerning the excessive duration of arbitral proceedings and their increasing complexity.[29] In this case, the term is used with a negative connotation: the judicialization of international commercial arbitration would turn this alternative method of dispute resolution into a slow and expensive process. Such an occurrence would put at risk the very existence of arbitration, once an idyllic, fast and simple procedure.[30] Yet 'judicialization' is also used to emphasize the adjudicative power of arbitrators. In this sense, the term is used to underline that arbitration is not purely a private endeavour stemming from a contractual agreement reached by the parties, but also the expression of a broader goal: the administration of civil justice.[31] In this context, judicialization refers to the similarities between arbitral justice and state justice, united in their effort to maintain social cohesion.[32] This is the meaning of judicialization that I will adopt in the present work, as well as the key concept that will allow me to consider how arbitral adjudication is structured and how the notion of arbitral award can be outlined.

To examine this concept, I will rely on two different theoretical approaches. The first is a sociological analysis of arbitration and, more specifically, a historically grounded one,[33] and the second is a comparative analysis. The sociological approach consists in a historical analysis of the foundational traits of contemporary international

---

29. See Rémy Gerbay, *Is the End Nigh Again? An Empirical Assessment of the Judicialization of International Arbitration*, 25 Am Rev of Int'l Arb 223, 230 (2014) ('[judicialization is] a phenomenon by which international arbitration procedure increasingly resembles domestic litigation, as a result of an increase in procedural formality/sophistication and litigiousness'); *See also* Günther J. Horvath, *The Judicialization of International Arbitration* in Stephan Kröll et al., *Liber Amicorum Eric Bergsten-International Arbitration and International Commercial Law* 251, 259 (Kluwer Law 2011); Artur W. Rovine, *Fast-Track Arbitration: A Step Away From Judicialization of International Arbitration* in Richard B. Lillich & Charles N. Brower, *International Arbitration in the 21st Century: Towards 'Judicialization' and Uniformity?* 45, 49 (New York: Transnational Publishers 1994).
30. *See* Giorgio Bernini, *Flexibility or Rigidity?* in Lew & Mistelis, *supra* n. 12, 47, 49; Klaus Sachs, *Time and Money: Cost Control and Effective Case Management* in Loukas A. Mistelis & Julian D.M. Lew, *Pervasive Problems in International Arbitration* 103, 112 (Kluwer Law 2006).
31. Cf. Andrea Marco Steingruber, *Consent in International Arbitration*, 329 (Oxford University Press 2012) ('Arbitration should be reconciled with its jurisdictional side, which is as important and practically relevant as its contractual nature ... as it is not fully settled whether arbitration is of a contractual, jurisdictional, or mixed nature, one should not unduly favour the contractual side over the jurisdictional element').
32. Alec Stone Sweet & Florian Grisel, *The Evolution of International Arbitration: Delegation, Judicialization, Governance* in Walter Mattli & Thomas Dietz, *International Arbitration and Global Governance: Contending Theories and Evidence* 22, 32 (Oxford University Press 2014).
33. *See* James Crawford, *Continuity and Discontinuity in International Dispute Settlement*, 1:1 J Int'l Disp Sett'l 3, 24 (2010) ('first, we must avoid thinking that all our bright ideas are new ideas, for sometimes their roots are to be found deep in the historical experience of international law; second, we must try to achieve a historical understanding of our own activities, for only in such a way we will be able to fully comprehend them – and, it may be, advance beyond them'). On the sociological approach, more generally, *see* Michael Freeman, *Law and Sociology* in Michael Freeman, ed., *Law and Sociology*, 1, 15 (Oxford University Press 2006); Roger Cotterrell, *From Living Law to the Death of Social–Sociology in Legal Theory* in Michael Freeman, *Law and Sociology* 16, 31 (Oxford University Press 2006).

commercial arbitration and, in particular, an analysis of the history of the institution that has had the most significant impact on its evolution, that is, the Court of Arbitration of the International Chamber of Commerce (ICC). As I shall explain in Chapter 2, the term 'institution' is here understood to refer to an ensemble of regulative and cognitive elements for ordering society. The analysis will suggest that international commercial arbitration is greatly influenced by institutions of this kind.[34] As a result, in order to apprehend the notion of award, one has to look at how the adjudicative power of arbitrators is shaped by such institutions. It is worth noting that the importance of this institutional setting is valid both with respect to administered and ad hoc arbitration. While in administered arbitration, the institutional setting is that of the arbitral centre administering the case, in ad hoc arbitration it will be constituted by the state court overseeing arbitral proceedings[35] and (where applicable) the arbitration rules chosen by the parties (e.g., the 2010 United Nations Commission on International Trade Law (UNCITRAL) *Arbitration Rules*).[36] In this respect, scholars have highlighted–and sometimes, criticized–[37]the role of UNCITRAL and its *Arbitration Rules* in the institutionalization of ad hoc arbitration.[38] These rules, in fact, not only provide for predetermined regulation of arbitral proceedings but also require support, in often cases, from an arbitral institution to ensure their application. It is not infrequent, therefore, that parties to an ad hoc arbitration clause will require an arbitral institution to administer their arbitration within the boundaries set by the ad hoc rules on which they have agreed.[39]

Despite its broad approach, an institutional analysis focusing on arbitral centres has some shortcomings. Essentially, it tends to neglect the role of important players, namely States. These latter entities, in fact, also contribute greatly to the preservation of an effective system of arbitral justice. In order to integrate such an important factor

---

34. Rémy Gerbay, *The Functions of Arbitral Institutions*, 46 and 184 ff. (Kluwer Law 2016).
35. Anne Véronique Schläpher & Angelina Petti, *Institutional v. Ad Hoc Arbitration* in Nathalie Voser & Elliott Geinsinger, *International Arbitration in Switzerland* 13, 14–15 (Kluwer Law 2013) ('A local court may be called upon to assist with the appointment of the arbitrator(s), any challenges to the arbitrator(s), as well as any questions linked to the jurisdiction of the arbitral tribunal ... with *ad hoc* arbitration there is, therefore, an unsettling reliance upon the legal system, be it at the seat of arbitration or in another jurisdiction, and its ability to handle arbitration-specific issues').
36. Pierre Lalive, *Avantages et inconvénients de l'arbitrage ad hoc* in *Études offertes à Pierre Bellet* 301, 318–319 (Litec 1991). *See also* Phillippe Fouchard, *Les institutions permanentes d'arbitrage devant le juge étatique*, 3 Rev Arb 225, 225 (1987) (the authors note that there is a nearly unanimous consensus as to the current prevalence of administered arbitration over ad hoc arbitration).
37. *See* Pierre Lalive, *De la fureur réglementaire*, 12:2 ASA Bull 213, 217 (1994); Phillipe Fouchard, *Une initiative contestable de la CNUDCI*, 12:3 ASA Bull 369, 378 ff. (1994).
38. Carita Wallgren-Lindholm, *Ad Hoc v Institutional Arbitration* in Giuditta Cordero-Moss, *International Commercial Arbitration–Different Forms and Their Features* 61, 76 (Cambridge University Press 2013); Crawford, *supra* n. 33, at 13.
39. *See ICC Statistics 2015*, 26:1 ICC Bull 1 (2016); Antoine Kassis, *Réflexions sur le règlement d'arbitrage de la Chambre de Commerce Internationale*, 25–26 (LGDJ 1988) ('[L]es parties ... peuvent légitimement ... redouter de *bricoler* un règlement d'arbitrage, alors que des modèles standard, soigneusement élaborés, sont disponibles gratuitement sur le marché et sans copyright. *On peut donc prendre le modèle de l'institution sans prendre l'institution elle-même*') [emphasis added].

into my analysis, I will supplement the aforementioned approach with a comparative one.

The comparative approach will allow me to describe how States contribute to the delineation of arbitral awards' boundaries. In particular, I will draw from Patrick Glenn's theory of legal traditions. According to this theory, law amounts to information produced by different entities (grouped as identities), capable of guiding behaviour, and bears some immanent characteristics that have remained unchanged throughout the centuries, despite the rise of new historical and cultural contexts.[40] I will thus argue that users of arbitration systems are deeply influenced by the Romano-canonical and common law traditions of civil litigation, as embedded in national arbitration legislation.[41] As a consequence, the notion of arbitral award in international arbitration will be compared with the equivalent notions found in two representatives of these traditions, that is, in French and English laws. Furthermore, due consideration will be given to the UNCITRAL *Model Law on International Commercial Arbitration*, in particular when analysing certain types of arbitral decisions (namely, consent awards, jurisdictional awards, and provisional decisions).

The decision to focus on these legal instruments has a twofold explanation. First, they were selected because a significant (and perhaps even preponderant) number of international commercial arbitrations are seated in either London or Paris.[42] Most importantly, however, this choice is justified by the fact that while the *English Arbitration Act 1996* was inspired by the 1985 UNCITRAL *Model Law on International Commercial Arbitration* (*Model Law*) with respect to the notion of award[43]—in some

---

40. Patrick Glenn, *Legal Traditions of the World*, 4 (Oxford University Press 2012).
41. I am using the terms 'Romano-canonical' and 'common law' (instead of 'inquisitorial' and 'adversarial') to underline the historical sources of such procedural traditions, rather than focusing on certain alleged contemporary differences. *See* CH van Rhee, *Public Justice: Some Historical Remarks* in Alan Uzelac & CH van Rhee, *Public and Private Justice*, 31, 36 ff. (Intersentia 2007); Cf. Fabien Gélinas et al., *Foundations of Civil Justice*, 77 (Springer 2015) ('The ALI/UNIDROIT principles arguably show signs of convergence in civil procedure between the adversarial and inquisitorial traditions ... yet, legal pluralism and cosmopolitanism suggest that civil procedure may be more diversified than a positivist account would show. Where such diversity does not seem obvious, legal pluralism and cosmopolitanism also point to the more normative issue of whether a diversification of civil procedure, rather than harmonization, should take place').
42. According to the Queen Mary University of London's 2015 survey on international commercial arbitration, 82% of arbitrations are seated in either Paris or London. *See* Loukas A. Mistelis & Paul Friedland, *2015 International Arbitration Survey: Improvements and Innovations in International Arbitration*, 12, www.arbitration.qmul.ac.uk/docs/164761.pdf (accessed 31 January 2017). It is likely that the importance of London as a seat of arbitration will not be affected by the consequences of the referendum held in June 2016 (the so-called 'Brexit' referendum). The key regulatory instruments of international arbitration, in fact, are not part of EU law, and will thus continue to apply whether or not the UK government will move forward with Brexit. For an overview, *see* Mohammad Salahudine & Abdal Wahhabism, *Brexit's Chilling Effects on the Choice of Law and Arbitration in the United Kingdom*, 33 JOIA 463, 472–474 (2016). There is however the possibility that London will lose some ground to the benefit of Geneva, especially if European companies were to start perceiving the UK as a 'hostile' jurisdiction (*see* Michael McIlwrath, *An Unamicable Separation: Brexit Consequences for London as a Premier Seat of International Dispute Resolution in Europe*, 33 JOIA 451, 454–455 (2016).
43. Mark Oliver Saville, *1996 Report on the Arbitration Bill*, 13:3 Arb Int 275, 276 (1997). Scholars have also underlined the lasting persuasive value of the English Courts' interpretation of the

instances, anticipating the 2006 amendments to the *Model Law*-, France developed its own peculiar legislative framework for arbitration in its *Code of Civil Procedure*,[44] and has hosted and contributed to the development of the Court of Arbitration of the ICC. This highlights a fundamental difference in terms of policy objectives pursued by these jurisdictions. By intervening on the boundaries of the notion of award, French Law and English Law have regulated in different ways the equilibrium between state justice and arbitral justice. While French law endorses a narrow definition of award (essentially confined to the notion of final decision on the merits), English law adopts a broader notion of award. This notion includes all decisions rendered following a judicial-like procedure, which either establishes the jurisdictional boundaries of the tribunal or leads to a resolution of a dispute or prevent the frustration of arbitral proceedings. As a result, these different conceptions will entail a definition of the interplays between state courts and arbitral tribunals, limiting or extending the intervention of the formers in the arbitral process.

§1.03 SCOPE AND LIMITATIONS

The sociological and comparative analysis of international commercial arbitration could be approached in several ways. I have chosen to focus my attention on the notion of arbitral award because it is a problematic concept in the field. Not only does it present an opportunity to address uncertainty among scholars and practitioners as to the actual boundaries of this notion, but an analysis of the meaning of arbitral award can also allow us to go beyond these practical concerns, so as to look at its broader function in the interplay between international commercial arbitration and state justice. Most importantly, clarifying the notion of arbitral award allows for a greater understanding of the functioning of international commercial arbitration and, especially, of its non-contractual aspects.

Among the avenues of study that I decided to exclude from my analysis is a particularly interesting one: the role of third parties in arbitration. In a nutshell, this issue concerns how parties that have not signed (or otherwise consented to) the arbitration agreement can take part in arbitration proceedings. If one is prepared to look at the issue from an adjudicative angle, evidence of consent to arbitration may not be the sole factor capable of determining whether third parties should join the proceedings. There are two reasons, however, for excluding this topic.

First, the literature on this issue is fairly saturated and includes heterogeneous contributions covering topics such as joinders, consolidations, and extension of

---

1996 Arbitration Act in other common law jurisdictions having adopted the *Model Law*. For a detailed analysis of the interpretation of the *Model Law*, see Dean Lewis, *The Interpretation and Uniformity of the Uncitral Model Law on International Commercial Arbitration* (Kluwer Law 2016). For a specific study of Singapore arbitration law, *see* Frédéric Bachand & Fabien Gélinas, *Interpreting the Model Law: Methodology and the Singapore Experience* in David Joseph & David Foxton, *Singapore International Arbitration*, 539, 552 ff. (LexisNexis 2014). For a recent example, *see also BLC and others v. BLB and another [2014] SGCA 40*.

44. Thomas Clay, *La Convention de New York vue par la doctrine française*, 27:1 ASA Bull 49, 51 (2009) [Clay, *La Convention de New York*].

arbitration agreements.[45] Second, a dissertation by Stavros L. Brekoulakis (which was published as a book in 2010) has already attempted to move the debate beyond the sole contractual dimension of arbitration, by focusing on how the problem posed by third parties can be tackled through the adjudicative power of arbitrators.[46]

Another issue that has been excluded from the scope of the present work is the decision-making process of arbitrators and, in particular, evidentiary matters relating to this process. The type of evidentiary powers that one is prepared to grant to an arbitral tribunal will certainly influence its final outcome (i.e., the award). Here, again, the answer to the problem of how broad evidentiary powers should be will depend on one's understanding of international commercial arbitration: a contractual understanding will result in the limitation of evidentiary powers to the ones allowed by the parties' agreement; an adjudicative understanding will recognize that arbitrators have independent (or ex officio) evidentiary powers.[47] Despite the interesting questions surrounding this topic, my decision to exclude it was dictated by the greater consensus on evidentiary powers found in the field of international arbitration.[48]

---

45. *See* Andrea Meler, *Multi-Party Arbitrations* in Manuel Arroyo, *Arbitration in Switzerland* 1325 (Kluwer Law 2013); John Gilbert, *Multi-Party and Multi-Contract Arbitration* in Julian D.M. Lew et al., *Arbitration in England, with Chapters on Scotland and Ireland* 455 (Kluwer Law 2013); Keechang Kim, *Voluntary Third-Party Intervention in International Arbitration for Construction Disputes: A Contextual Approach to Jurisdictional Issues*, 30:4 JOIA 407 (2013); Jeff Waincymer, *The Process of an Arbitration: Complex Arbitration* in Jeff Waincymer, *Procedure and Evidence in International Arbitration* 495 (Kluwer Law 2012). *See generally* Bernard Hanotiau & Eric A. Schwartz, *Multiparty Arbitration* (ICC Publications 2010); Stavros L. Brekoulakis, *Third Parties in International Commercial Arbitration* (Oxford University Press 2010); Christopher Koch, *Judicial Activism and the Limits of Institutional Arbitration in Multiparty Disputes*, 28:2 ASA Bull 380 (2010); Elena Gutiérrez Garcia De Cortazar, *Non-Signatories and Arbitration: Recent Developments* in Miguel Angel Fernandez-Ballesteros & David Arias, *Liber Amicorum Bernardo Cremades* 561 (Kluwer Law 2010); Ricardo Ugarte & Thomas Bevilacqua, *Ensuring Party Equality in the Process of Designating Arbitrators in Multiparty Arbitration: An Update on the Governing Provisions*, 27:1 JOIA 9 (2010); Romain Dupeyré, *La participatión de terceros en el arbitraje internacional*, 9 Revista del Club Español del Arbitraje 83 (2010); Nathalie Voser, *Multi-party Disputes and Joinder of Third Parties* in Albert van den Berg, *50 Years of the New York Convention* 343 (Kluwer Law 2009); Tobias Zuberbühler, *Non-Signatories and the Consensus to Arbitrate*, 26:1 ASA Bull 18 (2008); Alexis Mourre, *L'intervention des tiers à l'arbitrage*, 16:4 Revista Brasileira de Arbitragem 76 (2007); Julian D.M. Lew et al., *Multiparty and Multicontract Arbitration* in Julian D.M. Lew & Loukas A. Mistelis, *Comparative International Commercial Arbitration* 377 (Kluwer Law 2003); Martin Platte, *When Should an Arbitrator Join Cases?* 18:1 JOIA 67 (2002); Philippe Leboulanger, *Multi-Contract Arbitration*, 13:4 JOIA 43 (1996).
46. Brekoulakis, *supra* n. 45, at 200.
47. For a general overview, *see* Born, *supra* n. 4, at 2306 ff.; Poudret & Besson, *supra* n. 2, at 550 ff. On the need for flexible rules in order to combine the approaches of different legal traditions, *see generally* Philippe Landolt, *Arbitrators' Initiative to Obtain Factual and Legal Evidence*, 28:2 Arb Int 173 (2012); William W. Park, *Truth Seeking in International Arbitration* in Markus Wirth, Christina Rouvinez & Joachim Knoll, *The Search for the 'Truth' in Arbitration: Is Finding the Truth What Dispute Resolution Is About?* 1 (JurisNet 2011); Robert Pietrowski, *Evidence in International Arbitration*, 22:2 Arb Int 373 (2006); Yves Derains, *La Pratique de l'administration de la preuve dans l'arbitrage commercial international*, 4 Rev Arb 781 (2004).
48. *See generally* Fabien Gélinas & Giacomo Marchisio, *The Investigative Power of Arbitrators*, 26 Rev Arb Med 229 (2015).

§1.04 STRUCTURE AND SUMMARY OF THE ANALYSIS

The aim of this book is to provide an explanation of how the notion of arbitral award can be defined and, in particular, to challenge the assumption according to which the notion of arbitral award shall necessarily track that of a final judgment rendered by a state court (hereafter, the 'monodimensional model').[49] Adjudication in international commercial arbitration has been mainly conceived with reference to a contentious function, which describes arbitration as a 'mechanism by which a third party resolves a dispute between two or more parties, in a final manner, by virtue of the adjudicative mandate that was conferred to him by them',[50] hence the similarity to state courts and the analogy between arbitral award and final judgment.

As we shall see, however, the analysis of the notion of arbitral award found in the present book suggests that a broader descriptive model should be used. Such a model allows one to perceive that awards are not all the same. On the contrary, they pursue different goals and can be issued at the end of different proceedings. This observation suggests the need to rely on a 'multidimensional model' of arbitration, which takes into account that legal institutions are created and evolve in response to the needs of its constituents.[51] In a nutshell, the multidimensional model describes arbitral awards in light of the different types of adjudicative powers which arbitrators wield. It highlights the fact that adjudication goes beyond the mere final resolution of a substantive dispute between the parties (contentious decisions).

Consistently, other types of arbitral decisions can be identified (the following list is not exhaustive; it is rather based on the most visible and important arbitral practices): 'provisional decisions' – which consist of urgent orders directed against a party, prohibiting a certain conduct (e.g., emergency orders, interim measures, etc.), 'jurisdictional decisions' or 'awards on competence' (i.e., deciding whether the arbitral tribunal is the appropriate jurisdictional forum for litigating the parties' claims), and 'decisions to record a settlement' (which assess whether the parties' settlement can obtain an exequatur, that is, whether it can be recorded in the form of an award). The structure of the book is as follows.

First, I will set the scene by describing the framework of the analysis, presenting the differences between the monodimensional and the multidimensional models (Chapter 1). I will then explain that today's international commercial arbitration has strong institutional roots (Chapter 2). In this chapter, I will argue that the predominance of institutions is ultimately responsible for the existence of a broad bundle of arbitral decision types, which can be described by the multidimensional model.

---

49. *Infra*, §2.02.
50. Jarrosson, *supra* n. 16, at 372. A similar definition is found in Gaillard & Savage, *supra* n. 5, at 8 ('Arbitration is a device whereby the settlement of a question, which is of interest for two or more persons, is entrusted to one or more other persons – the arbitrator or arbitrators – who derive their powers from a private agreement, not from the authorities of a State, and who are to proceed and decide the case on the basis of such an agreement').
51. *See* Mikael Rask Madsen, *The Sociology of International Law* in Richard Nobles & David Schiff, *Law, Society and Community: Socio-Legal Essays in Honor of Roger Cotterrell* 242 ff. (Ashgate Publishing 2014).

Arbitral institutions, in fact, have evolved from authorities appointing arbitrators for the resolution of a dispute, to ones providing an infrastructure for administering justice. This was caused both by a significant increase in the number of users of arbitral systems and by an attempt to provide an exhaustive forum for the resolution of international commercial disputes. To illustrate this evolution, I will focus on the most influential arbitral institution, that is, the Court of Arbitration of the ICC. By adopting a historical perspective, I will show that the ICC has pursued, since its inception, the creation of an arbitration regime that allows great autonomy for arbitral institutions and a high degree of flexibility in the administration of arbitrations. After this, I will consider three types of arbitral awards, which are each the expression of different adjudicative functions. Each of these awards was selected because of its practical relevance. These considerations lead us to Chapter 3.

Chapter 3 of the book will present an analysis of the notion of contentious award (a decision resolving a dispute on the merits by speaking the law), which can be regarded as an imitation of courts' final judgments on the merits. Consistently, I will consider the notion of judgment. By relying on a historical perspective, I will point out that judgments – whose function is to resolve the merits of the case, in a final manner, by speaking the law (*ius dicere*) – are a product of Roman law and, in particular, of the expansion of a centralized administrative system of civil justice. Further on, the chapter will also explain that the two major Western procedural traditions (common law and Romano-canonical) present convergent definitions of final judgment. The second part of Chapter 3 will analyse the notion of contentious award under English and French arbitration law. The study will show that while English arbitration law endorses a multidimensional model for the adjudicative role of arbitrators, French law adopts a monodimensional one. In practical terms, this means that French courts will tend to enforce mainly final awards resolving a dispute between the parties by speaking the law, whereas English courts will also accept other types of awards.

The following chapters will present a case study of specific types of arbitral awards. Each of them responds to a specific adjudicative function, which goes beyond the final resolution of a dispute between the parties (a contentious function).

The first of such awards can be termed a 'jurisdictional award' (or 'award on competence') (Chapter 4) and consists of a decision rendered by the arbitrators on their jurisdiction over the claims filed by the parties. Here, one can note the expansion of the power of arbitrators with respect to their decision to decline or retain a case, and such decisions are now considered as enforceable awards by a growing number of jurisdictions. Given the various existing trends, the dichotomy of French versus English arbitration law will be supplemented by an analysis of other jurisdictions. Due consideration will also be given to the UNCITRAL *Model Law*, which takes an ambiguous position with respect to the form of jurisdictional decisions.

Chapter 5 will extend the case study to the notion of 'consent awards', which are decisions rendered by arbitrators homologating a settlement reached by the parties. Here, the research confirms the validity of the descriptive dichotomy of French versus English arbitration law, for while the former fails to recognize such decisions, the latter does not hesitate to enforce them. The position and legislative history of the UNCITRAL

Model Law will further show that there is a general consensus in favour of the recognition of consent awards.

Similarly, Chapter 6 will focus on emergency decisions rendered by arbitrators during a new type of procedure called 'emergency arbitration'. Given the fact that this procedure is quite recent, most national laws on arbitration do not address the nature and enforceability of emergency measures rendered in that context. The case study will therefore concentrate on the most influential arbitration rules in order to understand how such decisions can be categorized. The analysis will show that emergency measures can, under certain conditions, take the form of an award.

Finally, in the Conclusion, I will argue that the debate on the notion of award can be re-centred around the public dimension of arbitration that is inherent to the adjudicative role of arbitrators. Furthermore, the comparative findings will allow me to present a complex (and non-unitary) notion of arbitral award, consistent with a multidimensional model of arbitral adjudication.

CHAPTER 2
Diverging Understandings of Arbitration

§2.01 INTRODUCTION

What is arbitration? At first glance, this question might seem banal. In his work *La notion d'arbitrage*,[52] Charles Jarrosson defines arbitration as 'the mechanism by which a third party resolves a dispute between two or more parties, by virtue of the jurisdictional mandate that was conferred to him by them'.[53] Similarly, Gary Born describes it as 'a means by which international business disputes can be definitively resolved, pursuant to the parties' agreement, by independent, non-governmental decision-makers, selected by or for the parties, applying neutral judicial procedures that provide the parties an opportunity to be heard'.[54] Along the same lines is Poudret and Besson's definition, according to which 'arbitration is a contractual form of dispute resolution exercised by individuals, appointed directly or indirectly by the parties, and vested with the power to adjudicate the dispute in place of state courts by rendering a decision having effects analogous to those of a judgment'.[55]

These definitions show the recurrence of two distinct legal notions: the *agreement* (to arbitrate) and the *adjudication* (of the dispute).[56] In other words, while the

---

52. Jarrosson, *supra* n. 16, at 372.
53. Author's translation. *See also* Gaillard & Savage, *supra* n. 5, at 8 ('Arbitration is a device whereby the settlement of a question, which is of interest for two or more persons, is entrusted to one or more other persons–the arbitrator or arbitrators–who derive their powers from a private agreement, not from the authorities of a State, and who are to proceed and decide the case on the basis of such an agreement').
54. Born, *supra* n. 4, at 68.
55. Poudret & Besson, *supra* n. 2, at 2.
56. Arbitration lies at the crossroads of contract law and civil procedure. *See* Alain Prujiner, *L'arbitre et le droit*, 1:1MJDR 33 (2014) (here lies not only the nature but also the legitimacy of arbitration: '[c'est] l'alliance du conventionnel et du juridictionnel, de sa source contractuelle et de son onction étatique qui confère sa légitimité à l'arbitrage'). *See also* Cadiet et al., *Théorie générale*, *supra* n. 28, at 181.

dispute is adjudicated by resorting to the paradigm of civil justice, the arbitrators' power remains deeply anchored to the agreement of the parties. This understanding was later transposed into modern arbitration instruments, such as the 1958 *New York Convention*,[57] in which Article IV(1) states that recognition and enforcement of the award can be obtained by providing an original or certified copy: (a) of the *arbitration agreement* and (b) of the *award*. Given the above, it seems natural to define international commercial arbitration by reference to two constitutive elements: first, the contractual source; second, the adjudicative role. This position enjoys broad consensus.[58]

Despite this dual nature, the prevailing approach in the literature has placed emphasis on the contractual pillar of arbitration and, as a result, on party autonomy.[59] The arbitration agreement would, in this view, represent the source and limits of the entire system. However, this contractual focus has ended up overemphasizing the private features of international arbitration and, in particular, its degree of autonomy (if not predominance) over other normative orders.[60] This has inevitably led to a re-enactment of the debate regarding the relationship between private normative sources and state normativity. Conversely, little attention has been devoted to the second pillar of arbitration, that is, the *adjudicative* role of arbitrators and, in particular, the decisions that they render.[61] The neglect of this dimension has taken place despite the occurrence of significant developments: while theories on the arbitration agreement have simply evolved by advocating the need to reduce courts' intervention regarding matters covered by said agreement,[62] arbitrators' decisions have changed in more significant ways,[63] especially in terms of content, without any theorization of this new development in methods of adjudicating.[64]

---

57. *Convention on the Recognition and Enforcement of Foreign Arbitral Awards*, 10 June 1958, 330 UNTS 38, 21 UST 2517 [*New York Convention*].
58. Gaillard & Savage, *supra* n. 5, at 10.
59. Born, *supra* n. 4, at 216.
60. While, based on Santi Romano's definition of social order, Gaillard argues that private autonomy in arbitration has created a transnational and independent legal order, Paulsson arrives at the same conclusion by placing arbitration in a context of social and normative pluralism. *See* Gaillard, *Legal Theory*, *supra* n. 12, at 46; Jan Paulsson, *Arbitration in Three Dimensions*, 7 TDM 1, 30–32 (2010).
61. Cf. Thomas Clay, *L'arbitre*, 43 ff. (Dalloz 2001) [Clay, *L'arbitre*].
62. Emmanuel Gaillard & Yas Banifatemi, *Negative Effects of Competence-Competence: The Rule of Priority in Favour of the Arbitrators* in Emmanuel Gaillard & Domenico di Pietro, *Enforcement of Arbitration Agreements and International Arbitral Awards* 257 (Cameron May 2008).
63. *See* e.g., the flourishing of emergency arbitration and the use of consent awards described in Chapters 5 and 6.
64. Not only has the content changed but so has the number of awards rendered. This has affected, notably, the world's most influential arbitration centre, the ICC International Court of Arbitration. In 2015, 498 awards were rendered under the auspices of the institution (*ICC 2015 Statistical Report*, 26:1 ICC Bulletin 9 (2016)). In 1993, the number of final awards was 112 (*ICC 1993–1997 Statistical Report*, 9:1 ICC Bulletin 1 (1998)).

§2.02 OVERVIEW OF THE MONODIMENSIONAL MODEL: THE ARBITRATOR RESOLVES A DISPUTE IN A FINAL MANNER

The various definitions of international arbitration described in the Introduction to this chapter draw extensively on arbitrators' duty to resolve a dispute between the parties. This understanding, based on a narrow definition of adjudicative power dating back to Roman times (*jurisdictio contentiosa*),[65] is outlined in the following paragraphs.

By virtue of this conception of arbitration, the award is regarded as a decision enforceable before state courts;[66] from the perspective of the state, the award and the arbitrator are functional equivalents, respectively, of a judgment and of a court.[67] Both arbitration and state courts would rely on a common adjudicative model: two parties with opposite positions have an impartial third party resolve their dispute, in a final manner, by speaking the law (*ius dicere*).[68] From a philosophical standpoint, the goal of this adjudicative model is that of restoring justice between the litigants, that is, giving each of them what they rightfully deserve.[69] Since this model exclusively focuses on the resolution of a dispute on the merits between two litigants by means of a contentious decision, it can be defined as monodimensional. This understanding of arbitration has a venerable ancestry. In fact, according to classical Roman law, arbitration had to be conducted in the same manner as a trial in court and was intended to put an end to litigation.[70] Therefore, the adjudicative role of arbitrators and courts would be the same: resolving the dispute by speaking the law and rendering a final and

---

65. Paul Frédéric Girard, *Manuel élémentaire de droit romain*, 1033 (Rev. Ed., Dalloz 2003).
66. *See e.g.*, *Arbitration Act 1996* (England and Wales) section 66(1) ('An award made by the tribunal pursuant to an arbitration agreement may, by leave of the court, be enforced in the same manner as a judgment or order of the court to the same effect').
67. Jean-Pierre Ancel, *L'arbitre juge*, 4 Rev Arb 717, 722 (2012) ('L'arbitre est un juge pour la simple raison ... qu'il juge. Or le juge est bien la personne qui – tous comptes faits – dit dans sa décision ce qui doit être selon le droit et le juste').
68. Guinchard, *supra* n. 22, at 103 ('L'hypothèse où des parties, ayant des prétentions opposées, attendent d'un juge qu'il dise le droit pour y mettre un terme définitivement, au terme d'une procédure ritualisée'). A similar notion is found in canon law. *See* Émile Jombart, *Manuel de droit canonique*, 469 (Beauchesne et fils 1958) ('Un jugement ou procès est dit contentieux ... s'il s'agit de trancher un différend entre deux personnes'). The *Codex Iuris Canonici* codified this model under the provisions dealing with the 'contentious trial' (Can. 1501-1670: *De Iudicio contentioso*). It should be noted that the role of speaking the law is absent in case of *amiable composition*. This type of arbitration can be defined as granting 'the arbitrators ... power not to restrict themselves to applying rules of law, thereby allowing them not only to ignore the rules of law altogether, but also to depart from them to the extent that their conception of equity requires' (Gaillard & Savage, *supra* n. 5, at 837). ICC statistics show that this type of arbitration has disappeared: in the last ten years, only ten awards were rendered by arbitrators acting as *amiables compositeurs*.
69. The same theory of justice is found in both Greek philosophy and classical Roman law. *See* Ernest Weinrib, *Corrective Justice in a Nutshell*, 52 UTLJ 349 (2002); *Institutiones*, I, I ('Justitia est constans et perpetuas voluntas jus suum cuique tribuendi' – justice is the constant and perpetual desire to give each one what is rightfully his).
70. *Corpus Iuris Civilis*: *Digestum*, Book IV, Title VIII, n. 1. Translation by Samuel Parsons Scott, *The Civil Law* 116 (Central Trust Company 1932) ('compromissum ad similitudinem judiciorum regitur: et ad finienda lites pertinent').

binding decision.[71] The arbitrator can thus be regarded as a judge, and the award as a judgment.[72]

In light of the above, the monodimensional model can be defined by three essential elements. The first element consists of the contentious adjudication of a *dispute* on the merits between two or more parties (*litige, controversia*). The second element is a neutral third party (the adjudicator)[73] who is expected to resolve the dispute. His or her neutrality arises from impartiality and independence from the parties to the case.[74] The third element amounts to the notion of res judicata. The award, just as a judgment, shall be final: this prevents one of the parties from having the same dispute retried.[75] As I shall explain in the following chapters, this narrow understanding of arbitration is championed by French law and leads to a narrow definition of award. While the *Code de procédure civile* fails to provide an explicit definition, French courts have constantly held – mainly in the context of annulment proceedings – that an award is 'a final decision, resolving in full or in part the dispute submitted to the arbitrators, concerning either the merits, the competence of the tribunal, or another preliminary objection putting the proceedings to an end'.[76] In passing, it is worth noting that while *finality* is an indispensable attribute of this conception, nothing suggests that awards per se have a *final* nature. Finality seems rather to be an effect granted by an external norm (be it a general legal principle or a specific provision of a domestic arbitration act, such as Article 1484(1) of the French *Code de procédure civile*), ensuring that the decision is res judicata.[77] Despite the above definition's wide acceptance by French scholars, a careful analysis points to the conclusion that this

---

71. Clay, *L'arbitre, supra* n. 61, at 85 ('c'est-à-dire qu'un litige est 'tranché' par une décision ayant l'autorité de chose jugée').
72. *Ibid.* at 90, 96 ff. (on the basis of the above, the same author suggests that arbitrators would also have a power of *imperium*, that is, the power to order, of which the jurisdictional power would be only one manifestation; the author explains that this conclusion is dictated by the fact that: (a) *iurisdictio* is a mere manifestation of the *imperium* – the power to order something; (b) the arbitrator is only lacking the coercive power – the *imperium merum* (the sheer power to order), while benefitting from the *imperium mixtum*, that is, the power of ordering measures that are not strictly related to the proceedings; (c) given the pro-enforcement approach of state courts vis-à-vis arbitral awards, the coercive power seems to be held, de facto, by the arbitral tribunal). On the Roman taxonomies (*imperium-iurisdictio*), see Girard, *supra* n. 65 at 1032–1033.
73. *See* D. 2, I, 10 ('Qui jurisdictioni praest, neque sibi jus dicere debet, neque uxori, vel liberi suis, neque libertis, vel caeteris quos secum habet' – one ought not to be a judge in one's own case). *See also Regent Company v. Ukraine*, 3 April 2008, n. 773/03 ECHR, para. 54 (since arbitral awards are 'treated as equivalent to an enforceable court judgment', arbitral tribunals are bound by Art. 6§1 of the European Convention on Human Rights: in the determination of one's civil rights and obligations, everyone is entitled to a fair hearing by an independent and impartial tribunal).
74. Fabien Gélinas, *The Dual Rationale of Judicial Independence* in Alain Marciano, *Constitutional Mythologies* 146 (New York 2011); Dominique Hascher, *Les perspectives françaises sur le contrôle de la sentence internationale ou étrangère*, 1:2 MJDR 12 (2015).
75. Jarrosson, *supra* n. 16, at 28.
76. Cass Civ 1e, 12 October 2011, No 09-72.439 (author's translation). *See also* CA Paris, 29 October 2009, No 08/18544. These decisions are based on a 1994 case rendered by the Paris Court of Appeal (Sardi sud). *See* CA Paris, 25 March 1994, 2 Revue de l'arbitrage 391 (Annotation Charles Jarrosson).
77. Cadiet et al., *Théorie générale, supra* n. 28, at 894; Gaillard & Savage, *supra* n. 5, at 780. The res judicata effects of the decision are not granted by the decision itself but are enforced by a

conception of awards is only partially in line with the general notion of arbitration elaborated by the French doctrine. Arbitration, in fact, is usually defined through a reference to: (i) its contractual dimension (the arbitration agreement between the parties) and (ii) its adjudicative dimension (the arbitrators' power to resolve disputes).[78] According to Henri Motulsky, for example, arbitration would be 'une justice privée, dont l'origine est normalement conventionnelle' (a private justice, whose origin is usually contractual).[79] The blending of the contractual and adjudicative dimensions is clearly identifiable in this definition. Motulsky's work was later expanded on by Charles Jarrosson in an acclaimed monograph, entitled *La notion d'arbitrage*. Here, Jarrosson specified that arbitration is a private form of justice because of the adjudicative mandate (*mission juridictionnelle*) conferred on the arbitrators. In defining the nature of arbitrators' mandates, Jarrosson introduced a reference to the doctrine of *acte juridictionnel*[80] – an act rendered by an adjudicator at the end of a specific procedure, which, based on his or her findings, resolves the dispute between the parties in a final manner.[81] It is worth noting that the notion of *acte juridictionnel* did not explicitly appear in Motulsky's works, which simply referred to the adjudicative function of arbitrators (*fonction juridictionnelle*). While Jarrosson seemed to be cautious in his reference to this doctrine,[82] emphasizing that it is essentially needed to distinguish arbitration from other institutions, such as the *arbitrato irrituale, arbitraggio*, mediation, or expert determination, the *Cour de cassation* was dogmatic in incorporating the *acte juridictionnel* doctrine into the definition of arbitral award. One of the elements of the model – the *fonction juriditionnelle* – became the *conditio sine qua non* for the definition of arbitral award. This occurred despite the fact that the *acte juridictionnel* doctrine was originally developed only to distinguish decisions rendered by administrative courts – deprived of the power to speak the law (*ius dicere*) – from those rendered by ordinary courts of law.[83]

§2.03 OVERVIEW OF THE MULTIDIMENSIONAL MODEL: THE ARBITRATOR RENDERS JUSTICE

Under Roman law, the notion of speaking the law was very broad – *jus dicentis officium latissimum est*[84] – and was exercised by means of broad powers ('he who has

---

   principle or norm external to that decision, preventing the same arbitral tribunal or a different one from rehearing the case. It is in the enforcement of these effects that the true final character of the decision lies.
78. Kassis, *supra* n. 17, at 27. *See also* Eric Loquin, *L'arbitrage du commerce international*, 2 (Lextenso 2015) ('une certaine incertitude règne en droit français sur la notion d'acte juridictionnel et donc sur le concept d'arbitrage, dès lors que celui-ci dépend de cette notion') [Loquin, *Arbitrage international*].
79. Motulsky, *supra* n. 14, at 6.
80. Jarrosson, *supra* n. 16, at 76.
81. Jacques Héron & Thierry Le Bars, *Droit judiciare privé*, 268 (Lextenso 2012).
82. Jarrosson, *supra* n. 16, at 260.
83. Guinchard, *supra* n. 22, at 704.
84. D. 2, I (*De Jurisdictione*) 1.

jurisdiction, shall also have the necessary powers that are required for its exercise').[85] Accordingly, three different types of adjudicative powers were in place: (i) the *jurisdictio voluntaria*, whereby parties were able to conclude certain agreements by resorting to formalized rituals in the presence of a certain authority (*in jure cessio, emancipatio*, etc.);[86] (ii) *jurisdictio contentiosa* (a third party resolving a dispute); (iii) *imperium mixtum cui jurisdictio* (orders issued by magistrates resulting from free-standing liabilities: *missiones in possessionem, interdicta*, etc.).[87] While modern codifications have abandoned the above taxonomy, several jurisdictions have maintained a broad notion of adjudicative power, consistent with the central role of judges in the administration of civil proceedings.[88] This broad notion of adjudicative power is based on the different functions that adjudicative institutions fulfil.[89] For this reason, it can be referred to as the multidimensional model. The term 'multidimensional' underlines that the analysis of adjudicative power can be understood in light of the different types of decisions that are rendered in order to administer justice. In the context of international arbitration, the *multidimensional* model highlights the fact that adjudication goes beyond the mere resolution of the dispute. In addition to the contentious power, by which the arbitral tribunal resolves a dispute in a final manner by speaking the law, three other types of adjudicative powers can be identified: (i) the provisional power – which consists of orders directed against a party, prohibiting or imposing a certain conduct (e.g., emergency orders, interim measures, etc.),[90] (ii) the power to rule on the tribunal's jurisdiction, and (iii) the power to record a settlement, which entails an assessment of whether the parties' settlement can be recorded in the form of an award. While it may be noted that the above adjudicative powers are usually

---

85. The definition recalls the doctrine of inherent powers of the tribunal. *See* D. 2, I, 2 ('Cui jurisdictio data est, ea quoque concessa esse videntur, sine quibus juirisdictio explicari non potuit').
86. This was usually achieved through sacred trials known as *legis actiones*. *See* Silvio Perrozzi, *Istituzioni di diritto romano*, 57 (Vallardi 1928).
87. Girard, *supra* n. 65, at 1033 (sub n. 5).
88. John Jolowicz, *On Civil Procedure*, 78–79 (Oxford University Press 2000). The centralized role of the judge should not to be confused with the 'inquisitorial' label. *See* Loïc Cadiet, *Sources and Destiny of French Civil Procedure in a Globalized World* in Colin Picker & Guy Seidman, *The Dynamism of Civil Procedure-Global Trends and Developments* 63, 81 ff. (Springer 2016) [Cadiet, 'Sources and Destiny'].
89. Crisanto Mandrioli, *Diritto processuale civile*, 9 (Giappichelli 2011); Cf. Roger Cotterrell, *Sociology of Law*, 222 (Butterworths 1984) ('The problem with seeing dispute processing as central to the work of courts is twofold. First, there are good grounds for saying that the adjudicative process of courts is extremely poorly fitted for dispute resolution. Secondly, there seems to be considerable evidence that a great deal – probably the major part in terms of total number of cases – of courts' work is concerned with matters other than disputes').
90. When the court has been seized of a matter, it will exercise both an adjudicative and provisional jurisdiction; however, if the court has not yet been seized, the provisional jurisdiction will be exercised by a different court (*ante causam*). On the first scenario, *see generally* Sébastien Besson, *Arbitrage international et mesures provisoires*, 81 (Schulthess 1998); Olivier Mignolet, *Les mesures provisoires et conservatoires prises par les arbitres* in Achille Saletti et al., *L'arbitre et le juge étatique* 161 (Bruylant 2014). On the second scenario, *see generally* Cécile Chainais & Charles Jarrosson, *L'urgence avant la constitution du tribunal arbitral* in Guy Keutgen, *L'arbitrage international et l'urgence* 61 (Bruylant 2014).

Chapter 2: Diverging Understandings of Arbitration §2.03

ancillary to the general goal of resolving a dispute between the parties, they deserve nonetheless to be considered separately, especially in light of their specific scopes.

As I will explain in the following chapters, English law endorses this broader understanding of arbitration, which in turn, leads to a broad definition of arbitral award. A potential explanation for this approach can be found in the criterion used in English law to distinguish arbitration from similar dispute resolution mechanisms such as expert determination. Several cases indicate that unlike French law, which gives pivotal importance to the *acte juridictionnel* doctrine, the *conditio sine qua non* for arbitration in England is not related to the nature of the decision rendered by the third party (the arbitrator) but rather to the nature of the procedure that led to that decision. Unlike an expert, an arbitrator resolves a dispute by taking into account the evidence and arguments submitted by the parties.[91] Awards, therefore, amount to decisions on the parties' claims based 'on the evidence and arguments presented',[92] directing the parties to the 'nature and extent of [their] duties'.[93] In other words, the distinctive feature of arbitration is that its procedure has 'something in the nature of a judicial inquiry'.[94] The above explains the flexibility of the *Arbitration Act 1996*, which specifies (section 47) that 'the tribunal may make more than one award at different times on different aspects of the matters to be determined', which include 'a part only of the claims or cross-claims' (section 47(b)). The act further accommodates provisional decisions under the umbrella of arbitral award (section 49), including orders for the payment of money or the disposition of property as between the parties (section 49(2)(a)). Much like under the UNCITRAL *Model Law*, these decisions can take the form of an award, despite the fact that their effectiveness has an expiration date.[95] At the same time, these decisions are not final, for the tribunal will be able to reconsider their subject matter in the final award dealing with the merits of the dispute (section 47(3)).[96] Similarly, the act includes within the concept of award other important decisions rendered by arbitral tribunals, such as awards by consent (section 51) recording a settlement reached by the parties.[97] Much like provisional awards, consent awards have not found uniform recognition in France.[98]

---

91. *Halifax Life Ltd v. The Equitable Life Assurance Society* [2007] EWHC at paras 45 and 48; *Bernhard Schulte GmbH & Co v. Nile Holdings Ltd* [2004] EWHC 977 at para. 95; *Hussmann (Europe) Ltd v. Al Ameen Development & Trade Co* [2000] EWHC 210 at para. 47. *See also* Redfern, *supra* n. 1, at 2.
92. David St John Sutton, Judith Gill & Matthew Gearing, *Russel on Arbitration*, 305 (Sweet & Maxwell 2007).
93. *Ibid.* at 307.
94. *Wilky Property House Holdings Plc v. London & Surrey Investments Ltd* [2011] EWHC 2226 at para. 27. *See also Jivraj v. Hashwani* [2011] UKSC 40 at para. 41; *David Wilson Homes Ltd v. Survey Services Ltd* [2001] 1 EWCA Civ 34 at paras 13–14.
95. *See Konkola Copper Mines v. U&M Mining Zambia Ltd* [2014] EWHC 2374 at paras 88–97. Cf. Art. 17, *2006 UNCITRAL Model Law*.
96. Cf. Robert Merkin & Louis Flannery, *Arbitration Act 1996*, 156 (Routledge 2014).
97. *See* Section 51(3) *Arbitration Act 1996* ('An agreed award shall state that it is an award of the tribunal and shall have the same status and effect as any other award on the merits of the case' [emphasis added]); Art. 30, *2006 UNCITRAL Model Law*.
98. For an overview, *see* Éric Loquin, *L'arrêt de mort des sentences d'accord-parties*, Rev trim dr com 476 (2013) [Loquin, *L'arrêt de mort*].

§2.04 THE SILENCE OF THE NEW YORK CONVENTION

Unsurprisingly, the notion of award is an unsettled concept in international commercial arbitration. Critiques are raised whenever decisions of arbitrators depart from the model of final judgment found in state justice (and, therefore, from the monodimensional model). This is certainly the case for consent awards (i.e., decisions recording the parties' settlement in the form of an award).[99] However, arbitration practice seems quite indifferent to these critiques and relies on a model of award characterized by a high degree of pragmatism: the label of award is often given to a very heterogeneous group of decisions, mainly with a view to ensuring enforcement (especially under the *New York Convention*). In light of this puzzling scenario, scholars took two different positions.

The first one consisted in adopting a broad definition of award, capable of encompassing a wide range of decisions. Accordingly, it was suggested that '[a]n arbitral award can be defined as a final decision by the arbitrators on all or part of the dispute submitted to them, whether it concerns the merits of the dispute, jurisdiction, or a procedural issue leading them to end the proceedings'.[100] Similarly, another author suggested that an award would be a 'final and binding legal instrument, generally having immediate legal effects and creating immediate legal rights and obligations for the parties'.[101] One cannot, however, look at these definitions without a bit of scepticism: while the former fails to grasp the temporary validity of some decisions rendered by arbitral tribunals (e.g., a decision rendered by emergency arbitrators), the latter is so broad as to encompass even the civilian notion of contract (precisely, an instrument creating rights and obligations).

The second position consisted in arguing that the notion of award was an empty box. In particular, in this view, when examining the decision rendered by an arbitral tribunal, one should not ask oneself whether it is an award but rather whether it *should* be one.[102] Therefore, the analysis would ultimately be a matter of policy. As we shall see in the Conclusion, this position is appealing, as it shows that the notion of award is a essentially a regulative instrument which manages the interplays between arbitral and state justice.

The struggle facing arbitration scholars is also a consequence of the ambiguous position taken by the *New York Convention* and the 1985 UNCITRAL *Model Law*.[103] As far as the *Model Law* is concerned, despite intense discussions during the *travaux préparatoires*, the following definition was rejected for its controversial character:[104]

---

99. *See* Jean-Marie Tchakoua, *Le statut de la sentence arbitrale d'accord parties: les limites d'un déguisement bien utile*, 2 Int'l Buss J 784 (2002).
100. Gaillard & Savage, *supra* n. 5, at 735.
101. Born, *supra* n. 4, at 2897.
102. Kirby, *supra* n. 3, at 477.
103. Domenico Di Pietro, *What Constitutes an Award Under the New York Convention* in Gaillard & Di Pietro, *supra* n. 62, 139 at 140.
104. United Nations Commission on International Trade Law, *Report of the Working Group on International Contract Practices on the Work of its Seventh Session* (New York, 6–17 February 1984), UN Doc. A/CN.9/246, para. 192.

[A]ward means a final award which disposes of all issues submitted to the arbitral tribunal and any other decision of the arbitral tribunal which finally determine[s] any question of substance or the question of its competence or any other question of procedure but, in the latter case, only if the arbitral tribunal terms its decision an award.

The irreconcilable disagreement between those in favour of a more liberal definition of award also encompassing jurisdictional and procedural decisions and those in favour of a narrower one eventually led to its withdrawal.[105] Likewise, the 2006 amendments have failed to address this matter. This is particularly noticeable in the new articles dealing with provisional measures. Notably, Article 17(2) of the UNCITRAL *Model Law* laconically provides that provisional measures can either take the form of awards or orders.

Similarly, the *New York Convention* does not contain a definition of award. As noted by Sébastien Besson, 'the lacuna is not an omission that could have been avoided, but rather the result of the difficulties in identifying a unitary definition of arbitral award'.[106] This explains why it is unhelpful to attempt to uncover a meaning – whether objective or subjective – of the term 'award' by resorting to the *Vienna Convention on the Interpretation of Treaties (Vienna Convention)*,[107] for the meaning itself lies outside the *New York Convention*.[108] Moreover, this latter instrument demonstrates the severe limits of the rules of interpretation enacted in the *Vienna Convention*. As a matter of principle, the rules of interpretation of the *New York Convention* should not differ from those enacted in the *Vienna Convention*.[109] But said instrument being a multilateral treaty, with a set of core obligations to be performed by the national courts of each contracting state, the uniform interpretation of its provisions is not something that can be taken for granted. As observed by Albert van den Berg:[110]

The significance of the New York Convention for international commercial arbitration makes it even more important that the Convention is interpreted uniformly by the courts [of the contracting states]. A review of the court decisions on the Convention shows that such a uniform interpretation is lacking in several respects.

---

105. Gaillard & Savage, *supra* n. 5, at 735.
106. Besson, *supra* n. 90 at 326.
107. *Vienna Convention on the Law of Treaties*, 23 May 1969, entered into force on 27 January 1980, 1155 UNTS 331, 8 ILM 679 [*Vienna Convention*]. For a commentary, *see* Olivier Corten & Pierre Klein, *The Vienna Convention on the Law of Treaties* (Oxford University Press 2011); Mark E. Villiger, *Commentary on the 1969 Vienna Convention on the Law of Treaties* (Martinus Nijhoff Publishers 2009); Ulf Linderfalk, *On the Interpretation of Treaties* (Springer 2007); Richard K. Gardiner, *Treaty Interpretation* (Oxford University Press 2008).
108. Marike Paulsson, *The 1958 New York Convention in Action*, 31 (Kluwer Law 2016).
109. Cf. Art. 1 of the *Vienna Convention* ('The present Convention applies to treaties between States').
110. Albert van den Berg, *The New York Arbitration Convention of 1958*, 1 (Kluwer Law 1981). *See also* Christoph Liebscher, *Preliminary Remarks* in Reinmar Wolff, *The New York Convention* 1, 19 (Hart Publishing 2012).

This situation is further exacerbated by the fact that some contracting states systematically refuse to apply the *New York Convention*, on the ground that their national legislation would be more favourable to enforcement.¹¹¹

Divergent interpretations of international provisions are not a rare occurrence. Public international law scholars have described the implications of this phenomenon with the expression 'fragmentation of international law'.¹¹² Such fragmentation would derive from conflicting interpretations of international norms.¹¹³ In order to cope with the risk of fragmentation, courts and scholars have been developing sui generis rules for the harmonization of the interpretation of the *New York Convention*, which supplement the classic canons dictated by the *Vienna Convention*.

The first type of harmonization rule was advanced by Albert van den Berg, who, in his well-known commentary to the *New York Convention*, recommended the harmonization of the judicial interpretation of its provisions 'by means of the comparative case law method'.¹¹⁴ In his own words:¹¹⁵

> This approach has the objective to formulate one possibly acceptable interpretation on the basis of a comparison of court decisions given in respect of the convention, which could be followed by the courts in the contracting States.

The second type of harmonization rule, which is derived from Article 31(1) of the *Vienna Convention* (the 'object' of the treaty), aims to resolve issues of interpretation by referring to the 'pro-enforcement bias' of the *New York Convention*.¹¹⁶

---

111. This interpretation is based on Art. VII(1) of the *New York Convention* ('The provisions of the present Convention shall not ... deprive any interested party of any right he may have to avail himself of an arbitral award in the manner and to the extent allowed by the law or the treaties of the country where such award is sought to be relied upon'). *See* Clay, *La Convention de New York*, *supra* n. 44, at 50 ff.
112. William W. Burke-White, *International Legal Pluralism*, 25 Mich J Int'l L 963, 966 (2003). *See also* Jean D'Aspremont, *The Systemic Integration of International Law by Domestic Courts: Domestic Judges as Architects of the Consistency of the International Legal Order* in Ole K. Fauchald & André Nollkaemper, *The Practice of International and National Court and the (De-)Fragmentation of International Law* 141 (Hart Publishing 2012). For a Canadian perspective *see*: Joshua Karton & Samantha Wynne, *Canadian Courts and Uniform Interpretation: An Empirical Reality Check*, 1 Unif L Rev 1, 24–25 (2013).
113. Burke-White, *supra* n. 112, at 967. There are multiple causes for such divergence. According to Eyal Benvenisti, the protection of short-term national interests could be one. *See* Eyal Benvenisti, *Judicial Misgivings Regarding the Application of International Law: An Analysis of Attitudes of National Courts*, 4 EU J Int'l L 159, 161 (1993). *See also* Ole K. Fauchald & André Nollkaemper, *The Practice of International and National Courts and the (De-) Fragmentation of International Law – Conclusions* in Fauchald & Nollkaemper, *supra* n. 112, 343 at 352–353 ('In view of the interplay between domestic and international law, and the engagement of national courts in the international legal order, national judicial practice is a central factor for the level and characteristics of the fragmentation of international law. The fragmentation caused by divergent national receptions of international law is "an ephemeral reflection of a more fundamental, multidimensional fragmentation of global society itself". Such differences are not necessarily a matter of non-compliance with international obligations. They also can result from different constructions and interpretations that may even go beyond what is required by international law').
114. Van den Berg, *supra* n. 110, at 2. *See also* Di Pietro, *supra* n. 103, at 142.
115. Van den Berg, *supra* n. 110, at 2.
116. *See* Herbert Kronke, *The New York Convention Fifty Years on* in Kronke, *supra* n. 8, 1 at 3; Peter Sanders, *The New York Convention as an Instrument of International Law*, 15 (ICCA 2011). For

The above therefore reinforces the need for a comparative analysis. Furthermore, the special rules on the harmonization of the *New York Convention* point out that this comparative undertaking must take into consideration the importance of legal traditions, which are ultimately responsible for the reception of international law at the domestic level. This is why the often expressed view, according to which 'to fall under the Convention, awards must resolve a difference between the parties and be final in nature' is not entirely convincing.[117] The fact that Article 1(1) refers to a 'difference between persons', and Article V(1)(e) states that only 'binding' decisions will be enforceable as awards, is not enough to support the view restricting the notion of award to final decisions on a 'difference'.[118] This interpretation is in fact contingent to the definition of two terms–'binding' and 'difference'–which are quite general, in that they may also accommodate decisions that are all but final awards.

§2.05 CONCLUSION

The present chapter has outlined the academic debate on the adjudicative power of arbitrators and on the notion of award. In particular, it has summarized the distinctions between the monodimensional adjudicative model and the multidimensional model. In light of this overview, it is now the time to consider how international commercial arbitration functions. To do so, I will conduct a historical analysis, which will allow me to posit that the multidimensional adjudicative model is a natural development of international commercial arbitration, deriving from its institutional roots and international sources.

---

an application, *see Dardana v. Yukos* [2002] 2 Lloyd's Rep 326 at 10 (the pro-enforcement bias results in 'a prima facie right to recognition and enforcement').
117. Paulsson, *supra* n. 108, at 115.
118. *Ibid.* at 116.

CHAPTER 3
The Influence of Arbitral Institutions on Today's International Commercial Arbitration

§3.01 INTRODUCTION

In Western legal history, arbitration can be regarded as a form of dispute resolution as old as adjudication. There is, in fact, a palpable disagreement as to which came first.[119] It is probably impossible to tell since, as observed by Bruno Oppetit, the idea of arbitration grew in parallel with the notion of justice.[120] Arbitration, in fact, is at least as old as the Roman *Twelve Tables* (a collection of laws enacted in the fifth century BC),[121] which can be regarded as the foundations of modern litigation. While this book is not the appropriate place for providing an exhaustive historical account of arbitration, it is worth pointing out that arbitration has always been an available forum for the resolution of private disputes (whether or not commercial), coexisting with the public administration of justice. Therefore, the *idea* (or the *notion*) of arbitration itself – the reader can pick whatever term he or she prefers – has also evolved over time.[122]

After a few remarks on methodology (section §3.02), this chapter will describe the relationship between state litigation and arbitration in the nineteenth century, before the emergence of arbitral institutions (section §3.03). It will then address the rise of institutions in the first half of the twentieth century (section §3.04). In particular, it will elucidate the role of the ICC and its pursuit of preserving broad autonomy in the

---

119. Ernest Metzger, *An Outline of Civil Procedure*, 9 Rom L Trad 1, 9 (2013); Michel Humbert & Bruno de Loynes de Fumichon, *L'arbitrage à Rome*, 2 Rev Arb 285, 291–292 (2003).
120. Oppetit, *supra* n. 15, at 13.
121. Derek Roebuck & Brunoroede Loynes de Fumichon, *Roman Arbitration*, 67 (Oxford University Press 2004); Clay, *L'arbitre, supra* n. 61, at 6.
122. Jan Paulsson, *The Idea of Arbitration*, 5–6 (Oxford University Press 2013); Jarrosson, *supra* n. 16, at 369.

creation of a specialized procedure for the resolution of international commercial disputes. Next, it will show how the ICC obtained recognition of its aspirations through the 1923 Geneva *Protocol on Arbitration Clauses*, the 1927 *Convention on the Execution of Foreign Arbitral Awards*, and the 1958 *New York Convention* (section §3.05). The chapter will then consider how this recognition constituted an important opportunity for other actors interested in the growth of international commercial arbitration (section §3.06). In particular, it will describe how new arbitration centres took advantage of the liberalization of arbitral procedure and how states encouraged the development and increase of alternative fora for the resolution of civil disputes. Finally, the chapter will address the implications of the institutional foundations of contemporary international commercial arbitration (section §3.07).

§3.02 A THEORETICAL OVERVIEW OF INSTITUTIONALISM

The term 'institution' has deep historical roots and comes across as both intuitive and complex at the same time.[123] At a basic level, it alludes to an entity capable of constraining individual behaviour 'within the context of [its] organization'.[124] There are, nonetheless, many types of institutionalism, as well as many different definitions of 'institution'. A first type of institutionalism can be found in political sciences. Here, institutions vary from a 'collection of norms, rules, understandings, and ... routines'[125] to 'a process, ... a settled structure or an identifiable pattern'.[126] A second type of institutionalism can be found in sociological studies. The basic requirements for an institution are similar (albeit looser) in this field. Institutions are either an ensemble of 'regulative, normative, and cultural-cognitive elements'[127] or 'assemblages of practices within larger social fields or more generally devices for ordering society'.[128] For the present purposes, I will adopt the basic meaning of institutionalism in sociology, according to which an institution is a collection of regulative and cognitive elements.

While similar definitions of 'institution' can be found in sociology and political science, these fields' research goals relating to institutionalism are quite different. In

---

123. Yves Sassier, *Reflexion autour du sens d'instituere, institutio, instituta* in Jean-Philippe Bras, *L'institution* 19, 26 (L'Harmanattan 2008) ('*instituere, institutio*, signifient à la fois l'action de fondation, et l'action d'établir une personne dans une fonction préexistante, avec cette première idée que, lorsque on l'on fonde, on établit en même temps une règle, un cadre imposé de fonctionnement de l'objet créé'). *Ibid.* at 31 ('Plus encore que le mot *institutio*, assez souvent cantonné à désigner un modèle ou une règle de vie spécifique, c'est dans le domaine du droit, le mot *institutia*, substantif neutre pluriel construit à partir du participe passé *institutus*, qui traduira durant le Moyen Âge le cadre légal général dans lequel devra se mouvoir l'action des dirigeants et des dirigés').
124. Brainard Guy Peters, *Institutional Theory in Political Science*, 179 (Continuum International Publishing Group, 2012).
125. *Ibid.* at 29.
126. *Ibid.* at 116. *See also* Mark A. Pollack, *Political Science and International Adjudication* in Romano, *supra* n. 26, 357 at 363–364.
127. W. Richard Scott, *Approaching Adulthood: The Maturing of Institutional Theory*, 37:5 Theory and Society 427, 428 (2008). *See also* W. Richard Scott, *The Adolescence of Institutional Theory*, 32.4 Adm Sci 493, 493–511 (1987).
128. Mikael Rask Madsen, 'Sociological Approaches to International Courts' in Romano, *supra* n. 26, 388 at 391.

very general terms, if the overarching objective of political science studies is that of understanding the functioning of an institution and predicting its (present and future) behaviour in politics, sociological studies are rather interested in what institutional organizations per se aim to achieve.[129] A similar dualism can be found in arbitration literature. On the one hand, some arbitration specialists focus on the central role and functioning of arbitral institutions.[130] Their analysis starts from the premise that international commercial arbitration is a type of justice. Arbitration centres would contribute to the administration of justice just as state courts would do.[131] In particular, while the accounts on the nature and contribution of arbitral institutions have often depicted them as being relegated to the exercise of administrative functions, some scholars have recently started to question this view, arguing that these institutions participate in the overall adjudication of the dispute between the parties.[132] On the other hand, a second group of scholars concentrates on the (hidden), or socio-economic, goals of arbitral institutions. By drawing on an ample pool of interviews with arbitration scholars and practitioners, Dezalay and Garth, the fathers of this school of thought, posited that the international commercial arbitration regime is grounded in the activity of arbitral institutions, among which is the International Court of Arbitration of the ICC.[133] These institutions would serve as hubs of a network composed of a number of individuals, around which the legitimacy of international commercial arbitration is constructed.[134] The overarching goal would be that of controlling – or at least enjoying a preponderant influence over – a specific portion of the legal market: the sector concerned with international dispute resolution.[135]

---

129. Samuel Barkin, *International Organization: Theories and Institutions*, 27 (Macmillan 2006) (referring to the literature on international organizations). The roots of this analysis are found in Max Weber, *Economy and Society*, 246 ff. (University of California Press 1978). These sociological definitions draw therefore on Weber's view, according to which institutions are a transformation of authority (a legitimate mode of domination) from a charismatic, individual level to a collective, organized one. *See also* David Armstrong, Theo Farrell & Hélène Lambert, *International Law and International Relations*, 100 ff. (Cambridge University Press 2012).
130. The most important proponents of this analysis are Bruno Oppetit and Philippe Fouchard. *See generally* Philippe Fouchard, *Où va l'arbitrage international*, 34 MLJ 435 (1989); Philippe Fouchard, *Typologie des institutions d'arbitrage*, 2 Rev Arb 281 (1990).
131. Jarrosson, *supra* n. 16, at 369. *See also* Gerbay, *supra* n. 34, at 213 (the author describes arbitral institutions as 'ancillary participants in the adjudicative process [of the arbitrators]').
132. *Ibid.* at 185, and 190 ff.
133. Yves Dezalay & Brian Garth, *Dealing in Virtue*, 5 (Chicago University Press 1996); Gerbay, *supra* n. 34, at 46.
134. Dezalay & Garth, *supra* n. 133, at 46.
135. *Ibid* at 197 ff. *See* Madsen, *supra* n. 128, at 400 ('[Dezalay and Garth's work] is based on two different research traditions which are brought together via a set of broader conceptual frameworks provided by the sociologist Pierre Bourdieu: first, a sociology of professions with a view to analysing how professions increasingly compete with one another in the construction of new transnational markets and arenas; secondly, a sociology of elites with the aim of exploring how a set of distinct social groups of (legal) agents hold the power to define new areas of legal practice, with consequences not only for the profession at large, but also for international politics and society. Drawing on Pierre Bourdieu, they frame these battles as social *fields*, that is, as spaces of contestation over defining the law in which different agents occupy positions relative to the portfolio of capitals they can muster and which are "capitalized" according to the logic of the specific field in question').

This chapter will attempt to provide arguments in support of the first school of thought, according to which arbitral institutions and arbitral tribunals constituted under their aegis fulfil in a cooperative manner a set of adjudicative functions. In particular, by relying on a historical approach, I will look at the birth and evolution of what can be regarded as the most influential international arbitration centre – the International Court of Arbitration of the ICC – as the motor for the creation of a stable system of arbitral justice. In a nutshell, the theoretical assumption is that in order to understand how an institution operates in its current form, one has to look at its historical foundations.[136] This static character – or slow evolution around founding pillars – results from the allegiance that actors of a given institution have vis-à-vis its traditional objectives.[137]

Before turning to the history of the ICC, however, it is important to indulge in a brief historical excursus on the relationship between state justice and arbitration. This will allow me to highlight the historical circumstances that permitted the emergence of the ICC and of the institutional setting of international commercial arbitration.

§3.03 ARBITRATION IN THE NINETEENTH CENTURY: A WEAK COMPETITOR OF STATE JUSTICE

After a long period of tranquil proliferation (especially during the Italian Renaissance and the growth of the mercantile society in France),[138] the role of arbitration in continental Europe was greatly reduced after the fall of the *ancien régime*, when the concentration of normative power and civil justice in the hands of a centralized political authority was finally achieved. This occurrence can be regarded as a response to the maze of normative sources and the excesses of local parliaments in the administration of justice.[139]

---

136. *See* Sven Steinmo, *Historical Institutionalism* in Donatella Della Porta & Michael Keating, *Approaches and Methodologies in The Social Sciences* 118, 127 (Cambridge University Press 2008); Mikael Rask Madsen & Mikkel Jarle Christensen, *Global Actors: Networks, Elites, Institutions*, 44 iCourts WPS 1, 21 (2016) ('Historical institutionalism builds on the development of institutions themselves. This perspective is not completely unrelated to either formalism or realism and in fact incorporates elements of both, namely how political space formats institutions, and how institutions themselves co-create their boundaries by following their own internal logic. To explain the development of this logic, the institution is studied in a wider field in which its foundational dynamics help define how it evolves, what is also referred to as path dependency. In other words, the path dependency of institutions is shaped by their political mandate as well as by the organizational formats, normative preferences, and professional balances').
137. This 'allegiance' has been defined as 'path-dependency' of a given institution. For a critical analysis of the term, *see* Roy Suddaby, William M. Foster & Albert J. Mills, *Historical Institutionalism* in Marcelo Bucheli & R. Daniel Wadhwani, *Organizations in Time* 100, 110 (Oxford University Press 2014).
138. *See generally* Yves Jeanclos, *La pratique de l'arbitrage au XIIème et XVème siècle*, 3 Rev Arb 417 (1999).
139. *See* e.g., Albert N. Hamscher, *The Parlement of Paris after the Fronde*, 155 (Pittsburgh University Press 2009); William Beik, *Absolutism in France*, 77 ff. (Cambridge University Press 1985); Henry A. De Colyar, *Jean-Baptiste Colbert and the Codifying Ordinances of Louis XIV*, 13:1 J Soc Comp Leg 56, 58 (1912) ('In Colbert's time, and indeed before the great Revolution,

Following a brief period of popularity in the aftermath of the French revolution,[140] arbitration was relegated to a minor role under Napoleon (and the *Code de procédure civile* of 1806), akin to a form of private conciliation rather than a type of justice.[141] The mistrust of arbitration culminated in a decision rendered in 1843 by the *Cour de cassation*, declaring arbitration clauses null and void.[142] From a technical point of view, the only valid way to resort to arbitration was through the conclusion of a submission to arbitration (*compromis, compromissum*), that is, an agreement to arbitrate an existing dispute. At its highest point, the European glorification of the centralization of normative and adjudicative power in the hands of the sovereign resulted in a view of arbitration as a threat. René David sums up this perception very aptly: 'arbitration is a loose cannon, capable of threatening state justice. As such, it must be scrutinized, and limits must be imposed on the possibility to conclude arbitration agreements'.[143] This negative conception was further transposed into most of the European jurisdictions influenced by Napoleonic codes[144] and, as result, also in Latin America.[145] Similar ideas can also be found in common law jurisdictions, though the motives for opposing arbitration were very different.

In the United States (US), for example, the principle according to which parties to a contract 'cannot oust the jurisdiction of the courts by any agreement to submit the matters in difference to arbitration' is found in several nineteenth century decisions.[146]

---

the civil legislation of France was divided into two general systems, namely, the customary and the written law, each of which branched into a multitude, of subdivisions. There were upwards of 180 customs, extending more or less over the various provinces of France. In many parts of the country, though less in Provence and Languedoc, the Roman law had gone back into that shape of a body of customs from which it had emerged a thousand years before, while in Northern and Middle France some customs, and especially those relating to land, were not Roman at all. Independently of customary law and written law, considered as local law, France was also governed by Roman law, the laws of the Prince, and the decisions of the local Parliaments').

140. Jean Hilaire, *L'arbitrage dans la période moderne (XVIème-XVIIIème siècle)*, 2 Rev Arb 187, 225 (2000). *See also* Carine Jallamion, *Arbitrage forcé et justice d'état pendant la révolution française*, 4 Annales historiques de la Révolution française 69, 70–71 (2007) ('La faveur des révolutionnaires pour l'arbitrage se révèle rapidement, au cours de la réforme de la justice dont le chantier commence dès le mois d'août 1789, et elle est corrélative de la méfiance des révolutionnaires envers la justice traditionnelle. La réforme entreprise par les Constituants aboutit ainsi à la loi des 16-24 août 1790 qui contient deux séries de dispositions sur l'arbitrage, lesquelles reposent sur la foi quasi dogmatique du pouvoir politique dans la résolution extrajudiciaire des conflits. ... Le titre Ier de la loi présenté d'abord l'arbitrage volontaire comme "le moyen le plus raisonnable de terminer les contestations entre citoyens"').
141. Carine Jallamion, *Arbitrage et pouvoir politique en France du XVIIème au XIXème siècle*, 1 Rev Arb 2, 37 (2005).
142. Cour de cassation, 10 July 1843, as cited by René David, *Arbitrage du XIXème et arbitrage du XXème siècle* in *Mélanges offerts à René Savatier*, 219, 220 (Dalloz 1965) ('On ne compromet pas valablement, lorsqu'on ne désigne pas l'objet du litige et le nom des arbitres ... la distinction entre une convention compromissoire et un compromis, n'est établie par aucune disposition de la loi, et on [ne pourrait] l'admettre sans méconnaitre le véritable esprit du Code de procédure au titre des arbitrages').
143. *Ibid.* at 221.
144. René David, *L'arbitrage dans le commerce international*, 40 (Economica 1982).
145. Born, *supra* n. 4 at 60–61.
146. *See*, e.g., *Trott v. The City Ins. Co.* (1860) 1 Cliff. 439 (Maine). For an overview, *see* Addison C. Burnham, *Arbitration as a Condition Precedent*, 11:4 HLR 234, 243 (1897).

England, albeit with a different timing, also displayed great loathing for arbitration. A quite sincere explanation for despising arbitration is provided by Lord Campbell in *Scott v. Avery*:[147]

> Somehow the Courts of law had, in former times, acquired a horror of arbitration; and it was even doubted if a clause for a general reference of prospective disputes was legal. I never could imagine for what reason parties should not be permitted to bind themselves to settle their disputes in any manner on which they agreed ... This doctrine had its origin in the interests of the judges. There was no disguising the fact that, as formerly, the emoluments of the judges depended mainly, or almost entirely, on fees, and as they had no fixed salaries there was great competition to get as much as possible of litigation into Westminster Hall and there was a great scramble in Westminster Hall for the division of the spoil. ... And they had great jealousy of arbitration whereby Westminster Hall was robbed of those cases.

Among the last bastions defending this negative conception of arbitration one can find French and Québec law, in which up until 1981 and 1983, respectively, arbitration clauses were considered void for breach of public policy.[148]

At the end of the nineteenth century, a significant shift occurred, growing exponentially in importance at the beginning of the twentieth century. The impulse came from private institutions, which managed to change the perception entertained by national legislators of international commercial arbitration. A few words are thus necessary to explain, first, why such a shift occurred and, second, how it was implemented.

§3.04 ARBITRATION IN THE FIRST HALF OF THE TWENTIETH CENTURY: THE RISE AFTER INSTITUTIONALIZATION

The first half of the twentieth century witnessed a significant evolution of arbitration. While this evolution essentially concerned international commercial arbitration, important consequences also ensued for domestic arbitration. It is most difficult to provide an exact description of this evolution. With some approximation, it is nonetheless possible to conclude that the creation of the ICC constitutes the most significant motor of this process. I will thus focus my study on the ICC, conscious of the fact that other arbitration centres, such as the London Court of International Arbitration (LCIA) are as old as, if not simply older, than the ICC, and have had a significant impact on international commercial arbitration. Such institutions are further described below in section §3.06.

---

147. *Scott v. Avery* [1856] 5 H.L. Cas. 811, 853 (House of Lords). The excerpts are reproduced in Born, *supra* n. 4, at 36–37.
148. Fouchard, 'Où va l'arbitrage international?', *supra* n. 130, at 437–438 ('[Au Canada] dans les provinces de *common law*, l'arbitrage a été soumis à une tutelle judiciaire étroite, inspirée du droit anglais, tandis qu'au Québec, sous l'influence du droit français, la clause compromissoire a été prohibée ou contestée jusqu'à l'intervention de la Cour suprême du Canada, le 17 mai 1983'). *See Zodiak International Productions Inc. c. The Polish People's Republic*, [1983] 1 SCR 529.

Chapter 3: The Influence of Arbitral Institutions §3.04[A]

[A] A Historical Overview of the ICC

The decision to found the ICC was made in 1919, in the aftermath of World War I, at the International Trade Conference held in Atlantic City,[149] with a view to safeguarding peace through economic prosperity. This explains why its founders have been described since its inception as the 'merchants of peace'.[150] The initiative to create the chamber was mooted by a group of 'influential industrialists and traders from Belgium, France, Italy, the UK and the United States, all of whom were called together by the US Chamber of Commerce'.[151] The ICC's headquarters were established in Paris. As reported by the ICC itself:[152]

> The world had few working international structures in the immediate aftermath of the first of the 20th century's global conflicts. There was no world system of rules to govern trade, investment, finance or commercial relations. That the private sector should start filling the gap without waiting for governments was groundbreaking. It was an idea that took hold.
>
> Although they did not know it at the time, the pioneers were creating an organization that would become essential to the global economy ... From the very beginning, ICC spoke out on behalf of business in making representations to governments and intergovernmental organizations. [As an illustration,] three ICC members served on the Dawes Commission, which drew up the international treaty on war reparations in 1924.

Besides the noble considerations behind the decision to found the ICC, the initiative constituted a concrete response to the need to reconstruct Europe's economic foundations after the disaster of World War I.[153] To contemporary observers, it may look somehow ironic that the reins of an institution aiming at the liberalization of markets and trade were taken, in 1923, by Étienne Clémentel, a second-class French politician often regarded as a socialist sympathizer[154] but who was also one of the founding figures of the ICC.[155] Yet the contradictions are only apparent. Clémentel's efforts in international relations were focused on the creation of an economic union with Western European countries and the US.[156] It is probably the failure of such

---

149. Dominic Kelly, *The International Chamber of Commerce*, 10:2 NPE 259, 260 (2005).
150. *See The Merchants of Peace*, http://www.iccwbo.org/about-icc/history/ (accessed 31 January 2017); *see also* Florian Grisel et al., *Aux origines de l'arbitrage commercial contemporain: l'émergence de l'arbitrage CCI (1920–1958)*, 2 Rev Arb 403, 434 (2016) [Grisel, *Aux origines*].
151. Dominc Kelly, *The Business of Diplomacy: The International Chamber of Commerce meets the United Nations*, 74:1 CSGR 1, 10 (2001).
152. *Merchants of Peace*, *supra* n. 150.
153. George L. Ridgeway, *The Merchants of Peace*, 21 (Columbia University Press 1938).
154. Clotilde Druelle-Korn, *De la pensée à l'action économique: Étienne Clémentel (1864–1936), un ministre visionnaire*, 16:1 Histoire-Politique 1, 8 (2012) ('Si l'on cherche à confronter les réflexions de politique économique de Clémentel au programme économique du parti radical, plusieurs intersections se dessinent ... En matière économique, l'élu pratique volontiers l'éclectisme tout en puisant aux grandes options du radicalisme économique: primauté de l'État et solidarisme'). *See also* Marc Trachtenberg, *A New Economic Order: Etienne Clémentel and the French Economic Diplomacy during the First World War*, 10:2 Fre Hist'l Std 315, 318 (1977).
155. Ridgeway, *supra* n. 153, 21.
156. David Stevenson, *The First World War and European Integration*, 34:4 Int'l Hist Rev 841, 856 (2012).

project that brought him to the ICC, in a broader attempt to consolidate diplomatic relations with the US, an attempt that proved successful (thanks in part to the pressure exercised by large American companies wishing to start investing in Europe and needing to get rid of the post-war *dirigisme*).[157] Clémentel's appointment can also be regarded as a form of recognition for his political work, despite his work's lack of prestige at the national level. On this point, an author has observed that:[158]

> Clémentel was not a political figure of the first order. A deputy since 1900 and a minister three times before the war, he never headed a government and does not seem to have personally had a large political following. He was not even able to keep his seat in the elections of November 1919, which in other respects represented a landslide victory for the government.

Be that as it may, Clémentel's merits are certainly to be praised, for he was able to see the full potential of the ICC, aiming to use it as an important diplomatic instrument. In this regard, the proximity of the old Paris headquarters (38 cours Albert 1er) to several embassies is eloquent.

Coming back to the history of the ICC, a major turning point was the creation of the International Court of Arbitration (*Cour internationale d'arbitrage*), which took place in 1923, the year of Clémentel's appointment.[159] The International Court of Arbitration was established with a view to providing an alternative method of dispute resolution, characterized by the application of equity and the non-provision of reasons in awards.[160] According to this equitable vision of arbitration, also favoured by Clémentel, the model of dispute resolution that was to be preferred was one where the arbitrator decided in equity, free from any legalistic constraints.[161] This is why, for instance, the first rules enacted by the ICC insisted on the importance of conciliation, as a primary tool for preserving business relationships.[162]

We know that this type of arbitration has now been abandoned, save in some industries, in favour of law-based arbitration, bringing the procedure significantly closer to the standard paradigm of state justice, and far away from the alternative equitable model that served as its source of inspiration.[163] The ICC's law-based

---

157. Geir Lundestad, *Empire by Invitation in the American Century*, 23:2 Dipl Hist 189, 192 (1999) (the author underlines the vain insistence on keeping the United States involved in European politics via membership in several post-war councils regulating shipping and commercial raw materials). *See also* Andrew Knapp & Vincent Wright, *Government and Politics of France*, 18 (4th ed., Routledge 2001).
158. Trachtenberg, *supra* n. 154, 317.
159. Phillippe Fouchard, *L'arbitrage commercial international*, 215 (Dalloz 1965).
160. Florian Grisel, *Droit et non droit dans les sentences arbitrales CCI: une perspective historique*, 25:2 ICC Bull 13, 14 (2014) [Grisel, *Droit et non droit dans les sentences CCI*].
161. *International Commercial Arbitration – Practical Hints* (ICC Publishing 1935) at 5, as cited by Grisel, *supra* n. 160, at 14.
162. Grisel, *Aux origines*, *supra* n. 150, at 439.
163. Pierre Mayer, *L'arbitre et la loi* in *Études offertes à Pierre Catala*, 225, 240 (Litec 2001) ('Les rapports de l'arbitre avec la loi sont plus complexes que ceux que le juge entretient (ou devrait entretenir) avec elle. Extérieur des ordres juridiques, il jouit d'une grande liberté, surtout en matière internationale, où il est le maître du choix du système, non nécessairement étatique, dans lequel il puisera les règles. Il est exposé à la tentation de l'équité, et à celle de la valorisation excessive du contrat qui lie ceux dont il tient sa mission. Pourtant la loi a bien des

Chapter 3: The Influence of Arbitral Institutions   §3.04[B]

arbitration paradigm is now a constant in international arbitration, despite evidence of the continued response to non-legalistic concerns via the application of trade usages and *lex mercatoria*.[164]

[B]   The ICC's Impetus in Favour of Arbitration

The decision to create an International Court of Arbitration was prompted by the general feeling that state litigation was inadequate, and this for several reasons. Essentially, the proponents of a 'world court of business' felt that state litigation lacked rapidity and understanding of the commercial practices surrounding international commercial matters.[165] To be fair, arbitration also established itself at the ICC thanks to the previous satisfactory experiences of some European and American chambers of commerce with this form of dispute resolution.[166] A resolution adopted at the 1914 International Congress of Chambers of Commerce and Commercial and Industrial Associations, held in Paris, acknowledged that the development of an international private arbitration mechanism had already been explored a few years before.[167] On this occasion, the delegates had expressed the intention to consider a form of arbitration based on:[168]

> the arbitration rules of the International Cotton Federation and by those of the International Publishers' Congress, also taking into account the important results of the inquiry conducted by the Berlin Chamber of Commerce, and of the proposed rules compiled by the New York Chamber of Commerce, with a view to organizing international colleges of arbitrators for all trades or groups of trades.

In 1921, after the end of the war, the first ICC Congress, in London, recognized that the idea of creating a 'world court of business' was to be supported by 'the securing of legal sanction through national acceptance of foreign arbitrators and their decisions

---

mérites ... elle garantit contre l'arbitraire et rassure les parties, elle prend en compte les intérêts généraux de la société. Cela devrait conduire l'arbitre à lui manifester, mieux que de l'obéissance, du respect. Les usagers de l'arbitrage, et les États, n'attendent pas autre chose'). Cf. David, *supra* n. 144, at 568 ('L'opposition entre arbitrage selon le droit et amiable composition est finalement un leurre. En dehors de cas spéciaux, dont on ne saurait nier l'existence, il est permis de dire que tous les arbitres sont, dans une large mesure, des amiables compositeurs, parce que leur préoccupation, conforme à la volonté des parties, est d'arriver à une solution de justice plus que d'appliquer rigoureusement un droit étatique donné').
164. Cf. Joshua Karton, *The Culture of International Arbitration and the Evolution of Contract Law*, 147 ff. (Oxford University Press 2013) (the author underlines the persistent differences from state litigation that exist regarding the application by the arbitrators of the substantive law). *See also* Grisel, *Droit et non droit dans les sentences CCI*, *supra* n. 160, at 17 ff. (the author argues that the equitable aspects of early ICC arbitration were transposed into today's paradigm via provisions on trade usages and the *lex mercatoria* doctrine); Emmanuel Jolivet, Giacomo Marchisio & Fabien Gélinas, *Trade Usages in ICC Arbitration* in Fabien Gélinas, *Trade Usages and Implied Terms in the Age of Arbitration* 211 (Oxford University Press 2016).
165. Ridgeway, *supra* n. 153, at 317.
166. Claire Lemercier & Jérôme Sgard, *Arbitrage privé international et globalisation(s)*, 11 ff. (CNRS 2015).
167. Grisel, *Aux origines*, *supra* n. 150, at 438.
168. Ridgeway, *supra* n. 153, at 318.

and the unification of laws on arbitration in an international convention'.[169] The diplomatic efforts of the ICC under the leadership of Clémentel led to the successful conclusion of the 1923 Geneva *Protocol on Arbitration Clauses* (*Geneva Protocol*).[170] Similar circumstances led to the drafting of the Geneva *Convention on the Execution of Foreign Arbitral Awards* of 1927 (*Geneva Convention*),[171] an ancillary instrument to the *Protocol on Arbitration Clauses* that was concluded with a view to fostering the effectiveness of arbitral decisions, allowing the enforcement of awards in jurisdictions other than the one in which the arbitration took place.[172] The first sign of the revolution in states' perception of arbitration thus became apparent.

Nevertheless, the 1927 *Convention on the Execution of Foreign Arbitral Awards* revealed a certain carefulness, exemplified by its Article I. According to this article, in order to obtain recognition and enforcement of an award, the applicant had to meet the following (onerous) conditions by proving:

(a) That the award has been made in pursuance of a submission to arbitration which is valid under the law applicable thereto;
(b) That the subject-matter of the award is capable of settlement by arbitration under the law of the country in which the award is sought to be relied upon;
(c) That the award has been made by the Arbitral Tribunal provided for in the submission to arbitration or constituted in the manner agreed upon by the parties and in conformity with the law governing the arbitration procedure;
(d) That the award has become final in the country in which it has been made, in the sense that it will not be considered as such if it is open to *opposition*, *appel* or *pourvoi en cassation* (in the countries where such forms of procedure exist) or if it is proved that any proceedings for the purpose of contesting the validity of the award are pending;
(e) That the recognition or enforcement of the award is not contrary to the public policy or to the principles of the law of the country in which it is sought to be relied upon.

---

169. *Ibid.* at 327 ('Clémentel ... introduced a bill designed to insure the validity in France of arbitration clauses agreed to with nationals of other countries. ... Events were moving in a similar direction at Geneva where the Economic Committee had been preparing a draft protocol dealing with the question of the validity of arbitration clauses. On September 24, 1923, a protocol designed to secure the international validity of the arbitration clause was approved by the Assembly and opened for signature. Such was the French enthusiasm for commercial arbitration that although Clémentel's bill had not at that time become law, the French delegation at Geneva, under the leadership of Hanotaux, nevertheless accepted the principles of the bill as embodied in the protocol and signed the protocol for the nation. The council of the ICC, through the national committees, waged a vigorous campaign to secure national signatures and ratifications for the protocol').
170. *Protocol on Arbitration Clauses of 1923*, 27 League of Nations Treaty Series (1924) 158. It appears that the ICC's interests were successfully lobbied by British representatives before the League of Nations, after a first failed attempt by the ICC itself. *See* Lemercier & Sgard, *supra* n. 166, at 98 ff.; Eugenio Minoli, *Rapport introductif* in IIIrd International Arbitration Congress 1969 189, 189 (UTED 1970) ('Entre les deux guerres, l'institution de la CCI seule avait été suffisante pour obtenir la signature du Protocole de 1923, puis de la Convention de Genève de 1927'); Grisel, *Aux origines*, *supra* n. 150 at 451.
171. *Geneva Convention on the Execution of Foreign Awards of 1927*, 92 League of Nations Treaty Series (1929-1930), 302. *See* Lemercier & Sgard, *supra* n. 166, at 105 ff.; Minoli, *supra* n. 170, at 189; Grisel, *Aux origines*, *supra* n. 150, at 452.
172. Ridgeway, *supra* n. 153, at 328-329.

Despite the harsh conditions imposed on applicants looking to enforce foreign arbitral awards, these two international instruments certainly had the potential to shift the state of the law. In particular, the 1923 *Geneva Protocol* managed to revive the use of arbitration clauses, that is, clauses providing for arbitration before any dispute has arisen, and to subvert the rule requiring the existence of a dispute before an arbitration agreement was allowed to be concluded.

[C] The ICC's Difficulties Implementing International Commercial Arbitration

Not entirely satisfied with its success, the ICC continued to solicit the ratification of the 1923 *Geneva Protocol* and the 1927 *Geneva Convention*, and with a resolution adopted at the ICC Vienna Congress on 2 June 1933, it invited all those states that had not already done so to sign and ratify these two international conventions.[173] The declaration was an implicit reference to the US, which had refused to sign the protocol and the convention.[174] At the same time, the 1927 *Convention on the Execution of Foreign Arbitral Awards* had only been ratified by a limited number of countries (albeit those among the most important from an economic standpoint).[175] Most importantly, however, not only was the ICC struggling to bring about an effective implementation of the international regime it had designed, but it also began to face competition from another international institution, namely, the Institute for the Unification of Private Law (UNIDROIT).[176] Two years after the ICC Vienna Congress, the institution received, from UNIDROIT, a copy of a proposed international law on arbitration, which had been drafted in 1935, along with a request for comments.[177] At first, the draft was received with mild enthusiasm. The type of observations submitted by René Arnaud, *conseiller technique* of the International Court of Arbitration, were of two kinds.[178]

---

173. Vienna Congress, International Commercial Arbitration, Minutes of the Meeting of June 2nd, 1933 (unpublished), n. 5288 AB/CL.
174. *Protocol on Arbitration Clauses*, Ratifications, Registration n. 678, 2 League of Nations Multilateral Treaties 1 (Part II).
175. *Convention on the Execution of Foreign Arbitral Awards*, Ratifications, Registration n. 2096, 7 League of Nations Multilateral Treaties 1 (Part II).
176. The organism, with headquarters in Rome, was founded in 1926 by an act of the League of Nations and was later reaffirmed by an independent treaty in 1940. For a historical overview, *see* Mario Matteucci, *The History of Unidroit and the Methods of Unification*, 66 LLJ 286 (1973).
177. Committee on International Commercial Arbitration, 12th session, December 4th, 1935, ICC Doc. 5743 (unpublished) ('The International Institute for the Unification of Private Law at Rome has submitted to the International Chamber of Commerce this preliminary draft recently worked out by its Committee of experts on arbitration, requesting the Chamber to present its observations. Although this is not an official consultation since the draft is not final, the matter appeared sufficiently important to call for a searching study being made by the Committee on International Commercial Arbitration. An explanatory memorandum drafted by the Institute, as well as a covering letter, are attached to the preliminary draft. The members of the Committee will receive before the meeting a commentary prepared by Mr René Arnaud, technical advisor of the Court of Arbitration, with the cooperation of the headquarters of the ICC').
178. René Arnaud, *Observations sur l'Avant-projet d'une loi internationale sur l'arbitrage en droit privé, élaborée par l'Institut international de Rome pour l'unification du droit privé*, 5 December 1935, CCI doc. 5745 AB/CL (unpublished).

On the one hand, certain innovations suggested by UNIDROIT were clearly praised – this was the case of Article 28 (*effet universel de l'exequatur*), which provided that once an award has been declared enforceable by a state, enforcement could not be refused in another state, save for the following cases: (i) the award has already been enforced; (ii) the award is against the public policy of the forum where the enforcement is sought; and (iii) the award deals with a matter that is not arbitrable in the place of enforcement. René Arnaud did not contain his enthusiasm and stated in his commentary that the draft provision adopts the same view expressed by the ICC, simplifying and facilitating the enforcement of arbitral awards.[179] On the other hand, however, certain draft provisions were dismissed with severe critiques. This is the case, for instance, of Article 4 (form of the arbitration agreement), which stated that unwritten and unsigned arbitration agreements were invalid unless the party waived its right to challenge such validity.[180] In this regard, Arnaud observed that the provision excluded the validity of arbitration clauses contained in the terms and conditions of many sale contracts. As a result, the tacit approval of these terms would no longer suffice for a validly concluded arbitration clause, something that was completely against the business practices.[181]

Another example of the ICC's criticism concerned the provision on the replacement of arbitrators, which suggested that in case of difficulties in the constitution of the arbitral tribunal, the interested party could seek the intervention of state courts. The observations submitted to UNIDROIT in this regard underlined that the decisions on the challenges against arbitrators ought to be an exclusive prerogative of the ICC.[182]

Yet the mild enthusiasm expressed at first was only the initial position of the ICC. Criticism was on the rise. Roughly a year after the report of René Arnaud, Henri

---

179. *Ibid.* at 13 ('L'exposé des motifs [de UNIDROIT] marque la hardiesse de cette innovation, qui consacre l'effet universel de l'exequatur accordé dans un pays donné. Il y a lieu d'applaudir à cette disposition qui est parfaitement conforme à l'esprit qui anime la Cour d'Arbitrage de la CCI, en simplifiant et facilitant autant que possible les difficultés d'exécution des sentences arbitrales').
180. Article 4, *Projet de loi uniforme* ('La convention arbitrale doit être stipulée par écrit et signée par les parties sous peine de nullité. Elle peut être modifiée de la même manière. La nullité, toutefois, est couverte, en ce qui concerne une contestation donnée, s'il résulte du procès-verbal ou de la sentence que les parties ont comparu devant la juridiction arbitrale et que, par leur conduite, elles ont renoncé à se prévaloir de cette nullité').
181. Arnaud, *supra* n. 178, at 3 ('Pareil article exclut du domaine d'application de la loi les cas, très fréquents dans le commerce, où une partie fait figurer une clause arbitrale dans ses conditions générales de vente, imprimées en marge ou au verso de son papier à lettres commercial et où l'acceptation de cette clause par l'autre partie se déduit du consentement tacite de cette dernière. Cette exclusion est d'autant plus regrettable que plusieurs lois ou jurisprudence nationales considèrent ces clauses acceptées tacitement comme des engagements parfaitement valables. ... Il serait fâcheux que l'adoption de la loi internationale en matière d'arbitrage eût pour effet d'imposer aux tribunaux une attitude moins libérale ... et d'interdire pratiquement tout recours à l'arbitrage à des milliers de commerçants et d'industriels qui traitent quotidiennement de petites ou grosses affaires sans qu'il y ait contrat signé des deux parties').
182. *Ibid.* at 7 ('Cette disposition semble exiger l'intervention du tribunal dans tous les cas de récusation. Mais certains organismes d'arbitrage, et notamment la Cour d'arbitrage de la CCI, prévoient qu'ils pourront statuer eux-mêmes en cas de récusation et remplacer l'arbitre récusé. *Il serait fâcheux que la loi nouvelle interdît aux organismes d'arbitrage de mettre eux-mêmes de l'ordre chez eux en pareil cas, et rende obligatoire le recours aux tribunaux*').

Sambuc (vice-president of the International Court of Arbitration) submitted another set of observations, which were circulated as an internal document during the fourteenth session of the ICC Committee on International Commercial Arbitration.[183] The opening remarks are eloquent:[184]

> The draft model law constitutes a severe threat against ICC arbitration. First, it is difficult to foresee what its impact will be, once formally enacted, on our clauses. Second, while the provisions aligning with our arbitration rules will not be problematic, the same cannot be said of those that depart from it. This begs the question as to whether or not the model law will prevail over our rules.

As reported in the same document, after solicitation from the ICC, UNIDROIT had already agreed in 1936 to modify the draft of the arbitration law by adding 'save contrary agreement of the parties', whenever the provisions diverged from the ICC *Arbitration Rules* (*ICC Rules*), and specifying, in a separate article, that the provisions of a given set of arbitration rules chosen by the parties must be interpreted as equivalent to the terms 'arbitration agreement' or 'agreement of the parties'.[185] Yet the above was considered as insufficient to protect ICC arbitration. Fearing that the wording 'save contrary agreement of the parties' would suggest the imperative character of the other provisions contained in the draft arbitration law, the report by Henri Sambuc called for the implementation of a stronger guarantee, specifically that Article 2 of the draft arbitration law be modified by introducing a provision according to which 'when the parties' arbitration agreement refers to a set of arbitration rules, the latter exclude the application of all contrary provisions contained in the present law'.[186] This, moreover, was advanced as a *conditio sine qua non* for the approval of the draft.[187] This condition, however, was not implemented by UNIDROIT in the new draft of its uniform law on arbitration.[188] The spirit of the *Model Law* will only see the light of day fifty years later, with the adoption by UNCITRAL of the 1985 *Model Law on International Commercial Arbitration*.

Along with dealing with UNIDROIT's competition, the ICC was also struggling to develop its clientele and attract new arbitrations. In the years following the signing of the *Geneva Convention*, the number of arbitrations administered by the ICC grew rapidly but remained a modest number of cases, never exceeding the number of eighty. Moreover, during the years of the Great Depression and World War II, the caseload dropped dramatically: between 1933 and 1947 the average number of new requests for arbitration plunged to twelve.[189] Despite such challenges, the ICC continued its

---

183. Comité d'études de l'arbitrage commercial international, 14th session, 26 February 1937, *Projet d'une loi internationale sur l'arbitrage en droit privé élaborée par l'Institut International de Rome pour l'unification du droit privé – Note de M. Henri Sambuc, Vice-président de la Cour d'arbitrage* ICC doc. 6167 (unpublished).
184. *Ibid.* at 1.
185. *Ibid.*
186. *Ibid.* at 3.
187. *Ibid.*
188. Institut International pour l'Unification du Droit Privé, *Avant-projet d'une loi uniforme sur l'arbitrage dans les rapports internationaux en droit privé et rapport explicatif*, UDP 1940, Projet III (1), Rome, December 1940.
189. *ICC 1998 Statistical Report*, 10:1 ICC Bull 1, 4 (1999).

activities. Even during World War II, the International Court of Arbitration continued to administer cases, although with difficulty, by moving from Paris to Stockholm.[190] It is worth noting that despite the political context, members of countries at war still appeared at meetings of the members of the court.[191]

§3.05 ARBITRATION IN THE SECOND HALF OF THE TWENTIETH CENTURY: THE ICC'S SUCCESS IN CREATING AN EFFECTIVE INTERNATIONAL REGIME

In the aftermath of World War II, the ICC's most significant efforts were put into the drafting of a new convention for international arbitral awards.[192] These efforts eventually led to the 1958 *New York Convention*. In fact, contrary to certain otherwise

---

190. For an account of the transition from Paris to Stockholm, *see* Sigvard Jarvin, *La Cour d'arbitrage de la chambre de commerce internationale pendant la deuxième guerre mondiale*' in Laurent Lévy & Yves Derains, *Liber Amicorum en l'honneur de Serge Lazareff* 331–347 (Pedone 2011).
191. *Ibid.* at 344 (*see*, for instance, the account of the 1940 April session of the International Court of Arbitration in Stockholm, where – among others – members from Germany and the United Kingdom appeared).
192. United Nations – Economic and Social Council (ECOSOC), *Statement submitted by the International Chamber of Commerce, a non-governmental organization having consultative status in category A*, 10 September 1953, E/C.2/373, at 7–8:

> At its Lisbon Congress (1951), the ICC adopted a resolution which it was hoped would be followed up by an International Conference with a view to obtaining the adoption of a new international system of enforcement of arbitral awards.
> It should be recalled that the studies and research undertaken by the Commission on International Commercial Arbitration in 1950 on the initiative of the Chairman, Sir Edwin S. Herbert, had borne out the ICC in its conviction that the system established under the 1927 Geneva Convention no longer corresponded to the requirements of international trade. Criticizing the Convention's main defect, which consists in the enforcement of only those awards that are strictly in accordance with the rules of procedure laid down in the law of the country where the arbitration took place – consequently, national awards only – the ICC considered that there could be no progress without full recognition of the conception of international awards.
> In actual fact, the idea of an international award, i.e., an award completely independent of national laws, corresponds precisely to an economic requirement. It is certain that a commercial agreement between the parties, even for international transactions, will always be linked up with a given national system of law. Nevertheless, the fact that an award settling a dispute arising in connection with this agreement will produce its effects in different countries, makes it essential that it should be enforced in all these countries in the same way. The development of international trade depends on this.
> Only by giving full value to the autonomy of the will can this result be attained in the field of conflict of laws.
> Legal circles have until recently shown a marked opposition to recognizing autonomy of the will as a valid source of private international law which, being ideally the science of conflict of laws, presupposes that all legal relationships are subject to some national law.
> But at the same time, it would be hard to imagine the sense of frontier and sovereignty disappearing, economically to start with and later politically, without the simultaneous establishment of international forms of procedure along similar lines.
> Furthermore, it should be pointed out that at the very moment when a supposedly scientific approach is tending to repudiate autonomy as a source of law, the texts of conventions (and in particular the Rome Institute's Draft Uniform Law) are emphasizing in many cases that the provisions set forth will only be valid if the parties have not arranged otherwise, thus confirming the autonomy of the will. Finally, important as may be the opinion of legal circles, it is nevertheless to meet the

Chapter 3: The Influence of Arbitral Institutions §3.05

convincing accounts,[193] this convention is essentially a product of the ICC. A recent article made this point very convincingly, describing the extent and success of the ICC's lobbying.[194] There is therefore no need to go into these details again. What should be emphasized, nonetheless, is that even conventional authorities affirm that the *New York Convention* was aligned with the requests of the ICC. As explained by Gaillard and Savage, the United Nations Economic and Social Council (ECOSOC), which rejected the 1953 ICC's proposed draft in 1955, ended up drafting a text that was very close to ICC's proposals. Gaillard and Savage observe, in fact, that 'the text which it adopted on June 10, 1958 was considerably more liberal ... and came closer to the ideas, if not the wording, of the ICC draft'.[195]

One further point on which I shall dwell has to do with the most important goal pursued by the ICC: the protection of its arbitral procedure and its detachment from the law of the seat of arbitration.[196] This goal was pursued because the institution in question already had an efficient way to handle arbitration proceedings, the only weak spot being the effectiveness of the ultimate product of this procedure, that is, the enforcement of the award.[197] It is not a coincidence that the UNCITRAL *Model Law on*

---

requirements of international trade, which are perfectly clear, that conventions are elaborated. However, since the aim is more particularly to facilitate the enforcement of awards relating to international commercial disputes, it is necessary to give a precise definition thereof. The present report and preliminary draft convention were drawn up to meet all these considerations.

193. Cf. Yves Fortier & Annie Lespérance, *La contribution des Nations Unies à l'arbitrage international*, 1:1 MJDR 56, 61 (2014).
194. Grisel, *Aux origines*, *supra* n. 150, at 472 ff.
195. Gaillard & Savage, *supra* n. 5, at 122.
196. van den Berg, *supra* n. 110, at 7.
197. United Nations – Economic and Social Council (ECOSOC), *Statement submitted by the International Chamber of Commerce*, E/C.2/373/Add. 1, at 2–3 ('The 1927 Geneva Convention originated in an ICC resolution requesting the League of Nations to study the question of the recognition of arbitral awards with respect to the private character of arbitration ... [it] was an important step forward since it recognized the voluntary submission of disputes to arbitration as a legal process. Moreover, a number of countries which were parties to the Convention introduced legislation permitting the enforcement of international awards by registration, instead of by ordinary court action. However, registration is only effective against the defendant within limitations, and certain difficulties arose from these limitations. The Geneva Convention stipulated that to be enforceable an award must conform not only to the will of the parties, but to the law of the country. It is the reference to the latter which caused the difficulties ... Naturally, if the laws of the various countries relative to arbitration could be brought into line, these difficulties would be overcome. Since such a process is slow, the ICC suggests a more limited reform, namely, that the automatic enforceability of arbitral awards based on the will of the parties be established. For an international award to obtain legal sanction, it should be sufficient for it to conform to the procedure laid down in the parties' contract. This is implied in the principle of freedom of contract. However, in the present state of law relative to arbitration in the various countries, it is not as a rule permissible to substitute a procedure based merely on the will of the parties, for proper legal procedure. Nonetheless there is valid justification for discriminating between the submission of the parties to procedure established by the law of a particular country and their submission stipulating the application of rules of procedure agreed upon in the contract. International awards should be recognized as valid in every country, if the procedure applied is in accordance with the rules agreed upon, irrespective of whether they are drawn up by the parties themselves or established through an arbitral body. Since the basic principle of the will of the parties was included in the Geneva Protocol on Arbitration Clauses of 1923, it should be possible to draw up a new diplomatic instrument

International Commercial Arbitration was not enacted until thirty years after the *New York Convention*'s enactment, despite the ECOSOC being well aware of the sophisticated uniform arbitration law draft, prepared by UNIDROIT.[198] In addition to the 'denationalization' of arbitral procedure, the *New York Convention* introduced a liberal regime for the enforcement and recognition of awards. The first pillar of this regime establishes that awards are presumed to be enforceable:[199]

> All the party seeking enforcement must do according to Article IV is to supply the arbitration agreement and the award. It is then up to the other party to prove the existence of one of the grounds for refusal imitatively set out in Article V(1).

This means that awards will be held to be enforceable unless the resisting party is able to prove otherwise. The only limit to this mechanism is that of Article V(2), according to which national courts can refuse to enforce the award, on their own motion, if the subject matter of the dispute is not arbitrable or the recognition would result in a violation of public policy.

The second pillar of this liberal regime relates to the presumptive validity of arbitration agreements.[200] The court of a contracting state, when seized of an action in a matter in respect of which the parties have made an arbitration agreement, shall, at the request of one of the parties, refer the parties to arbitration. This referral can be impeded by the opposing party upon proof of the invalidity or ineffectiveness of said agreement (Article II(3)).

The entry into force of the *New York Convention* proved to be extremely beneficial to the ICC and to its institutional model of administered arbitration.[201] In the years following the enactment of the *New York Convention*, the ICC's case load

---

which would expressly state this and simultaneously allow the prompt enforcement of international awards, subject to reservations relative to validity, fraud or infringement of principles of natural justice. With this in mind the ICC drew up a Preliminary Draft Convention to overcome the main defect of the Geneva Convention, namely, the enforcement of only those awards that were strictly in accordance with the rules of procedure laid down in the law of the country where the arbitration occurred, hence only national awards. The ICC believes there can be no progress without full recognition of the conception of international awards (i. e. independent of national laws), and, in fact, the development of international trade depends upon this concept. The ICC proposal amends the Geneva Convention on only two important issues: (1) by stating that awards to which the future convention applies would relate to commercial disputes between persons subject to 'the jurisdiction of different States, or to disputes involving legal relationships on the territory of different States; and (2) since the finality of the awards rendered is essential to arbitration and in most cases resort to means of recourse is merely for delaying purposes, an international convention should not encourage such tactics by over-emphasizing the means available for opposing enforcement. Therefore, it did not seem advisable to retain the last paragraph of article 2 and all of article 3 of the Geneva Convention') [references omitted].

198. United Nations – Economic and Social Council (ECOSOC), *Report of the Committee on the Enforcement of International Arbitral Awards*, 28 March 1955, E/AC.42/4/Rev.1, at para. 69.
199. van den Berg, *supra* n. 110, at 9.
200. Albert Jan van den Berg, *The New York Convention of 1958: An Overview* in Gaillard & Di Pietro, *supra* n. 62, 39 at 39.
201. *ICC 1998 Statistical Report*, 10:1 ICC Bull 1 (1999). *See also* Fouchard, *supra* n. 36, at 226 ('Les conventions internationales et les systèmes juridiques nationaux ont réagi, et ont donné à l'arbitrage institutionnel les moyens de se développer. D'une part, les négociateurs de la Convention de New York de 1958 ont tenu à affirmer la licéité de principe de l'arbitrage

increased significantly. From 1959 to 1998, the annual number of cases grew from 41 to 466.[202] Nowadays, despite the great increase of cases (966 new cases were filed in 2016),[203] the nature of ICC arbitration has remained the same, as the similarity of the provisions contained in the *ICC Rules* of 1955, 1975, 1988, 1998, and 2012 shows. Analogously, the 2017 *ICC Rules* maintain the same essential structure: the ordinary administration of the proceedings is carried out by the Secretariat under the supervision of the International Court of Arbitration (Article 1), which directly intervenes (where applicable) in important phases of the procedure, such as the prima facie review of the existence of an arbitration agreement (Article 6(4)), the replacement of arbitrators (Article 15), and, most importantly, the approval of the draft of the arbitral award (Article 34).

§3.06 ARBITRATION AT THE BEGINNING OF THE TWENTY-FIRST CENTURY: THE CONSECRATION OF INSTITUTIONS

[A] Further Actors Contributing to Institutionalization: An Overview

The above overview of the ICC's contribution to the development of the arbitral regime has shown that the creation of an arbitral regime introducing a liberalization of arbitral procedure was not necessarily a response to the merchants' demands for simplification and increased flexibility, but was rather a way to entrench the ICC's own procedural model. It was a form of legitimization.

In order to provide a complete overview, the above analysis needs to be supplemented by examining new actors that are further contributing to the institutional setting governing international commercial arbitration. This will be done by briefly presenting these actors and explaining what their impact is. *In limine*, it is worth noting that all such actors align with the institutional vision first embraced by the ICC and operate with similar mechanisms (albeit while pursuing different national and business platforms).

Starting with the most obvious, the first set of new actors are other institutions, be they arbitration centres administering disputes or other international institutions promoting the use of international commercial arbitration. Currently, several arbitral institutions compete in the market of dispute resolution, which is now regarded as a type of 'service industry'.[204] Most of these institutions use a national platform to attract

---

institutionnel ... D'autre part, la force obligatoire du règlement de procédure établi par le centre d'arbitrage est très largement affirmée en droit positif, spécialement si l'arbitrage est international').
202. *Ibid.*
203. International Chamber of Commerce (ICC), *ICC Reveals Record Number of New Arbitration Cases Filed in 2016*, https://iccwbo.org/media-wall/news-speeches/icc-reveals-record-number-new-arbitration-cases-filed-2016/ (accessed 31 January 2017).
204. Pieter Sanders, *Quo Vadis Arbitration?* 10 (Kluwer Law 1999); Emmanuel Gaillard, *Sociology of International Arbitration*, 31:1 Arb Int 1, 5 (2015). *See also* Gerbay, *Institutions*, *supra* n. 34, at 32 ff. (commenting on the increase in the number of institutions).

clients: in other words, they rely on the potential of the city or region where their headquarters are set.

In Europe, the LCIA reported 326 new arbitrations (in its 2015 report),[205] whereas the Arbitration Institute of the Stockholm Chamber of Commerce (SCC) declared 181 new cases (in its 2015 report).[206] While the former relies on London's central financial importance (attracting disputes regarding commodity transactions, financial agreements and loans, joint ventures, and oil and gas industry agreements),[207] the latter lives off its reputation as a neutral country for the arbitration of matters between Eastern and Western Europe (and North America).[208] As such, it mainly attracts disputes regarding service agreements, supply agreements (including energy), and business acquisitions.[209] Finally, the German Institute of Arbitration (DIS) reported 140 cases in 2015,[210] and the Milan Chamber of Arbitration (CAM) indicated 131 new cases.[211]

In the US, the International Centre for Dispute Resolution (ICDR) administered 1052 cases in 2015 (although it is unclear how many new arbitrations were filed in the same year).[212] Like the DIS and CAM, the ICDR mostly relies on local companies and the domestic market.[213]

In Asia, one can observe three major centres. In 2015, the Hong Kong International Arbitration Centre (HKIAC) reported 271 new arbitration cases.[214] The Singapore International Arbitration Centre (SIAC) also received 271 new cases in 2015.[215] While the HKIAC and SIAC mostly rely on international dealings involving sales, maritime or shipping contracts, and the corporate sector, the China International Economic and Trade Arbitration Commission (CIETAC) – which reports that 1968 cases were accepted in 2015 – mostly relies on domestic cases (1531 domestic arbitration, versus 437 international cases).[216]

True, the ICC remains by far the institution with the highest number of new international cases per year (roughly 75% of the disputes filed at the ICC in 2015 were

---

205. *LCIA – Registrar's Report 2015*, http://www.lcia.org/LCIA/reports.aspx (accessed 31 January 2017).
206. *SCC Statistics 2015*, http://www.sccinstitute.com/statistics/ (accessed 31 January 2017).
207. *Registrar's Report*, supra n. 205, at 1.
208. Dezalay & Garth, *supra* n. 133, at 182.
209. *SCC Statistics*, supra n. 204, at 2.
210. *DIS Statistics 2015*, http://www.dis-arb.de/upload/statistics/DIS-Statistiken%202015.pdf (accessed 31 January 2017).
211. *CAM 2015 Report*, http://www.camera-arbitrale.it/Documenti/CAMarbitration_facts&figures 2015.pdf (accessed 31 January 2017).
212. *2015 ICDR Statistics*, http://globalarbitrationnews.com/parties-preferences-in-international-arbitration-the-latest-statistics-of-the-leading-arbitral-institutions-20150805/#982971-v1-GAN _Article_Arbitration_Institutions.docx (accessed 31 January 2017).
213. *See* e.g., the nationality of the parties arbitrating under the rules of the CAM, *supra* n. 211.
214. *HKIAC 2015 Case Statistics*, http://www.hkiac.org/about-us/statistics (accessed 31 January 2017).
215. *SIAC Statistics*, http://www.siac.org.sg/2014-11-03-13-33-43/facts-figures/statistics/64-why-siac (accessed 31 January 2017).
216. *CIETAC Statistics 2006–2015*, http://www.cietac.org/index.php?m=Page&a=index&id=40& l=en (accessed 31 January 2017).

international cases).²¹⁷ Yet the above shows the significant importance (at least in terms of aggregate numbers) of other arbitral institutions. Within this first group of actors, one should also mention UNCITRAL. This institution plays a significant role in at least two respects: (i) it aims to harmonize arbitration laws, with the promotion of its *Model Law* on international arbitration;²¹⁸ and (ii) it creates informal instruments to regulate arbitral proceedings. These goals have either been achieved through the promotion of instruments such as the *Notes on Organizing Arbitral Proceedings* (which can be used in the context of both ad hoc and administered arbitration)²¹⁹ or through the use of UNCITRAL's arbitration rules in ad hoc arbitration.²²⁰

Finally, a second group of actors can be identified: the states.²²¹ We have discussed how the ICC has secured states' approval and support of international commercial arbitration. A second internal movement, nonetheless, can be further identified. I allude to the states' implementation of neo-liberal policies resulting in a contraction of their role as administrators of civil justice, which consecrated the alternative dispute resolution (ADR) movement.²²² The relative complexity of this matter requires a separate discussion.

[B] The Privatization of Justice as an Important Motor of Arbitration's Institutionalization

The ADR movement, which brought about intense modifications to Western civil justice systems, originated in the late 1970s in the US.²²³ It is usually regarded as comprising three different types of dispute resolution: (i) negotiation, (ii) mediation, and (iii) arbitration. Furthermore, it falls under a general trend favouring the privatization of civil justice,²²⁴ tolerated (if not encouraged) by liberal states. As noted by Oppetit, in an ideal system of justice, the State no longer aspires to monopolize the resolution of private conflicts, favouring instead party autonomy and the spontaneous solutions elaborated by private individuals.²²⁵

---

217. *2016 Statistical Report*, *supra* n. 203.
218. For an overview, *see* Fabien Gélinas & Frédéric Bachand, *The Unictral Model Law after Twenty-Five Years: Global Perspectives on International Commercial Arbitration* (JurisNet 2013).
219. United Nations Commission on International Trade Law, *UNCITRAL Notes on Organizing Arbitral Proceedings*, 1 (United Nations 2012) ('The purpose of the Notes is to assist arbitration practitioners by listing and briefly describing questions on which appropriately timed decisions on organizing arbitral proceedings may be useful. The text, prepared with a particular view to international arbitrations, may be used whether or not the arbitration is administered by an arbitral institution').
220. Crawford, *supra* n. 33, at 13; Schläpher & Petti, *supra* n. 35, at 14–15; Lalive, *supra* n. 36, at 318–319; Wallgren-Lindholm, *supra* n. 38, at 76; Kassis, *supra* n. 39, at 25.
221. Alec Sweet Stone & Martin Shapiro, *On Law, Politics and Judicialization*, 337 ff. (Oxford University Press 2003).
222. Gélinas, *supra* n. 41, at 119.
223. Stephen B. Goldberg et al., *Dispute Resolution*, 5 (Kluwer Law 2012).
224. Trevor C.W. Farrow, *Civil Justice, Privatization, and Democracy*, 72 (University of Toronto Press 2014).
225. Oppetit, *supra* n. 15, at 21.

The contemporary origins of ADR are found, more specifically, in a 1976 conference organized by Warren Burger, Chief Justice of the US Supreme Court (the so-called Pound Conference),[226] which aimed at revisiting the causes of dissatisfaction with the administration of justice, 'as well as ways in which the justice system could be made more efficient and effective'.[227] The core of the movement shared a major concern: that US civil justice was being affected by a severe crisis, expressed in terms of several negative effects such as excessive delays, costs, complexity of litigation, and high lawyer fees.[228] This state of affairs was a result of a dramatic rise in the number of cases litigated, a symptom of an overly litigious society.[229] To these observations, early critics replied that the increase in the caseload could not be legitimately regarded as a failure of the justice system, because 'ninety percent of all cases [would be] settled without adjudication'.[230] To be fair, however, the movement had noble origins, for it grew as a response to the general need for the increase of access to justice. In other words, the *access to justice* theme preceded ADR's emergence. More specifically, ADR was to be a response to the access to justice debate, by permitting the delegation of adjudicative or other dispute resolution functions to nonjudicial entities.[231]

The ADR movement, moreover, ascribed itself within a pre-existing practice of delegating the resolution of disputes to administrative bodies. The difference with ADR was that it involved a further step, namely, a delegation in favour of private entities, be they arbitrators, mediators, or negotiators. While accepted in the US, this delegation to private entities was initially rejected in Europe in favour of the creation of a set of administrative bodies with adjudicative functions, based on the French administrative model.[232] The only notable exception was England. It was, in fact, through the *Woolf Report* of 1996 and the 1998 reform of civil procedure that ADR made its appearance in this jurisdiction.[233] The introduction of ADR mechanisms was justified on the basis of concerns similar to the ones raised in the US, those of attempting to reduce the complexity and cost of litigation.[234] As aptly summarized by Trevor Farrow, the core arguments in favour of the privatization of justice through the use of ADR, have been 'efficiency', and 'increased access to justice'.[235]

It is worth noting that the causes behind the crisis of civil justice have not been the same in each of the above countries. In the common law world, for instance, the cost of legal representation has been identified as a central factor limiting access to

---

226. Leonard L. Riskin et al., *Dispute Resolution and Lawyers*, 27 (West Academic Publishing 2014).
227. *Ibid*.
228. Katherine V.W. Stone, *Private Justice: The Law of Alternative Dispute Resolution*, 2 (Foundation Press 2000).
229. *Ibid*. at 3.
230. Harry T. Edwards, *Alternative Dispute Resolution: Panacea or Anathema?* 99:3 HLR 668, 670 (1986).
231. Mauro Cappelletti, *The Judicial Process in a Comparative Perspective*, 222 (Clarendon Press 1989).
232. *Ibid*. at 234.
233. Jolowicz, *supra* n. 88, at 392.
234. *Ibid*. at 386 (the author observes that '[t]his, so far as is known, was the first time that the courts have sought actively to turn away business in favour of what might formerly have been considered a rival institution'); *Ibid*. at 392.
235. Farrow, *supra* n. 224, at 61.

justice. In the civil law world, and particularly in Continental Europe, the problem has been the opposite–'cheap' legal representation has caused an impressive overload of state courts, and, as a result, an excessive duration of proceedings. In this respect, some scholars have suggested that the main causes of the state of crisis are to be found in the growth of the welfare state. Citing Roosevelt's New Deal, Mauro Cappelletti observed that the twentieth-century state had encouraged 'increasingly frequent intervention in the economy, regulation of property, and control over enterprise'.[236] Focusing on the increase in regulation, François Ost suggested that the legislative changes undertaken by the welfare state have resulted not only in more legislation but also in a greater involvement of judges in their cases. The 'juge-arbitre' of the liberal state, called to apply the law to a set of facts, is replaced by the 'juge-entraineur', that is, a judge becoming involved in the parties' interests by managing them in light of the policies pursued by the welfare state:[237]

> As much as their predecessors did, judges still adjudicate and resolve disputes … but they are now expected to do so much more. In the pre-trial phase, they manage, orient and prevent; in the post-trial phase, they keep track of the case, taking further decisions so as to take into account new facts and circumstances … Today's judges have become more interested in the quality of the outcome, rather than the purity of the law.

However, while it is certainly true that judges are today expected to play a more active role in modern day litigation, it seems that other basic factors may also have had a significant impact on the caseload of state justice systems, such as the growth of the adversarial culture, and lawyer's monopoly over legal services.[238] The growth of population as well as the process of gentrification have also been blamed. Increased interactions, restricted space, and complex allocation of limited resources all became sources of social tension.[239]

In any event, whatever the causes behind the crisis of civil justice, it is a well-known fact that such growth was not matched by an increase in resources for state justice. Neo-liberal policies have, in fact, progressively pushed toward a contraction of state budgets, hence, to a contraction of states' involvement in civil justice.[240] In this context, the implementation of ADR was often justified as an attempt to bring justice closer to its users. A more 'user-friendly' and efficient justice system has been the leitmotiv of several reforms in the EU and North America, as well as in England.[241]

This consideration of the ADR movement has allowed me to place contemporary arbitration in the broader context of states' retreat from the administration of civil justice. Thanks to the movement toward privatization of justice, arbitration has received significant recognition of its legitimacy, reinforcing its institutional role in the

---

236. Cappelletti, *supra* n. 231, at 224.
237. François Ost, *Dire le droit, faire justice*, 104 (Bruylant 2007).
238. Some literature suggests that the lawyer-to-population ratio may also play an important role. See e.g., Steven Vago, *Law and Society*, 284–286 (Pearson 2008).
239. Marc Galanter, *The Travails of Total Justice* in Robert W. Gordon & Morton J. Horwitz, *Law, Society, and History* 103, 104 ff. (Cambridge University Press 2011).
240. Farrow, *supra* n. 224, at 54.
241. *Ibid.* 77 ff.

administration of justice. At this point, a question becomes inevitable: what are the consequences of the institutionalization of international commercial arbitration? Some hypotheses are explored in the following section.

§3.07 THE CONSEQUENCES OF THE INSTITUTIONAL ROOTS OF INTERNATIONAL COMMERCIAL ARBITRATION

According to Dezalay and Garth, the first consequence of the institutional predominance of arbitration was the 'bureaucratization' of arbitral institutions, which was necessary to accommodate new individuals serving as arbitrators and not accustomed to their role. This led, in their view, to the transformation of 'an informal justice centred on the European grand professors into a US-style "offshore litigation"'.[242] The examples of bureaucratization given by these authors are those of the use of the ICC terms of reference and the review of draft awards by the ICC International Court of Arbitration.[243]

Yet this analysis does not appear to be entirely satisfactory. The terms of reference and the review of draft awards are in fact essential characteristics of ICC procedure: each of them precede in time the arrival of new parties, US law firms, and North-South disputes. They are, in other words, original ICC hallmarks. The terms of reference, can be regarded as a precaution against the insecurity surrounding the enforcement of arbitration clauses before the existence of the 1923 *Geneva Protocol*. They have their origin in the historical requirement of a 'submission agreement' (*compromis*) between the parties and the arbitrators, that is, an agreement to arbitrate a present dispute.[244] At the same time, the review of draft awards consists of a supervisory role that has existed since the dawn of ICC arbitration, for 'the institution has an interest in ensuring that an award bearing the ICC cachet have international currency and be entitled to execution in the largest possible number of States. ... [I]t is important that there be a central authority having experience with recognition and enforcement practices throughout the world'.[245]

What is certainly true, nonetheless, is that ICC procedure has undergone some changes since the beginnings of this institution. The new set of rules on emergency arbitration proceedings are an eloquent example. The same goes for the new provisions on expedited proceedings.[246] However, the most important changes are rather found in the institution's perception of its role. An interesting hypothesis is that the institutional character of international commercial arbitration has made arbitral institutions aware

---

242. Dezalay & Garth, *supra* n. 133, at 10.
243. *Ibid.*
244. L. William Craig et al., *International Chamber of Commerce Arbitration*, 252 (ICC Publishing 1990).
245. *Ibid.* at 341.
246. For an overview, *see* José Ricardo Feris, *The 2017 ICC Rules of Arbitration and the New ICC Expedited Procedure Provisions – A View from Inside the* Institution, 1 ICC Bull 63 (2017); Giacomo Marchisio, *Recent Solutions to Old Problems: A Look at the Expedited Procedure Under the Newly Revised ICC Rules of Arbitration*, 1 ICC Bull 76 (2017); Michael Bühler & Pierre Heitzmann, *The 2017 ICC Expedited Rules: From Softball to Hardball?*, 34:2 JOIA 121 (2017).

of their role as administrators of justice. The institutional setting has given a permanent character to the ephemeral nature of arbitral tribunals, thus transforming it into a stable system of justice, functioning in ways that resemble those of international tribunals.[247] This stable character has also allowed for the emergence of concerns that go beyond the parties' claims before the arbitral tribunal, involving wider social interests,[248] which include, most notably, the application and development of the law.[249]

The similar roles that arbitral tribunals share with other international tribunals are not the only relevant observable phenomenon. Unsurprisingly, if one turns to the literature dealing with international adjudicative bodies,[250] it can be noted that international commercial arbitration has seen incremental developments analogous to those of other international adjudicative institutions, such as the Court of Arbitration for Sport and the International Court of Justice. Such developments, which usually concern the expansion of jurisdiction and an increase of the types of measures that can be granted, are noticeable both in international commercial arbitration and other international courts.[251] A preliminary confirmation of the fact that the institutional nature of international commercial arbitration has transformed it into a system of justice can be found in the case law of the European Court of Human Rights (ECHR), according to which arbitral tribunals can be regarded as 'tribunals' where a party's right to a fair trial is applicable (Article 6§1 of the *1950 European Convention on Human Rights*)[252] and as a legitimate alternative to state courts.[253] As a result, for the ECHR, an arbitral tribunal and a state court are functionally equivalent, for they operate in a similar manner and pursue analogous objectives.[254]

Be that as it may, this overview has allowed us to underline an increasingly acknowledged public dimension inherent to international commercial arbitration and ensuing from the exercise of adjudicative functions similar to those exercised by civil courts and international tribunals. Furthermore, this approach has emphasized that justice exists outside the boundaries of state litigation and that the stateless nature of international commercial arbitration does not make it a subordinate or less sophisticated justice. It is thus even more important to analyse how arbitrators exercise their adjudicative power, which, in turn, means looking at what type of decisions they render.

---

247. Gary Born, *A New Generation of International Adjudication*, 4 Duke LJ 775, 828 (2012).
248. Stone Sweet & Grisel, *supra* n. 32, at 31.
249. *See* Jolowicz, *supra* n. 88, at 73 ff.
250. For an overview, *see* Cesare Romano, Karen Alter & Yuval Shany, *Mapping International Adjudicative Bodies, The Issues, and Players* in Romano, *supra* n. 26, 3 at 10.
251. Cf. Karin Oellers-Frahm, *Expanding the Competence to Issue Provisional Measures – Strenghtening the International Judicial Function* in Armin Von Bogdandy & Ingo Venzke, *International Judicial Law Making* 389, 401 (Springer 2011).
252. *See* e.g., *Regent Company v. Ukraine*, ECHR, 3 April 2008, at para. 54.
253. *Klausecker v. Germany*, ECHR, 6 January 2015 at para. 76. *See also* Guido Carducci, *Remarques sur la nature juridique de l'arbitrage en droit italien et français à partir de l'arrêt Corte di Cassazione, 8 octobre 2013*, 1 Rev Arb 139, 142–143 (2015).
254. *See* Oppetit, *supra* n. 15, at 217 (the author observed that in recent years, arbitration has tended to come closer to the judicial model of state courts, with a view to upholding a similar idea of justice and due process).

The consequences brought about by this new context on the field have been described by some as the 'judicialization of arbitration'. While certain authors have used this term to indicate the increasing complexity of arbitral proceedings,[255] others have adopted it to underline the quasi-public role now played by international commercial arbitration, as a type of private justice which has benefitted from the delegation of state courts' adjudicative functions.[256] These considerations are key to understand the paradigmatic shift that has occurred in the field–from the central role played by the will of the parties (central expression of a private understanding of international commercial arbitration), we have assisted to the emergence of a further competing principle, i.e., the will of the constituents of the field. This phenomenon can be observed on two distinct levels.

First, as empirical works have shown, arbitral institutions now fulfil functions that contribute to the exercise of arbitral adjudication.[257] In simple terms, this means that international commercial arbitration now consists of an ensemble of complex adjudicative institutions, i.e., arbitral centres and the arbitral tribunals constituted under their aegis. The support of the adjudicative functions is mostly visible in the preliminary screenings of jurisdictional objections (e.g., Article 6(4) *ICC Rules*), and in the decisions regarding joinders of cases (Article 10 *ICC Rules*), the appointment and challenges of arbitrators (Articles 12 and 15 *ICC Rules*), the scrutiny of awards (Article 34 *ICC Rules*), and the determinations concerning costs and arbitrators' fees.[258] This state of affairs has been consecrated by the *New York Convention*. In particular, thanks to the liberal wording of Article V(1)(d), the rules enacted by arbitral institutions have become the prevailing way to arbitrate.[259] As such, these institutions have become the source and limit of the adjudicative power of arbitrators.[260] This should not be a shocking conclusion, especially in light of the role played by the ICC in the drafting of the Convention.[261] This means that these institutions have a vested interest in controlling and regulating the type of decisions that are capable of being enforced before state courts, which explains the tendency, as I shall show in the following chapters, to use the label of 'award' for very different types of decisions.

Second, the paradigmatic shift can be observed in the institutions' perception of their role. This explains the growing display of legitimacy concerns, particularly with respect to the transparency of arbitral institutions, and the impartiality of arbitrators.[262]

In light of the above, the following chapters will analyse the decision-making areas in the context of which the notion of arbitral award is invoked. I shall start with the least controversial one–i.e., the final determination of a dispute on the merits–to continue with mildly controversial scenarios–such as in the case of jurisdictional decisions and decisions recording settlement agreements. I will then conclude with the

---

255. Gerbay, *supra* n. 29, at 230.
256. Stone Sweet & Grisel, *supra* n. 32, at 31.
257. Gerbay, Institutions, *supra* n. 34, at 213.
258. *Ibid.* at 213.
259. Motulsky, *supra* n. 14 at 302.
260. Stone Sweet & Grisel, *supra* n. 32, at 31.
261. Grisel, *Aux origines*, *supra* n. 150, at 436 ff.
262. *Infra*, §8.

highly controversial emergency decisions. The analysis will attempt to show the existence of a trend favouring the expansion of the notion of award, with a view to guaranteeing a uniform and wide enforcement of important arbitral decisions. Furthermore, it will show that this expansion concerns decisions having significant consequences on the entirety of arbitral proceedings and the resolution of the dispute. This explains why, in the context of state court proceedings, equivalent decisions are always enforceable, regardless of the form that they take.

§3.08 CONCLUSION

This chapter has provided a socio-historical account of the evolution of international commercial arbitration. The above account showed how the modern institutional roots of arbitration have influenced the way in which arbitral justice is organized.

I first explained that in the nineteenth century, normative centralism and the idea of nation-state relegated arbitration to a secondary role. Secondly, I explained how international commercial arbitration has evolved in the twentieth century. In particular, I pointed out that this type of dispute resolution was used as a diplomatic tool to reconstruct the European economy, by encouraging international trade between private companies. Thirdly, I provided an account of the emergence of international commercial arbitration, thanks to the creation of the ICC. In particular, I have explained how the ICC managed to negotiate favourable conditions at the international level: the Geneva instruments and the *New York Convention*, in fact, recognized the decisions rendered under the auspices of the ICC as a type of foreign judgment. I have also noted that other projects, such as the uniform law of international arbitration proposed by UNIDROIT, were put aside.

Furthermore, I argued that the *New York Convention* liberalized arbitration procedure by detaching it from national laws. This occurrence, coupled with an increase in the number of users and a decrease in states' intervention in the administration of justice, has entrenched international commercial arbitration as a type of adjudication sustained by international institutions. Finally, I considered the consequences of the institutional framework described above by pointing out that it allowed the emergence of a public dimension in international commercial arbitration, inherent to the adjudicative functions of arbitrators.

In light of the above, I will now look at the notion of award, keeping an awareness of the framework in which contemporary international commercial arbitration has developed.

CHAPTER 4
Contentious Awards

§4.01 INTRODUCTION

By drawing on Glenn's theory of legal traditions,[263] the present chapter will deal with the notion of contentious award and the parallel notion of judgment (section §4.02). It will first present a historical analysis of the notion of judgment in Western law. Such a historical excursus will examine judgments – contentious decisions speaking the law (*ius dicere*) – as a product of Roman law and, in particular, of the expansion of a centralized system for the administration of civil cases (section §4.02[A]). Consequently, the chapter will point out that the two major Western procedural traditions (common law and Romano-canonical) present convergent definitions of judgment (section §4.02[B]).

The second part of the chapter analyses the notion of contentious award under English and French arbitration law (section §4.03). The law of these two countries was selected because most international commercial arbitrations are seated in either Paris or London (also as a result of the importance of these countries' respective arbitration institutions).[264] This section first sets out the scope of enquiry for this analysis (section §4.03[A]). The analysis will show that while French arbitration law adopts a purely monodimensional adjudicative model for arbitrators (section §4.03[B]), English law endorses a multidimensional one (section §4.03[C]). In practical terms, this means that, as a matter of principle, French courts will tend to enforce mainly final awards resolving a dispute over substantive claims between the parties, whereas English

---

263. *Supra* §1.02. *See also* W. Laurence Craig, William W. Park & Jan Paulsson, *International Chamber of Commerce Arbitration*, 367 (Oceana Publishing 2000) ('Awards rendered by civil-law arbitrators tend to follow the example of the civil-law court judgments, structured as an outline of tightly reasoned conclusions following legal and logical premises. Common law arbitrators, on the other hand, tend to deal with the factual issues in much greater detail and to discuss and weigh the evidence at length').
264. *See* Mistelis & Friedland, *supra* n. 42, at 12 (according to the 2015 survey, 82% of arbitrations are seated in either Paris or London).

courts will also accept provisional awards containing urgent measures as well as consent awards.

Finally, section §4.04 of the chapter will briefly discuss the notion of contentious award in arbitral practice. As we shall see, this is a fairly unregulated area of the arbitral process. The sets of arbitration rules taken into account in this analysis show that there is a natural inclination to consider contentious awards as the natural fulfilment of arbitrators' main mandate.

§4.02 THE NOTION OF CONTENTIOUS JUDGMENT IN WESTERN LAW

A few preliminary words are necessary to clarify the scope of section §4.02. The core of this book revolves around the notion of arbitral award. Its findings will be used to reflect on the adjudicative model found in international arbitration. Yet, as shown in the following subparts, the idea of adjudication is an element common to state courts and arbitral tribunals. In fact, the historical introduction contained in the following subparts points out that state justice in civil matters is simply a peculiar evolution of an overarching, Western model of justice. This observation indicates an intimate, *traditional* bond between the notion of judgments and final arbitral awards. In other words, the notion of arbitral award must be understood alongside that of judgment. As stated by Jolowicz, in the preface to his well-known book *On Civil Procedure*,[265] we are all men and women of our time, and while we learn from the past, we never manage to escape from it.

Trying to give a definition of what is meant by *judgment* (even when limited to a Western perspective) is a colossal task. The idea of judgment can be analysed from many angles. The only one that I will pursue, however, is a historical and legal angle. This analysis will not, of course, be a biopsy of the *ius positum* but merely an enquiry into the historical foundation and evolution of the legal notion of judgment. While section §4.02[A] will depict the origin of judgment in Western law, section §4.02[B] – by drawing on a study of the Romano-canonical and common law traditions – will describe the contemporary meaning of judgment. Finally, section §4.02[C] will deal with the effects of judgments.

[A] Historical Inceptions

In this chapter, I will explain that judgments represent the bond between the adjudicative role of a judge (i.e., resolving a dispute) and the act of speaking the law (i.e., *ius dicere*), a connection that became easily identifiable in early Roman law (more specifically, in the *legis actiones* and the formulary trial). Let us consider each of these procedures in turn.

---

265. Jolowicz, *supra* n. 88, at ix.

[1] Classic Roman Procedure and the Absence of Ius Dicere

The *legis actiones* are usually presented as the most ancient model of litigation between Roman citizens.[266] Before their introduction, it is contended – in a romantic fashion – that relationships between individuals were exclusively governed by force and self-defence.[267] According to a long-standing line of scholarship, the *legis actiones* are regarded as having replaced an archaic method of arbitration, probably conducted by a local *rex* or *supreme pontiff*.[268] Be that as it may, the only certain fact is that the *legis actiones* were introduced before the *Twelve Tables*, which, in turn, were enacted as formal laws sometime around 450 BC.[269] This type of civil litigation was characterized by a high degree of formalism,[270] which bordered on sacred ritual, where every actor had a particular part to play. The fragments of writings by the Latin jurist Gaius contain records of five actions: the *per sacramentum*, *per iudicis postulationem*, *per condictionem*, *per manus iniectionem*, and *per pignoris capionem*.[271]

The formulary procedure (also known as *ordo iudiciorum*) was probably introduced in 242 BC[272] and eventually (around 17 BC) became the most common type of civil litigation, thus replacing the *legis actiones*.[273] Its major innovation consisted in the introduction of litigation *per concepta verba*, that is, using words adapted to the type of dispute between the parties:[274]

> Under the new system the question at issue is submitted to the *iudex* in a form of words making plain to him that if he finds certain assertions of the plaintiff to be true it is his duty to condemn the defendant, and that if he does not find them to be true he is to absolve him.

This type of procedure extended the jurisdiction of the praetor, who became capable of settling disputes falling under the *ius civile*.[275] The magistrate was put in charge of enacting an annual *edictum* containing all the procedural measures or remedies (*formulae*) that were going to be granted in order to correct and amend the *ius civile*.[276] While the new procedure was characterized by a reduced formalism, it left untouched the two-phase trial of the *legis actiones*. The *in iure* phase was centred on

---

266. Vincenzo Arangio Ruiz, *Istituzioni di diritto romano*, 99 (Jovene 1927).
267. Perrozzi, *supra* n. 86, at 52. Cf. René Girard, *Des choses cachées depuis la fondation du monde*, 59 ff. (Bernard Grasset 1978).
268. Ibid.
269. Metzger, *supra* n. 119, at 13; Pasquale Voci, *Istituzioni di diritto romano*, 170 (Giuffrè 2004).
270. Girard, *supra* n. 65, at 1030.
271. Arangio Ruiz, *supra* n. 266, at 102.
272. Metzger, *supra* n. 119, at 13.
273. Voci, *supra* n. 269, at 179.
274. Herbert Felix Jolowicz & Barry Nicholas, *Historical Introduction to the Study of Roman Law*, 176 (Cambridge University Press 1972).
275. Originally, the jurisdiction of the praetor was divided between the *praetor peregrinus* – in charge of administering justice between foreigners (*peregrini*), and between foreigners and Roman citizens – and the *praetor urbanus*, administering justice between Roman citizens (in order to fill the gaps of the *ius civile*).
276. D. 1.1.7.1 (in Papinianus's elegant words: 'ius praetorium est quod praetores introduxerunt adiuvandi vel supplendi vel corrigendi iuris civilis gratia propter utilitatem publicam').

the *formula*. First, in the *intentio*,[277] the praetor would enucleate the actual question 'upon the answering of which the judgment depends'.[278] The *intentio* was followed by the *condemnatio*: should the *iudex* or *arbiter* find the *intentio* grounded, he would proceed by granting the remedy sought; otherwise, he would dismiss the claim.[279] The praetor would then conclude the *in iure* phase with the formalization of the *formula*, that is, with the *litis contestatio*: the plaintiff would read to the defendant the *formula* in the presence of witnesses.[280] The praetor would then appoint the *iudex* indicated by the parties, ordering him to rule over the dispute in the so-called *apud iudicem* phase.

Based on this overview of the traits of Roman litigation, it is now the time to consider the system's most important distinctive element – the separation between the *in iure* and *apud iudicem* phases. According to an influential authority, the division in question would assimilate Roman litigation to a form of voluntary submission to state-sanctioned arbitration,[281] where the decision maker was purely a creation of the parties. Even if the role of the magistrate was identified as *iuris dictio*, the *in iure* phase was rather close to the notarized procedure of a submission to arbitration. In the Roman procedural model, speaking the law was therefore purely limited to stating the claims of the parties and appointing a third party who had a function similar to early juries in England.[282] The *in iure* phase was centred around a formal agreement known as *litis contestatio*. In the words of Arangio Ruiz, the *litis contestatio* (i.e., the central act of the *in iure* phase) was, in fact, a mere agreement between the parties.[283] Even if some indirect sanctions were in place against contumacious defendants, under classical Roman law (both in the *legis actiones* and the formulary trial), the role of resolving a dispute was a purely private activity conducted by a layman, which necessarily required the participation of both parties.[284] Most importantly, such a function (i.e., that of resolving the dispute) had nothing to do with the judicial activity of the magistrate. This public figure was therefore a mere accessory, whose function was that of recording the *litis contestatio* and declaring it valid.[285]

---

277. GAI 4, 41: 'Ea pars formulae, qua actor desiderium suum concludit' (the *intentio* could be *certa*, if the claim referred to a *certa res*, or *incerta*, if the claim did not refer to a specific performance or thing).
278. Leopold Wenger, *Institutes of the Roman Law of Civil Procedure*, 141 (Veritas Press 1940).
279. GAI 4, 43: 'Ea pars formulae, qua iudici condemnandi absolvendive potestas permittitur; GAI 4,40: Principio ideo inseritur, ut demonstretur res, de qua agitur' (the plaintiff would then describe in the *demonstratio* the facts grounding his claim).
280. Voci, *supra* n. 269, at 197.
281. Metzger, *supra* n. 119, at 9; van Rhee, *supra* n. 41, at 31.
282. Jolowicz & Nicholas, *supra* n. 274, at 178. For a detailed analysis, *see* Herbert Felix Jolowicz, *The Judex and the Arbitral Principle*, 2 RIDA 477–492 (1949).
283. Arangio Ruiz, *supra* n. 266, at 123.
284. Jill Harries, *Creating Legal Space: Settling Disputes in the Roman Empire* in Catherine Hezser, *Rabbinic Law in its Roman and Near Eastern Context*, 63, 69 (Mohr 2003) (the author observes that the close ties of Ancient Roman society would have nonetheless weakened the 'voluntary' element, for social pressure would have been capable of forcing a defendant to accept litigation).
285. *Ibid. See also* José Javier De Los Mozos Touya, *Dire le droit, interpreter le droit dans l'expérience juridique romaine* in Barbara Anagnostou-Canas, *Dire le droit: normes, juges, juriconsultes* 99, 101 (LGDJ 2006) ('Le magistrat dit le droit dans le procès, établissant le cadre du jugement. Il est curieux que cette activité prenne la dénomination de *dicere*, car à proprement parler il ne dit plus le droit, il autorise le jugement, il donne la possibilité de juger *iudicium dare*').

Finally, the sui generis bond between adjudication and law telling is confirmed by the existence of a plethora of special proceedings. This is what led Justinian to provide the following remarks in the *Digestum*: under Roman law the notion of jurisdiction is very broad (*jus dicentis officium latissimum est*)[286] and is exercised by means of broad powers ('he who has jurisdiction, shall also have the necessary powers that are required for its exercise').[287]

[2]   The Extra Cognitio *and the Emergence of* Ius Dicere

The bond between speaking the law and adjudication evolved considerably with the rise of the *Dominate*, when the emperor obtained a great concentration of powers, both normative and adjudicative. The imperial *cognitio extra ordinaria* slowly grew to be the most relied-upon means of litigation[288] and led to the formal abolition of the formulary procedure in AD 342.[289] This shift in favour of a direct form of administration of justice had significant consequences. The most important consequence ensuing from the adoption of this new procedure, however, was the end of the distinction between the *in iure* and *apud iudicem* phases, and the creation of a unitary phase before a public official.[290] As Johnston puts it:[291]

> The central characteristic of these extraordinary proceedings is that they had a single stage only, and the case was not remitted in a separate stage of trial by a judge but was disposed only by the magistrate ... the judge was for the first time an official.

Furthermore, Wenger reports that under the new procedure, three different types of judgments were available:[292]

> Judgments are either *interlocutory judgements* ... which take up preliminary questions which have been raised in the case, and the decision which is made in advance of the final judgment, or they are *final judgements*, ... which finally dispose of either the whole or a part of the litigation; *partial judgements* ... are permitted by Justinian if the matter is divisible into several points suitable to individual decisions.

The end of the distinction between *in iure* and *apud iudicem* meant that the judge was now in charge of speaking the law in order to respond to the parties' claim. In other words, the substantive legal aspects of the claim were not predetermined before a magistrate in light of the parties' requests but rather were left for the judge to decide.

---

286. D. 2, I (*De Jurisdictione*) 1.
287. The definition recalls the doctrine of inherent powers of the tribunal. D. 2, I, 2: 'Cui jurisdictio data est, ea quoque concessa esse videntur, sine quibus juirisdictio explicari non potuit'.
288. Girard, *supra* n. 65, at 1140 (scholars are not in agreement as to the exact period during which the *cognitio* became the usual method for resolving civil disputes).
289. Craig Anderson, *Roman Law*, 106 (Dundee University Press 2009).
290. Johnston, *supra* n. 296, at 122.
291. Ibid.
292. Leopold Wenger, *Institutes of the Roman Law of Civil Procedure*, 304–305 (Rev. Ed., Liberal Arts Press 1986).

Moreover, one can easily note how this occurrence allowed for the creation of a more elaborate taxonomy of judgments.

For the first time in Western history, the notion of *ius dicere* became assimilated to the act of resolving a dispute between the litigants, and lawyers' pleadings abandoned a legal reasoning based on actions and *formulae* in favour of a reasoning in terms of substantive law.[293] The administration of justice became a prerogative of the centralized political power, which organized its officials in a bureaucratic hierarchy.

[B] Contemporary Epiphanies: The Purpose(s) of Judgments

Since the *cognitio extra ordinem*, the central paradigms of civil procedure in the West have remained essentially the same.[294] To prove this point, let us consider the Romano-canonical and common law traditions. Despite having been often presented with the dissonance between the inquisitorial and adversarial approaches, it is now generally accepted that the outstanding differences concerning these systems mainly affect evidentiary matters and fact finding, rather than the final product of the procedure.[295] For this reason, I have preferred to use the terms 'Romano-canonical' and 'common law', as they focus on the historical sources of these traditions rather than their alleged differences. In this respect, it has been submitted that such distinctions between adversarial and inquisitorial models should be avoided, for Western procedural systems now tend toward a convergence of models.[296] There is considerable truth in this statement if it is made with reference to the European context. Here, sectorial reforms and landmark rulings of the European Court of Justice have pushed toward a lurking harmonization of civil justice in the various Member States.[297] It remains, however, that traditions continue to influence the way in which central notions and problems are addressed.[298]

It has been observed that '[i]n all systems of procedure doing justice means arriving at decisions which give the parties before the court what is legally due to them'.[299] This amounts to a legal understanding of justice, for a decision will be just if

---

293. Jolowicz & Nicholas, *supra* n. 274, at 440 (the authors suggest nonetheless that the formulary system may have survived within the *cognitio*, especially thanks to the magistrate's practice of delegating the hearing of cases to a *iudex pedanus*. The use of *formulae* would have, in fact, facilitated this delegation and allowed for the intervention of laymen). *See also* van Rhee, *supra* n. 41, at 31–32.
294. Cf. Cotterrell, *supra* n. 89, at 217 ff.
295. Jolowicz, *supra* n. 88, at 214.
296. Nicolò Trocker & Vincenzo Varano, *Concluding Remarks* in Nicolò Trocker & Vincenzo Varano, *The Reforms of Civil Procedure in a Comparative Perspective* 243, 245 (Giappichelli 2005).
297. Andrea Biondi, *The Impact of EC Law on National Procedural Law* in Trocker & Varano, *supra* n. 296, 233 at 234–235.
298. *See* e.g., Lac D'Amiante du Québec Ltée v. Québec Inc [2001] 2 RSC 743.
299. Adrian A.S. Zuckerman, *Justice in Crisis: Comparative Dimensions of Civil Procedure* in *Civil Justice in Crisis* 3, 3 (Oxford University Press 1999) [Zuckerman, 'Justice in Crisis']. Cf. John Sorabji, *English Civil Justice After the Woolf and Jackson Reforms*, 3 (Cambridge University Press 2014), the author argues that substantive justice is now being replaced by a form of proportionate justice: "A limit is now placed on the amount of resources individuals and the State can properly expend on securing substantive justice in any particular case. The limit

Chapter 4: Contentious Awards §4.02[B]

it gives the litigants what they *legally* deserve.[300] Moreover, justice will be done if the true facts have been established and the relevant law, correctly applied.[301] If we accept these propositions, then a judgment can be defined as the act giving the parties what is legally due to them. Let us consider how this general definition is articulated in the Romano-canonical and common law traditions.

In the Romano-canonical tradition, a judgment can be defined as a reasoned decision on a claim made by one of the parties to the proceedings.[302] The ordinance (also known as an order) is an ancillary, albeit conceptually different, act. It can be defined as 'an act regulating the proceedings'.[303] It is therefore a means rather than an end. A similar distinction can be found in the common law tradition. According to Zuckerman, a judgment 'disposes of an action or part of an action', and, as such, it should not be confused with a procedural decision (usually in the form of an order), which 'directs a party or another person to do something or refrain from doing something, or which determines the course of the proceedings'.[304] Yet the different functions accomplished by judgments and orders are not the only possible basis for distinguishing between them. These acts are also distinguishable in light of the different kinds of reasoning that they imply. Canon law, for instance, explicitly sets out

---

      operates in two ways. In some cases it requires the court to refuse to allow a claim to proceed to judgment. It thus denies substantive justice in its entirety. In other cases – the majority – it restricts the amount of time and money that is spent on litigation. As such, it reduces the court's ability to achieve substantive justice."
300. Cf. Ulpian, D.I.1: 'Iustitia est constans et perpetua voluntas ius suum cuique tribuendi' ('Justice is the constant and perpetual desire to give to each one that to which he is entitled').
301. *Ibid.* Cf. Sorabji, *supra* n. 299, at 3.
302. Mandrioli, *supra* n. 89, at 469 ('La funzione decisoria alla quale assolve la sentenza quando non si ferma ad una pronuncia sul processo per il rilievo d un ostacolo, [corrsponde] all'esigenza di tutela prospettata nella domanda attraverso l'esercizio dell'azione'). *See also* Code of Canon law, can. 1611-*sentenstia debet*:

    1° definire controversiam coram tribunali agitatam, data singulis dubiis congrua responsione;
    2° determinare quae sint partium obligationes ex iudicio ortae et quo modo implendae sint;
    3° exponere rationes seu motiva, tam in iure quam in facto, quibus dispositiva sententiae pars innititur;
    4° statuere de litis expensis.

      Cf. Guinchard, *supra* n. 22, at 698 ('En théorie, le mot "jugement", qui est susceptible d'acceptions différentes, devrait être synonyme d'acte juridictionnel. ... [D]ans "jugement" il y a "jus" et juger, c'est répondre en droit à une demande'). *See also* Ernest Caparros, Hélène Thériault & Jean Thorn, *Code of Canon Law Annotated*, 1261 (2ed, Wilson & Lafleur 2004) (sub Can. 1611: '[T]he judgment must settle the controversy and answer each of the questions of the parties, as expressed in the legally formulated and approved *dubia*').
303. Mandrioli, *supra* n. 89, at 477; Guinchard, *supra* n. 22, at 716 ('Les mesures d'administration judiciaire ont deux objectifs principaux. Elles tendent, tantôt, au bon fonctionnement du tribunal, tantôt, au bon déroulement de la procédure').
304. Adrian Zuckerman, *On Civil Procedure*, 1058–1059 (3ed, Sweet & Maxwell 2013) (the author further notes (at 1059) that 'while the distinction between dispositive decisions and interim or procedural decisions is fairly clear, there are no generally accepted terms that encapsulate it. At one time the term judgment was reserved for dispositive decisions while the term order was used to describe procedural decisions. However ... these terms are no longer used exclusively in relation to one or other type of court decisions') [Zuckerman, *Civil Procedure*].

a methodological distinction based on the different intellectual activity that is involved in each:

> [Unlike] an order (imperium), a judgment is a mental act and the fruit of human reason (iudicium). Therefore, it must be well founded and studied by the judge in relation to the facts on which it is based and the law that it applies.[305]

This passage is very suggestive. While an order is presented as a *command*, the judgment would be a *reasoned answer*. However, a definition based exclusively on these characteristics could be problematic, for an order (or ordinance) can also contain reasons,[306] and a judgment can contain commands.[307]

In light of the above, the similarities between the two traditions are grounded in a common understanding of 'action' and 'claim'. The common law tradition has, in fact, adopted the Roman notion according to which a claim (or action) consists in a request for a remedy, based on a set of facts.[308] Now, by this I do not mean that the common law has endorsed the view according to which rights precede remedies[309] but, quite simply, that an action is a request for the intervention of an adjudicative body. In the words of Zuckerman:

> Once ... a dispositive decision has been given, the original cause of action is merged in the decision, *transit in rem judicatam*, and any further enforcement of the rights in question must be by means of enforcement of the judgment.

This passage highlights a shared conception of the remedial character of civil justice as the crystallization of a right, an occurrence that can be explained through the

---

305. Caparros et al., *supra* n. 302, at 1262. *See also* Can. 1608:

    §1. Ad pronuntiationem cuiuslibet sententiae requiritur in iudicis animo moralis certitudo circa rem sententia definiendam.
    §2. Hanc certitudinem iudex haurire debet ex actis et probatis ... .

    (The authors further add (at 1258 (sub can. 1608): 'The moral certainty that the judge must have about the matter or the object of the trial ... is neither an absolute certainty (either physical or metaphysical), a mere probability, or a subjective conviction. It must be supported by the laws of logic and ethics by which human conduct is governed').
306. *See* e.g., Art. 134 of the Italian *Code of Civil Procedure*, according to which, ordinances shall contain summary reasons.
307. Zuckerman, *Civil Procedure*, *supra* n. 304, at 1059; Mandrioli, *supra* n. 89, at 471. Cadiet et al., *Théorie générale*, *supra* n. 28 at 684 ('La motivation d'une décision renvoie à ses motifs. Cependant, elle peut aussi être perçue comme l'indication des mobiles psychologiques du juge qui a décidé').
308. Jolowicz, *supra* n. 88, at 81 (here, the author describes the common notion of action, shared by the two traditions) and 185 ff., 202 (discussing the principle *Da mihi factum dabo tibi jus* and concluding that 'in both countries [France and England,] the allegation of facts is for the parties, while the ultimate determination of their legal consequences is for the judge').
309. Hedge Dedek, *From Norms to Facts: The Realization of Rights in Common and Civil Private Law*, 56:1 MLJ 77, 85 (2010) (discussing the dichotomy *ubi remedium ibi ius, ubi ius ibi remedium*, and noting the contribution of theorists such as Peter Birks in bridging this classic divergence between the two traditions). *See also* Jolowicz, *supra* n. 88, at 82–83 (where he identifies the separation of right and remedy and, as a result thereof, the rapprochement of the two traditions in the *Judicature Acts* of 1873 and 1875).

similarities between early English procedure based on writs and the Roman formulary trial.[310] The only notable theoretical difference between the two revolves around the fact that the Romano-canonical tradition conceives such a realization of a right as *secondary*, in the sense that the norms enacted in the civil codes already constitute a type of *primary* realization.[311] A judgment, therefore, is defined by both traditions as a reasoned decision disposing of a claim or action. Such decisions are justified in normative terms: that is, they give to each party what that party legally deserves.

A further area where significant convergence has occurred relates to the fundamental condition that should characterize any type of civil action, that is, the existence of a dispute. It is commonly stated, for instance, that a judgment consists in a decision resolving a dispute between two parties. This, however, is not always the case. Consent judgments, for instance, which are judgments recording a private settlement between the parties, are now a common occurrence in both procedural traditions.[312] Also, declaratory judgments can be regarded as an example of a decision not requiring the existence of a dispute. They rather consist of 'a binding declaration concerning a legal state of affairs'.[313] The English declaratory judgment echoes the Italian judgment of *accertamente mero* ('mere ascertainement').[314] Even in France, where the doctrine of *acte juridictionnel* (originally developed to distinguish a decision rendered by an administrative court from one rendered by an ordinary court of law)[315] is often said to imply that a judgment (or *acte juridictionnel*) constitutes the resolution of a dispute (*litige*), there is broad consensus as to the possibility of entering judgments in the absence of a dispute.[316] The changing nature of judgments is also said to be the result of the growing importance of alternative means of dispute resolution: accordingly, 'civil litigation should no longer be seen as limited to the resolution of disputes'.[317] The contentious model of judgments has, as a result, been significantly eroded by the above developments.

Having examined the nature of contentious judgments, let us now consider the effects of contentious judgments (i.e., resolving disputes) inherent to the final character (res judicata) of these decisions.

[C] The Effects of Judgments

If we adopt a procedural perspective, a judgment resolves a dispute by ricochet rather than directly. If a Court of First Instance declares that a defendant has breached a contract entered with the claimant for the delivery of goods, and the defendant is ordered to pay damages, what will prevent the same defendant, once the judgment has

---

310. Glenn, *supra* n. 40, at 240–241.
311. Giuseppe Chiovenda, *Istituzioni di diritto processuale civile*, 7 (Jovene 1936).
312. *See*, e.g., Section 40(6) of the 1998 English Civil Procedure Rules; Art. 1567 of the French *Code of Civil Procedure*.
313. Zuckerman, *Civil Procedure*, *supra* n. 304, at 1061.
314. Chiovenda, *supra* n. 311, at 191.
315. Cadiet et al., *Théorie générale*, *supra* n. 28, at 411.
316. Guinchard, *supra* n. 22, at 713; Cadiet et al., *Théorie générale*, *supra* n. 28, at 416.
317. Jolowicz, *supra* n. 88, at 394.

been rendered, from continuing to withhold its performance? What resolves the dispute between the parties, in effect, is the res judicata effect attached to the judgment of the court, rather than the act itself: a decision per se does not resolve a dispute; it merely answers the parties' claims. In other words, what is considered to be a central effect of judgments is actually the product of an external norm. It is immaterial whether this rule is implemented in an external legal provision or if it is an unwritten rule followed by courts themselves. Not only is the finality of judgments a characteristic shared by both legal traditions, it can also be regarded as an attribute of the rule of law itself (and thus, a constitutional-like principle). Unsurprisingly, res judicata is also described as a general principle of law within the meaning of Article 38 of the *Statute of the International Court of Justice*:[318] 'The principle of finality demands that a judgment disposing of a dispute should leave no room for further litigation of the same subject matter. ... [T]here is a general public interest in not allowing an issue to be litigated all over again.'[319] Such principle of finality is usually presented as a synonym of res judicata, which, in turn, can be defined as follows:[320]

> The term res judicata refers to the general doctrine that an earlier and final adjudication by a court or arbitral tribunal is conclusive in subsequent proceedings involving the same object or relief, the same legal grounds and the same parties.

More precisely, res judicata was defined by the International Law Association by reference to two distinct effects:[321]

> a positive effect (namely, that a judgment or award is final and binding between the parties and should be implemented, subject to any available appeal or challenge); and, a negative effect (namely, that the subject matter of the judgment or award cannot be re-litigated a second time, also referred to as *ne bis in idem*).

Both effects show that it is not in the nature of the judgment itself to finally resolve the dispute but rather that this finality flows from the attributes of the res judicata doctrine. This observation underlines that res judicata effects could also (in theory) be attributed to non-contentious or provisional decisions.

In light of the above, it is now time to consider the notion of arbitral award. Before looking at how this concept is defined in French and English law, I will underline that central transnational and international instruments fail to provide sufficient guidance on the definition of the notion of award.

---

318. Luca Radicati di Brozolo, *Res Judicata* in Pierre Tercier, *Post Awards Issues* 127, 129 (JurisNet 2011); Norah Gallagher, *Parallel Proceedings, Res Judicata, and Lis Pendens: Problems and Possible Solutions* in Loukas A. Mistelis & Julian D.M. Lew, *Pervasive Problems in International Arbitration* 329, 335 (Kluwer Law 2006); Bernard Hanotiau, *Complex Arbitrations: Multiparty, Multicontract, Multi-Issue and Class Actions*, 238–239 (Kluwer Law 2006).
319. Zuckerman, *Civil Procedure*, supra n. 304, at 1238.
320. Audley Sheppard, *The Scope and Res Judicata Effect of Arbitral Awards* in Guy Keutgen, *Arbitral Procedure at the Dawn of the New Millenium* 263, 267 (Bruylant 2005).
321. Filip de Ly & Audley Sheppard, *Res Judicata* in *Report of the International Law Association* 2 (2004).

Chapter 4: Contentious Awards   §4.03[B]

§4.03 THE NOTION OF CONTENTIOUS AWARD IN NATIONAL ARBITRATION ACTS

[A] The Scope of the Enquiry

'At the end of the day, what can be regarded as an award?' is a question that may often come up in practice. Many will confirm that the need to address the confusion around the definition of arbitral award is extremely relevant, since, most of the time, such definitional questions are asked at delicate moments in the arbitration, when time is of the essence (e.g., at the phase of enforcement or of annulment). Users of international arbitration tend to have a preconception according to which an arbitral award must look more or less like a final judgment, that is, a decision rendered by a judge that resolves a dispute in a final manner. After all, arbitrators are seen as functional equivalents of state courts and, as such, are called upon to exercise similar functions.

'What is an award?' is a question that can be asked at numerous levels. One could ask, for example, 'What is an award under the *New York Convention*?' or 'What are the requirements of an arbitral decision for the purpose of a request for annulment under the French *Code of Civil Procedure*?' Despite the many possible questions, for the sake of clarity and predictability of international arbitration, it is important to give a single answer to all of them. As the *New York Convention* demonstrates, the effectiveness of the entire system of commercial arbitration lies in the possibility of enforcing arbitrators' awards. Despite their central role, neither the *New York Convention* nor the UNCITRAL *Model Law* provide a univocal definition of arbitral award.[322]

In light of the above, the analysis should be complemented by a study of national arbitration acts. Given their prominence in international commercial arbitration and their place within to two different legal traditions (Romano-canonical and common law), the following subparts will analyse the notion of arbitral award in the French *Code of Civil Procedure* and in the English *Arbitration Act 1996*.

[B] France

As previously explained, the analysis carried out in this book is limited to international commercial arbitration. As a result, this subpart will not focus on the requirements for domestic awards. It should be noted, in passing, that French arbitration legislation presents more stringent requirements for domestic awards.[323] Let us now consider, therefore, the general requirements that international awards have to fulfil in this jurisdiction. According to authoritative scholars, 'an award is a decision putting an end to all or part of the dispute; it is therefore final with regard to the aspect (or aspects) of

---

322. Although, as we shall *see* throughout the book, the UNCITRAL *Model Law*, do provide some guidance by indicating that certain decisions can take the form of awards. *See* in particular, Arts 16(3) (implicitly), 17(2) [2006 amendments], 30(2), and 31.
323. Mathieu de Boisséson & José Pinto, *Le nouveau droit français de l'arbitrage*, 32 Rev Arbitragem 7, 14 (2011).

the dispute that it resolves'.[324] This implies that arbitrators can also make partial awards, deciding 'a particular aspect of a dispute (such as jurisdiction, the governing law or liability)'.[325] The French *Code of Civil Procedure* devotes a set of specific provisions to arbitral awards.[326] Nevertheless, these provisions merely identify *formal* requirements, leaving to courts the role of uncovering the *substantive* ones.

[1] Formal Requirements

As far as formal requirements are concerned, Article 1513 of the French *Code of Civil Procedure* states that an award shall be signed by all arbitrators. However, Article 1513(2) clarifies that 'if a minority among them refuses to sign the award, the others shall so state in the award'.[327] The provision also implies that the decision shall be made in *writing*.[328] It imposes the writing requirement *ad probationem* but not *ad validitatem*.[329] Article 1506, moreover, by referring to Article 1481 on domestic arbitrations, makes further requirements applicable to international arbitral awards rendered in France. The international arbitral award should thus indicate:[330]

(1) the full names of the parties, as well as their domicile or corporate headquarters;
(2) if applicable, the names of the counsel or other persons who represented or assisted the parties;
(3) the names of the arbitrators who rendered it;
(4) the date on which it was rendered;
(5) the place where the award was rendered.

---

324. Gaillard & Savage, *supra* n., 5 at 741. *See also Ibid.* at 737 ('An arbitral award can be defined as a final decision by the arbitrators on all or part of the dispute submitted to them, whether it concerns the merits of the dispute, jurisdiction, or a procedural issue leading them to end the proceedings').
325. *Ibid*, at 741.
326. *See generally* Thomas Clay, *Le nouveau droit français de l'arbitrage* (Lextenso 2011); Charles Jarrosson & Jacques Pellerin, *Le droit français de l'arbitrage après le décret du 13 janvier 2011*, 1 Rev Arb 5 (2011).
327. Article 1513(2), French *Code of Civil Procedure*: 'Toutefois, si une minorité d'entre eux refuse de la signer, les autres en font mention dans la sentence'.
328. Christophe Seraglini & Denis Mouralis, *L'arbitrage commercial international* in Jacques Beguin & Michel Menjucq, *Traité de droit du commerce international*, para. 1964 (LexisNexis 2011). Cf. Gaillard & Savage, *supra* n. 5, at 760. *See also* Loquin, *Arbitrage International*, *supra* n. 78, at 382.
329. Born, *supra* n. 4, at 3032.
330. Article 1481, French *Code of Civil Procedure*: La sentence arbitrale contient l'indication :

    1° Des noms, prénoms ou dénomination des parties ainsi que de leur domicile ou siège social ;
    2° Le cas échéant, du nom des avocats ou de toute personne ayant représenté ou assisté les parties ;
    3° Du nom des arbitres qui l'ont rendue ;
    4° De sa date ;
    5° Du lieu où la sentence a été rendue.

In addition, Article 1482 provides that the award shall succinctly set forth the respective claims and arguments of the parties, and state the reasons upon which it is based.[331] It is worth noting that, pursuant to Article 1506, the above provisions are applicable, 'absent a contrary agreement of the parties'. Yet there seems to be uncertainty as to the boundaries of private autonomy[332] and especially as to the possibility of absolving the arbitrators of their obligation to state the reasons for their decision.[333] With respect to this latter case, several decisions rendered before the 2011 reform of the *Civil Code of Procedure* suggest that a lack of reasons constitutes a valid ground of annulment, regardless of the parties' agreement in this regard.[334]

Now, since the French legislator has established several formal requirements for international awards, it is important to discuss the potential consequences of a failure to comply. Unfortunately, the French *Code of Civil Procedure* provides little guidance in this regard. While Article 1483, referring to domestic arbitration, states that only a lack of: (i) the name of the arbitrators, (ii) their signatures, (iii) the date of rendition, or (iv) reasons will result in an award being void, no equivalent provision is to be found in the chapter on international arbitral awards. The doctrine has raised questions regarding the consequences attached to such a failure to comply, and there has been a tendency to argue that Article 1483 would indeed only be applicable to domestic awards.[335]

Upon a closer look, however, a contrary interpretation should be preferred, and Article 1483 should be deemed applicable to international arbitral awards. It should be noted that the *Code of Civil Procedure*'s chapter on international arbitration is composed of fewer rules and that Article 1506 declares a significant number of provisions enacted for domestic arbitration to be applicable by reference. The absence, in Article 1506, of a direct reference to Article 1483, should not be considered conclusive.[336] In other words, the absence of an explicit reference would only entail a more important place for flexibility, something that may be necessary in international arbitration in order to account for the circumstances of the case as well as the legal traditions of the parties to the dispute.[337] In particular, French courts would maintain discretion in deciding whether the failure to comply with a formal requirement may justify, given the circumstances of the case, the annulment of the award. The extensive application of Article 1483 also seems in line with the case law preceding the entry into force of the 2011 reform. Let us consider an illustration.

While the Paris Court of Appeal rejected a request for annulment based on the fact that one arbitrator had not signed an award on the same date as the other arbitrators,[338] in a previous case, the same court held that an omission of arbitrators'

---

331. Article 1482, French *Code of Civil Procedure*: (1) La sentence arbitrale expose succinctement les prétentions respectives des parties et leurs moyens. (2) Elle est motivée.
332. Jarrosson & Pellerin, *supra* n. 326, at 61.
333. Dominique Vidal, *Droit français de l'arbitrage interne et international*, 280 (Lextenso 2012).
334. *See* e.g., Cass Civ 1e, 14 June 2000, 4 Rev Arb 729 (2001).
335. Laure Bernheim – Van de Casteele, *Les principes fondamentaux de l'arbitrage*, 587 (Bruxelles 2012).
336. Cf. Jarrosson & Pellerin, *supra* n. 326, at 60.
337. William W. Park, *Truth Seeking in International Arbitration* in Markus Wirth, *The Search for the 'Truth' in Arbitration: Is Finding the Truth What Dispute Is About?* 1, 12 (JurisNet 2011).
338. CA Paris, 17 June 1997, 3 Rev Arb 584 (1997) (Annotation Dominique Bureau).

signatures entails the nullity of an award.[339] These cases could mean that if a flaw results in a mere irregularity, the award will not be considered void. Conversely, a complete omission of a formal requirement (such as reasons[340] or the date[341]) would entail the nullity of the award, which could be obtained pursuant to a request for annulment under Article 1520(3) (on the grounds that 'the arbitral tribunal ruled without complying with the mandate conferred upon it').[342]

We note, moreover – and this can be regarded as a further reason supporting the interpretation favouring the extensive application of Article 1483 to international awards – that if a lack or omission of a formal requirement did not entail the nullity of the award (and therefore the admissibility of a *recours en annulation*), one would be left without a clear procedure for challenging such pathological decisions.[343] This circumstance would force the parties to seize a national court in order to obtain an order declaring that the formally flawed decision is not an arbitral award (*jugement déclaratoire*).[344] This could easily turn into a very complicated and time-consuming procedure.

Finally, it should be noted that the omissions and errors mentioned in Article 1483 amount to a case of partial nullity. The arbitral tribunal, in fact, can always rectify the mistake or omission (Article 1485(2)) upon a request from a party. In this regard, the Paris Court of Appeal stated that the arbitrator can also proceed *sua sponte* by issuing an award rectifying mistakes or omissions, provided that all parties are given an opportunity to submit their observations.[345]

As a corollary to the rule of partial nullity, the award cannot be annulled on the ground of errors or omissions if the party seeking annulment has not previously sought

---

339. CA Paris, 27 October 1988, 4 Rev Arb 908 (1990) (Annotation Bertrand Moreau). *See also* Sophie Crépin, *Le contrôle des sentences arbitrales par la Cour d'appel de Paris depuis les réformes de 1980 et 1981*, 4 Rev Arb 521, 575 (1991). A similar decision was reached with respect to domestic arbitration. *See* Cass Civ 1e, 3 October 2006, 1 Rev Arb 85 (2008) (Annotation Charles Jarrosson).
340. Dominique Hascher, *Les perspectives françaises sur le contrôle de la sentence internationale ou étrangère*, 2:1 MJDR 1, 6 (2015) (The judicial review of the reasons of the award consists of a 'constatation matérielle et non d'une critique intellectuelle du raisonnement de l'arbitre').
341. Liebscher, *supra* n. 8, at 128.
342. Cf. CA Paris, 29 September 2011, No 11/06269 ('Considérant que les articles 1471 et 1472 devenus les articles 1480 et 1481 du code de procédure civile sont applicables en matière d'arbitrage international en vertu de l'article 1506 nouveau du même code ... il résulte des dispositions de l'article 1502 devenu l'article 1520 du code de procédure civile que les critiques concernant la date et la signature de la sentence arbitrale ne constituent pas des cas d'ouverture du recours en annulation en matière d'arbitrage international').
343. *See* e.g., CA Paris, 21 November 1991, 3 Rev Arb 494 (1992) 494 (Annotation Marie-Claire Rivier).
344. This would probably force the interested party to invoke the doctrine of 'non-existing act' (*inexistence de l'acte de procédure*), which can be found in continental civil procedure. *See* Guinchard, *supra* n. 22, at 673 ff.
345. CA Paris, 29 September 2011, No 11/06269 ('Si la sentence dessaisit l'arbitre de la contestation qu'elle tranche, l'arbitre a néanmoins le pouvoir d'interpréter la sentence, de réparer les erreurs ou omissions matérielles qui l'affectent et de la compléter lorsqu'il a omis de statuer sur un chef de demande').

out the arbitral tribunal and requested that it rectify the situation with an award, unless it is objectively impossible to reconvene the tribunal.[346]

[2] The Substantive Requirements

As a preliminary observation, one should note that only decisions rendered by arbitrators (or permanent arbitral institutions) can have the potential to amount to arbitral awards. This criterion is not necessarily useful in order to categorize decisions rendered by arbitrators but may become handy in order to separate awards from decisions rendered during the course of other dispute resolution mechanisms.[347] In this respect, it is a generally accepted proposition that, unlike an expert, the arbitrator resolves a dispute regarding a legal entitlement (*litige sur une prétention juridique*),[348] exercising the power to speak the law (*pouvoir juridictionnel*) conferred to him or her by the parties.[349]

From a theoretical point of view, French jurisprudence endorses a peculiar notion of international arbitral award, which is qualified as a 'decision of international justice detached from any national legal order, whose validity shall be appreciated in light of the rules of the country in which its recognition and enforcement are sought'.[350]

A much more precise definition is found in cases dealing with annulment proceedings,[351] where courts assess if the arbitral decision at hand meets the minimum requirements to be an arbitral award. Where these minimum requirements are not

---

346. CA Paris, 27 October 2011, No 10/12982 ('[I]nfra petita constitue une omission de statuer et non une violation de la mission dans le cadre de l'article 1520 3° du code de procédure civile. ... [D]'autre part, les appelants ne démontrent pas qu'ils se trouvaient dans l'impossibilité de saisir l'arbitre en omission de statuer alors que le règlement d'arbitrage de la Chambre de Commerce Internationale (C.C.I.) sous l'empire duquel les parties s'étaient placées en vertu de la clause compromissoire, s'il ne prévoit pas expressément dans sa rédaction applicable cette possibilité, ne l'interdit pas et que par ailleurs, aucune impossibilité matérielle de reconstituer le tribunal arbitral n'est invoquée').
347. CA Paris, 28 November 2002, 2 Rev Arb 445 (2003) (the adjudicative power is, in fact, the central element that allows one to distinguish arbitration from other forms of dispute resolution such as expert determination). On this point, *see* Cass Civ 2e, 3 October 2013, 3 Rev Arb 643 (2014) (Annotation Vincent Chantebout).
348. Jarrosson, *supra* n. 16, at 254–255 ('On dira qu'il y a litige, contestation ... dès lors qu'une partie résiste en pouvant s'appuyer sur une argumentation juridique, au point de vue qu'une autre partie essaye d'imposer, et qui diffère du sien').
349. *Ibid.* at 260; Clay, *L'arbitre*, *supra* n. 61, at 18 ('l'arbitre [est] un juge privé désigné par ceux dont il doit trancher le litige').
350. CA Paris, 20 November 2012, No 11/12192 (this definition was first adopted in the *Putrabali* case). *See* Cass Civ 1e, 29 June 2007, 3 Rev Arb 507 (2007) 507 (Annotation Emmanuel Gaillard). *See also* Emmanuel Gaillard, *Ordre juridique arbitral: réalité, utilité, spécificité*, 55 MLJ 891, 905 (2010). *See* most recently: Cass Civ 1e, 8 July 2015, No 13-25.846 ('[L]a sentence internationale, qui n'est rattachée à aucun ordre juridique étatique, est une décision de justice internationale dont la régularité est examinée au regard des règles applicables dans le pays où la reconnaissance et l'exécution sont demandées; qu'il résulte [de la Convention de New York de 1958] que l'exequatur des sentences arbitrales rendues à l'étranger est exclusif de tout jugement sur le fond et relève de la compétence des juridictions judiciaires').
351. Article 1520, French *Code of Civil Procedure*: 'An award may only be set aside where: (1) the arbitral tribunal wrongly upheld or declined jurisdiction; or (2) the arbitral tribunal was not properly constituted; or (3) the arbitral tribunal ruled without complying with the mandate

fulfilled, the challenge would be inadmissible (*non-recevable*). As stated by the *Cour de cassation*:[352]

> [S]eules peuvent faire l'objet d'un recours en annulation les véritables sentences arbitrales, c'est-à-dire les actes des arbitres qui tranchent de manière définitive, en tout ou en partie, le litige qui leur est soumis, que ce soit sur le fond, sur la compétence ou sur un moyen de procédure qui les conduit à mettre fin à l'instance.
>
> Translation:
>
> Only arbitral awards, that is, decisions by which the arbitrators resolve in a final manner, whether in whole or in part, a dispute put before them (whether on the merits, jurisdiction, or another procedural objection leading to the termination of proceedings), can be challenged with the annulment procedure.

An arbitral award, therefore, shall resolve a dispute between the parties in a final manner, that is, by resolving its substantive or procedural facets. To give a few examples, the decision will be considered to be an award if it resolves, in a final manner, a dispute on a legal entitlement or the performance of a contract (substantive facets), or if it resolves matters related to the jurisdiction of the tribunal or questions of inadmissibility of the claims submitted before the arbitrators (procedural facets). This type of decision is often referred to as an *acte juridictionnel*, that is, a decision through which the adjudicator speaks the law (*ius dicere*) and dispenses justice.[353] While it is fairly simple to imagine the content of an award, it is much more difficult to grasp the notion of finality (in the words of the *Cour de cassation*, 'trancher de manière définitive'), which is presented as the quintessential element of an arbitral award. Such a notion, in fact, ultimately refers to the effects of the decision rather than to its subject matter. The French *Code of Civil Procedure* addresses this point in two separate provisions, namely Articles 1484 and 1485.

These norms embody the principle according to which an award shall bear a res judicata effect. While Article 1484(1) states that 'as soon as it is made, an arbitral award shall be res judicata with regard to the claims adjudicated in that award',[354] Article 1485(1) introduces the ancillary *functus officio* doctrine: 'Once an award is made, the arbitral tribunal shall no longer be vested with the power to rule on the claims adjudicated in that award.'[355] The exceptions to this doctrine are contemplated in

---

conferred upon it; or (4) due process was violated; or (5) recognition or enforcement of the award is contrary to international public policy'.
352. Cass Civ 1e, 12 October 2011, No 09-72.439. *See also* CA Paris, 29 October 2009, No 08/18544.
353. Jarrosson, *supra* n. 16, at 372; Clay, *L'arbitre*, *supra* n. 61 at 175; Bernheim – Van de Casteele, *supra* n. 335, at 596.
354. Article 1484(1), French *Code of Civil Procedure*: 'La sentence arbitrale a, dès qu'elle est rendue, l'autorité de la chose jugée relativement à la contestation qu'elle tranche'.
355. Article 1485(1), French *Code of Civil Procedure*: 'La sentence dessaisit le tribunal arbitral de la contestation qu'elle tranche'. These are usually defined as the preclusive effects of an arbitral award; *see* Born, *supra* n. 4, at 2900 ('Once a final award is made, the tribunal becomes *functus officio* and its mandate generally comes to an end; if post-award proceedings relating to the award are necessary, these are matters for the parties and, if necessary, national courts'); Alexis Mourre, *Is There Life After An Award?* in Pierre Tercier, *Post Award Issues* 1, 2 (JusriNet 2011) ('The two principles of *functus* and *res judicata* do not, however, have exactly the same domain. There are situations in which an arbitrator may become *functus* without having accomplished his jurisdictional mission. Such is the case when an arbitrator validly resigns,

Article 1485(2), allowing the tribunal to 'interpret the award, rectify clerical errors and omissions, or make an additional award where it failed to rule on a claim. ... '[356]

As one will recall, the res judicata effect does not pertain to the act itself but is an attribute conferred by an external norm.[357] This is why, for instance, the *Code of Civil Procedure* confers, in ordinary litigation, such an effect on orders rendered on the basis of successful procedural objections entailing the termination of proceedings.[358] Article 1484(1) of the *Code of Civil Procedure*, which confers a res judicata effect on arbitral awards rendered in France, 'is primarily directed at French courts, which must hold inadmissible any action seeking resolution of a dispute which has already been decided by the arbitration'.[359] But what is the essence of this notion? Res judicata has two different connotations.

According to the first connotation (*conception positive*), a decision bearing res judicata effects can be invoked in another trial or dispute, with respect to the actual order or orders contained therein.[360] It is worth noting that according to the prevalent case law of the *Cour de cassation*, such effects are limited to the *dispositif* (i.e., the court order) and do not apply to the reasons and factual findings of the decision.[361] According to the second connotation (*conception négative*),[362] res judicata entails that the same dispute (or matter decided by the decision) cannot be reheard by the same (or a different) decisional body. For this rule to apply, the following conditions have to be met:[363]

(i) The *parties* to the dispute shall be the same.
(ii) The *causae* (i.e., the facts and juridical reasons giving rise to the claims of the parties) shall be the same.
(iii) The *petita* (i.e., claims of the parties) shall be identical as well.

In this respect, it should be noted that the *Cour de cassation* has held that there is identity of *causae* even if the claims are grounded on different norms or invoke different rules.[364] By referring to the principle of *concentration des moyens*

---

when a challenge is successful or if, after the constitution of the arbitral tribunal, a competent court decides that there is no valid arbitration agreement between the parties. ... The arbitrator will also be *functus* if the parties settle or if they waive their arbitration agreement, subject however to the principle of competence-competence').

356. Article 1485(2), French *Code of Civil Procedure*: 'Toutefois, à la demande d'une partie, le tribunal arbitral peut interpréter la sentence, réparer les erreurs et omissions matérielles qui l'affectent ou la compléter lorsqu'il a omis de statuer sur un chef de demande. Il statue après avoir entendu les parties ou celles-ci appelées'.
357. Cadiet et al., *Théorie générale*, *supra* n. 28, at 894.
358. Article 775, French *Code of Civil Procedure*.
359. Gaillard & Savage, *supra* n. 5, at 780.
360. *Ibid.* at 297.
361. Cass Civ Ass Plen, 13 March 2009, No 08-16.033 ('l'autorité de chose jugée n'a lieu qu'à l'égard de ce qui fait l'objet d'un jugement et a été tranché dans son dispositif'). *See also* Cadiet et al., *Théorie générale*, *supra* n. 28, at 897. For an overview of the special cases in which the principle can be extended to other parts of the judgment (such as the reasons), *see* Guinchard, *supra* n. 22, at 785 ff.
362. Cadiet et al., *Théorie générale*, *supra* n. 28, at 895.
363. Héron & Le Bars, *supra* n. 81, at 288–289.
364. Cass Civ Ass Plen, 7 July 2006, No 04-10.672.

(concentration of claims), the same court has held that claimants shall file all the claims arising out of the same facts and juridical reasons in the same procedure ('le demandeur doit présenter dans la même instance toutes les demandes fondées sur la même cause').[365] A failure to do so will result in inadmissibility (*fin de non recevoir*) on the basis of res judicata. The same principle applies to arbitral awards.[366]

Under French law, one should avoid confusing res judicata (*autorité de chose jugée*) with *finality* of a decision (*decision passé en chose jugée*). In fact, *finality* of a decision simply means that the decision can no longer be challenged through suspensive proceedings (e.g., appeal),[367] whereas res judicata prevents one from relitigating the same case. For the sake of clarity, it should be noted that the term 'finality' is used in different ways in international arbitration: it can either indicate a decision 'on the last aspect of a dispute and which, as a result, terminates the arbitrators' jurisdiction ... [or be used] to describe an award which puts an end to at least one aspect of the dispute'.[368] As a result, a decision can be res judicata without being final.[369] For example, a judgment at first instance bears res judicata effects, despite being potentially subject to an appeal.[370] Similarly, an arbitral award can be considered *final* only if the term for bringing forth an action to set aside has expired, that is, one month after the notification of the award (Article 1519(2)). In cases where annulment proceedings are initiated, the award will become *final* upon rejection of the claim for annulment by the Court of Appeal having jurisdiction over the claim.

In light of the above, how should one interpret the attribute of finality ('trancher de manière définitive') employed by the *Cour de cassation* in the definition of arbitral award? On this point, Gaillard and Savage stated that 'an award is a decision putting an end to all or part of the dispute; it is therefore final with regard to the aspect or aspects of the dispute that it resolves'.[371] Another author observes that the *final* character is actually expressed by the irrevocable nature of the decision.[372] In practical terms, according to a relatively recent decision by the *Cour de cassation*, finality means that the decision cannot be reheard by the same (or a different) arbitral tribunal. Parties to an arbitration agreement cannot validly stipulate that once an award has been rendered, the same dispute can be reheard by a new arbitral tribunal upon a request from one of them.[373] Such a stipulation, in other words, would exceed the boundaries

---

365. Ibid.
366. Cass Civ 1e, 28 May 2008, No 07-13.266; Cass Civ 1e, 12 April 2011, No 11-14.123.
367. Article 500(1) of the French *Code of Civil Procedure*. See Héron & Le Bars, *supra* n. 81, at 423 ('Il résulte de l'article 500 du Code de procédure civile qu'est passé en force de chose jugée le jugement qui n'est pas susceptible d'aucun recours suspensif ou qui, ayant été passé d'un tel recours, a cessé de l'être à l'expiration du délai pour ce recours').
368. Gaillard & Savage, *supra* n. 5, at 740–741.
369. Article 480 of the French *Code of Civil Procedure*: 'Le jugement qui tranche dans son dispositif tout ou partie du principal, ou celui qui statue sur une exception de procédure, une fin de non-recevoir ou tout autre incident a, dès son prononcé, l'autorité de la chose jugée relativement à la contestation qu'il tranche'.
370. Guinchard, *supra* n. 22, at 779.
371. Gaillard & Savage, *supra* n. 5, at 741.
372. Bernheim – Van de Casteele, *supra* n. 335 at 601.
373. Cass Civ 1e, 5 March 2014, No 12-29.112 ('Alors, d'une part, que constitue une sentence susceptible de recevoir l'exéquatur, tout acte des arbitres qui tranche, de manière définitive, en

of party autonomy (without affecting the validity of the 'first' final award rendered). This decision of the *Cour de cassation* constitutes a marked departure from the previous case law.[374] In effect, it was generally admitted that an arbitration agreement providing for the constitution of a second tribunal, appointed to rehear the dispute between the parties, would eliminate the final nature of the award rendered by the first tribunal, thus impeding its enforcement or rendering inadmissible a claim for annulment.[375] Yet the decision rendered by the *Cour de cassation* only refers to a case where the dispute

---

tout ou partie, le litige qui leur est soumis; que tel est le cas de "la sentence définitive", qui comme celle en cause en l'espèce, a été rendue dans le cadre d'une procédure arbitrale soumise à réexamen dans laquelle les parties disposent de la possibilité, une fois la sentence rendue, de faire réexaminer l'affaire par un autre tribunal arbitral dès lors que cette sentence a tranché le litige soumis aux arbitres et ce, même si les parties ont usé de leur faculté de faire réexaminer l'affaire; que la cour d'appel, qui a jugé l'inverse, a violé les articles 1484, 1514 et 1516 du code de procédure civile;

> Alors, d'autre part, que l'exéquatur doit être prononcé au regard de la régularité intrinsèque de la décision soumise au juge et sans égard au sort qui pourrait lui être réservé du fait de l'exercice des voies de recours ouvertes contre celle-ci par la convention d'arbitrage ou la loi du lieu du siège de l'arbitrage; que la cour d'appel, qui a refusé l'exéquatur en raison de la demande de réexamen formulée par la République tchèque, a violé l'article 1516 du code de procédure civile;
> Alors, de troisième part, que sauf le recours en révision prévu à l'article 1502 du code de procédure civile, le droit français de l'arbitrage international interdit l'exercice de toute voie de recours contre la sentence; qu'en affirmant que l'institution par la Convention d'arbitrage d'une procédure de réexamen ne heurte aucune règle du droit français quand une telle procédure, qui vise à faire réexaminer l'entier litige par une nouvelle formation arbitrale, constitue une voie de recours offerte aux parties contre la sentence, la cour d'appel a violé les articles 1502, 1506, 1516, 1520 et 1525 alinéa 4 du code de procédure civile').

374. CA Paris, 8 October 1998, 1 Rev Arb 128 (2000).
375. CA Paris, 20 November 2012, No 11/12192 ('Considérant qu'aux termes de l'article V de [la convention d'arbitrage] les parties ont également convenu que la sentence arbitrale serait susceptible d'être réexaminée par d'autres arbitres que les parties choisiront de la même manière, si une demande de réexamen parvient à l'autre partie dans un délai de 30 jours après la date à laquelle la sentence arbitrale est parvenue à la partie demandant le réexamen (…);

> Considérant qu'il est constant que cette dernière décision a été notifiée aux deux parties le 13 août 2008 et que le 22 août 2008, la République Tchèque a notifié à Diag Human une demande de réexamen contenant désignation de son arbitre dans la nouvelle instance; que la procédure de constitution du second tribunal arbitral est toujours en cours;
> Considérant que si, suivant l'article 1484 alinéa 1er du code de procédure civile, applicable en matière d'arbitrage international en vertu de l'article 1506 4° du même code, la sentence arbitrale a, dès qu'elle est rendue, l'autorité de la chose jugée relativement à la contestation qu'elle tranche, il n'en va ainsi que pour autant que l'acte en cause s'analyse en une véritable sentence; qu'il appartient au juge de l'exequatur de se prononcer sur ce point et, le cas échéant, de requalifier un acte inexactement dénommé;
> Que si, en l'espèce, le document soumis à l'exequatur s'intitule sentence arbitrale définitive, ce dernier qualificatif faisant du reste seulement référence à la circonstance que s'y trouvent examinés les derniers points en litige après qu'ont été rendues plusieurs sentences partielles, il résulte clairement des stipulations précitées de la convention d'arbitrage, que la commune intention des parties était de refuser à un tel acte la qualité de sentence dès lors qu'une demande de réexamen était formée dans le délai convenu;
> Considérant que de tels aménagements conventionnels ne heurtent aucune règle du droit français qui n'attache l'autorité de chose jugée qu'aux seules sentences arbitrales; [par ces motifs infirme l'ordonnance d'exequatur]').

resolved by the award could have been reheard by the same arbitral tribunal. In other words, it transforms the decision rendered in something that can or cannot be followed by the parties. It would be rather different if the parties decided to introduce a form of arbitral appeal into their arbitration agreement. In this case, would the 'first instance' award be a valid decision? To answer this question, it is sufficient to go back to the definition of negative effects of res judicata.

The 'arbitral appeal', according to the definition of res judicata found in the doctrine, could neither be affected nor barred by the previous decision because of a lack of the simultaneous presence of the three elements giving rise to the negative effects of res judicata: identity of: (i) parties, (ii) *causae*, and (iii) *petita*. While, in fact, the parties to the appeal would be the same, there would be different *causae* (the juridical reason giving rise to the claim) and, more importantly, different *petita*.

In conclusion, it should be stated that there is no single requirement that will allow for the identification of an award with certainty but rather there are a bundle of elements that must be considered. Among such elements, some are more conclusive then others. For instance, an act rendered by the arbitrators that includes their names, signatures, and the date of rendition tells us little as to the nature of the act. Even the presence of reasons, which is an important sign, is not conclusive. Also, the presence of a substantive requirement alone is weak and inconclusive. As explained, in fact, such requirements ultimately boil down to the attributes conferred by an external norm (res judicata). Likewise, the doctrine of the *acte juridictionnel* is useful yet insufficient to establish whether the decision at hand is an award.[376] As a result, the nature of a decision can only be established by identifying several formal and substantive requirements. Therefore, it is the accumulation of such characteristics that allows for the identification of an arbitral award.[377] The implication is that one cannot limit the analysis of the nature of the act to the label chosen by the arbitrators.[378]

[C] England

The English *Arbitration Act 1996* applies to all international and domestic arbitration seated in England, Wales, or Northern Ireland (section 2(1)). As a result, it introduces a common notion of award, for both international and domestic arbitration.

English law does not provide a statutory definition of arbitral award, and nor is there a common law definition of the term.[379] As with French arbitration law, therefore, the concept of award will be analysed by presenting its formal and substantive requirements.

---

376. Bernheim – Van de Casteele, *supra* n. 335, at 595.
377. *Ibid.* at 604 ('La qualification de la sentence obéit à un faisceau d'éléments dont l'appréciation peut être pondérée par le principe d'efficacité de la justice arbitrale').
378. *See* Cass Civ 1e, 12 October 2011, No 09-72439, cited by Bernheim – Van de Casteele, *supra* n. 335, at 603; CA Paris, 7 October 2004, 4 Rev Arb 737 (2005); Gaillard & Savage, *supra* n. 5, at 737.
379. Liebscher, *supra* n. 8, at 123.

[1] Formal Requirements

Section 52 of the English *Arbitration Act 1996* states:

(1) The parties are free to agree on the form of an award.
(2) If or to the extent that there is no such agreement, the following provisions apply.
(3) The award shall be in writing signed by all the arbitrators or all those assenting to the award.
(4) The award shall contain the reasons for the award unless it is an agreed award or the parties have agreed to dispense with reasons.
(5) The award shall state the seat of the arbitration and the date when it is made.

As a preliminary matter, it should be noted that the provision at hand was greatly inspired by Article 31 of the UNCITRAL *Model Law on International Commercial Arbitration*.[380] Moreover, it is similar to corresponding provisions in other jurisdictions, such as Germany (section 1054 of the *Code of Civil Procedure* (ZPO)), Hong Kong (section 67 of the 2014 *Arbitration Ordinance*), Singapore (section 3 of the *International Arbitration Act*, giving force of law to Article 31 of the *Model Law*), and Switzerland (Article 189(2) of the *Federal Statute on Private International Law*).[381]

It is worth starting the discussion on section 52 of the English *Arbitration Act 1996* by saying that while the statute grants ample liberty to the parties (they can agree on the form of the award), rarely, in fact, is such discretion exercised.[382] The literature is unanimous as to the boundaries of party autonomy in this respect. Not only is it self-evident that parties can absolve the arbitrators of the duty to give reasons, it is also clear that they can dispense with the arbitrators' duty to render an award in writing.[383] This observation, however, should be tempered by some prudent remarks, as 'having the tribunal's decision in written form facilitates both the enforcement of the award and any challenge to it'.[384] Moreover, it is also clear that a failure to comply with the statutory requirements or those agreed by the parties will constitute a valid ground for

---

380. Article 31 (Form and Contents of Award) UNCITRAL *Model Law*:
    (1) The award shall be made in writing and shall be signed by the arbitrator or arbitrators. In arbitral proceedings with more than one arbitrator, the signatures of the majority of all members of the arbitral tribunal shall suffice, provided that the reason for any omitted signature is stated.
    (2) The award shall state the reasons upon which it is based, unless the parties have agreed that no reasons are to be given or the award is an award on agreed terms under article 30.
    (3) The award shall state its date and the place of arbitration as determined in accordance with article 20(1). The award shall be deemed to have been made at that place.
    (4) After the award is made, a copy signed by the arbitrators in accordance with paragraph (1) of this article shall be delivered to each party.
381. *See* Poudret & Besson, *supra* n. 2, at 664. Article 189(2): 'In the absence of [an agreement reached by the parties], the arbitral award shall be made by a majority, or, in the absence of a majority, by the chairman alone. The award shall be in writing, supported by reasons, dated and signed. The signature of the chairman is sufficient'.
382. Merkin & Flannery, *supra* n. 96, at 224.
383. Sutton et al., *supra* n. 92, at 291 (referring to the so-called parol awards).
384. *Ibid.*

challenging the award under section 68(2)(h), that is, for a failure to comply with the requirements as to the form of the award.[385] Pursuant to section 70(2) of the act, however, a challenge under Article 68 will be rejected if there is any available recourse under section 57 (correction of award).[386] Such a provision allows the tribunal, on its own initiative (or upon the application of a party), to 'correct an award so as to remove any clerical mistake or error arising from an accidental slip or omission or clarify or remove any ambiguity in the award'.[387] As a result, the challenging party must first request a correction of the award before filing a challenge for annulment.

For an application under section 68 to be upheld, the applicant must prove the existence of a serious irregularity resulting in a substantial injustice.[388] Courts, in fact, 'will look for more than a merely technical or formalistic failure to comply with the terms of the arbitration agreement'.[389] The only formal requirement that follows a different regime is the one concerning the award's reasons (provided that the parties have not indicated that reasons are unnecessary).[390] In fact, according to section 70(4) of the act, the court may order the tribunal to state the reasons for its award in sufficient detail, if the award: (a) does not contain the tribunal's reasons or (b) does not set out the tribunal's reasons in sufficient detail to enable the court properly to consider the application. This is a discretionary power that should be exercised sparingly, and while a failure to apply to the arbitral tribunal for a correction under section 57 'may be a factor against the court exercising its section 70(4) power, ... it does not provide a jurisdictional bar'.[391]

In light of the above, one can conclude that the formal requirements are similar under English law to those provided for by French law, with the notable exception of reasons, which, under English law, are a requirement that can be excluded by the parties' agreement. This possibility does not change the fact that nowadays reasons are virtually always present and are regarded as a common characteristic of decisions

---

385. *Ibid.* at 290; Liebscher, *supra* n. 8, at 122.
386. David Wolfson & Susanna Charlwood, *Challenges to Arbitration Awards* in Lew, *supra* n. 45, 526 at 541.
387. Section 57(3)(a) of the *Arbitration Act 1996*.
388. *Terna Bahrain Holding Company v. Ali Marzook Al Bin Kamil Al Shamsi and others* [2012] EWHC 3283 at para. 85 ('[O]nly an extreme case will justify the Court's intervention. Relief under s. 68 will only be appropriate where the tribunal has gone so wrong in its conduct of the arbitration, and where its conduct is so far removed from what could be reasonably be expected from the arbitral process, that justice calls out for it to be corrected. ... In determining whether there has been substantial injustice, the Court is not required to decide for itself what would have happened in the arbitration had there been no irregularity. The applicant does not need to show that the result would necessarily or even probably have been different. What the claimant is required to show is that had he had an opportunity to address the point, the tribunal might well have reached a different view and produced a significantly different outcome').
389. Craig Tevendale & Andrew Cannon, *Enforcement of Awards* in Lew, *supra* n. 45, 563 at 577.
390. Merkin & Flannery, *supra* n. 96, at 340 ('under section 70(4), the court may still require reasons, or adequate reasons ... for the purposes of exercising its powers under the challenge provisions').
391. *Navios International Inc v. Sangamon Transportation Group* [2012] EWHC 166 Comm at para. 37.

rendered by 'all judicial and quasi-judicial bodies'.[392] The possibility of excluding the obligation to give reasons is mostly a historical vestige.[393]

Finally, a notable difference between the two legal systems concerns the possibility of correcting and remedying a mistake or omission made by the arbitrators. English law seems more effective than its counterpart and is clear in providing that a failure to fulfil formal requirements may ground a challenge for annulment. While the results reached are similar, French law certainly requires some interpretative efforts.

[2] Substantive Requirements

As far as the substantive requirements are concerned, unsurprisingly, the golden rule in English law is that the award is a decision rendered by an arbitrator. This means that a decision rendered by an expert,[394] even if appointed by the parties as a decision maker required to give reasons in support of his or her decision in relation to findings of fact,[395] is not an award. The golden rule alone (i.e., an award is a decision rendered by an arbitrator), however, provides little guidance. It presupposes a distinction between arbitration and other dispute resolution mechanisms such as expert determination. What is, then, the distinctive feature of arbitration? In short, that the arbitrator is appointed by the parties to adjudicate a dispute following a judicial-like inquiry. In other words, an arbitral tribunal adjudicates a dispute after taking account of any evidence and arguments of the parties to that dispute.[396] Such a decision, moreover, cannot be delegated.[397] The adoption of a *procedural* criterion for the distinction between expert determination and arbitration is a departure from the standard adopted under French law, summarized by the doctrine of *acte juridictionnel*. More specifically, the law-speaking character of the decision is absent under English law.

It is worth pointing out that the procedural criterion can be perceived as unsatisfying, for experts can indeed take into account evidence and arguments submitted by the parties. In order to counter this weakness, courts attach significant importance to the intent of the parties, which shall be that of referring a dispute 'to the *adjudication* of some selected person whose decision on the matter they agree to accept'.[398] The procedural criterion can be particularly problematic when legal experts

---

392. Merkin & Flannery, *supra* n. 96, at 226. *See also* Neil Andrews, *England and Wales* in Silvia Barona & Carlos Esplugues, *Global Perspectives on ADR* 103, 119 (Intersentia 2014) (the authors note that arbitrators *should* give reasons and that, in practice, most awards are reasoned ones).
393. Born, *supra* n. 4, at 3039.
394. Liebscher, *supra* n. 8, at 120.
395. *Halifax Life Ltd v. The Equitable Life Assurance Society* [2007] EWHC 503 (Comm) at paras 45 and 48.
396. Sutton et al., *supra* n. 92, at 7. *See also Agrimex Ltd v. Tradigrain SA* [2003] EWHC 1656 at para. 33.
397. Merkin & Flannery, *supra* n. 96, at 224.
398. *Sutcliffe v. Thackrah* [1974] 1 All ER 859 at 870 (House of Lords) [emphasis added]. *See also* John Kendall, *Expert Determination* 222–223 (Sweet & Maxwell 2001).

are involved in the arbitration. The difficulties reach a pinnacle whenever the arbitrators decide to appoint an expert to determine the content of the applicable law.

In an interesting case, a tribunal-appointed expert was requested to report on a relevant principle of Saudi law applicable to the dispute between the parties.[399] The opinion expressed in the expert's report, however, was not limited to a substantiation of the applicable principles and rules, but included advice as to the proper decision to make with respect to the parties' claims.[400] The court, based on the following declaration rendered by the arbitral tribunal, found that there had been no irregularity under section 68 of the *Arbitration Act 1996* and rejected the challenge against the award:[401]

> It would be almost impossible for any expert on foreign law to give his opinion on law divorced from the facts and issues in the case. We are of the view that this is precisely what [the expert] has done giving his views on the law in the light of the issues and written materials with which he was supplied. Of course [the expert]'s opinion on factual matters will have no room in our deliberations. These will be the subject of submissions in the light of the evidence and both his factual and legal views can be, and no doubt will be, if the Claimant wished to cross examine him before us. At the end of the day the tribunal will come to their own conclusions on the evidence as a whole and make their own findings on Saudi law without we hope being coloured in any way by the views of [the expert] or anyone else.

Let us consider a subsequent case for a stay of proceedings under the *Arbitration Act 1996*, in relation to a dispute resolution clause contained in the contract entered by the applicant for the stay and the respondent. While the former suggested that the clause at hand amounted to an arbitration agreement, the opposing party demanded that it be declared a mere expert determination clause. The relevant part of the clause provided that in case of disputes as to the meaning of the terms of the contract or as to the calculation of the price to be paid thereunder, an expert was to determine the dispute and the liability for costs.

The court first found that 'the way in which the dispute resolution process is described or labelled by the parties in their agreement is not conclusive as to the true character of that process [; however], the language used by the parties may well provide an important indication of the nature of the process that they intend'.[402] After

---

399. *Hussmann (Europe) Ltd v. Al Ameen Development & Trade Co* [2000] EWHC 210 (Comm).
400. *Ibid.* at paras 34–35 ('The main report of [the expert] first set out the documents he had seen. Then, with great clarity, he set out the principles of Saudi law relating to construction, the rules as to liability, evidence and commercial agency regulation. ... The second part of his report then addressed the issues in dispute as set out in the draft terms of reference. In this part of the report, he proceeded to give his opinion as to all the points in issue before the tribunal, applying the principles of law to the facts as he saw them and reaching various conclusions on the matters that had been submitted to the tribunal for their decision').
401. *Ibid.* at para. 47.
402. *Wilky Property Holdings Plc v. London & Surrey Investments Ltd* [2011] EWHC 2226, at para. 27. The case refer to further authorities. *See: Arenson v. Casson & Others* [1977] AC 405; *David Wilson Homes Ltd v. Survey Services Ltd* [2001] 1 All ER (Comm) 449.

concluding that the wording of the clause suggested, prima facie, the appointment of an expert rather than an arbitrator, the court concluded that a number of factors should be considered in order to establish whether a process qualifies as arbitration or expert determination. A decision that: '(i) is binding on the parties and (ii) which resolves a dispute which is already formulated'[403] is not necessarily an arbitration. Ultimately, the relevant test is that of ascertaining whether the dispute should be resolved by 'something in the nature of a judicial inquiry'.[404]

Further confirmation of this test can be found in another case dealing with the status and functions of an expert:[405]

> There is an essential distinction between judicial decisions and expert decisions, although the reason for the distinction has been variously expressed. ... A person sitting in a judicial capacity decides matters on the basis of submissions and evidence put before him, whereas the expert, subject to the express provisions of his remit, is entitled to carry out his own investigations, form his own opinion and come to his own conclusion regardless of any submissions or evidence adduced by the parties themselves. Although, contrary to what is said in some of the authorities, there are many expert determinations of matters where disputes have already arisen between the parties, there is a difference in the nature of the decision made, ... namely that there is no requirement for the rules of natural justice or due process to be followed in an expert determination in order for that determination to be valid and binding between the parties.

In light of the above, one can conclude that English law treats the distinction between expert determination and arbitration mostly as a matter of contract interpretation. It follows that the words used by the parties are indicative, yet not determinative, of a decision to appoint an expert or an arbitrator. Ultimately, the relevant test will be to ascertain if the person in question exercises, or is called upon to exercise, a judicial-like function, deciding matters put before him or her on the basis of arguments and evidence submitted by the parties.[406]

Echoes of this approach can be found in an often-cited Canadian judgment – *Sport Maska v. Zittrer* – rendered by the Supreme Court in 1988.[407] In this case, the

---

403. *Wilky Property Holdings*, at *para*. 41.
404. *Ibid*. at para. 57. *See also* Kendall, *supra* n. 398, at 230 ('To be an arbitrator, the referee has to be shown, in deciding the matter between the parties, to have exercised the function of a judge. It is not the function of a judge to use his or her own expertise in a given area outside the law and the administration of justice').
405. *Bernhard Schulte GmbH & Co Kg & Ors v. Nile Holdings Ltd* [2004] EWHC 977, at para. 95.
406. *See also Jivraj v. Hashwani* [2011] UKSC 40, at para. 41 ('The arbitrator is in critical respects independent of the parties. His functions and duties require him to rise above the partisan interests of the parties and not to act in, or so as to further, the particular interests of either party. ... [H]e must determine how to resolve their competing interests. He is in no sense in a position of subordination to the parties; rather the contrary. He is in effect a quasi-judicial adjudicator') [references omitted]. *See also* Kendall, *supra* n. 398, at 232 (the author explains how an arbitrator can only decide on the basis of the evidence and arguments submitted by the parties, whereas an expert can ground a decision exclusively on his or her technical expertise).
407. *Sport Maska Inc v. Zittrer* [1988] 1 SCR 564 [*Sport Maska*. *See* Richard Boivin & Nicola Mariani, *International Arbitration in Canada*, 20:5 J Int'l Arb 507, 508 (2003). For a commentary, *see*

contractual clause at the forefront of the litigation between the parties provided that one of the inventories sold to the appellant should be 'counted or verified by representatives of ... the Vendor and the Purchaser [and that such] count and valuation of the inventory [should] be verified' by the vendor's auditors.[408] Furthermore, the clause added that '[u]pon delivery of such opinion, the inventory count and valuation shall be deemed to be definitively determined for all purposes in connection with this Offer'.[409] Roughly a year after said evaluation had been rendered, the appellant, that is, the buyer of the inventory, brought an action for damages against the auditors, alleging that the actual value of the inventory was inferior to what they had declared in their opinion.[410] A key issue, which had led to the dismissal of the appellant's claims before the Quebec Court of Appeal, was whether the auditors could raise an immunity exception on the grounds that they had acted as arbitrators rather than mere experts.[411] To answer this question, and in the absence of a specific legal provision in Quebec law, the Supreme Court of Canada turned to an analysis of French law and the common law.

Starting from the latter, the court referred to the House of Lords' decision in *Arenson v. Casson Beckman Rutley*,[412] which emphasized that the distinction between arbitration and expert determination lies in the adjudicative function that arbitrators and judges exercise but that experts do not. Turning to French law, the court affirmed that the relevant criterion for distinguishing between experts and arbitrators was the existence of a dispute, coupled with the parties' intention to have recourse to arbitration.[413] At this point, and turning to Quebec law, Justice L'Heureux-Dubé's majority decision noted that 'it [was] crucial to identify the precise function the parties intended to entrust to this third party'.[414] Justice L'Heureux-Dubé then discussed a list of relevant criteria for identifying the will of the parties, adding, however, that they:[415]

> are not necessarily exhaustive, nor are they mutually exclusive, in the sense that they may occur together and even merge into one another. *They do not all have to be existing, still less be unanimously in favour of one position or another.* The criteria, as their name suggests, are in fact only tools used to determine the intention disclosed by the documents and other instruments, in order to establish the function the parties actually meant to assign to the third party chosen by them.

Sabine Thuilleaux, *L'arbitrage commercial au Québec*, 20–24 (Éditions Yvon Blais 1991); Babak Barin & Marie-Claude Rigaud, *L'arbitrage consensuel au Québec*, 37–40 (Éditions Yvon Blais 2012).
408. *Sport Maska*, supra n. 407 at para. 7.
409. *Ibid.*
410. *Ibid.*
411. *Ibid.* at para. 19.
412. *Ibid.* at para. 61; *Arenson v. Casson Beckman Rutley & Co.*, [1975] 3 All E.R. 901.
413. *Sport Maska*, supra n. 407, at para. 70 (i.e., the intention of appointing a private judge to resolve in a final manner the dispute by rendering a law-speaking decision).
414. *Ibid.* at para. 94.
415. *Ibid.* at para. 99 [emphasis added].

More specifically, the court insisted on the importance of two criteria:[416] 'the similarity that must exist between arbitration and the judicial process',[417] and compliance with the concept of impartiality and other mandatory legal provisions.[418]

Coming back to English law, the second rule of English arbitration law is centred on a distinction between awards and orders, according to their different purposes. Orders would merely 'address the procedural mechanisms to be adopted in the reference',[419] whereas awards would amount to a decision on a legal claim filed by the parties ('based solely on the evidence and argument presented by the parties'[420] and imposing clear directions as to the 'nature and extent of the duties it imposes on the parties'[421]).

The third rule is that awards are final decisions, even if they do not deal with the dispute in its entirety. In this regard, section 47 of the *Arbitration Act 1996* states:

(1) Unless otherwise agreed by the parties, the tribunal may make more than one award at different times on different aspects of the matters to be determined.
(2) The tribunal may, in particular make an award relating–
    (a) to an issue affecting the whole claim, or
    (b) to a part only of the claims or cross-claims submitted to it for decision
(3) If the tribunal does so, it shall specify in its award the issue, or the claim or part of a claim, which is the subject matter of the award.

In light of this statutory provision, an arbitral award can also be defined as 'a final determination of a particular issue or claim in the arbitration'.[422] This means that a tribunal can issue several awards, dealing with different aspects of the dispute. Such decisions are often called partial awards.[423] The term 'final award' is generally reserved for 'an award that disposes of all of the issues in dispute',[424] that is, all the remaining issues.

The dichotomy of *final* (in the sense of global determination of the dispute) versus *partial* award (in the sense of determining a single claim or aspect of the claim)

---

416. See Babak Barin, *Harry Potter, Five and a Half Supreme Court Decisions and the Reflections on the Future of Arbitration in Canada: Expecto Patronum!* In *Mélanges Alain Prujiner* 25, 32 (Éditions Yvon Blais 2011) (discussing the context in which the decision was rendered: 'By all counts the years 1986 to 2007 were rather stable years for arbitration in Canada').
417. *Sport Maska*, *supra* n. 407, at para. 96 ('The greater the similarity, the greater the likelihood that reference to a third party will be characterized as arbitration. The facts that the parties have the right to be heard, to argue, to present testimonial or documentary evidence, that lawyers are present at the hearing and that the third party delivers an arbitration award with reasons establish a closer likeness to the adversarial process than the expert opinion').
418. *Ibid.* at *para.* 98 ('if the third party is to be an arbitrator, he cannot act as the mandatory of one of the parties. For example, the fact that he has a special connection with one of them or that he is paid by only one of them seems inconsistent with the concept of impartiality, a fundamental characteristic of arbitration'). *See also* Louis Marquis, *La notion d'arbitrage commercial international en droit québécois* 37 MLJ 448, 456 (1992) (explaining that the criteria also have relevance in the context of international commercial arbitration).
419. Sutton et al., *supra* n. 92, at 271.
420. *Ibid.* at 305.
421. *Ibid.* at 307.
422. *Ibid.* at 271. *See also* Liebscher, *supra* n. 8, at 123.
423. Merkin & Flannery, *supra* n. 96, at 212.
424. *Ibid.* at 212.

is not the only one existing in English law. Awards can be also distinguished in relation to the *duration* of their effects: a *final* award is a decision that will not be modified by the tribunal, whereas a *provisional* award is, subject to certain conditions, a decision that can be modified by the arbitrators. On this point, section 39 of the *Arbitration Act 1996* reads as follows:

> Power to make provisional awards.
> (1) The parties are free to agree that the tribunal shall have power to order on a provisional basis any relief which it would have power to grant in a final award.
> (2) This includes, for instance, making –
>   (a) a provisional order for the payment of money or the disposition of property as between the parties, or
>   (b) an order to make an interim payment on account of the costs of the arbitration.
> (3) Any such order shall be subject to the tribunal's final adjudication; and the tribunal's final award, on the merits or as to costs, shall take account of any such order.
> (4) Unless the parties agree to confer such power on the tribunal, the tribunal has no such power. This does not affect its powers under section 47 (awards on different issues, &c.).

Section 39 is an opt-in provision: parties are thus required to provide the tribunal with such a power, either expressly in their arbitration agreement or by reference to a set of arbitration rules.[425]

In a nutshell, the provision at hand will allow the arbitral tribunal to issue an award subject to the tribunal's final adjudication. As such, 'it must therefore be taken into account and finally determined in a subsequent award ... dealing with the merits of the dispute and/or costs'.[426]

Because of the possibility of modifying such an award, the provision at hand has been subject to criticism. First, a certain ambiguity was noted in the text of the provision, due to incoherence as to whether it refers to the power to make an award or an order.[427] In effect, while the title of the section makes reference to 'provisional *awards*', the remainder of the text merely speaks of *orders*. The second critique concerns the use of the term 'provisional'. By drawing on the report of the Departmental Advisory Committee (DAC),[428] the critics insist that the provision would merely

---

425. *Konkola Copper Mines*, *supra* n. 95, at para. 16 ('Section 39 provides that the parties are free to agree that the tribunal shall have power to order on a provisional basis any relief which it would have power to grant in a final award, a power which is confirmed by the LCIA rules, under which this arbitration proceeded. The Rules provide that the tribunal can order on a provisional basis, subject to final determination in an award any relief which the Arbitral Tribunal would have power to grant in an award, including a provisional order for the payment of money'). *See also*: Sutton et al., *supra* n. 92, at 280.
426. *Ibid.* at 281.
427. Merkin & Flannery, *supra* n. 96, at 155.
428. Saville, *supra* n. 43, at paras 202–203 ('There is a sharp distinction to be drawn between making provisional or temporary arrangements, which are subject to reversal when the underlying merits are finally decided by the tribunal; and dealing severally with different issues or questions at different times and in different awards, which we cover in Clause 47. It is for this reason that in this provision we draw attention to that Clause. These considerations have led

'confer on the arbitrators the power to grant interim financial relief in the form of an award, which may not be entirely dispositive as to the arbitration ... but it would be final it its own right'.[429] The awards in question would not, therefore, be reversible ones.[430] A closer reading of the same passage, however, suggests quite the contrary. With regard to such temporary arrangements, which can later be modified when the merits of the case are finally decided by the arbitrators, the drafters of the *Arbitration Act 1996* noted that:[431]

> subject to the safeguards of the parties' agreement and the arbitrators' duties (Clause 33) ... this enlargement of the traditional jurisdiction of arbitrators could serve a very useful purpose, for example in trades and industries where cash flow is of particular importance.

A confirmation of the *temporary* and thus reversible character of provisional awards – contrary to the opinion in the literature mentioned in the previous paragraph – can be found in the decision rendered by Mr Justice Cooke in *Konkola Copper Mines v. U&M Mining Zambia Ltd.*[432]

In this case, the applicant argued, among other things, that a partial award rendered by the arbitrators was defective given that it ordered the payment of certain sums 'unless [defendant] show[ed] cause, supported by evidence, within 14 days of the Award, why such an order should not be made'.[433] In rejecting the request for setting aside under section 68 of the *Arbitration Act 1996*, Mr Justice Cooke stated that arbitral decisions have to be reviewed in light of the objective set out in section 1 of the same act (i.e., to 'obtain the fair resolution of disputes ... without unnecessary delay and expense'):[434]

> The Second Award was plainly designed to avoid further delay and expense whilst not shutting out the absent party, [defendant], from adducing material to justify a defence, in circumstances where the tribunal was satisfied that it had received an adequate opportunity to put its case but had failed to do so. The form of order 'to show cause' and similar forms of order giving an absent party one final opportunity to apply to reverse an order made against it in the Courts is well recognised as part of the armoury of judicial orders. There was debate as to the distinction between an order and a final award but the terminology is, in my judgment, of little or no importance. An award will frequently include orders or declarations and it matters not how they are expressed. ... The tribunal did not purport to order a

---

us firmly to conclude that it would only be desirable to give arbitral tribunals power to make such provisional orders where the parties have so agreed. Such agreements, of course, will have to be drafted with some care for the reasons we have stated. Subject to the safeguards of the parties' agreement and the arbitrators' duties (Clause 33) we envisage that this enlargement of the traditional jurisdiction of arbitrators could serve a very useful purpose, for example in trades and industries where cash flow is of particular importance').
429. Merkin & Flannery, *supra* n. 96, at 156.
430. *Ibid.*
431. Saville, *supra* n. 43, at para. 202.
432. *Konkola Copper Mines*, *supra* n. 95.
433. *Ibid.* at para. 83.
434. *Ibid.* at paras 88–97.

payment of sums which were not due and owing nor to take a 'rough look' and determine a minimum sum that would in any event be payable: nor did it purport to order a payment on account or a provisional payment subject to final determination later. The arbitrators found that the sums in question were due and owing on the evidence presented to them. In order, however, to give [defendant] one final chance to adduce any defence, the tribunal gave it one last opportunity to show cause within 14 days why the orders it had made should not be operative. I do not see why, as matter of principle … an award cannot be final and conclusive in its terms where it clearly provides for specific relief, including payments of money, which only bites at a point in the future, in the absence of submission and evidence from an absent party to the contrary. The tribunal has made decisions which are final and complete and are not subject to further decisions on its part or of any other person or body unless a specified contingency occurs. Such an award is complete and final on its own terms, albeit conditional. Whilst this might present difficulties for enforcement purposes, that is nothing to the point and does not prevent it from being an award which binds the parties.

Finally, the fourth principle of English arbitration law (which obviously does not apply to provisional awards until they have, as the case may be, become final) is the res judicata effect. Only final awards render arbitral tribunals *functus officio*, exhausting and concluding their jurisdiction over the matters decided therein.[435] A decision therefore creates 'an estoppel with regard to the matters with which it deals, preventing either party from pursuing those matters in a later stage of the arbitration or in subsequent proceedings'.[436] The estoppel ensuing from res judicata and the doctrine of *functus officio* closely track notions also found in French and in other common law jurisdictions.[437]

From a technical point of view, res judicata can be invoked by pleading a *cause of action estoppel* ('precluding a party asserting or denying the existence of a particular cause of action, the non-existence or existence of which had been determined by a court of competent jurisdiction in previous litigation between the same parties') or an

---

435. *Dawes v. Treasure & Son Ltd* [2011] BLR, at para. 27.
436. *See* Sutton et al., *supra* n. 92, at 339; *Associated Electric & Gas Insurance Services Ltd v. European Reinsurance Company of Zurich* [2003] UKPC 11, at para. 15 ('[The] award has conferred upon [the parties] a right which is enforceable by later pleading an issue estoppel. It is a species of the enforcement of the rights given by the award just as much as would be a cause of action estoppel. It is true that estoppels can be described as rules of evidence or as rules of public policy to stop the abuse of process by relitigation. But that is to look at how estoppels are given effect to not at what is the nature of the private law right which the estoppel recognises and protects. For example, a party who has attorned to another is estopped from denying that he holds the relevant goods for that other; the attornment has created a legal relationship and legal rights which the attorning party must recognise. The same applies to where arbitrators have, pursuant to the submission of a dispute to them, decided an issue; that decision then binds the parties and neither party can thereafter dispute that decision').
437. *See* e.g., *T.Co Metals LLC v. Dempsey Pipe & Supply Inc*, 592 F. 3d 329 (2010), at para. 29 ('The functus officio doctrine dictates that, once arbitrators have fully exercised their authority to adjudicate the issues submitted to them, their authority over those questions is ended, and the arbitrators have no further authority, absent agreement by the parties, to redetermine those issues'.) *See also Trade & Transp., Inc. v. Natural Petroleum Charterers Inc.*, 931 F.2d 191, 195 (1991).

issue estoppel ('[precluding] a party in subsequent proceedings from contradicting an issue of fact or law that has already been distinctly raised and finally decided in earlier proceedings between the same parties').[438] At the same time, it should also be noted that the *abuse of process* doctrine can be invoked against parties attempting to relitigate matters or arguments raised in arbitral proceedings but not directly decided by the arbitrators. This doctrine is more wide-reaching; it impedes relitigation not only of the findings of the tribunal but also of incidental matters.[439]

In conclusion, the main aspects and characteristics of an award under the English *Arbitration Act 1996* were addressed in the present part. The formal requirements enacted in section 52 of the act are default ones, in the sense that parties can agree on a different form. The most striking difference from French law is that parties may elect to have an award without reasons. This would likely constitute a breach of public policy according to French courts. In any event, a failure to comply with statutory or contractual requirements dealing with the form of the award will constitute a valid ground for challenging the decision.

As far as the substantive aspects of awards are concerned, English law does not focus on an award's function of speaking the law (i.e., the French *acte juridictionnel* doctrine) in order to distinguish arbitration from other forms of dispute resolution mechanisms. Furthermore, one can observe the existence of four main requirements:

(1) To be considered an award, the decision must be rendered by an arbitrator.
(2) Only decisions following a judicial-like procedure may qualify as awards.
(3) An award must resolve a dispute between the parties or otherwise determine their rights.
(4) An award can either be final, thus rendering the arbitral tribunal *functus officio* with respect to the issues dealt with, or provisional, allowing said tribunal to modify the decision, if appropriate.

As we shall see in the following chapters, the flexible criterion on which English law relies to distinguish between arbitration and other ADR mechanisms, is ultimately responsible for the implementation of a non-unitary notion of award, allowing to accommodate under it also a number of non-contentious decisions.

---

438. Sheppard, *supra* n. 320 at 269. *See also* The International Law Association, *Report on Res Judicata*, 7 (2004). *See generally* Varun N. Ghosh, *An Uncertain Shield – Res Judicata in Arbitration*, 31:4 Arb Int 661 (2015).
439. *OMV Petrom SA v. Glencore International AG* [2014] EWHC 242, at para. 27 ('It can, in my view, be an abuse of process for a party which was successful overall in earlier proceedings to seek to relitigate an issue on which it was unsuccessful. Likewise, whilst it may be decisive under the doctrine of res judicata to identify whether or not a particular finding was obiter, there is no reason to take such a restrictive view in the case of abuse of process. The focus in the latter case is not so much on the binding nature of the finding, but upon the undesirability of having the same matter adjudicated upon again where it would be manifestly unfair to do so, or would bring the administration of justice into disrepute'). Cf. Sutton et al., *supra* n. 92, at 340 ('The bar to fresh proceedings applies to claims coming within the reference whether or not the claims were actually brought before the tribunal').

§4.04 THE NOTION OF CONTENTIOUS AWARD IN ARBITRAL PRACTICE

Contentious awards are not explicitly addressed by specific provisions of institutional arbitration rules. This can be explained by the fact that the way in which arbitration was originally conceived by certain arbitral institutions, was not entirely adjudicative in nature.[440] As far as the ICC is concerned, for instance, the adjudicative model was gradually developed at the end of the first half of the twentieth century.[441] As for the other arbitral institutions, the non-adjudicative nature of arbitration in many industries and sectors is likely to have had an impact on their arbitration rules, preventing them from defining the nature of arbitrators' dispute resolution functions.

As far as the *ICC Rules* are concerned, a contentious award amounts to a final, reasoned decision on the parties' claims,[442] as specified in the terms of reference.[443] The decision will be rendered after the proceedings have been declared closed,[444] that is, after the tribunal has heard the parties and examined the evidence.[445] This decision, moreover, must be rendered within a specific time limit (usually six months).[446] As observed by Craig, Park, and Paulsson, contentious awards will, in practice, closely mimic state courts' judgments:[447]

> It is in the interest of the arbitral tribunal and of the Court of Arbitration that the award be considered by the parties to constitute a fairly reasoned judgment on the issues and controversies presented. For this reason, the arbitral award should not only do justice to the parties, but also be so drafted that justice is seen to have been done.

Moreover, the award shall be signed and dated,[448] and mention the place of arbitration.[449] Finally, it should be noted that an ICC award will be such only if approved by the International Court of Arbitration.[450] The approval will be obtained if

---

440. Michael Mustill, *Comments on Fast-Track Arbitration*, 10:4 J Int'l Arb 121, 122 (1993).
441. *Supra* §3.04[A].
442. Articles 21(1) and 32(2) 2017 *ICC Rules*. *See* Thomas Webster & Michael Bühler, *Handbook of ICC Arbitration*, 486 (Sweet & Maxwell 2014); Andreas Reiner & Christian Aschauer, *ICC Rules* in Rolf A. Schütze, *Institutional Arbitration* 25, 153 (Beck & Nomos 2013). Cf. Art. 42(1) 2017 SCC *Arbitration Rules* (' The Arbitral Tribunal shall make its award in writing, and, unless otherwise agreed by the parties, shall state the reasons upon which the award is based').
443. Articles 23(1)(c) and 23(4) 2017 *ICC Rules*. *See* Webster & Bühler, *supra* n. 442, at 488–491.
444. Cf. Art. 30(1) 2014 ICDR *International Arbitration Rules*.
445. Article 27 2017 *ICC Rules*. *See also* Art. 32(1) 2016 SIAC *Arbitration Rules* ('The Tribunal shall, as promptly as possible, after consulting with the parties and upon being satisfied that the parties have no further relevant and material evidence to produce or submission to make with respect to the matters to be decided in the Award, declare the proceedings closed. The Tribunal's declaration that the proceedings are closed shall be communicated to the parties and to the Registrar').
446. Article 31(1) 2017 *ICC Rules*.
447. Craig, Park & Paulsson, *supra* n. 263, at 364–365.
448. Article 32(3) 2017 *ICC Rules*.
449. Jason Fry, Simon Greenberg & Francesca Mazza, *The Secretariat's Guide to ICC Arbitration*, 323 (ICC Publishing 2012).
450. Article 34 2017 *ICC Rules*. A similar provision may be found in Art. 32(3) 2016 SIAC *Arbitration Rules* ('Before making any Award, the Tribunal shall submit such Award in draft form to the

Chapter 4: Contentious Awards §4.04

the court is satisfied with the form of the award as well as with the way in which the arbitral tribunal has addressed the claims submitted by the parties,[451] that is, whether the decision reached by the arbitrators has been carefully justified both in legal and factual terms.[452]

Another example of contentious awards in the rules of a prominent arbitration centre can be found in Article 26 of the 2014 *LCIA Arbitration Rules*. The relevant provisions read as follows:

> (1) The Arbitral Tribunal may make separate awards on different issues at different times, including interim payments on account of any claim or cross-claim (including Legal and Arbitration Costs). Such awards shall have the same status as any other award made by the Arbitral Tribunal.
>
> (2) The Arbitral Tribunal shall make any award in writing and, unless all parties agree in writing otherwise, shall state the reasons upon which such award is based. The award shall also state the date when the award is made and the seat of the arbitration; and it shall be signed by the Arbitral Tribunal or those of its members assenting to it.

From the above provision, it follows that a contentious award is a final decision on one or more claims filed by the parties.[453] Moreover, awards will generally be in writing and contain reasons (unless otherwise agreed by the parties).[454] They must also be dated and signed by the tribunal, and mention the seat of the arbitration.[455] Once the tribunal has drafted the award, it must transmit it to the LCIA Court, which is the entity that will formally 'render' the award. The court will then authenticate the award and send it to the parties.[456] Before doing so, it will conduct an informal review of the decision, ensuring that the applicable formal requirements have been complied with and that the award does not contain clerical or computational errors.[457]

Registrar. Unless the Registrar extends the period of time or unless otherwise agreed by the parties, the Tribunal shall submit the draft Award to the Registrar not later than 45 days from the date on which the Tribunal declares the proceedings closed. The Registrar may, as soon as practicable, suggest modifications as to the form of the Award and, without affecting the Tribunal's liberty to decide the dispute, draw the Tribunal's attention to points of substance. No Award shall be made by the Tribunal until it has been approved by the Registrar as to its form').

451. Fry, Greenberg & Mazza, *supra* n. 449, at 327–328.
452. Webster & Bühler, *supra* n. 442, at 504–505.
453. Maxi Scherer, Lisa M. Richman & Rémy Gerbay, *Arbitrating Under the 2014 LCIA Rules*, 335 (Kluwer Law 2015) ('An award may be defined as an instrument made by the arbitrator(s) which contains the Arbitral Tribunal's final decision on a particular claim or issue relating to the merits of the dispute, the Tribunal's jurisdiction or any other important substantial issue of the arbitration').
454. *See* Art. 42(1) 2017 SCC *Arbitration Rules* ('The Arbitral Tribunal shall make its award in writing, and, unless otherwise agreed by the parties, shall state the reasons upon which the award is based'); Art. 30(1) 2014 ICDR *International Arbitration Rules*.
455. Simon Nesbitt & Michael Darowski, *LCIA Arbitration Rules – Article 26* in Loukas A. Mistelis, *Concise International Arbitration* 546, 546 (Kluwer Law 2015).
456. Article 26(7) 2014 LCIA *Arbitration Rules*.
457. Scherer et al., *supra* n. 453, at 344.

Finally, while arbitration rules will usually state that a contentious award is a binding decision,[458] they do not explicitly state that such a decision shall bear res judicata effects.[459] In the few awards that have been published and address this matter, it is nonetheless possible to observe that arbitrators recognize the res judicata effects of previous arbitral decisions.[460] This may suggest that, from the arbitrators' perspective, the res judicata doctrine operates as a substantive principle (*règle matérielle*) rather than a formally enacted one.[461]

§4.05 CONCLUSION

The present chapter has illustrated the notion of contentious judgment (a final decision on the parties' claims or actions resolving a dispute by speaking the law), as well as that of contentious arbitral award. First, I analysed the historical procedural meaning of judgment, which emerged in Imperial Rome. I described the initial notarized procedure of submission to arbitration (*legis actiones*) and explained how the subsequent emergence of *cognitio extra ordinem* changed adjudication by equating the act of deciding with a legal reasoning based on substantive law (hence, the 'law-speaking' activity). Judgments, therefore, give the parties what they legally deserve; they answer a request for intervention.[462] This definition tails that both answers to specific claims and single answers to all claims can be regarded as judgments, creating the dichotomy of partial versus final (in the sense of comprehensive) judgments. With this in mind, I looked at two key arbitration laws, the French *Code of Civil Procedure* and the English *Arbitration Act 1996*. While they converge in some respects, I pointed out the existence of significant divergences.

As far as the *validity* of the award is concerned, reasons are a mandatory requirement under French law, whereas English law allows parties to choose, by

---

458. *See* e.g., Art. 35(6) 2017 *ICC Rules*; Art. 26(8) 2014 LCIA *Arbitration Rules*; Art. 32(11) 2016 SIAC *Arbitration Rules*; Art. 30(1) 2014 ICDR *International Arbitration Rules*.
459. Bernard Hanotiau, *The Res Judicata Effect of Arbitral Awards*, ICC Bull Suppl 43, 39 (2003) ('It is true that even if the ICC Rules of Arbitration do not contain any provisions concerning res judicata, it would be difficult to imagine the ICC International Court of Arbitration approving a second arbitral award between the same parties on the same subject matter that contradicts a prior award already approved by the Court').
460. *See* ICC final award n. 9800/2000 in Jean-Jacques Arnaldez et al., *Collection of ICC Arbitral Awards 2001–2007* 659, 666–667 (Kluwer Law 2009); ICC Award 12226/2004, cited by Arnaldez et al. at 667 ('Le principe de l'autorité de la chose jugée appartient à l'ordre juridique international. Il s'impose d'abord pour des motifs évidents de sécurité et d'économie. Lorsque une autorité compétente, qu'il s'agisse d'un juge ou d'un arbitre, a tranché définitivement une difficulté opposant deux parties, la décision qui est prise a pleine force juridique: "le droit est dit"'); *A v. Z*, Order No 5 (2002), 21:4 ASA Bulletin 810 (2003); SCC Award n. 17/1997 in Sigvard Jarvin & Annette Magnusson, *SCC Arbitral Awards 1999–2003* 17, 22 (JurisNet 2006); ICC award n. 6233/1992 in Jean-Jacques Arnaldez, *Collection of ICC Arbitral Awards 1991–1995* 332, 335 (Kluwer Law 1997); ICC Award n. 3267/1989 in Sigvard Jarvin, Yves Derains & Jean-Jacques Arnaldez, *Collection of ICC Awards 1986–1990* 43. 44–45 (Kluwer Law 1994); ICC Award n. 3540/1980 in Sigvard Jarvin & Yves Derains, *Collection of ICC Arbitral Awards 1947–1985* 105, 111 (Kluwer Law 1990).
461. Cf. Dominique Hascher, *L'autorité de la chose jugée des sentences arbitrales* in *Travaux du Comité Français de DIP*, 17 (Pédone 2004).
462. The request directed to an adjudicative body is expressed in terms of a claim or action.

agreement, to exclude the obligation of arbitrators to provide reasons. Both jurisdictions dictate as a condition of validity that awards must be in writing, signed by the arbitrators, and indicate the seat of arbitration. These requirements can all become grounds for invalidity of the decision.

As far as the *existence* of the award is concerned, in France, an arbitral award must be final (i.e., it must preclude new arbitration) and must resolve the dispute on the merits by speaking the law; English law, on the contrary, recognizes that provisional decisions (i.e., decisions that can later be modified by the tribunal) can also amount to awards.

These differences can be explained by the different criteria used in French and English law in order to distinguish arbitration from other types of dispute resolution. The French doctrine of *acte juridictionnel* holds that if a third party renders a decision similar to a judgment, then one must be in the presence of an arbitration; English authorities, on the contrary, hold that if the procedure administered by a third party has a judicial-like nature, then it must be an arbitration, unless the parties intended otherwise. Both these defining paradigms lead to distortions. While the goal of English law is to expand the number of enforceable decisions, it fails to provide clear guidance concerning the nature of arbitration. At the same time, French law bases the condition for the existence of an award on a restrictive understanding of adjudication, limited to contentious decisions.

Finally, I looked at contentious awards in arbitral practice. Their most evident indicator is their characteristic of finally resolving a dispute by speaking the law and providing reasons. True, only in French law is the latter requirement mandatory. Yet, as explained above, English law also shows a marked preference for the inclusion of reasons in an award. Be that as it may, arbitration rules clearly favours the inclusion of reasons.

CHAPTER 5
Jurisdictional Awards

§5.01 INTRODUCTION

International commercial arbitration does not exist in a vacuum. In effect, it coexists (and cooperates) with other fora and, in particular, with national jurisdictions.[463] As a result, arbitrators may sometimes be seized in a matter over which they do not have jurisdiction (*compétence*). Similarly, a state court can be seized despite the existence of a valid and applicable arbitration agreement.[464] The present chapter will deal with the jurisdictional power of arbitrators, that is, with the power of an arbitral tribunal to decide whether it is the appropriate forum for litigating the dispute before it.[465] At the same time, the chapter will also explain how such a power is articulated and what type of decisions is rendered in its exercise.[466]

---

463. *See* Andreas Bucher, *Court Intervention in Arbitration* in Richard B. Lillich & Charles N. Brower, *International Arbitration in the 21st Century: Towards 'Judicialization' and Uniformity?* 1, 29 ff. (Irvington, New York: Transnational Publishers, 1994).
464. For a discussion on Art. 8 of the *Model Law*, *see* Frédéric Bachand, *Does Article 8 of the Model Law Call for Full or Prima Facie Review of the Arbitral Tribunal's Jurisdiction?* 22:3 Arb Int 463 (2006); Wiliam W. Park, *Determining Arbitral Jurisdiction: Allocation of Tasks Between Court and Arbitrators*, 8 Am Rev Int'l Arb 133 (1997); Frédéric Bachand, *Court Intervention in International Arbitration: The Case for Compulsory Judicial Internationalism*, 1:6 J Disp Res 83 (2012).
465. Cf. Yuval Shany, *Assessing the Effectiveness of International Courts*, 67 (Oxford University Press 2014) ('The ability of international courts and tribunals to attain the goals prescribed by their mandate providers is decisively influenced by their jurisdictional powers. ... This is because the ability of international courts to fulfill their various functions depends on the level of actual and potential business that they can expect to attract or generate. The scope of such judicial activity is delimited, in turn, by the jurisdictional provisions found in the relevant courts' constitutive instruments, as such provisions dictate who can access the courts, which issues may be litigated, what legal claims may be raised in the course of litigation and, at times, which remedies can be sought').
466. The research used in this chapter draws on an article on the legal theory of international commercial arbitration and the allocation of jurisdiction between state courts and arbitral

As far as the categorization of awards is concerned, the jurisdictional power responds to a specific function, that is, assessing whether the parties have validly invoked the jurisdiction of the arbitral tribunal. As a prerequisite to carrying out this assessment, the arbitrators have to positively conclude that there is a valid and applicable arbitration agreement existing between the parties. According to an authoritative commentator, the valid constitution of the tribunal would also fall under the notion of jurisdiction.[467] However, this extremely well-argued interpretation is not entirely convincing, for the term 'jurisdiction' seems to refer to the immediate underlying arbitration agreement, rather than covering the procedure agreed upon by the parties. The notion at hand, therefore, should be understood with reference to an abstract arbitral tribunal, so that the relevant question becomes whether the claims under a given contract are subject to arbitration rather than ordinary litigation.[468] By contrast, the constitution of the tribunal refers to a concrete situation, revolving around whether a *given* arbitral tribunal can render a valid decision. It should be noted, moreover, that not all procedural irregularities (even those concerning the constitution of the tribunal) will inevitably lead to an invalid decision. This is not the case where the tribunal lacks jurisdiction, an occurrence which can ground an annulment claim irrespective of the outcome reached by the arbitrators. As soon as we turn to the concrete case – is *this* arbitral tribunal the appropriate forum? – we are thus distancing ourselves from the notion of jurisdiction, and turning to the compliance with the applicable procedure. This conclusion is also confirmed by the fact that the irregular constitution of an arbitral tribunal is generally treated as a distinct ground for challenging the award, as it is the case under Article V(1)(d) of the *New York Convention*. Had the irregular constitution of the tribunal been subsumed under Article V(1)(a) of the same Convention, this separate additional ground would be clearly redundant.

Arbitral tribunals can take two types of jurisdictional decisions – they can either retain or decline jurisdiction over a case. While the decision to retain jurisdiction is compatible with the contractual theory of arbitration, the decision to decline it presents several difficulties. In fact, it is quite challenging to recognize that a decision rendered under an invalid contract (the arbitration agreement) can produce valid legal effects (a decision declining jurisdiction). And what about the compatibility of such decisions with the adjudicative theory of arbitration and its monodimensional model? As

---

tribunals. *See* Giacomo Marchisio, *Jurisdictional Matters in International Commercial Arbitration: Why Arbitrators Stand on an Equal Footing with State Courts*, 31:4 J Int'l Arb 455 (2014) [Marchisio, *Jurisdictional Matters*].

467. Frédéric Bachand, *L'intervention du juge canadien avant et durant un arbitrage commercial international*, 310-311 (Éditions Yvon Blais 2005) (the author draws on section 30(1) of the English *Arbitration Act* – according to which 'the arbitral tribunal may rule on its own substantive jurisdiction, that is, as to … (b) whether the tribunal is properly constituted' – arguing that the extension of the notion of jurisdiction allows for the immediate intervention of state courts in case of an irregularity in the constitution of the tribunal. While the concern is certainly justifiable in ad hoc arbitration, it seems less cogent in institutional arbitration. This is so because the arbitration rules enacted by the institution will often set up appropriate procedural mechanisms preventing potential irregularities). *See also* Poudret & Besson, *supra* n. 2, at 383.

468. Clay, *L'arbitre*, *supra* n. 61, at 141.

outlined earlier,[469] the monodimensional model is defined by reference to three essential elements. The *first* element consists of the contentious adjudication of a dispute on the merits between two or more parties, which is articulated in the form of claims (*litige, controversia*). The *second* element, is a neutral third party (the adjudicator), who is expected to resolve the dispute. The *third* element amounts to the notion of res judicata (the award, just like a judgment, shall be final, preventing one of the parties from having the same dispute retried). A priori, the jurisdictional power recognized to arbitrators and the decisions that result from its exercise are not consistent with two of the above elements (i.e., resolution of a dispute on the merits and the finality of the decision) for:[470]

(i) The decision on the jurisdiction does not resolve a dispute on the merits of the case.
(ii) The decision is not final, for it can be retried in full by a state court.

With a few stretches, it may be possible to overcome the first point, by arguing that the resolution of the parties' dispute regarding the tribunal's jurisdiction can indeed amount to a dispute on the merits (provided that one is able to show that invoking the jurisdiction of the arbitrators can be regarded as a right). It seems rather obvious, however, that the dispute on the jurisdiction is purely ancillary to the main dispute, the one in relation to which the arbitrators were seized in the first place. Deciding on a jurisdictional issue, therefore, is a mere condition to proceeding with the merits of the case, but not an end in itself.

Be that as it may, no interpretative effort could ever overcome the second point: generally speaking, jurisdictional awards can be retried in full by a state court (i.e., they do not possess res judicata effects). While the above affects both decisions retaining jurisdiction (positive jurisdictional rulings) and declining it (negative jurisdictional rulings), an extra set of problems applies to the latter type of rulings. In fact, negative rulings put into question whether the arbitral tribunal rendering them can truly be regarded as an arbitral tribunal, for the arbitrators may have rendered a decision in the absence of a valid arbitration agreement. Despite this, such a negative ruling will prevent parties from constituting a new arbitral tribunal, unless a state court declares said ruling to be null.

In light of the above, the goal of this chapter is to address the above inconsistencies and explain how jurisdictional decisions (both positive and negative) are compatible with a broader understanding of arbitral adjudication as exemplified by the multidimensional adjudicative model.

---

469. *Supra* §2.02.
470. In some cases an additional inconsistency can be observed. Sometimes the arbitral tribunal will render a jurisdictional decision on its own motion. This will often happen in a case of default by the defendant. In such a case, therefore, the jurisdictional decision is rendered in the absence of an actual dispute regarding jurisdiction. For an application, *see* Final Award, ICC Case No. 17020/2011, 40 YB Comm Arb 294, 308 (2015) ('The first question of law to be decided is whether the Sole Arbitrator has jurisdiction to hear and decide on Claimant's Claims – an issue which the Sole Arbitrator considers he must look at in default proceedings where the Respondent is not expressing itself').

The following section of this chapter will explore the coexistence of arbitrators and state courts, and how jurisdiction is allocated between these two fora in the pre-award phase (challenges to final awards for lack of authority of the arbitrators will therefore not be considered) (section §5.02). For the usual reasons, the focus of this chapter will be on the English *Arbitration Act 1996* and French arbitration legislation. However, given the fact that multiple approaches to jurisdictional matters are endorsed internationally, the comparative analysis will be supplemented (when appropriate) by further references to other jurisdictions.

Section §5.03 will begin with an overview of the Romano-canonical and common law approaches to jurisdictional decisions (section §5.03[A]), and will then address jurisdictional decisions rendered by arbitrators whereby they decide to retain jurisdiction (section §5.03[B]) or to decline it (section §5.03[C])). Section §5.03[D] will then examine the position taken by the *UNCITRAL Model Law*, enshrined in Article 16(3). Finally, Section §5.04 will discuss these decisions in light of the multidimensional model of international commercial arbitration.

I will conclude by explaining that jurisdictional decisions are now generally considered as full-fledged awards. In particular, these awards, which are the expression of the arbitrators' willingness to administer justice in a given case, constitute decisions on legal entitlements of the parties. In other words, these decisions concern the parties' access to arbitral justice. While partly contentious (the parties may well disagree on the jurisdiction of the arbitral tribunal), they cannot be regarded as truly contentious awards, for they are merely an accessory to the resolution of the substantive dispute.

§5.02 A COMPARATIVE OVERVIEW OF THE ROLE OF STATE COURTS IN THE PRE-AWARD PHASE

[A] France

Under French law, the arbitral tribunal will generally be the first forum to consider challenges related to its jurisdiction.[471] In this case, if a party commences an action in breach of an arbitration agreement, the French court will automatically refer it to the arbitral tribunal (provided that the other party has objected to the jurisdiction of the court,[472] and is able to show that there is an existing arbitration agreement).[473] These operative rules are based on a key policy choice, i.e., that 'the [arbitral] tribunal alone has jurisdiction to rule on the validity or limits of its appointment',[474] subject to an ex-post judicial review of its decision.

---

471. Gaillard & Banifatemi, *supra* n. 62, at 258.
472. Gaillard & Savage, *supra* n. 5, at 405 ('[A state] court cannot declare on its own motion that they lack jurisdiction as a result of the existence of an arbitration agreement').
473. Loquin, *Arbitrage International*, *supra* n. 78, at 217; Cf. Jarrosson & Pellerin, *supra* n. 326, at 13.
474. Cass Civ 1e, 10 May 1995, 4 Rev Arb 617 (1995) (Annotation Emmanuel Gaillard).

French scholars present the rules on the allocation of jurisdiction as an application of the competence-competence principle, a substantive rule (*règle matérielle*) of French arbitration law.[475] Taken to the extreme, this principle would justify a very permissive test in order to obtain a stay of proceedings. French courts have labelled it the 'prima facie' test:[476]

> [T]he Courts, when making a *prima facie* determination that there exists an arbitration agreement and that it is valid, leave it to the arbitrators to rule on the question and recover their power of full scrutiny at the end of the arbitral process, after the award is rendered by the arbitral tribunal.

This principle is now enshrined in Article 1448(1) of the French *Code of Civil Procedure* (which, pursuant to Article 1505, also applies to international arbitrations). The provision at hand states that if a dispute falling under an arbitration agreement is brought before a court, then said court must decline to hear the case, unless the tribunal has not been constituted and the arbitration agreement is manifestly void or manifestly inapplicable.

The limited intervention of state courts is deemed to arise from the 'negative effect' of the competence-competence principle, which would exclude the jurisdiction of French courts over matters falling under the scope of an arbitration agreement.[477] Furthermore, the competence-competence principle (and its derivation, that is, the prima facie test) are consistent with another substantive rule (*règle matérielle*) according to which the validity of the arbitration agreement 'shall be assessed independent from any national law'.[478] This legal standard is indispensable for the effective implementation of the prima facie test. In its absence, in fact, it would be difficult to establish whether or not the arbitration clause is prima facie valid under, say, the law of a remote and little known jurisdiction. Yet the same could be said of a sophisticated legal system which French courts are simply not familiar with. It is worth noting that the position taken by France is an isolated one. Several common law jurisdictions have adopted a different criterion for the allocation of jurisdiction between state courts and arbitral tribunals in the pre-award phase. This criterion reduces the jurisdictional power of the arbitrators, for courts will be able to make an assessment of the validity and applicability of the arbitration agreement between the

---

475. Bernhein – Van de Casteele, *supra* n. 335, at 291; Cass Civ 1e, 7 June 2006, 4 Rev Arb 945 (2006) (Annotation Christophe Seraglini).
476. Gaillard & Banifatemi, *supra* n. 62, at 261.
477. Cass Civ 1e, 9 January 2008, XXXIII YB Comm Arb 478 (2008). A recognition of this principle is usually also found in institutional arbitration rules (*see* e.g., Art. 23 of 2010 UNCITRAL Arbitration Rules). One may wonder if it should not be regarded as a pure product of the negative effect of the arbitration agreement. Since the parties have undertaken to submit certain disputes to arbitration (positive effect), it would violate such an undertaking to have state courts intervene in directly connected disputes that are derivative of the main substantive disputes (negative effect). In other words, it would be incoherent to allow parties to have arbitrators resolve the merits of a dispute but not its procedural aspects, such as aspects concerning whether a claim has been validly filed (standing, capacity, quality, etc.).
478. Cass Civ 1e, 7 June 2006, XXXII YB Comm Arb 290 (2007).

parties if seized with a dispute falling under the scope of such agreement. These jurisdictions are considered in the following subpart.

[B]   England

According to section 30(1) of the English *Arbitration Act 1996*, 'unless otherwise agreed by the parties, the arbitral tribunal may rule on its own substantive jurisdiction', that is, it may determine (i) whether there is a valid arbitration agreement, (ii) whether the tribunal has been properly constituted, and (iii) if the matters were submitted to arbitration fall within the scope of the arbitration agreement.[479] This means that, generally speaking, English law recognizes the competence-competence principle.[480] At the same time, the provision makes clear that the parties can derogate (in writing) from this rule in their arbitration agreement.[481] While it is uncontroversial that arbitrators can rule on their jurisdiction, it remains to be seen what role state courts will play in cases where a party seeks their intervention in a matter purportedly covered by an arbitration agreement. The relevant provision of the *Arbitration Act 1996* (section 9(1)) reads as follows:

> Section 9(1) – Stay of Legal Proceedings
>
> A party to an arbitration agreement against whom legal proceedings are brought (whether by way of claim or counterclaim) in respect of a matter which under the agreement is to be referred to arbitration may (upon notice to the other parties to the proceedings) apply to the court in which the proceedings have been brought to stay the proceedings so far as they concern that matter.

This is a mandatory provision, which applies even to arbitrations seated abroad or for which the seat has not yet been determined.[482] Other mechanisms – such as *anti-suit* injunctions – are further available if the seat is abroad.[483]

When there is an application for a stay of legal proceedings under section 9, courts will usually grant the stay to allow the arbitrators to determine whether they have jurisdiction,[484] provided that the interested party is able to show that there is an *existing* arbitration agreement.[485] However, things are more complex in cases where a

---

479. See Jonathan Mance, *The Review of Arbitral Awards in England* in Emmanuel Gaillard, *The Review of International Arbitral Awards* 119, 124 (JurisNet 2008).
480. Merkin & Flannery, *supra* n. 96, at 102.
481. Sutton et al., *supra* n. 92, at 208.
482. *Ibid.* at 358.
483. Merkin & Flannery, *supra* n. 96, at 41. *See also* Sutton et al., *supra* n. 92 at 349–350 (discussing the availability of anti-suit injunctions).
484. *Accentuate Limited (UK) v. Asigra Inc (Canada)*, XXXV YB Comm Arb 460, paras 11–13 (2009) (for a court to decline such a request, the opposing party will have to 'show that it has a good arguable case that the court has jurisdiction'). *See also Trust Risk Group SPA v. Amtrust Europe Ltd* [2015] EWCA Civ 437, at para. 16.
485. *Dallah Real Estate v. Ministry of Religious Affairs* [2010] UKSC 46, at *para.* 97 [*Dallah Real Estate*]; *Al-Naimi (t/a Buildmaster Construction Services) v. Islamic Press Agency* [2000] 1 Lloyd's Rep 522 (CA) [*Al-Naimi*]; *Albon (t/a NA Carriage Co) v. Naza Motor Trading Sdn Bhd (No 4)* [2007] EWCA Civ 1124, [2008] 1 Lloyd's Rep 1.

Chapter 5: Jurisdictional Awards §5.02[B]

party wishes to raise a plea of invalidity or inapplicability of the arbitration agreement. The court will have to decide whether the question should be resolved by the arbitrators or in court proceedings. As held in *Joint Stock Company 'Aeroflot Russian Airlines'*:[486]

> Under section 9(4) the court shall grant a stay unless satisfied that the arbitration agreement is null and void or inoperative. This means ... that once the first party has established the existence of an apparently concluded relevant arbitration agreement and that it covers the matters in dispute in the proceedings, it is for the party resisting a stay to satisfy the court that the apparently existing arbitration agreement is null and void ... the standard of proof which must be attained in order that the court should refuse a stay is one of the balance of probabilities'.

Unless 'the court [was] virtually certain that an arbitration agreement exists',[487] under the traditional position, courts tended to prefer to carry out a full review of the jurisdictional question.[488] Recent cases, however, indicate that a different course of action should be favoured. According to such decisions, particularly the often cited *Fiona* case, if the court is not prepared on the basis of written evidence (or simply by construing the agreement) to resolve the matter,[489] it should always refer the parties to the arbitrators.[490] More precisely, according to Merkin and Flannery, since the *Fiona* case, the presumption would be 'that the arbitral tribunal will usually be the first port of call in any jurisdictional determination'.[491] While this *iter* does not come close to the prima facie test endorsed by French courts, it shows the attempt to give precedence to the arbitrators as far as jurisdictional matters are concerned.

---

486. [2013] EWCA Civ 784, at paras 74–77.
487. Merkin & Flannery, *supra* n. 96, at 42 (citing *British Telecommunications plc v. SAE Group Inc* [2009] EWHC 252 (TCC), at para. 50).
488. Born, *supra* n. 4, at 1085; Amokura Kawharu, *Arbitral Jurisdiction*, 23:2 NZUL Rev 247 (2008). *See* e.g., *Law Debenture Trust Corp Plc v. Elektrim Finance BV* [2005] EWCH 1412.
489. *JSC BTA Bank v. Ablyazov & Ors* [2011] 2 Lloyd's Rep 129, at para. 29. *See also Al-Naimi, supra* n. 485 (this course of action is open only if both parties agree that the court can examine written evidence).
490. *See Fiona Trust & Holding Corp v. Privalov* [2008] 1 Lloyd's Rep 254 HL. *See also A v. B* [2006] EWHC 2006 (Comm) ('The structure of Section 9 of the 1996 Act leaves no doubt that once the existence of an arbitration agreement has been established by the applicant, a stay will be granted unless one of the section 9(4) matters is established. The respondent to the application must therefore make good the existence of one of those matters. If the court is unable to determine whether it is so satisfied on the witness statements before it, consideration has to be given to whether to order a trial of the issue or whether a stay should be granted and the question of substantive jurisdiction under Section 9(4) left to the arbitrators. Whether the latter course is adopted may in many cases depend heavily on the extent to which the resolution of that issue will involve findings of fact which impact on substantive rights and obligations of the parties which are already in issue and whether in general the trial can be confined to a relatively circumscribed area of investigation or is likely to extend widely over the substantive matters in dispute between the parties. If the latter is the case the appropriate tribunal to resolve the jurisdictional issues is more likely to be the arbitration tribunal, provided it has Kompetenz-Kompetenz').
491. Merkin & Flannery, *supra* n. 96, at 43.

It is worth noting that more prima facie oriented-positions have been adopted in other common law jurisdictions,[492] yet there is not a clear trend in this direction.[493]

[C] Allocation of Jurisdiction and Arbitral Practice: The Issue of Bifurcation

This brief comparative overview has shown that there is no uniform standard of review at the pre-award phase. Courts can choose to conduct a review of jurisdictional objections or refer the parties to arbitration, provided that the arbitration agreement is not manifestly invalid or inapplicable (the so-called prima facie test) or that written evidence is sufficient to conclude that the agreement is invalid or inapplicable (the *Fiona* test). There are arguments in support of each of these positions. Without going into the details, the prima facie test has a dogmatic appeal: it reduces the intervention of state courts and reinforces the jurisdictional power of the arbitrators. Conversely, the *Fiona* test applied by English courts has a pragmatic appeal. If the court seized in a matter covered by an arbitration agreement is capable of assessing its validity and applicability, then there is no need to defer the decision to the arbitrators. True, a valid and applicable arbitration agreement confers jurisdiction over the disputes falling under its scope to the arbitral tribunal.[494] Yet, according to the proponents of this test, allowing state courts to perform a review does not necessarily frustrate the purpose of such agreement.

Notwithstanding the above rules, arbitrators maintain autonomy as to the timing of their jurisdictional decisions. In fact, they may decide to deal with a jurisdictional challenge through a preliminary decision (bifurcation), or to postpone the ruling until the rendering of the final award dealing with the merits of the dispute.[495] Leading

---

492. Cf. the position endorsed in Singapore in *The Titan Unity* [2013] SGHCR 28; *Tomolugen Holdings Ltd v. Silica Investors Ltd and Ors* [2015] SGCA 57 at para. 63 ff.
493. For a Canadian perspective, *see*: *Dell Computer Corp v. Union des consommateurs*, 2007 SCC 34, 4 Rev Arb 593 (2007) (Annotation Alain Prujiner) (describing the Canadian approach, regardless of the province). Justice Deschamps laid down the following test: 'I would lay down a general rule that in any case involving an arbitration clause, a challenge to the arbitrator's jurisdiction must be resolved first by the arbitrator. A court should depart from the rule of systematic referral to arbitration only if the challenge to the arbitrator's jurisdiction is based solely on a question of law ... if the challenge requires the production and review of factual evidence, the court should normally refer the case to arbitration, as arbitrators have, for this purpose, the same resources and expertise as courts. Where questions of mixed law and fact are concerned, the court hearing the referral application must refer the case to arbitration unless the questions of fact require only superficial consideration of the documentary evidence in the record. Before departing from the general rule of referral, the court must be satisfied that the challenge to the arbitrator's jurisdiction is not a delaying tactic and that it will not unduly impair the conduct of the arbitration proceeding. This means that even when considering one of the exceptions, the court might decide that to allow the arbitrator to rule first on his or her competence would be best for the arbitration process' (paras 84–86).
494. According to a controversial decision, the breach of the obligation to resort to arbitration could give rise to equitable damages, granted by the arbitral tribunal itself. *See* e.g., *West Tankers Inc v. Allianz SPA & Generali Assicurazione Generali SPA* [2012] EWHC 854 (Comm).
495. For an illustration, *see* Final Award, ICC Case No. 14667/2011, 40 YB Comm Arb 51-144 (2015).

arbitration rules usually leave the decision with the arbitrators.[496] In this respect, Article 6(5) of the 2017 *ICC Rules*, for instance, does not specify when the tribunal should render its jurisdictional decision.[497] Authoritative commentators have noted:[498]

> Jurisdictional objections can and often are decided in a discrete, preliminary phase of the arbitration. An early decision on jurisdiction can have the advantage of saving time and unnecessary expense where the arbitral tribunal finds that it has no jurisdiction.

This view does not necessarily make consensus. Gary Born, for instance, has underlined that if the jurisdictional decision is intertwined with the merits, then it may be preferable to postpone the jurisdictional determination to the final award on the merits.[499] Redfern & Hunter expressed a similar position, stating that 'the tribunal's decision will usually depend on whether the objection is a self-contained legal question that can be properly addressed without detailed knowledge of the underlying facts ... or a question that is linked to the merits and facts of the case'.[500] Only in the former scenario do they express a preference for a preliminary decision on jurisdiction.[501] Along the same lines, Marc Blessing has argued that the possibility of isolating the legal and factual questions concerning the jurisdictional objections is a key factor in the tribunal's decision on the bifurcation of proceedings.[502] He also added that whether or not the objection is dilatory in nature is also an important factor.[503] At the same time, the recent imperatives of saving time and costs have urged commentators to add a further criterion on which arbitrators should base their decision concerning bifurcation. More specifically, the preliminary decision on jurisdiction should be preferred only if it results in a more efficient conduct of the proceedings.[504] This suggests that where the challenge to the jurisdiction is manifestly ill-founded, the tribunal's determination on jurisdiction can be postponed to the final award dealing with the merits of the case. This may also be the case where the objection is intertwined with the merits.

---

496. Clyde Croft et al., *A Guide to the UNCITRAL Arbitration Rules*, 257 (Cambridge University Press 2013); Jacob Grierson & Annet van Hooft, *Arbitrating Under the 2012 ICC Rules* 109 (Kluwer Law 2012). *See also* Art. 23(4) 2014 *LCIA Rules*; Art. 28(4) 2016 *SIAC Rules*.
497. Fry, Greenberg, Mazza, *supra* n. 449, at 87.
498. *Ibid.*
499. Born, *supra* n. 4, at 1244. *See also* Jeff Waincymer, *Procedure and Evidence in International Arbitration*, 612 (Kluwer Law 2012).
500. Redfern & Hunter, *supra* n. 1, at 344.
501. *Ibid.*
502. Marc Blessing, *The Arbitral Process–Part III: The Procedure Before the Arbitral Tribunal*, 3:2 ICC Bull 18, 27 (1998).
503. *Ibid.*
504. Philipp Habegger, *Saving Time and Costs* in Manuel Arroyo, *Arbitration in Switzerland* 1393, 1399 (Kluwer Law 2013). *See also* Francisco Blavi, *Bifurcation of ICC Arbitral Proceedings – A Selection of Recent Procedural Orders*, 1 ICC Bull 46, 46 (2017) ('The eight procedural orders published here confirm that the decision on bifurcating arbitral proceedings ultimately hinges on an efficiency analysis. When dealing with bifurcation, arbitrators have considered the following: (i) the issue(s) on which an early decision is sought and its connection to the merits of the dispute; (ii) the impact that bifurcation may have in terms of time and costs; (iii) the different interests at stake; and (iv) the effects of the decision on the enforceability of the final award, when the parties raise due process concerns').

Conversely, where the jurisdictional objection appears to be well-founded, a preliminary decision could spare the parties further delays and costs.[505] Summing up with a particularly instructive ICC procedural order:[506]

> In deciding whether to bifurcate proceedings, there is no bright line rule to follow as such a decision will largely depend on the particular circumstances of each case. That said, the following factors are among those frequently considered when deciding whether to bifurcate arbitral proceedings: (1) whether the issue to be dealt with is capable of being separated from the other parts of the arbitration; (2) whether the parties have had an opportunity to brief their position on the question of bifurcation; (3) whether the arbitrator has a sufficient view of the dispute as a whole; (4) the amount and type of evidence needed to be taken in relation to the issue to be separated; (5) whether the bifurcation will operate so as to expedite the proceedings and conduct them in a cost-effective manner; (6) whether bifurcation will result in prejudice or unfair advantage; and (7) whether a partial award will help to decide the remaining questions'.

Turning now to the form of the jurisdictional decision (when taken separately from the decision on the merits), arbitrators are free to determine it, unless the parties have decided otherwise.[507] However, the practice of some arbitral institutions may influence the form of such decisions. In ICC arbitration, jurisdictional decisions will usually 'take the form of awards rather than procedural orders ... since describing such decisions as awards for ICC purposes ensures that they will be scrutinized by the [International Court of Arbitration] ... under article 33 [of the 2012 *ICC Rules*]'.[508] The same goes for the LCIA Rules, under which jurisdictional decisions shall take the form of awards.[509] Both institutions express such preference knowing that this will increase the chances of review before the courts at the seat.[510] The above raises a central question: can jurisdictional decisions really become awards? While some arbitral institutions may take it for granted, the following subpart demonstrates that in some jurisdictions, the answer depends on the content of the decision rendered by the arbitral tribunal and, in particular, on whether the arbitrator retains jurisdiction (section §5.03[B]) or declines it (section §5.03[C]). Preliminarily, however, let us spend some time considering how this issue is conceptualized in the Romano-canonical and common law traditions (section §5.03[A]).

---

505. *See* e.g., ICC Procedural Order n. 18864/2013 ('The tribunal notes that the nature of [Repondent]'s jurisdictional and admissibility objections is such that these objections may lead to the conclusion that some or all of [Claimant]'s claims brought in this arbitration ... are to be denied without the need to entertain the merits of those claims ... In the Tribunal's view, this indeed speaks in favor of bifurcation, considering that doing so is likely to result in a more time-and cost-efficient resolution of the case').
506. ICC Procedural Order n. 14338/2008 at para. 18.
507. Webster & Bühler, *supra* n. 442, at 116.
508. Fry, Greenberg, Mazza, *supra* n. 449, at 88. *See also* Art. 34, 2017 *ICC Rules* ('Scrutiny of the Award by the Court': 'Before signing any award, the arbitral tribunal shall submit it in draft form to the Court. The Court may lay down modifications as to the form of the award and, without affecting the arbitral tribunal's liberty of decision, may also draw its attention to points of substance. No award shall be rendered by the arbitral tribunal until it has been approved by the Court as to its form'. *See also* Blessing, *supra* n. 502, at 27.
509. Scherer et al., *supra* n. 453, at 85.
510. *Ibid.*

§5.03 JURISDICTIONAL DECISIONS CAN TAKE THE FORM OF AWARDS AND ARE THUS ENFORCEABLE

[A] The Romano-Canonical and Common Law Traditions on Jurisdictional Rulings

[1] The Romano-Canonical Perspective

State courts are often subject to jurisdictional challenges. In the Romano-canonical tradition, a defendant (or, under certain circumstances, even the court on its own motion) may invoke either a lack of (i) territorial jurisdiction or (ii) jurisdiction with respect the subject matter of the dispute.[511] This gives rise to an incidental procedure establishing whether the application is founded (*déclinatoire de compétence*; *eccezione di competenza*).[512] In general, such a defence shall be raised *in limine litis*, that is, before the interested party has raised any defences on the merits or on the inadmissibility of the claims.[513] The most interesting aspect of this procedure lies in the form of the court's decision. Within the same tradition, two different approaches can be identified: according to the first approach, the decision on the lack of jurisdiction will take the form of a judgment; according to the second one, the decision will take the form of an order. In France, but the same is also true for Germany, the court will decide on the defence of lack of jurisdiction in a judgment, and the interested party will be able to file an appeal.[514] In Italy, however, the decision will take the form of an order, unless the jurisdictional objection is either intertwined with the merits or the court needs to hear evidence in order to render its decision – moreover, in this case, the challenge will be dealt with directly by the Court of Cassation (*Corte di Cassazione*).[515]

From the foregoing, it appears that as far as this procedural tradition is concerned, jurisdictional decisions can either take the form of a judgment or of an order. In both cases, such decisions can be challenged in front of a higher court.

---

511. Pierre Mayer & Vincent Heuzé, *Droit international privé*, 199 (LGDJ 2014) ('On distingue la compétence d'attribution (ou ratione materiae) et la compétence térritoriale (ou ratione loci); la première sert à départager entre eux les tribunaux des divers types (de l'ordre administratif, de l'ordre judiciaire, de grande instance, de commerce, etc.), la seconde à départager les tribunaux des divers ressors territoriaux'). A third type of jurisdiction can be identified, that is, the *compétence internationale* (dealing with cases where several jurisdictions could be seized regarding the same matter).
512. Guinchard, *supra* n. 22, at 1131; Mandrioli, *supra* n. 89, at 249.
513. *See*, e.g., Art. 74 of the French *Code of Civil Procedure*: 'Les exceptions doivent, à peine d'irrecevabilité, être soulevées simultanément et avant toute défense au fond ou fin de non-recevoir. Il en est ainsi alors même que les règles invoquées au soutien de l'exception seraient d'ordre public.'; Art. 38(1) of the Italian *Code of Civil Procedure*: 'L'incompetenza per materia, quella per valore e quella per territorio sono eccepite, a pena di decadenza, nella comparsa di risposta tempestivamente depositata. L'eccezione di incompetenza per territorio si ha per non proposta se non contiene l'indicazione del giudice che la parte ritiene competente'.
514. Guinchard, *supra* n. 22, at 1141; Peter L. Murray & Rolf Stürner, *German Civil Justice System*, 149 (Carolina Academic Press 2004).
515. Mandrioli, *supra* n. 89, at 281. *See also* Arts 42 and 43 of the Italian *Code of Civil Procedure*.

[2] The Common Law Perspective

As far as the notion of jurisdiction is concerned, while the common law tradition also endorses a dichotomy between subject-matter jurisdiction and territorial jurisdiction, there is no clear taxonomy – the notion of jurisdiction is, in fact, intimately tied to the constitutional setting of a given common law jurisdiction.[516] While it is impossible to trace a general position of the common law on jurisdictional matters, it is worth mentioning at least the position of English law. One key point that should be borne in mind, is the residual discretion that English courts have – this means that even when the court has jurisdiction, it may decide not to exercise it. In the civilian tradition, there is no equivalent discretionary ground.

In England, a defendant can challenge the jurisdiction of a court with an incidental procedure. In this regard, rule 11(1) of the 1998 *Civil Procedure Rules* (*CPR*) states:

> 1) A defendant who wishes to –
>   (a) dispute the court's jurisdiction to try the claim; or
>   (b) argue that the court should not exercise its jurisdiction
>   may apply to the court for an order declaring that it has no such jurisdiction or should not exercise any jurisdiction which it may have.

This application must be filed along with the acknowledgement of service and shall contain a response in which the defendant states its intention to contest the court's jurisdiction.[517] Furthermore, according to rule 11(4)(b) *CPR*, the applicant is required to give evidence.[518] The question of whether the provision at issue deals with both the subject-matter and territorial jurisdiction of the court has been subject to debate.[519] In an interesting decision, it was found that the term 'jurisdiction' in rule 11 *CPR* amounted to 'a reference to the court's power or authority to try a claim'.[520] This would suggest that rule 11 should be interpreted broadly, as encompassing both territorial and subject-matter jurisdiction. Interestingly enough, according to Zukerman, the claimant bears the burden of 'establish[ing] that the court has jurisdiction or, as the case may be, that it should exercise it'.[521] Yet this position contrasts with the requirement of rule 11(4)(b) *CPR*, by which evidence must be submitted by the applicant contesting the jurisdiction of the court. The author is probably alluding to a case where the defendant is able to establish that the court does not have jurisdiction

---

516. Adrian Briggs, *Civil Jurisdiction and Judgments*, 380 (Routledge 2015). *See also* John Fitzpatrick, *The Lugano Convention and Western European Integration: A Comparative Analysis of Jurisdiction and Judgments in Europe and the United States*, 8 Conn. J Int'l L 695, 714 (1993).
517. Zuckerman, *Civil Procedure*, *supra* n. 304, at 291. Yet the court has discretion to extend the term. *See Sawyer v. Atari Interactive Inc* [2005] EWHC 2351 (QB).
518. *See also Texan Management Ltd & Ors v. Pacific Electric Wire & Cable Company* [2009] UKPC 46, at para. 28.
519. Stuart Sime, *Civil Procedure*, 170 (Oxford University Press 2010).
520. *Hoddinott & Ors v. Persimmon Homes (Wessex) Ltd* [2007] EWCA Civ 1203, at *para.* 23.
521. Zuckerman, *Civil Procedure*, *supra* n. 304, at 292.

(or should not exercise it, pursuant, for instance, to the forum non conveniens doctrine), thus shifting the burden of proof onto the claimant.

Finally, the decision rendered by the court will take the form of an order.[522] If the court rejects the application, then the defendant will be able to contest the jurisdictional determination through an appeal of the judgment on the merits. To do so, the defendant will have to refrain from filing a new acknowledgment of service.[523] This *iter* appears to be quite different from the one described in the preceding subpart. In particular, the decision on the jurisdictional objection will take the form of an order, and if the court rejects the application, the defendant can only challenge this determination by appealing the judgment regarding the claims brought forth by the plaintiff.

This brief excursus has shown that there is no unanimous approach in state litigation as to the form, content, and possibility of challenging jurisdictional decisions. Surprisingly enough, a higher degree of uniformity can be found in national arbitration laws. For the sake of clarity, the analysis of these arbitration laws will be divided in two parts. First, I will consider arbitral decisions retaining jurisdiction (section §5.03[B]). Second, I will address those declining it (section §5.03[C]). It is important to clarify that the following section will only deal with a positive jurisdictional decision taken separately from the final award on the merits, as it is uncontroversial that this latter kind of award can be annulled or refused enforcement if the arbitrators lacked jurisdiction (as provided for under Article 34(2)(a)(i), and (iii) of the UNCITRAL *Model Law*, and Article V(1)(a) and (c) of the *New York Convention*).

[B] Positive Jurisdictional Rulings Are Enforceable Awards: The Convergence of French and English Law

Most of today's arbitration acts provide that the arbitrators' preliminary decisions to retain jurisdiction may be challenged in the courts of the seat of arbitration.[524] Such a decision is usually considered enforceable and is regarded as an award. This choice constitutes a first exception to the pure monodimensional model of the adjudicative power of arbitrators. In fact, if compared with the three essential elements of the exercise of arbitral power under such a model (resolution of a dispute; third neutral party; final decision), the jurisdictional power and the decisions resulting from its exercise are inconsistent with two of the above elements: they do not resolve a substantive dispute between the parties, and they are not final (they can, in fact, be fully reviewed by a state court). Let us consider how national legislators deal with the topic. Since the possibility of enforcing (and of challenging) a positive jurisdictional ruling of the arbitrators (i.e., a decision retaining jurisdiction over the claims) is a

---

522. *CPR* 11(1), (6).
523. *CPR* 11(8): 'If the defendant files a further acknowledgment of service in accordance with paragraph (7)(b) he shall be treated as having accepted that the court has jurisdiction to try the claim'.
524. *See* e.g., Art. 16(3) of the 2006 UNCITRAL *Model Law*.

nearly universal standard, the following subpart will present, at the same time, the overall concept in French arbitration legislation and in the English Arbitration Act.

The relevant provisions are found in the French *Code of Civil Procedure* (Article 1520(1)) and in the English *Arbitration Act 1996* (section 67(1)).[525] They both make clear that positive jurisdictional rulings are subject to review before state courts. Furthermore, parties cannot necessarily opt out of this type of provision. English authorities are clear on this point: section 67(1) of the *Arbitration Act 1996* is a mandatory provision.[526] Conversely, Article 1522 of the French *Code of Civil Procedure* states that the parties can agree to exclude annulment proceedings (*recours en annulation*).[527] A stipulation to this effect can be included in the arbitration clause or in a separate agreement; in either case, the parties will have to expressly state their intention to waive such an important right.[528]

While the possibility of challenging positive rulings is uncontroversial in both jurisdictions, some differences can be observed with respect to the applicable standard of review. In short, there is a broad consensus as to the need for fully reviewing the decision rendered by the arbitrators.[529] This option is favoured by English courts, where the decision rendered by the court will replace the arbitrators' ruling.[530] As stated by a commentator:[531]

> No decision by the arbitral tribunal as to its own jurisdiction binds the court if and when the matter comes to court: when the court rules on substantive jurisdiction, it reviews both the factual and the legal basis of substantive jurisdiction, receives

---

525. Article 1520(1) French *Code of Civil Procedure*: 'Le recours en annulation n'est ouvert que si: 1° Le tribunal s'est déclaré à tort compétent ou incompétent'; section 67(1) *Arbitration Act 1996*:

    'A party to arbitral proceedings may (upon notice to the other parties and to the tribunal) apply to the court–

    (a) challenging any award of the arbitral tribunal as to its substantive jurisdiction; or
    (b) for an order declaring an award made by the tribunal on the merits to be of no effect in whole or in part, because the tribunal did not have substantive jurisdiction'.

526. Merkin & Flannery, *supra* n. 96, at 292. It should be emphasized that the Arbitration Act allows the parties to agree upon a review of the tribunal's jurisdiction even in the absence of an explicit ruling (*see* section 32(1)).
527. Article 1522, French *Code of Civil Procedure*: 'Par convention spéciale, les parties peuvent à tout moment renoncer expressément au recours en annulation'.
528. Jarrosson & Pellerin, *supra* n. 326, at 70.
529. Cf. Amokura Kawharu, *Rehearings of Jurisdiction Issues: A Fresh Look at the Judicial Task*, 32 Arb Int 1, 5 (2016) (noting, however, that the full review of the arbitral decision does not turn the challenge into a form of 'appeal', but rather in sui generis procedure based on the need for maintaining a supervisory role over arbitral proceedings seated in the jurisdiction where the jurisdictional challenge is filed).
530. *See* e.g., *C v. D1, D2, and D3* [2015] EWHC 2126 (Comm), at para. 72 ('A challenge under sections 67 and 68 of the 1996 Act proceeds by way of rehearing, not review. Nevertheless, the Court will have regard to the Tribunal's reasoning if helpful. However, as has happened in this case, the arguments on challenge de novo can be and are presented in fresh and different ways, and with different emphases'). *See also Dallah Real Estate*, *supra* n. 485, at paras 25–26; *Film Finance Inc v. Royal Bank of Scotland* [2007] 1 Lloyd's Rep 382.
531. Mance, *supra* n. 479, at 126.

such evidence, written or oral, as may be necessary, and determines the question for itself.

Furthermore, the evidence on which the parties intend to rely in a section 67(1) challenge is not limited to what was adduced in the arbitral proceedings.[532]

Likewise, French courts will review all the available legal and factual elements to assess the arbitrators' jurisdiction.[533] Finally, it is also clear that the arbitrators' decision on jurisdiction can take the form of an award.[534] In this respect, as explained in the following subpart, the nature and enforceability of negative jurisdictional decisions (whereby the arbitrators decide to decline jurisdiction over the case) is much more problematic.

[C] Negative Jurisdictional Rulings Can Be Enforced as Awards

Arbitrators can decide to decline jurisdiction over parties' claims. The most important question to ask is whether such a decision is an enforceable one. Arbitration laws and court decisions endorse contrasting positions on the matter. The various approaches can be summarized as follows.

Reference will first be made to the jurisdictions where challenges against negative jurisdictional awards are inadmissible. This situation can be traced back to the contractual model of arbitration: a decision rendered by an arbitrator on the basis of an invalid contract cannot have legally binding effects, for there is no valid contractual basis for the authority of the adjudicator in the first place (section §5.03[C][1]). I will then show that there is a favourable trend toward the enforcement of negative jurisdictional decisions (section §5.03[C][2]). In most cases, the enforceability of such decisions is guaranteed by specific statutory provisions.

---

532. *Central Trading & Exports LTD v. Fioralba Shipping Co* [2014] EWHC 2397, at para. 30.
533. CA Paris, 17 December 2013, 4 Rev Arb 948, 949 (2014) (Annotation Daniel Cohen) ('Le juge de l'annulation contrôle la décision du tribunal arbitral sur la compétence en recherchant tous les éléments de droit et de fait permettant d'apprécier l'existence et la portée de la convention d'arbitrage'). *See also* Dominique Hascher, *The Review of International Awards in France* in Emmanuel Gaillard, *The Review of International Arbitral Awards* 97, 99 (JurisNet 2008) ('It is therefore possible for the court to come to a completely different conclusion to that of the arbitral tribunal. In order to come to a decision, the judge may of course rely on those arguments put forward by the parties on which the arbitrators based their award – it is precisely because the arguments were relevant that they are taken into consideration by the arbitrators; but the court may also take into account their arguments to uphold the award or, conversely, to set it aside. This is why the parties should even be allowed to submit evidence that was not put before the arbitrators. The court needs to determine whether the arbitrators are true arbitrators, as opposed to private individuals giving an unsolicited opinion. It is the arbitrators' jurisdiction that is subject to review here, and not the reasons of the award').
534. *See* section 31(4) of the *Arbitration Act 1996* ('Where an objection is duly taken to the tribunal's substantives jurisdiction and the tribunal has power to rule on its own jurisdiction, it may – (a) rule on the matter in an award as to jurisdiction, or (b) deal with the objection in its award on the merits'). *See also* Loquin, *Arbitrage International, supra* n. 78, at 236.

[1] Negative Jurisdictional Rulings Are Not Awards: An Out-dated Conception

On the face of it, the UNCITRAL *Model Law* seems to preclude challenges against negative jurisdictional rulings (Articles 16(3) and 34).[535] Such provisions state only that decisions holding that the arbitrators have jurisdiction can be challenged. Both Romano-canonical and common law jurisdictions have one representative still endorsing this out-dated conception, that is, Hong Kong[536] and Germany.[537] The latter example is very instructive.

While, in Germany, an arbitrator's negative jurisdictional ruling can be regarded as an award,[538] challenges against it will automatically be rejected as the grounds for annulment contained in section 1059 *ZPO* (the German *Code of Civil Procedure*) would not be applicable. This outcome can be explained by the fact that the grounds of annulment set out in section 1059 *ZPO* were mainly conceived for challenges against contentious awards. At the same time, it is unclear whether a wrongful decision to decline jurisdiction could amount to a violation of public policy.[539]

The inadmissibility of challenges against these decisions is thus a question of policy: while courts may review whether an arbitral tribunal wrongfully retained jurisdiction, thus annulling a positive jurisdictional ruling, they may not, on the contrary, rule that the tribunal wrongfully declined jurisdiction. The argument behind this choice, is that the parties will always be able to resort to state courts. In this respect, it does not seem enough to say that the problem has little practical relevance in light of arbitrators' tendency to retain jurisdiction over their cases; precluding challenges against negative rulings and re-opening the jurisdiction of state courts goes against the general policy objective of preserving arbitral jurisdiction and the validity of arbitration agreements.[540] If we take into account the institutional traits of international commercial arbitration, in fact, the question of jurisdiction should be treated in terms of an access to justice issue. A wrongful decision to decline jurisdiction would then result in a denial of justice. Hence, the importance of allowing the possibility of challenging such decisions.

---

535. Poudret & Besson, *supra* n. 2, at 407. *See also* Laurence GS Boo, *Ruling on Arbitral Jurisdiction – Is That an Award?* 3:2 As Int'l Arb J 125, 131 (2007); Klaus Peter Berger, *International Economic Arbitration*, 361 (Kluwer Law 1993). For an application, *see* e.g., the case law in Singapore, and in particular *PT Asuransi Jasa Indonesia (Persero) v. Dexia Bank S.A.* [2007] SLR(R) 597.
536. *See* section 34(4) of the 2014 *Arbitration Ordinance*, which re-enacts Art. 16(3) of the 2006 UNCITRAL *Model Law. See also Kenon Engineering Ltd. v. Nippon Kokan Koji Kabushiki Kaisha* [2003] HKCFI 568.
537. *See* generally Stephan Kröll, *Recourse Against Negative Decisions on Jurisdiction*, 20:1 Arb Int 55 (2004). *See also* Poudret & Besson, *supra* n. 2, at 407–408.
538. BGH (German Supreme Court), III ZB 44/01 of 6 June 2002, Schieds VZ, 2003, 39.
539. Kröll, *supra* n. 537, at 56 (nevertheless, the author suggests the possibility of invoking the ground of *infra petita* pursuant to section 1059(2)(c) ZPO). Cf. Poudret & Besson, *supra* n. 2, at 408; Frédéric Bachand, *Kompetenz-Kompetenz, Canadian-Style*, 25:3 Arb Int 431, 443 (2009).
540. *See* Berger, *supra* n. 535, at 362. *See also* Jean-Baptiste Racine, *La Sentence d'incompétence*, 4 Rev Arb 729, 730 (2010) ('Les arbitres ont une propension naturelle à s'estimer compétents').

As explained in the following subparts, a growing consensus shows a clear intention to consider these rulings as enforceable decisions.

[2] Negative Jurisdictional Rulings Are Enforceable Awards

It has been argued that the admissibility of challenges against negative jurisdictional rulings is now a prevalent trend.[541] This admissibility has been achieved either through statutory reforms or thanks to an expansive judicial interpretation of the provisions dealing with jurisdictional challenges. The English *Arbitration Act 1996* is an example of the latter case.

With respect to the English statute, while the possibility of challenging a negative jurisdictional award is broadly accepted among scholars,[542] the only case that has accepted this proposition is *L G Caltex Gas Co Ltd v. National Petroleum Corporation & Anor*,[543] where the Court of Appeal of England and Wales found, *obiter*, that section 67(1)(a) of the act did apply to negative jurisdictional rulings.[544] More recently, in *Monde Petroleum SA v. Westernzagros Ltd*,[545] the High Court of England and Wales has provided a further confirmation that this is the correct interpretation of the act:[546]

> Section 67(1)(a) applies both when a tribunal finds that it has jurisdiction and also, as in the present case, when it declines jurisdiction. Such challenges involve a full rehearing of the question of the arbitral tribunal's jurisdiction as opposed to a review of its decision; the Court's role is to decide whether or not the tribunal reached the correct decision and not simply to decide whether the tribunal was entitled to reach the decision it did.

Furthermore, this judgment has reaffirmed that courts should proceed with a full review of the jurisdictional decision.

Contrary to the English *Arbitration Act 1996*, the 2011 French arbitration reform introduced a new article in the *Code of Civil Procedure* (Article 1520(1)) addressing challenges against negative jurisdictional rulings.[547] This provision states that an award may be set aside where 'the arbitral tribunal wrongly upheld or declined jurisdiction'.[548] As a result, if the award deals with a question of admissibility rather than one of jurisdiction, it cannot be annulled pursuant to Article 1520(1) of the *Code*

---

541. *Ibid.* at 779.
542. Merkin & Flannery, *supra* n. 96 at 294.
543. [2001] EWCA Civ 788.
544. *Ibid.* at *paras* 70–71. Section 67 of the *Arbitration Act 1996* reads as follows:

> Challenging the award: substantive jurisdiction.
> (1) A party to arbitral proceedings may (upon notice to the other parties and to the tribunal) apply to the court –
> (a) challenging any award of the arbitral tribunal as to its substantive jurisdiction'.

545. [2015] EWHC 67 (Comm).
546. *Ibid.* at para. 28.
547. Decree n° 2011-48, 13 January 2011.
548. Article 1520(1) French *Code of Civil Procedure*: 'An award may only be set aside where: (1) the arbitral tribunal wrongly upheld or declined jurisdiction.'

of Civil Procedure.[549] It is worth noting that the *Cour de cassation* had already interpreted former Article 1502(1) – now replaced by the new Article 1520(1) – as allowing challenges against decisions wrongfully declining jurisdiction over the case.[550] Be that as it may, it is important to keep in mind that despite the fact that the admissibility of the *recours en annulation* has been extended to negative jurisdictional awards,[551] the annulment of such decisions will simply allow the parties to commence a new arbitration.[552] In other words, the provision at hand does not allow the court to compel the arbitrators to move forward with the proceedings.

Finally, with respect to the applicable test for reviewing an arbitrator's negative jurisdictional award, French courts have held in several cases that the standard will be one of full review.[553] This means that the court will assess, on the basis of the parties' submissions during the course of the proceedings,[554] whether the decision of the arbitral tribunal was correct in the light of the applicable law.

The present section has highlighted that after some struggles – which can be explained by the resilience of the contractual model of the adjudicative power of the arbitrators – negative jurisdictional rulings are now also treated as enforceable awards. Moreover, a wrongful decision of the arbitrators to decline jurisdiction is conceptualized in a way that comes closer to state litigation. In order to ensure that these decisions are fully challengeable, the label of 'award' is often utilized. Furthermore, it was pointed out that recent reforms show a trend to uphold challenges against negative arbitral rulings. One final question remains to be answered, that is, is this trend justified, and if so, why? I wish to suggest that, despite valid arguments against it, there are good reasons to answer in the affirmative.

To understand the usefulness of a recourse against a decision to decline jurisdiction, we have to make some distinctions in relation to its content. If the decision states that the arbitrators do not have jurisdiction over the dispute because it falls outside the scope of the arbitration agreement, the recourse has limited practical relevance. This is so because in the absence of such recourse the interested party can resume arbitral proceedings by constituting a new tribunal arguing that the claims brought forth are now different from the original submissions. We note in passing that this would be the same result stemming from a decision of a French court under section Article 1520(1) of the French Code of Civil Procedure, stating that the negative ruling was void. In such a case, the interested party would also be forced to constitute a new tribunal, which, however, would likely be bound to observe the content of the decision rendered by the French court. Conversely, the recourse becomes particularly important in presence of

---

549. Cass Civ 1e, 18 March 2015, No 14-13.336.
550. Racine, *supra* n. 540, at 739. *See also* Cass Civ 1e, 6 October 2010, 4 Rev Arb 813 (2010) (Annotation François-Xavier Train).
551. *See* Cass Civ 1e, 16 June 1988, 2 Rev Arb 309 (1989) (Annotation Charles Jarrosson).
552. *See* CA Paris, 17 December 2013, No 12/07231.
553. *Ibid.* ('[L]e juge de l'annulation contrôle la décision du tribunal arbitral sur sa compétence, en recherchant tous les éléments de droit et de fait permettant d'apprécier l'existence et la portée de la convention d'arbitrage').
554. This will obviously be mitigated by the applicable rules of evidence. That is to say that the parties will have to follow the rules of evidence that are applicable in the jurisdiction where the recourse against the negative award is filed.

a final declaration of invalidity of the arbitration agreement.[555] In this case, the arbitrators' rulings would prevent the constitution of a new tribunal on the motion of the party disagreeing with the decision. This is particularly true in the context of institutional arbitration. In this case, in fact, it is likely that the institution would oppose, in the presence of a negative arbitral ruling declaring the arbitration agreement null and void, the constitution of a new tribunal. This would be the case, for instance, under Article 6(3) of the 2017 ICC Rules. Said party, then, would be deprived of its access to arbitral justice, and be forced to seize state courts for a declaration on the validity of the arbitration agreement.

Finally, as a further consideration in favour of the enforceability of negative jurisdictional awards, it is worth mentioning that these decisions would also allow the successful party to directly recover costs from its opponent.

[D] The Peculiarities of the Recourse under Article 16(3) of the *Model Law*

According to Article 16(3) of 2006 UNCITRAL *Model Law*, positive jurisdictional rulings rendered prior to the final award on the merits can be challenged in front of the competent state court. The provision reads as follows:

> [I]f the arbitral tribunal rules as a preliminary question that it has jurisdiction, any party may request, within thirty days after having received notice of that ruling, the court specified in article 6 to decide the matter, which decision shall be subject to no appeal; while such a request is pending, the arbitral tribunal may continue the arbitral proceedings and make an award.

The provision is consistent with Article 16(1) of the UNCITRAL *Model Law*, which states that the tribunal may either rule on a jurisdictional objection 'as a preliminary question or in an award on the merits'. In this respect, it further aligns with the arbitration rules examined in section §5.02 [C], as it allows the arbitrators to opt for a bifurcation of proceedings when circumstances so require.

The peculiarities of Article 16(3) are found in the second phrase of the provision, according to which 'if the arbitral tribunal rules as a preliminary question that it has jurisdiction, any party may request, within thirty days after having received notice of that ruling, the court ... to decide the matter'. This raises two intertwined questions: what is the nature of the remedy, and what are its interplays with the enforcement and annulment provisions of the *Model Law*? Finally, does the provision take a stand with respect to the form of the tribunal's ruling?

Starting with the nature of the challenge, it has been stated that the provision at hand would involve a 'two-step challenge procedure': 'the first step requires the plea to be raised in front of the arbitral tribunal ... [t]he second step is that, if the tribunal rules that it has jurisdiction as a preliminary question, the party may ... request the

---

555. Berger, *supra* n. 535, at 361–362.

competent court to make a final decision on the matter'.[556] This qualification, however, seems to be imprecise, for the provision merely anchors the availability of the recourse under Article 16(3) to a jurisdictional objection before the tribunal. If, in fact, no such objection was raised, the arbitral tribunal would not need to opt for the bifurcation of proceedings in the first place. Similarly, it the tribunal decides to examine its jurisdiction on its own motion, it would be unreasonable to exclude the applicability of Article 16(3) on the basis that the interested party has not objected to the jurisdiction of the tribunal.[557]

Moving to the interplays of this challenge procedure with Articles 34 and 36 of the *Model Law* (dealing, respectively, with the annulment procedure, and the refusal of enforcement), it should be noted that the language of Article 16(3) is permissive, leaving room for different interpretations.[558] This is why courts have sometimes ruled in favour of the exclusive nature of the recourse under Article 16(3),[559] while in other instances they have held that the interested party can avail itself of Article 34 and/or 36 even if it has not challenged the preliminary ruling under Article 16(3).[560] There is, however, a key element that should provide guidance in addressing this point, namely, the form of the jurisdictional ruling rendered pursuant to Article 16(3). What would be the reason, in fact, to include a review of a preliminary decision, if arbitral tribunals can always render awards on competence? Couldn't that decision simply be challenged under the ordinary rules set out in Articles 34 and 36 of the *Model Law*?[561] A potential answer could be that Article 16(3) extends the possibility to challenge jurisdictional rulings when these are not rendered in the form of an award, and especially when they are provisional in nature. This would constitute a sensible solution meant to tackle

---

556. Peter Binders, *International Commercial Arbitration and Conciliation in UNCITRAL Model Law Jurisdictions*, 219 (Sweet & Maxwell 2010). *See also* Nata Ghibradze, *Preclusion of Remedies under Article 16(3) of the UNCITRAL Model Law*, 27:1 Pace Int'l L Rev 345, 348 (2015).
557. *See* UNCITRAL, *2012 Case Law Digest of the Model Law on International Commercial Arbitration*, 78 ('The travaux préparatoires indicate that the words "including any objections with respect to the existence or validity of the arbitration agreement" [found in article 16 (1)] were not intended to limit the "Kompetenz-Kompetenz" of the arbitral tribunal to those cases where a party raised an objection. Furthermore, the travaux préparatoires emphasize the arbitral tribunal's power to examine on its own motion issues of public policy bearing on its jurisdiction, including the arbitrability of the dispute').
558. *Ibid.* at 82.
559. Bundesgerichtshof, Germany, III ZB 83/02, 27 March 2003.
560. *PT First Media TBK v. Astro Nusantara International BV and others* [2014] 1 SLR 372, at *para.* 111. *See also* Ghibradze, *supra* n. 555, at 353; Kexian Ng, *Choice of Remedies under the UNCITRAL Model Law: PT First Media v. Astro and Beyond*, 7 J. E. Asia & Int'l L 256, 263 (2014) ('the failure to invoke an active remedy under Articles13(3) or 16(3) of the Model Law will preclude a subsequent active defence of setting aside the award under Article 34 of the Model Law is context-sensitive and resolved on the facts of every case').
561. Although it is true that the way in which the grounds for annulment and refusal of recognition are phrased, complicates the possibility of challenging a wrongful decision on jurisdiction. This issue arises in practice, and according to the German Supreme Court, while the challenge is admissible, it has to be rejected as it neither falls in any of the grounds listed in section 1059 ZPO (which mimics the grounds of annulment under Art. 34 of the *Model Law*), nor does it amount to a violation of the *ordre public*, given the fact that the rights of the parties are not affected (being still enforceable in front of a state court. *See* BGH (German Supreme Court), III ZB 44/01 of 6 June 2002, Schieds VZ, 2003, 39. It should be noted that, nevertheless, it could be possible to argue that the arbitrators' award is null for *infra* petita (Cf. Art. 1059(2)(c) ZPO).

Chapter 5: Jurisdictional Awards §5.04

cases that may often arise in practice, where tribunals issue an order declaring that they retain jurisdiction over the case, reserving to finally decide the matter in the award on the merits. It should be noted, however, that arbitral tribunals can also choose to finally decide on the issue of competence by way of an award. This is why the *Model Law* excludes that the challenge procedure at hand is extended to cases where the tribunal has ruled that it did not have jurisdiction. Where the tribunal were to render an award declining jurisdiction, then such a decision would be final; any form of challenge, even under Articles 34 and 36, would thus be excluded.[562] Conversely, if the arbitrators were to finally decide that they have jurisdiction over the case, then such an award could be challenged under Articles 34 and 36 of the *Model Law*.

§5.04 CONCLUSION

The present chapter has dealt with decisions rendered by arbitrators in the exercise of their jurisdictional power. Such a power allows them to decide whether arbitration is the appropriate forum for adjudicating the parties' claims.

After noting the lack of uniformity within the Romano-canonical tradition, and the diverging terminology and taxonomy in the common law tradition, regarding jurisdictional rulings, I explained that jurisdictional awards (either those retaining or declining jurisdiction) are usually considered to be enforceable. The label of 'award' is often attributed to them by a specific legislative provision, in order to allow challenges before the competent state courts. State courts, in fact, will review jurisdictional decisions to the same extent that they would do in the case of a decision rendered by a lower national court. This review by state courts can be explained by the fact that jurisdictional awards are able to affect the legal entitlements of the parties just as much as contentious awards do. They contain a decision regarding the possibility of seeking recourse to arbitral justice.

These rulings, therefore, are not a mere administrative assessment but rather the expression of arbitrators' willingness to administer justice in a given case, hence the possibility of enforcing and challenging them, and the label of award. At the same time, these determinations of jurisdiction cannot be regarded, given their subject matter, as pure contentious awards, for they are only ancillary to the resolution of the substantive dispute, and they do not necessarily amount to a response to a party's claim (jurisdictional issues can, in fact, be raised by an arbitral tribunal on its own motion, for example, in the case of default proceedings). Moreover, they are not final decisions,

---

562. Poudret & Besson, *supra* n. 2, at 407. *See also*: Bachand, *L'intervention du juge*, *supra* n. 467, at 304; *2012 Digest*, *supra* n. 556, at 81 (citing the *Official Records of the General Assembly, Fortieth Session, Supplement No. 17* (A/40/17), annex I, para. 163): 'Article 16(3) only deals explicitly with the reviewability of interim decisions in which the arbitral tribunal rules that it has jurisdiction over the claim; nothing is said in that provision about the reviewability of arbitral decisions denying jurisdiction, also known as negative jurisdictional decisions. However, the travaux préparatoires are clear on that matter: while noting that as article 16(3) does not address the judicial review of negative jurisdictional decisions ... it is nevertheless recognized ... that "a ruling by the arbitral tribunal that it lacked jurisdiction [is] final as regards its proceedings since it [would be] inappropriate to compel arbitrators who had made such a ruling to continue the proceedings."'

for they can, except for negative rulings under the *Model Law*, be reviewed in full by a state court. This means that jurisdictional awards can be regarded as the expression of a distinct adjudicative power, which is now increasingly acknowledged by national legislators. This is particularly evident when one considers the fact that the arbitrators are allowed to issue final awards on competence whereby they decline jurisdiction over the case. By recognising that these decisions can be qualified as awards, and that they can be subject to a challenge before state courts, not only can we assist to the recognition of a distinct adjudicative power, but also to one which is independent from the will of the parties, in open conflict against the pure contractual theory of arbitration.

In conclusion, the jurisdictional power of the arbitrators and the jurisdictional awards resulting from the exercise of this power are a first confirmation of the fact that the access to arbitral justice is now dealt with in a manner similar to how issues of access to state justice are conceptualized.

Having analysed jurisdictional awards, I will now consider a second type of award, this time relating to the power of recognising and recording a private settlement between the parties in the form of an award (i.e., 'consent awards').

CHAPTER 6
Consent Awards

§6.01 INTRODUCTION

Consent awards are the expression of a non-contentious adjudicative power of arbitrators. After analysing some inconsistencies and difficulties that persist in the French and English arbitration legislation, relating to consent awards, the present chapter will conclude by providing an indication of the essential elements and content that a consent award should have in order to avoid any issues of enforcement.[563]

The possibility of enforcing an award that records a settlement between the parties to an arbitration has been a controversial matter.[564] As the *New York Convention* demonstrates, the effectiveness of the entire system of commercial arbitration lies in the possibility of enforcing the final decisions of arbitrators, whether or not the decisions record a settlement agreement. Despite its central role, however, the *New York Convention* does not provide a univocal definition of 'arbitral award', thus complicating any attempt to demonstrate that consent awards are, for all effects and purposes, *awards*.[565] This explains the fact that UNCITRAL has recently intensified its efforts to draft an international instrument on the enforcement of settlement agreements.[566] While such draft instrument does not appear to cover settlement agreements reached during the course of arbitral proceedings and recorded in the form of an

---

563. Excerpts of this chapter have been published in the following article: Giacomo Marchisio, *A Comparative Analysis of Consent Awards: Accepting Their Reality*, 32:2 Arb Int 331 (2016). They are reproduced in this book with the permission of Oxford University Press.
564. Born, *supra* n. 4, at 3021. Given the lack of a relevant uniform legal framework, it is not surprising to find four synonyms indicating the same concept of a settlement recorded in an arbitral award: agreed award, award by consent, consent award, and award on agreed terms.
565. *Supra*, §2.04.
566. UNCITRAL, *International Commercial Conciliation: Preparation of an instrument on the enforcement of commercial settlement agreements resulting from conciliation*, A/CN.9/WG.II/WP.200 (28 November 2016), at para. 7.

arbitral award,[567] it highlights that their enforcement, even in the form of consent awards,[568] is not as straightforward as it should be.[569]

While arbitration instruments such as the *ICC Rules* (section §6.02) and the 2006 UNCITRAL *Model Law* (section §6.03) contain provisions on consent awards – with the aim of encouraging settlements (*see* Article 30 of the UNCITRAL *Model Law*) – national jurisdictions struggle with this notion. In England (section §6.04), the alleged contractual nature of consent awards expands the potential grounds for challenges, whereas in France (section §6.05), according to a regrettable decision rendered by the *Cour de cassation*, the enforcement of domestic consent awards is not possible.

§6.02 THE AWARD BY CONSENT IN ICC ARBITRATION

As explained in Chapter 2, the ICC had originally set up a dispute resolution model that was built around a central goal: attempting to preserve the commercial relations between the parties. To this effect, significant emphasis was placed on the role of conciliation.[570] Where this option was no longer viable, the arbitrators acting under the aegis of this institution were expected to resolve the disputes in an amicable manner, leaving room to equitable considerations that are now absent in ICC arbitration. Only in case of failure of the conciliation procedure could the parties bring the matter to arbitration. Even then, however, settlements were still encouraged. In particular, Article 19 of the 1927 *ICC Rules* provided that where the parties had reached a settlement during the course of the arbitration, this could be recorded either in an award by consent, or in the form of an agreement drawn up by the arbitrators and signed by them and by the parties.[571] It is clear that in the latter scenario, the arbitrators were mostly acting as conciliators rather than adjudicators, helping to draft an acceptable settlement to the parties.[572] Be that as it may, the provision at hand was

---

567. UNCITRAL, *Report of the Working Group II on the Work of its Sixty-Fifth Session*, A/CN.9/896 (30 September 2016), at para. 52; UNCITRAL, *Report of the Working Group II on the Work of its Sixty-Sixth Session*, A/CN.9/901 (16 February 2017) at para. 32.
568. Cf. *Ibid.* at para. 7 (interestingly enough, the Working Group is considering to extend the enforcement under the new instrument to settlements reached during arbitral proceedings, when their enforcement as consent awards is not possible in the State where such enforcement is sought).
569. *See generally* Stacie Strong, *Beyond International Commercial Arbitration? The Promise of International Commercial Mediation*, 45 Wash. U. J. L. & Pol'y 11 (2014).
570. 1927 ICC Rules, Art. 1: In the event of a business dispute arising between persons, firms or companies of different nationalities or which possesses an international element or character any of the parties to the dispute may seek the good offices of the Administrative Commission of the International Chamber of Commerce with a view *to settlement of the dispute by the acceptance of friendly suggestions made by that Commission* [emphasis added]. ICC Document No 2515, Arbitration Committee, 17 February 1927 [unpublished] (English).
571. ICC Document No 2515, Arbitration Committee, 17 February 1927 [unpublished] (English).
572. Cf. UNCITRAL, *Draft Instrument for the Enforcement of Mediated Settlements* (Art. 2(3)): '"Conciliation" means a process, regardless of the expression used and irrespective of the basis upon which the conciliation is carried out, whereby parties attempt to reach an amicable settlement of their dispute with the assistance of a third person or persons ("the conciliator") lacking the authority to impose a solution upon the parties to the dispute.' Cf. Art. 1(3) of the UNCITRAL *Model Law on International Commercial Conciliation* (2002) ('conciliation' means

introduced despite the scepticism expressed by the American committee, with the view to providing parties with the possibility of proving the existence of a settlement either during proceedings before a national court seized to re-examine the dispute or in the event of the opposing party's insolvency.[573]

The confusion between the role of conciliators and arbitrators disappeared as early as 1933, with a new version of the *ICC Rules*. Settlement agreements were addressed by Article 20, according to which in case of settlement during the course of the arbitration the parties could simply request the arbitrators to issue a consent award, thus excluding the possibility of having an agreement drawn up by the arbitrators.[574] The provision was modified in order to provide parties with a unique and clear outcome: an enforceable award.[575] It was felt that a simple agreement signed by the arbitrators and the parties was weak if compared to a consent award, which would be enforceable in case of failure to comply with its terms.[576] This choice was not unanimously welcomed. Concerns were expressed with respect to the ICC International Court of Arbitration's role of approving awards by consent. Since every award had to be reviewed and approved by the court, this approval process could stand as an obstacle to the recognition of the parties' agreement in its entirety.[577] To avoid the review by the ICC court, it was suggested that the award by consent in Article 20 should not be regarded as an actual award but rather as 'minutes recording a new agreement entered into by the parties'.[578] However, as rightly observed by Mr Sambuc, vice-president of the court, the powers of the court would be very limited in reviewing awards by consent, which, in any event, had previously been approved without modifications in the vast majority of cases.[579] Moreover, the court's intervention was considered essential. It could be, in fact, that the provisions of the parties' agreement were not accurately reflected in their award or that the same contained contradictions or evident omissions; in these cases, the court could draw the parties' attention to such defects and avoid any future issues of enforcement.[580]

---

a process, whether referred to by the expression conciliation, mediation or an expression of similar import, whereby parties request a third person or persons ('the conciliator') to assist them in their attempt to reach an amicable settlement of their dispute arising out of or relating to a contractual or other legal relationship. The conciliator does not have the authority to impose upon the parties a solution to the dispute).

573. ICC Document No 2583, Arbitration Committee, 4 February 1927 [unpublished] (French; intervention of Mr Henri Sambuc (representative of Indochina)).
574. Article 20, 1933 *ICC Rules* ('Should the parties reach an agreement before the arbitrators or arbitrator, this shall be recorded in the form of an award made by consent of the parties').
575. Craig, Park & Paulsson, *supra* n. 263, at 366 ('The primary concern of ICC Tribunals and the Court of Arbitration is to provide awards having international currency–awards which are recognized de facto in international business milieux as having the intrinsic value of persuasive and authoritative resolutions of disputes, and enforceable de jure in the greatest possible number of jurisdictions').
576. ICC Document No 5288, Arbitration Committee, 2 June 1933 [unpublished] (English; intervention of Mr René Arnaud (technical advisor)).
577. ICC Document No 5743, Arbitration Committee, 19 December 1935 [unpublished] at 4 (French).
578. *Ibid.* at 5.
579. ICC Document No 5747, Arbitration Committee, 19 December 1935 [unpublished] at 2 (French; observations presented by Mr Henri Sambuc).
580. *Ibid.*

It was also noted that it would be wise for arbitrators to invite parties to introduce an ICC arbitration clause into settlement agreements recorded in consent awards, so that, in case of breach or difficulties, the parties could avoid litigation in front of national courts.[581] In conclusion, the arbitration committee decided to confirm the power of review of the ICC court in cases of awards by consent, inviting it, however, to exercise such power in moderation and in a timely manner.[582]

The 1998 version of the *ICC Rules* introduced a significant amendment to the provision on settlement agreements (now contained in Article 33 of the 2017 *ICC Rules*). In particular, it recognized (in Article 26) that the arbitrators had discretion in agreeing to record the settlement in the form of an award, something for which the previous version of the rules had not explicitly allowed. The current version of the provision, which has remained unaltered, reads:

> If the parties reach a settlement after the file has been transmitted to the arbitral tribunal in accordance with Article 16, the settlement shall be recorded in the form of an award made by consent of the parties, if so requested by the parties and *if the arbitral tribunal agrees to do so*. [emphasis added]

As it has been correctly noted, the reason for requiring the tribunal's approval is essentially to avoid violations of relevant mandatory laws and other fraudulent or illegal terms.[583] This also explains why the request will be treated by the arbitrators themselves, once the tribunal has been constituted, which is the simplest way to permit them to familiarize with the facts of the case and the parties' claims.

As two commentators observed, this provision aims to avoid manipulations of the consent award, such as through 'the creation of a fictitious dispute designed to create a payment obligation for the purpose of tax deductibility or money laundering'.[584] To this effect, the tribunal may express comments directed to the parties – especially where the settlement agreement was presented in draft form – 'on potential problems that may arise to future disagreements, such as the allocation of costs, ... issues as to statements of fact accepted by the parties or [compliance with] the mandatory principles of applicable law'.[585] The provision also makes clear that the rendering of an award by consent is to be considered only pursuant to a joint request by the parties. In this respect, it should be noted that 'silence or apparent acquiescence is not sufficient'.[586]

From a practical point of view, statistics show that, in 2015, 29 out of 498 approved by the ICC Court were made by consent.[587] In 2014, 38 out of 459 ICC awards were made by consent.[588] To be fair, however, the number of consent awards should

---

581. *Ibid.* at 3.
582. ICC Document No 5761, Arbitration Committee, 19 December 1935 [unpublished] at 6 (Français).
583. Yves Derains & Eric Schwartz, *A Guide to ICC Rules of Arbitration*, 310 (Kluwer Law 2005).
584. Craig, Park & Paulsson, *supra* n. 263, at 359. Along the same lines, *see* Webster & Bühler, *supra* n. 453 at 496.
585. Webster & Bühler, *supra* n. 442, at 496.
586. Fry, Greenberg & Mazza, *supra* n. 449, at 326.
587. *ICC Statistics 2015*, 26:1 ICC Bull 9 (2016).
588. *2014 Statistical Report*, 25:1 ICC Bull 14 (2015).

be compared *exclusively* to the number of final awards,[589] thus excluding partial awards, which do not exclude a future settlement and arguably encourage it (126 interim awards were issued in 2015, and 105 in 2014). If we adopt this approach, the percentage of consent awards slightly increases (7,79% in 2015, and 10,73% in 2014). The sudden enthusiasm will quickly fade however: an even greater proportion of consent awards can be found in the 2003 statistics: 36 consent awards out of 234 final awards (over a total of 369 awards, 99 of which were interim awards), bringing the annual percentage of consent awards to 15.38% in 2003.[590] These statistics indicate a relative decrease in the number of consent awards, which is confirmed by comparing the 2009-2013 average (12.54%) against the 2004-2008 average (15.09%).[591] If we further take into account the 1999-2003 average (17.75%), the gradual decline in the number of consent awards in ICC arbitration becomes apparent.[592]

These figures should also be compared with the annual number of withdrawn cases, but there are no official statistics on the latter. The official Secretariat's commentary to the 2012 *ICC Rules* indicates that around 47% of cases are eventually withdrawn and that this will likely happen when the parties are able to reach a settlement.[593] In fact, a withdrawal may be preferred when there is no realistic need to enforce the settlement via the *New York Convention*, or when the increase in administrative expenses and arbitrator fees relating to an award by consent does not appear worthwhile.[594] Other reasons for favouring withdrawal of cases may involve matters of confidentiality, as confidentiality could be better preserved by avoiding divulgation of the terms of the settlement to the tribunal and the ICC International Court of Arbitration.

Strictly speaking, consent awards can take two different forms, the first one being that of attaching the settlement agreement to the award, while making all the necessary orders related thereto (including costs), and the second one being that of terminating the proceedings and merely awarding costs.[595] In any event, as explained in the Conclusion to this chapter, the main difference between incorporation and non-incorporation of the settlement within the award by consent lies in the fact that, in the former case, the agreement may have greater chances of being enforced under the *New York Convention*. Therefore, while generally speaking, the first option should be preferred, it may nonetheless become superfluous whenever the terms of the settlement have already been performed by the parties. Moreover, it is worth noting that the

---

589. A different approach was taken by Webster & Bühler (*supra* n. 442, at 493), who compared the number of consent awards against the total number of awards.
590. *2003 Statistical Report*, 15:1 ICC Bull 15 (2004).
591. All the figures are calculated on the basis of the annual report published in the *ICC International Court of Arbitration Bulletin*. In sum, the annual figures are the following: 12.23% (2013); 9.09% (2012); 11.81% (2011); 14.43% (2010); 14.71% (2009); 14.17% (2008); 13.45% (2007); 17.88% (2006); 15.86% (2005); 14.09% (2004). Over the past ten years, the average is 13.77%.
592. The annual figures are the following: 15.38% (2003); 17.31% (2002); 16.51% (2001); 16.13% (2000); 23.46% (1999).
593. Fry, Greenberg & Mazza, *supra* n. 449, at 323.
594. *Ibid.* at 324.
595. For an application, *see* ICC Final Award No 16426/2011 and No 12656/2006, discussed in Marchisio, *supra* n. 562, at 335-336.

UNCITRAL's instrument on the enforcement of settlements might allow for the enforcement of the agreement when this is not recorded in the form of an award, which could, in some instances, be a better option than attempting to enforce the settlement recorded in the form of a consent award.[596]

Finally, one should not forget that the basic scenario in which all parties decide to settle the dispute with respect to all claims brought forth is not the only existing one. For instance, a settlement may cover only part of the claims before the arbitrators. In this case, the arbitrators will likely issue only a partial award by consent and settle the remaining claims in a final award. Alternatively, a settlement may be reached only between the claimant and one of the respondents: in this case, the arbitration continues, but its scope is limited. Moreover, in order to avoid inconsistencies, the parties may wish to defer the formal entry of the consent award against one of the respondents until the tribunal has reached a decision on the claims against the others.

§6.03 THE AWARD BY CONSENT AND THE UNCITRAL *MODEL LAW* ON INTERNATIONAL COMMERCIAL ARBITRATION

In light of the ICC experience, it is unsurprising that a significant number of the leading jurisdictions in the field of international arbitration provide arbitrators with the power to record a settlement reached by the parties to an arbitration.[597] These provisions are strongly inspired by Article 30(1) of the UNCITRAL *Model Law*, which states:

> If, during arbitral proceedings, the parties settle the dispute, the arbitral tribunal shall terminate the proceedings and, if requested by the parties and not objected to by the arbitral tribunal, record the settlement in the form of an arbitral award on agreed terms.

The *travaux préparatoires* of the 1985 version of the *Model Law* indicate that there was no extensive discussion of this provision. This may be related, in part, to the existence of a similar provision in the 1976 UNCITRAL *Arbitration Rules* (Article 34.1).[598] UNCITRAL had in fact already worked on this topic: during the drafting of the *Arbitration Rules*, the inclusion of a provision addressing the possibility of recording a settlement in an award was presented as a necessity, already acknowledged in the provisions of several authoritative arbitration rules, including Article 43 of the 1968 International Centre for the Settlement of Investment Disputes (ICSID) *Arbitration*

---

596. Cf. Art. 1(3), UNCITRAL, *Draft Instrument on Enforcement of International Commercial Settlement Agreements resulting from Conciliation* (2017).
597. *Inter alia* section 51 of the English *Arbitration Act 1996* (UK), c 23; section 66 of the Hong Kong *Arbitration Ordinance* (Cap 609, No 38 of 2011); section 37 of the Singapore *Arbitration Act* (Cap 10, 2002 Rev. Ed. Sing); section 36 of the Ontario *Arbitration Act, 1991*, SO 1991, c 17; Art. 1712 of the Belgian *Code of Civil Procedure*; Art. 1053 of the German *Code of Civil Procedure*.
598. 'Si, avant que la sentence ne soit rendue, les parties conviennent d'une transaction qui règle le litige, le tribunal arbitral rend une ordonnance de clôture de la procédure arbitrale ou, si les deux parties lui en font la demande et s'il l'accepte, constate le fait par une sentence arbitrale rendue d'accord parties. Cette sentence n'a pas à être motivée'.

Rules.[599] In other words, settlement was correctly treated as a case of termination of the proceedings, which could, under certain circumstances, be recorded in an award.

According to the drafters of the *Model Law*, the main advantage of recording a settlement agreement was that the agreement would acquire 'the legal force of an award'.[600] The enthusiasm for such a convenient solution should have probably been tempered, given the failure to consider *how* the award by consent would obtain such legal force. Left aside in the discussion was that, contrary to the ICSID *Arbitration Rules* – which, being ancillary to the 1965 *Convention on the Settlement of Investment Disputes Between States and Nationals of Other States*,[601] were able to guarantee the legal force of awards on agreed terms – the *Model Law* was not able per se to attribute binding force to such awards given its nature as a soft law instrument. The power to give legal effect to awards on agreed terms was thus left to separate instruments, such as the 1958 *New York Convention*,[602] and, at the national level, to various domestic arbitration acts. In this particular scenario, the automatic inclusion of the notion of an award on agreed terms among the awards enforceable under the *New York Convention* could not be taken for granted.

An awareness of the possible difficulties relating to awards on agreed terms, in the legal framework of international commercial arbitration, is evinced in the UNCITRAL working group's decision to consider allowing the enforcement of settlement agreements as such – through a specific provision of the *Model Law* – without requiring their incorporation within an arbitral award.[603] This is a cure that would have probably killed the patient, as it would have opened the door to a high degree of discretion on the part of national legislators willing to adopt the *Model Law*, thus preventing the creation of a uniform setting for the enforcement of the agreements reached during arbitration proceedings. This proposition was thus rejected in light of a precise expectation that national courts would allow the enforcement of awards on agreed terms under the *New York Convention*, thanks to the clarification found in Article 30(2) of the *Model Law*, according to which an award by consent 'has the same status and effect as any other award on the merits of the case'.[604]

---

599. UNCITRAL, *Report of the Secretary General: Preliminary Draft Set of Arbitration Rules for Optional Use in Ad Hoc Arbitration Relating to International Trade (UNCITRAL Arbitration Rules)*, UN Doc A/CN.9/97 (1973) at 178 [UNCITRAL, *Arbitration Rules Draft*]. For a commentary on the 2006 version of the ICSID *Arbitration Rules*, see Christoph H. Schreuer et al., *The ICSID Convention: A Commentary*, 824 ff. (2nd ed., Cambridge University Press 2009).
600. UNCITRAL, *Arbitration Rules Draft*, supra n. 600, at 178.
601. *Convention on the Settlement of Investment Disputes between States and Nationals of Other States*, 18 March 1965, 575 UNTS 159, 17 UST 1270. See Yaraslau Kryvoi & Dmitry Davydenko, *Consent Awards in International Arbitration: From Settlement to Enforcement*, 40:3 Brook J Int'l L 827, 854–855 (2015).
602. See UNCITRAL, *Report of the Working Group on International Contract Practices on the Work of Its 4th Session*, UN Doc A/CN.9/232 (10 November 1982) at paras 174, 149 [UNCITRAL, *Model Law 4th Session*].
603. *Ibid.* at paras 173, 149.
604. UNCITRAL, *Report of the Working Group on International Contract Practices on the Work of Its 6th Session*, UN Doc A/CN.9/245 (22 September 1983) at paras 24, 95.

Two other points were considered in the *travaux préparatoires*, which I shall now address in turn: (i) the discretion of arbitrators in refusing to record a settlement; and (ii) the requirements of the request for an award on agreed terms. We know from the discussions of the 1976 UNCITRAL *Arbitration Rules* that the starting point with respect to awards by consent was to treat parties' settlements as a case of termination of the arbitration proceedings.[605] This starting point is confirmed by the current wording of the first sentence of Article 30(1) of the *Model Law*, which states that '[i]f, during arbitral proceedings, the parties settle the dispute, the arbitral tribunal shall terminate the proceeding'. What still needed to be decided by the drafters of the *Model Law*, then, were the conditions upon which an arbitral tribunal could record such a settlement.

During the drafting of the *Model Law*, a proposal was first made by the Australian delegation, suggesting that awards by consent ought to be automatically granted by the arbitral tribunal.[606] This line of reasoning was supported by the French representative, who stated that the tribunal should by no means interfere with the agreement of the parties, arbitration being a form of private justice.[607]

The American and Canadian delegations disagreed, maintaining that arbitrators should not be constrained by the parties' decision but rather are required to approve it and thus to consider – for instance – potential antitrust and tax issues.[608] Concerns were also expressed with respect to cases of 'suspected fraud, illicit or utterly unfair settlement terms'.[609] It is worth noting that, when similar objections were raised during the drafting of the UNCITRAL *Arbitration Rules*, it was agreed that arbitrators should have discretion regarding the decision to record a settlement, should it appear to be 'unlawful or against public policy'.[610]

These criticisms ultimately led to the withdrawal of the Australian proposal[611] and the preservation of the expression '[unless] objected by the arbitral tribunal' contained in Article 30(1) of the *Model Law*. Therefore, the idea that prevailed was that of granting a discretionary power to arbitrators, which would result in a form of scrutiny of the contents of the settlement on the basis, for instance, of applicable mandatory rules and public policy. It was, in fact, noted that excluding a discretionary power would have left arbitrators with the possibility of resigning in cases where they

---

605. UNCITRAL, *Arbitration Rules Draft*, supra n. 600, at 178.
606. UNCITRAL, *Summary Records of the 305th to 333rd Meetings Held at the Vienna International Centre, Vienna, 3–21 June 1985*, UN Doc A/CN.9/SR.305-333 (3–21 June 1985) at para. 4 [UNCTIRAL, *Model Law Summary Records*].
607. *Ibid.* at para. 11.
608. *Ibid.* at paras 6, 9.
609. UNCITRAL, *Report of the Secretary General: Analytical Commentary on Draft Text of a Model Law on International Commercial Arbitration*, UN Doc A/CN.9/264 (25 March 1985) at 65 [UNCITRAL, *Model Law Analytical Commentary*].
610. UNCITRAL, *Report of the Secretary General: Revised Draft Set of Arbitration Rules for Optional Use in Ad Hoc Arbitration Relating to International Trade (UNCITRAL Arbitration Rules)*, UN Doc A/CN.9/112 (7 November 1975) at 179.
611. UNCITRAL, *Model Law Summary Records*, supra n. 607, at para. 17.

held strong objections to the settlement,[612] a highly negative occurrence in the final stages of an arbitration, entailing a great loss of time and resources in order to appoint a replacement.

I should, however, stress the fact that no precise criteria were identified as certainly applicable in the exercise of such discretion; the decision ultimately rests on the sense of justice of the arbitral tribunal, which may also take into account whether third parties' interests are affected.[613]

As for the second condition, that is, the requirements relating to the request for an award by consent, the discussions addressed whether such a request should come from both parties. The Canadian delegation expressed some doubts, fearing that a joint request would confer a veto power to one of the parties, which could thus 'easily block the arbitral tribunal from recording a settlement in the form of an arbitral award'.[614] The Italian delegation objected to the Canadian proposal, since a request by only one of the parties 'could easily be understood as implying that no further agreement was needed to transform the contractual agreement into an award'.[615]

Despite the fact that a unilateral request would have been more simple, given that one of the parties usually has a greater interest in recording the settlement – either because it is a favourable one, or because of other economic reasons – it was felt that there would be less danger of injustice (e.g., in case of a great imbalance between the economic resources of the opposing parties) if a request from both parties was required.[616] From a practical point of view, the request may be forwarded to the tribunal by only one of the parties, provided that the opposing party agrees.[617]

The *travaux préparatoires* do not discuss how the settlement can be reached by the parties, thus allowing for a certain degree of liberty. Curiously enough, the commentary on the revised draft of the UNCITRAL *Arbitration Rules* explains that the parties may either chose to submit a written copy of a settlement agreement reached outside the arbitration proceedings or simply request that the settlement reached orally during the course of a hearing (possibly with the assistance of the arbitrators) be recorded.[618]

---

612. UNCITRAL, *Report of the United Nation Commission on International Trade Law on the Work of Its Eighteenth Session, 3–21 June 1985*, UN Doc A/40/17 (1985) at para. 249 [UNCITRAL, 18th Session Report].
613. The *Report of the United Nations Commission on International Trade Law on the Work of Its Eighteenth Session, 3–21 June 1985* concluded that 'arbitrators should not be forced to attach their signatures to whatever settlement the parties have reached since the terms of such settlement might, in exceptional cases, be in conflict with binding laws or public policy, including fundamental notions of fairness and justice' (*Ibid*).
614. UNCITRAL, *Report of the Secretary General: Analytical Compilation of Comments by Governments and International Organizations on the Draft Text of a Model Law on International Commercial Arbitration*, UN Doc A/CN.9/263, Add. 1 (15 April 1985) at 17.
615. UNCITRAL, *Model Law Summary Records, supra* n. 607, at para. 19.
616. UNCITRAL, *Model Law Analytical Commentary, supra* n. 610, at 65.
617. UNCITRAL, *18th Session Report, supra* n. 613, at para. 250.
618. *Arbitration Rules Draft, supra* n. 600, at 179. This conclusion was different from the one enshrined in the 1968 ICSID *Arbitration Rules* (Art. 43.2): 'If the parties file with the Secretary-General the full and signed text of their settlement and in writing request the Tribunal to embody such settlement in an award, the Tribunal may record the settlement in the form of its award'.

§6.04 CONSENT AWARDS IN ENGLAND

[A] The National Framework

Consent awards are dealt with by the *Arbitration Act 1996*. Pursuant to section 2(1), the act applies where the seat of the arbitration is in England and Wales or Northern Ireland. Section 51 of the act states:

> Settlement.
> (1) If during arbitral proceedings the parties settle the dispute, the following provisions apply unless otherwise agreed by the parties.
> (2) The tribunal shall terminate the substantive proceedings and, if so requested by the parties and not objected to by the tribunal, shall record the settlement in the form of an agreed award.
> (3) An agreed award shall state that it is an award of the tribunal and shall have the same status and effect as any other award on the merits of the case.
> (4) The following provisions of this Part relating to awards (sections 52 to 58) apply to an agreed award.
> (5) Unless the parties have also settled the matter of the payment of the costs of the arbitration, the provisions of this Part relating to costs (sections 59 to 65) continue to apply.

The above provision was strongly influenced by Article 30 of the *Model Law*.[619] However, regarding the relationship between the *Model Law* and section 51, as in other cases of legal transplant, a norm, once introduced into a given legal system, acquires a different form. The transplanted notion is, in fact, exposed to a pre-existing *humus* – what Patrick Glenn defines as 'legal tradition'[620] – and is re-elaborated in the light of other notions that together define a certain legal context. Therefore, in order to understand how section 51 of the *Arbitration Act 1996* operates, we should first analyse the notion of 'settlement' in English law.

Preliminarily, it should be noted that settlements can be achieved either with courts' cooperation (i.e., through orders by consent or Tomlin orders) or through a *pure* agreement (the so-called compromise).[621] While the following comparative overview will focus primarily on settlements embodied in court orders or judgments, I cannot refrain from first providing at least a very general definition of 'compromise', understood in purely contractual terms. In this respect, a well-regarded authority gives the following definition:

> In order to establish a valid compromise, it must be shown that there has been an agreement (accord) which is complete and certain in its terms, and that consideration (satisfaction) has been given or promised in return for the promised or actual forbearance to pursue the claim. It is a good defence to an action for breach of contract to show that the cause of action has been validly compromised. At common law, accord and satisfaction was no answer to claim on a specialty, but

---

619. Saville, *supra* n. 43, at 311.
620. Glenn, *supra* n. 40, at 4.
621. Neil Andrews, *Civil Procedure* in Andrew Burrows, *English Private Law* 1320, 1365 (3rd ed., Oxford University Press 2013). For further references, *see* generally David Foskett, *The Law and Practice of Compromise* (7th ed., Sweet & Maxwell 2010).

the rule was otherwise in equity and the latter now prevails. The accord need not be in writing even if the contract which is sought to discharge, or for the breach of which a claim is made, is required by law to be made or evidenced in writing. An oral accord will suffice unless the accord itself constitutes a contract or transaction which is required to be made or evidenced in writing.[622]

The essential element of a compromise, therefore, is the consideration given or promised in return for an actual or promised forbearance to pursue an identified claim. If the agreement is not executed spontaneously, the innocent party can bring suit for breach of contract. This may, however, be inconvenient at times. A higher degree of certainty, and much more effective enforcement, can be attained if the content of the agreement is reproduced in a measure emanating from a court. In this case, the *compromise* is the *conditio sine qua non* of the measure. Such measures can be of two types: (i) consent judgments and orders, and (ii) Tomlin orders.

Consent judgments and orders are addressed by rule 40.6 of the 1998 *CPR*,[623] which applies where 'all the parties agree the terms in which a judgment should be given or an order should be made' (paragraph 1). The most important judgments and orders subject to this rule are those concerning damages, specific performance (e.g., delivery of goods), dismissals, or stays of proceedings (paragraph 3). Similar results may be reached with a Tomlin order.[624] Such an order would usually provide that the 'proceedings be stayed save for the purpose of giving effect to the terms [attached to the order], for which there be liberty to apply'.[625] The difference between a consent order and a Tomlin order is that, while in the former, the settlement is incorporated into the order, in the latter 'the parties seek a stay of the proceedings on terms that the parties will comply with the agreement in the schedule'.[626] Therefore:

> [i]n the case of a Tomlin Order a stay is given on the basis that the agreement is complied with. The terms of the schedule are not ordered by the court. Frequently the terms of the agreement in the schedule to a Tomlin Order are detailed and contain matters which go beyond the scope of the original dispute in the proceedings.[627]

Moreover, as far as the interpretation of a Tomlin order is concerned, in *Sirius International Insurance Co v. FAI General Insurance Ltd*, it was held that:

> [t]he settlement contained in the Tomlin order must be construed as a commercial instrument. The aim of the inquiry is not to probe the real intentions of the parties but to ascertain the contextual meaning of the relevant contractual language. The inquiry is objective: the question is what a reasonable person, circumstanced as the actual parties were, would have understood the parties to have meant by the

---

622. Ewan McKendrick, *Discharge by Agreement* in Hugh Beale, *Chitty on Contracts* 1607, 1612 (31st ed., Sweet &Maxwell 2012).
623. *Civil Procedure Rules 1998* (UK), Part 40 ('Judgments and Orders'). For a commentary, *see* Lord Justice Jackson, *Civil Procedure: The White Book*, 1209 ff. (Sweet & Maxwell 2012).
624. *Dashwood v. Dashwood* (1927) 71 SJ 911.
625. *Community Care North East v. Durham County Council* [2010] EWHC 959 (QB) para. 5 [*Community Care*].
626. *Ibid.* at para. 25.
627. *Ibid.* at para. 26.

use of specific language. The answer to that question is to be gathered from the text under consideration and its relevant contextual scene.[628]

Each of these court measures, however, has certain downsides. Regarding Tomlin orders, essentially, a party cannot enforce the settlement attached in the schedule of the order: the contractual nature of the settlement prevails over the nature of the adjudicative measure.[629] Conversely, with a consent order, the party *can* enforce the terms of the settlement since they are incorporated into the order; moreover, said order is less vulnerable to the contractual pathologies of the underlying agreement (e.g., an unforeseen change of circumstances). This point requires further explanation: in particular, to what extent can a court vary the terms of these orders?

As far as Tomlin orders are concerned, the point is extensively discussed in *Community Care North East v. Dashwood* by Mr Justice Ramsey, who, after considering several authorities, concluded that the court has no general power to vary the agreement attached to the order unless such power arises as a matter of the law of contract.[630] The same is true for consent orders. As put by Mr Justice Warren:

> [A] consent order embodying an agreement which settles litigation can be set aside on the same grounds as any other agreement. This can occur, for instance, where a settlement agreement has been procured by fraud or as a result of misrepresentation or, perhaps more relevantly for present purposes, where the agreement is based on common mistake.[631]

Furthermore, the 'court will have jurisdiction to vary [or to set aside] ... [a consent] order, or part of it, which is void under the general law'.[632] Other grounds for setting aside or varying a consent order – which appear, however, to be limited to orders made in the Family Division[633] – are:

> (1) cases in which it is alleged there was at the date of the order an erroneous basis of fact e.g. misrepresentations or misunderstanding as to the position or assets. (2) cases in which there has been a material or unforeseen change in circumstances after the order so as to undermine or invalidate the basis of the consent order and known as a supervening event.[634]

Aside from these grounds, as held in *Hudson v. New Media Holding Company*,[635] courts will enjoy a residual power, pursuant to rule 3.1(6) *CPR*, to vary consent orders in matters related to case management, 'such as extending dates agreed for disclosure of documents'.[636]

---

628. *Sirius International Insurance Co v. FAI General Insurance Ltd* [2004] UKHL 54 at para. 18.
629. *Green v. Rozen* [1955] 2 All ER 796. Here, the application to enforce a settlement was rejected as the terms had been registered only in the counsels' briefs.
630. *Community Care*, supra n. 626, at para. 34.
631. *Ibid.* at para. 56.
632. *Ibid.* at para. 62.
633. *Hudson v. New Media Holding Company LLC* [2011] EWHC 3068 (QB) at para. 18 [*Hudson*] (commenting but not deciding on the matter). *See also Community Care*, supra n. 626, at para. 36.
634. *S v. S (Ancillary Relief: Consent Order)* [2003] Fam 1 at para. 4 [references omitted].
635. *Hudson*, supra n. 634.
636. *Ibid.* at para. 27.

Finally, as far as estoppels are concerned, I should mention that both Tomlin orders and consent orders:

> [are] capable of creating an estoppel such as will bar a party from bringing a second action and does create an estoppel if the parties to the second action are the same as the parties to the first and the issues raised in the second action were necessarily compromised in the first action. Whether this type of estoppel should properly be described as estoppel by res judicata or whether it would more accurately be described as estoppel by conduct does not greatly matter. It might be more logical if the term res judicata were reserved for cases in which the issues had been determined by a judge of competent jurisdiction.[637]

Closing this parenthesis, we can now return to the specific case of consent awards rendered in England under the *Arbitration Act 1996*.

[B] Consent Awards under the *Arbitration Act 1996*

[1] The Role of the Arbitrators

Arbitrators sitting in England play two essential roles with respect to settlement agreements. First, arbitrators are expected to exercise a form of control over the content of the compromise reached by the parties.[638] This does not entail that they should be playing an active role in the settlement negotiations, particularly with respect to the scope of the negotiations and the way in which they are conducted,[639] but rather that the tribunal should verify if the award has any 'objectionable feature'[640] capable of deceiving third parties (such as tax authorities),[641] or 'other public policy reasons that would justify' a refusal.[642] It should be noted that a decision to issue an award that forms part of an unlawful scheme can engender the criminal liability of the members of the tribunal.[643]

The control over the content of a settlement is a corollary of the jurisdiction of an arbitral tribunal. The settlement must never exceed the scope of the dispute submitted to the arbitrators. While some elements reasonably related to the original submissions may eventually become part of the settlement, the jurisdictional role of the arbitrators (assessing the conformity of the settlement with the applicable mandatory rules and public policy) can be exercised only after a review of the submissions, documents, and evidence related to the parties' claims. Therefore, in this case, requesting that the

---

637. *Zurich Insurance Company Plc v. Hayward* [2011] EWCA Civ 641 at paras 23, and 25.
638. Sutton et al., *supra* n. 92, at 237.
639. Merkin & Flannery, *supra* n. 96, at 223 (the authors further cite an interesting case, *Wicketts and Sterndale v. Brine Builders* [2001] CILL 1805, where '[a]n attempt by the arbitrator ... to control the settlement negotiations by directions in order to secure payment of his own fees, was described by HHJ Seymour QC as "outrageous" and merited the removal of the arbitrator under section 24 of the 1996 Act').
640. Saville, *supra* n. 43, at para. 242.
641. Merkin & Flannery, *supra* n. 96, at 223.
642. *Ibid.*
643. Saville, *supra* n. 43, at para. 242.

arbitrators record a settlement that goes beyond such scope in the form of an award cannot be regarded as a valid extension of the arbitrators' jurisdiction.[644]

Second, arbitrators are also 'the appropriate forum before which to bring the issue of validity of the compromise'.[645] This is consistent with section 30 of the *Arbitration Act 1996*, according to which an arbitral tribunal may rule on its own substantive jurisdiction, unless otherwise agreed by the parties. Since a compromise puts an end to their mandate and exhausts their jurisdictional power, arbitrators should be the judges of their own jurisdiction. It is immaterial whether, in making such a decision, they may be mere *putative* arbitrators (i.e., arbitrators who do not have jurisdiction over the dispute). This is confirmed by a recent trend in favour of giving effect to arbitrators' rulings by which jurisdiction over the subject matter is declined (a 'negative jurisdictional ruling').[646]

Finally, once parties have reached a settlement, the tribunal becomes *functus officio*; that is, it is deprived of its jurisdictional power over the dispute.[647]

This loss of jurisdiction, as explained by section 51 of the *Arbitration Act 1996*, can either result from an order declaring the end of the proceedings or from the award on agreed terms. We should be cautious however, for, when the settlement agreement is *infra petita* – that is, when its scope does not cover the entire dispute before the arbitrators – the tribunal will retain jurisdiction over the remaining questions. As stated in *Dawes v. Treasure and Son Ltd*:

> The settlement of a dispute after it has been referred to arbitration but before any final award does not generally, and certainly does not necessarily, bring to an end the jurisdiction. Section 51 suggests that even if the dispute is settled there remains a jurisdiction to terminate the substantive proceedings and to resolve issues of costs or indeed any other matters remaining in dispute at that time.[648]

In any event, 'unless the parties have also settled the matter of the payment of the costs of the arbitration', the tribunal retains jurisdiction over this matter (section 51(5) of the *Arbitration Act 1996*).

[2] Challenges

It is quite clear that the grounds in the *Arbitration Act 1996* for challenging an award rendered in England, including an award by consent, were not devised with this peculiar type of award in mind. This is so because most of the grounds would be excluded *ipso facto* by the settlement reached by the parties. In fact, as stated in section 73(1) of the act:

---

644. The rationale behind this conclusion can be better appreciated in the context of the ICC *Arbitration Rules*, where Art. 23(4) (*acte de mission*) limits the boundaries of the tribunal's jurisdiction following the inception of the procedure.
645. Michael Black, *Arbitrations* in Foskett, *supra* n. 622, at 523.
646. *See* Marchisio, *Jurisdictional Matters*, *supra* n. 466, at 467.
647. On the doctrine of *functus officio*, *see Chimimport Plc v. G d'Alesio SAS* [1994] 2 Lloyd's Law Reports 366.
648. *Dawes v. Treasure and Son Ltd* [2010] EWHC 3218 (TCC) at para. 29.

If a party to arbitral proceedings takes part, or continues to take part, in the proceedings without making, either forthwith or within such time as is allowed by the arbitration agreement or the tribunal or by any provision of this Part, any objection –

(a) that the tribunal lacks substantive jurisdiction,
(b) that the proceedings have been improperly conducted,
(c) that there has been a failure to comply with the arbitration agreement or with any provision of this Part, or
(d) that there has been any other irregularity affecting the tribunal or the proceedings,

he may not raise that objection later, before the tribunal or the court, unless he shows that, at the time he took part or continued to take part in the proceedings, he did not know and could not with reasonable diligence have discovered the grounds for the objection.

As a result, a party who becomes aware of a procedural irregularity is expected to raise an objection within the applicable time limit. If the parties have participated in the proceedings and obtained a settlement recorded in the form of an award, they cannot later claim, for instance, that the tribunal lacked jurisdiction or that there were other irregularities affecting the tribunal or the proceedings. The circumstances in which a settlement is reached are thus immaterial, as long as the parties have agreed upon the settlement. The agreement prevails over any potential irregularities that may have affected the proceedings or the arbitral tribunal.[649] The only exception amounts to a case where the parties have reached a settlement, and anchored the issuance of a consent award to one of the parties' failure to comply with said settlement. In this case, procedural irregularities committed before the issuance of the consent award could still be relevant, as it cannot be said that the parties have given *carte blanche* to the arbitrators. Similar arguments were raised In NRE *Coke Ltd v. Coeclerici Asia (PTE) Ltd.* In this case, the parties had reached–during the course of the arbitration–a settlement agreement containing the following provision:[650]

> In the event that NRE ... fail[s] to pay any of the Settlement Payments in accordance with this Payment Agreement, Coeclerici shall be entitled to resume the suspended arbitration proceedings ... In that event, NRE ... expressly and irrevocably agree[s] that Coeclerici will be entitled to *an immediate consent award*, without the need for any pleadings or hearings, for the following:
>
> (a) the Settlement Payments [set out at Clause 2 and amounting to US$8,500,000] less any sums paid after the date of this Payment Agreement;
> (b) all reasonable costs and expenses incurred after the date of default, including but not limited to legal costs, the costs of the Tribunal, arbitration costs and any legal or other costs ... .

---

649. Unless the interested party is able to show, under section 73(1) of the Arbitration Act, that despite a reasonable diligence, it was unaware of the grounds that could have supported a challenge.
650. [2013] EWHC 1987 at para. 4 [emphasis added].

According to the claimant, which sought the annulment of the award under section 68(2)(a) of the Arbitration Act (serious irregularity), the tribunal had only given it twenty-four hours to express its views as to whether the tribunal could issue a consent award.[651] As a result, the claimant would not have been afforded a reasonable opportunity to present its case.[652]

The court proceeded by identifying the proper test to deal with allegations of serious irregularities. To uphold a challenge under section 68(2), the court has to ask itself the following question: 'Is this an extreme case which justifies the court's intervention? Has the tribunal gone so wrong in its conduct of the arbitration, and is its conduct so far removed from what could be reasonably be expected from the arbitral process, that justice calls out for it to be corrected?'[653]

While the application to set aside the award was ultimately dismissed, the case underlines that it is still possible to commit procedural irregularities that might affect the consent award issued by the arbitrators. At the same time, these are truly

---

651. *Ibid.* at para. 19.
652. *Ibid.*
653. *Ibid.* at para. 25. The court relied on *Terna Bahrain-v-Al Shamsi* [2012] EWHC 3283, which spells the full test to deal with applications under section 68(2)(a) of the Arbitration Act. *See*, in particular, para. 85:

> (1) In order to make out a case for the court's intervention under s 68(2)(a), the Applicant must show:
>   (a) a breach of s 33 of the Act; ie that the tribunal has failed to act fairly and impartially between the parties, giving each a reasonable opportunity of putting his case and dealing with that of his opponent, adopting procedures so as to provide a fair means for the resolution of the matters falling to be determined;
>   (b) amounting to a serious irregularity;
>   (c) giving rise to substantial injustice
> (2) The test of a serious irregularity giving rise to substantial injustice involves a high threshold. The threshold is deliberately high because a major purpose of the 1996 Act was to reduce drastically the extent of intervention by the courts in the arbitral process.
> (3) A balance has to be drawn between the need for finality of the award and the need to protect parties against the unfair conduct of the arbitration. In striking this balance, only an extreme case will justify the court's intervention. Relief under s 68 will only be appropriate where the tribunal has gone so wrong in its conduct of the arbitration, and where its conduct is so far removed from what could be reasonably be expected from the arbitral process, that justice calls out for it to be corrected.
> (4) There will generally be a breach of s 33 where a tribunal decides the case on the basis of a point which one party has not had a fair opportunity to deal with. If the tribunal thinks that the parties have missed the real point, which has not been raised as an issue, it must warn the parties and give them an opportunity to address the point.
> (5) There is, however, an important distinction between, on the one hand, a party having no opportunity to address a point, or his opponent's case, and, on the other hand, a party failing to recognise or take the opportunity which exists. The latter will not involve a breach of s 33 or a serious irregularity.
> (6) The requirement of substantial injustice is additional to that of a serious irregularity, and the Applicant must establish both.
> (7) In determining whether there has been substantial injustice, the court is not required to decide for itself what would have happened in the arbitration had there been no irregularity. The Applicant does not need to show that the result would necessarily or even probably have been different. What the Applicant is required to show is that had he had an opportunity to address the point, the tribunal might well have reached a different view and produced a significantly different outcome.

exceptional circumstances, that are likely to arise only where the award by consent is issued at a later stage, after the parties have already reached a settlement agreement.

Other grounds for setting aside a consent award under English law are to be found in section 68(2) of the Arbitration Act *1996*, paragraphs (f) (uncertainty or ambiguity as to the effect of the award), (g) (award obtained by fraud or procured in a way contrary to public policy), (h) (failure to comply with the requirements as to the form of the award),[654] or (i) (any irregularity in the conduct of the proceedings or in the award that is admitted by the tribunal or by any arbitral or other institution or person vested by the parties with powers in relation to the proceedings or the award). Paragraphs (h) (form of the award) and (f) (uncertainty or ambiguity) do not require further consideration, for a court will not set aside an award 'unless it is satisfied that it would be inappropriate to remit the matters in question to the tribunal for reconsideration' (section 68(3) of the *Arbitration Act 1996*). It is clear that no authority is better suited than the arbitral tribunal to correct an issue of form and to clarify the terms of the award (in this case, the words of the parties' settlement). This is also dictated by section 57 of the act. Therefore, the most important grounds that may be relevant to consent awards are those covered by paragraphs (g) (award obtained by fraud or in a way contrary to public policy) and (i) (irregularity admitted by the tribunal).

While paragraph (i) 'provides the court with the power to intervene to correct admitted mistakes made by the tribunal which have not been corrected under the slip rule [section 57]',[655] paragraph (g) refers to 'an award being obtained by the fraud of a party to the arbitration or by the fraud of another to which a party to the arbitration was privy'.[656] In this latter case, the party making the complaint needs to show a causal link between the alleged conduct and the award. In the context of perjury and deliberate concealment of relevant documents, for instance, 'it will normally be necessary to satisfy the court that some form of reprehensible or unconscionable conduct on [the part of the opposing party] has contributed in a substantial way to obtaining an award in his favour'.[657] Furthermore, pursuant to section 68(2) of the act, the party challenging the award has to satisfy the court that it has suffered substantial injustice as a result of the alleged conduct.

---

654. Article 52 ('Form of award') of the *1996 Arbitration Act* provides as follows:

 (1) The parties are free to agree on the form of an award.
 (2) If or to the extent that there is no such agreement, the following provisions apply.
 (3) The award shall be in writing signed by all the arbitrators or all those assenting to the award.
 (4) The award shall contain the reasons for the award unless it is an agreed award or the parties have agreed to dispense with reasons.
 (5) The award shall state the seat of the arbitration and the date when the award is made.

655. David Wolfson & Susanna Charlwood, *Challenges to Arbitration Awards* in Julian D.M. Lew et al., *Arbitration in England, with Chapters on Scotland and Ireland* 527, 542 (Kluwer Law 2013).
656. *Elektrim SA v. Vivendi Universal SA* [2007] EWHC 11 (Comm) at para. 80. *See also Nestor Maritime SA v. Sea Anchor Shipping Co Ltd* [2012] EWHC 996 (Comm) at para. 13.
657. *Profilati Italia SRL & Painewebber Inc v. Painewebber International Futures Ltd* [2001] 1 Lloyd's Rep 715 at para. 17.

At this point, a question of paramount importance needs to be tackled. Given that consent is an essential element of awards on agreed terms, would it be possible to set these awards aside or to refuse enforcement for reasons other than those applicable to ordinary awards? As we shall see in a moment, this appears to be the case.

In general, grounds that would justify the setting aside of a contract 'would be sufficient to justify the setting aside of an arbitral award made by consent'.[658] In *Halpern v. Halpern*,[659] a party to a consent award – which dealt with the division of an estate pursuant to a will governed by Jewish law – sought specific performance of the compromise award and, alternatively, damages for repudiation of the compromise agreement.[660] One should note that the parties were of different nationalities and that the seat of the arbitration was in England. In their pleadings, the defendants put forth several defences, the most important being fraudulent misrepresentation, duress, mutual mistake, and frustration.[661]

The first observation that we ought to make is that this case presents a clear separation between the *instrument* containing the compromise and the *compromise agreement* itself. The award is thus presented as ancillary to the settlement. The second observation, which ensues from the first one, is that circumstances that would not normally affect an arbitral award now become relevant. The private *nature* of the settlement agreement becomes apparent. In particular, while an ordinary award will usually be expressed in the form of an *order* directed to one of the parties, a consent award will instead reproduce an *accord*. Therefore, in the former case, a party can either comply with the order or ignore it (in which case the other party can obtain a coercive enforcement). In the latter case, however, a lack of cooperation can be fatal as it will prevent performance of the entire agreement.

The above considerations explain why, under this line of reasoning, the applicable law may be relevant for the purposes of the enforcement of a consent award. In *Halpern*, the court first performed an analysis to determine the law applicable to the compromise agreement.[662] Absent a choice by the parties, the 1980 *Convention on the Law Applicable to Contractual Obligations*[663] dictated the application of the law of the country with which the agreement was most closely connected.[664] After concluding that there were no differences between Swiss law and English law (the two potentially applicable laws) in relation to duress, misrepresentation, mistake, or frustration, the court turned to the consideration of the merits of the claim. After dismissing a claim of fraud based on the supposed forgery of a document, the court considered the more substantial claim that the compromise agreement had been obtained by duress. Since

---

658. Black, *supra* n. 646, at 525.
659. *Halpern v. Halpern* [2006] EWHC 603 (Comm) [*Halpern I*].
660. *Ibid.* at para. 36.
661. *Ibid.* at para. 37.
662. *Halpern I*, *supra* n. 660, at paras 64 ff.
663. *Convention on the Law Applicable to Contractual Obligations*, 19 June 1980, 1605 UNTS 28023, OJ 1980 L 266.
664. *Halpern I*, *supra* n. 660, at para. 66.

the matter could not be decided by summary judgment, a trial was ordered. In the subsequent proceedings, the claim was dismissed since 'a party cannot avoid a contract procured by duress in circumstances where he cannot offer the other party substantial *restitutio in integrum*'.[665] The parties had in fact destroyed part of the documents relating to the arbitration in compliance with one of the terms of the settlement. Without going further into the details of the case, I note that the fate of a consent award is closely attached to the law applicable to the settlement agreement. In *Halpern*, for instance, had Jewish law been applicable, an agreement procured by duress would have been treated as void *ab initio* rather than as voidable.[666] Accordingly, the outcome of the case would have been significantly different.

In conclusion, it appears that, under English law, there are additional grounds for challenging a consent award. These grounds are anchored in the contractual nature of the agreement and rely heavily on English law as the law applicable to the compromise. This, however, seems to be an intrusion on the arbitrators' adjudicative decision to render an award by consent, which presupposes a positive assessment of an existing and valid agreement between the parties. Parties' counsel should thus be invited to consider inserting a specific stipulation in compromises, dealing with the applicable law.

[3]   Enforcement

As far as the enforcement of foreign awards is concerned, there can be no doubt as to the possibility of enforcing an award by consent in England. Without discussing the question of whether or not the *New York Convention* allows for the recognition of consent awards,[667] Article VII(1) of said convention requires the application of provisions of the law of the country where recognition is sought that are more favourable to enforcement than those of the convention. Since section 51 of the *Arbitration Act 1996* – applicable to awards rendered in England – clearly provides that consent awards should be treated as any other awards, English courts will not be reluctant to enforce foreign consent awards, which as stated in section 52(4) of the act, do not need to include reasons. For the same reasons identified with regard to Article 68(2) of the act, the only relevant grounds for challenging consent awards should be those regarding the violation of public policy.

---

665. *Halpern v. Halpern* [2006] EWHC 1728 (Comm) at para. 28.
666. *Halpern I*, *supra* n. 660, at para. 68.
667. A proposed amendment to article I aimed at including a reference to settlements reached before the arbitrators and made by the Federal Republic of Germany, the Austrian government, and the Polish Chamber of Commerce (respectively UNESCO, *Report of the Secretary General*, UN Doc E/2822 (31 January 1956), Annex I at 7; UNESCO, *Activities of Inter-governmental and Non-governmental Organizations in the Field of International Commercial Arbitration: Consolidated Report by the Secretary-General*, UN Doc E/Conf.26/4 (24 April 1958) at 26; UNESCO, *Consideration of the Draft Convention on the Recognition and Enforcement of Foreign Arbitral Awards*, UN Doc E/Conf. 26/L.26 (27 May 1958) at 1) was not upheld.

§6.05 CONSENT AWARDS IN FRANCE

[A] The National Legal Framework

The French *Code of Civil Procedure* does not deal expressly with consent awards. Moreover, the code only gives a basic definition of arbitral awards. Article 1482 – which, pursuant to Article 1506, is applicable to international arbitrations – states that an award shall summarize the parties' claims and give reasons. Given the above, we cannot avoid an analysis of the relevant notions in French law in order to provide a definition of consent awards and, in particular, the notion of *transaction* (settlement) and that of *jugement sur accord des parties* (judgment on agreed terms).

[1] Contrat de Transaction

The *transaction* is defined by Article 2044(1) of the French *Civil Code*:

> La transaction est le contrat par lequel les parties, par des concessions réciproques, terminent une contestation née, ou préviennent une contestation à naître.

This definition has been criticized on the basis that the notion of 'future dispute' (*contestation à naître*) is inaccurate. The dispute would rather always be a present one; the only distinction would be whether proceedings had yet been initiated by a party.[668] While this observation is most certainly correct, in our opinion the provision should be interpreted as providing a liberal definition of the notion of 'dispute', which can include situations of doubt as to the extent and consequences of a given legal relationship (*res dubia*). This interpretation was disapproved of by Louis Boyer, who posited an alternative interpretation according to which a settlement agreement could exist only in the presence of a *res litigiosa*, that is, a legal claim (whether or not brought before a court).[669] In particular, the notion of *contestation* would be more restrictive than that of *litige*, which can be interpreted as mere disagreement.[670] Both interpretations are now considered outdated,[671] and according to the prevailing doctrine, a *transaction* requires the existence at the same time of a *res dubia* (i.e., a situation of doubt as to a given legal relationship) and a *res litigiosa* (i.e., the existence of a dispute): only these requirements would be able to exclude cases of frivolous or fraudulent suits. Be that as it may, Article 2044 of the *Civil Code* seems quite clear in its alleged lack of precision; the use of the term *contestation* rather than *litige* or *différend* is not decisive. The essence of a settlement agreement should thus be found in the existence of a *disagreement* between two or more parties, revolving around facts with legal relevance or the extent and consequences of a legal entitlement (whether or not litigated in front of a court).

---

668. Loïc Cadiet & Emmanuel Jeuland, *Droit judiciaire privé*, 325 (LexisNexis 2013).
669. Louis Boyer, *La notion de transaction*, 45 (Sirey 1947).
670. Guinchard, *supra* n. 22, at 1314.
671. Laurent Poulet, *Transaction et protection des parties*, 85 (LGDJ 2005); Martine Lachance, *Le contrat de transaction*, 54 (Yvon Blais 2005).

The *transaction* is a 'nominate contract' (*contrat nommé*) providing a 'contractual resolution of the dispute' (*solution conventionnelle du litige*).[672] Its essential elements are: (i) the existence of a present or future dispute and (ii) a partial or comprehensive resolution of said dispute by means of (iii) reciprocal concessions.[673] This last requirement constitutes a barrier against potential abuses: both parties must give something up, though the economic value of what is forgone is not taken into account.[674] The written form is required only for evidentiary matters (*ad probationem*) and is not required in order for the act to be valid (*see* former Article 2044(2) of the *Civil Code*).[675]

The contractual nature of the *transaction* entails the usual possibility – provided that certain conditions apply – of terminating the agreement, rescinding it, or having it declared invalid. While the 2016 reform (Loi n. 2016-1547) has repealed Articles 2053–2058 of the *Civil Code*, thus making clear that termination and rescission are governed by the same general rules applicable to contracts, it is worth explaining how the previous regime operated.

The first hypothesis (termination) was quite straightforward and followed the general rules of contract law. The second one (rescission) had, by contrast, minor peculiarities.[676] Article 2053 of the *Civil Code* stated that a party to a settlement could rescind said agreement if it was procured by fraud or duress (paragraph 2), or alternatively, if it was affected by a mistake of fact as to the subject matter of the dispute or the identity of the opposing party (paragraph 1).

Likewise, a settlement could be rescinded if it was based on an invalid title (Article 2054 of the *Civil Code*). Under some circumstances, the *transaction* could be declared invalid *ex tunc* (from the outset). The most interesting cases were treated by Article 2055 of the *Civil Code*, which stated that a *transaction* based on false documents was void, and by Article 2056, according to which a *transaction* on a suit eventually resolved by a court order was void unless the parties were aware of the judgment. Errors of law were irrelevant (Article 2052(2)).

The 2016 reform has also modified the text of the most important provision on settlement agreements, i.e., Article 2052(1) of the *Civil Code*, which now reads as follow: 'La transaction fait obstacle à l'introduction ou à la poursuite entre les parties d'une action en justice ayant le même objet' (a settlement precludes each party to file a claim falling under its subject-matter). In other words, the settlement has a res

---

672. Cadiet et al., *Théorie générale*, *supra* n. 28, at 503. For a critique, *see* Lucie Mayer, *La transaction, un contrat spécial?* 3 RTD civ 523 (2014).
673. Alain Bénabent, *Droit des contrats spéciaux civils et commerciaux*, 668 (LGDJ 2013). According to the author, the notion of reciprocal concessions was introduced by the *Cour de cassation* in order to distinguish settlement agreements from donations. *See also* Charles Jarrosson, *Les concessions réciproques dans la transaction*, Rec Dalloz 267 (1997). The 2016 reform has explicitly introduced this requirement in Art. 2044 (Loi n. 2016-1547, 18 November 2016). *See* Thomas Clay, *L'arbitrage, les modes alternatifs de règlement des différends et la transaction dans la loi "Justice du XXIe siècle"*, 48 Semaine Juridique 2219, 2232 (2016).
674. Philippe Malaurie et al., *Les contrats spéciaux*, 600 (Defrénois 2012).
675. *Ibid.* at 611.
676. For a detailed analysis, *see* Paul-Henri Antonmattei & Jacques Raynard, *Droit civil: contrats spéciaux*, paras 587 ff. (LexisNexis 2013).

judicata effect.[677] In this respect, it has an effect of a declaratory nature on the rights of the parties.

Furthermore, pursuant to Article 1567 of the *Code of Civil Procedure*, a party can request homologation of a settlement by the court that would otherwise have had jurisdiction to hear the dispute. Homologation is a precondition to the enforcement of the *transaction*. While this enforcement procedure was only introduced quite recently (*Décret n° 2012-66 du 20 janvier 2012* and *Décret n° 2013-1280 du 29 décembre 2013*) and also covers other out-of-court settlements (such as those reached during conciliation and mediation), a similar procedure was provided by former Article 1441-4 of the French *Code of Civil Procedure*.

Finally, it should be noted that a *transaction* containing an arbitration clause can be enforced under the above provisions.[678] At the same time, a settlement with regard to a contract containing an arbitration clause would not extinguish the effectiveness of the clause.[679]

[2] **Jugement sur accord des Parties**

Settlements can also occur because of the court's intervention. There are two types of *jugement sur accord des parties* (on agreed terms): the *jugement d'expédient* and the *jugement de donner acte*.[680] These judgments are not regulated by the *Code of Civil Procedure*.

The difference between an ordinary judgment and a *jugement d'expédient* lies in the fact that, in the latter case, the parties have made concurring submissions and the dispute has been resolved, de facto, sometime after the beginning of the proceedings.[681] The content of the judgment is thus dictated by the parties' common view of the dispute. Despite being, to all effects and purposes, a judgment, the *jugement d'expédient* intervenes in a fictitious dispute.[682] It is subject to appeal as any other judgment would be.

---

677. Bénabent, *supra* n. 674, at 676. The reference to the res judicata effect, however, should not be interpreted literally. The provision does not indicate that the settlement has the same effect as a judgment; it rather provides a mere *fin de non-recevoir*, that is, a ground for inadmissibility of the claim. See Clay, *supra* n. 674, at 2232.
678. *See*, most recently: Cass civ 1e, 2 April 2014, No 11-14.692.
679. CA Paris, 21 January 2010, 2 Rev Arb 339 (2010) ('La transaction ne prive pas d'efficacité la clause compromissoire, d'autre part, que 'l'Accord transactionnel' trouve son origine dans l'inobservation du contrat de base, ... dont il est le complément, de sorte qu'il entre dans le champ des clauses d'arbitrages stipulées par ceux-ci'). *See also* CA Paris, 4 March 1986, 2 Rev Arb 167 (1987) ('La clause compromissoire possède une complète autonomie et que dès lors, la transaction ou la novation intervenue sur la convention contenant la clause compromissoire ne peut avoir pour effet de priver cette clause de son efficacité').
680. Patrick Chauvel, *Transaction* in *Répertoire de droit civil*, 64 ff. (2011).
681. Gérard Cornu & Jean Foyer, *Procédure civile*, 24 (3rd ed., Presses universitaires de France 1996).
682. Frédérique Eudier & Nicolas Gerbay, *Jugement* in *Répertoire de procédure civile*, para. 13 (2014).

Conversely, with the *jugement de donner acte* (an expression of the broader notion of *contrat judiciaire*)[683] the court will simply declare the existence of an agreement between the parties, reached during the course of the proceedings. Since the court is merely recording an agreement, the resulting order will not bear an adjudicative character.[684] Accordingly, such an order will neither be subject to appeal[685] nor enforceable as an ordinary judgment.[686] Furthermore, it does not have a res judicata effect. Nevertheless, the parties can have recourse to ordinary remedies against contractual pathologies (through termination, rescission, resolution).[687]

Therefore, as emphasized by the *Cour de cassation*, this type of judgment has a merely declaratory value – the decision rendered by the court does not resolve a dispute; it merely records the settlement reached by the parties:

> [U]n jugement de donner acte n'a pas la nature d'une décision judiciaire contentieuse dès lors qu'il ne tranche aucune difficulté, en se contentant de reprendre l'accord intervenu entre les parties. ... Il s'ensuit que le donné acte figurant dans le dispositif de l'arrêt litigieux ne peut pas être considéré comme ayant une portée juridique susceptible d'avoir un effet judiciaire (ou exécutoire) sur les obligations respectives des parties.[688]

[B] Consent Awards under French Arbitration Law

[1] Only International or Foreign Consent Awards Can Be Enforced in France?

As far as French arbitration law is concerned, there are no doubts as to the possibility of enforcing a foreign[689] or international[690] consent award under Articles 1514 and following of the *Code of Civil Procedure*,[691] which, pursuant to Article VII(I) of the 1958

---

683. Charles Jarrosson, *Transaction* in *Répertoire de droit international*, para. 32 (1998).
684. CA Paris, 5 November 2008, No 06/22858 ('Il n'y a lieu ni d'infirmer ni de confirmer un jugement de donné acte, la formule signifiant simplement que les juges constatent que les parties ont fait ou n'ont pas fait quelque chose dans le cours d'une procédure dont la réalité résulte de l'acte lui-même puisqu'il intervient dans une procédure écrite').
685. Gaëlle Deharo, *Contrat judiciaire* in *Répertoire de procédure civile*, para. 60 (2012).
686. CA Bastia, 20 January 2010, No 09/00094; Cass Civ 1e, 5 February 2008, No 04-19.861 ('[U]n jugement de donné acte ne peut créer aucun droit ni constituer aucun titre au profit ou à l'encontre de l'une des parties'). It goes without saying that it cannot have a res judicata effect either.
687. Cass civ 3e, 10 July 1991, No 90-11.847 ('[U]n contrat judiciaire est exposé aux seules voies de nullité ou de rescision susceptibles d'atteindre les contrats, et ne peut être attaqué par les voies de recours ouvertes contre les jugements').
688. Cass civ 2e, 31 March 2011, No 10-15.505.
689. Awards rendered outside of France.
690. Article 1504: 'Est international l'arbitrage qui met en cause des intérêts du commerce international'.
691. A single regime deals with the enforcement of international awards rendered in France and foreign awards. *See* Jarrosson & Pellerin, *supra* n. 326, at 66.

New York Convention become applicable given the fact that they set up a more favourable framework than the convention itself.[692]

In *Société Dansk Eternit Fabrik 1994 c Société Copernit & C SpA*,[693] the court analysed the scope of a settlement agreement entered by the parties that was recorded in an ICC award and later enforced pursuant to an ordinance of the *Tribunal de grande instance* of Paris.[694] Not once did the court hesitate in defining the ICC award as an enforceable award by consent.

Accordingly, the enforcement of a foreign award by consent will be subject to the general rules: the party wishing to enforce the award must prove its existence; the enforcement order will be granted provided that it does not result in a manifest violation of international public policy (Article 1514 of the *Code of Civil Procedure*).[695]

Unsurprisingly, in *Société Viva Chemical (Europe) NV c APTD*,[696] the Paris Court of Appeal annulled the ordinance of enforcement rendered by a lower court because the award by consent, issued by a sole arbitrator sitting in London, had occurred under suspicious circumstances. In particular, respondent was in a situation of great financial distress, and the court found that the settlement agreement was part of a fraudulent scheme to reduce the assets of respondent before an imminent declaration of bankruptcy. Given the fact that the enforcement of such a consent award would violate international public policy, the ordinance of the lower court was annulled.

Finally, pursuant to Article 1525(4) of the *Code of Civil Procedure*, the party resisting enforcement may appeal an order of enforcement on one of the grounds provided by Article 1520.[697] However, challenges may rarely succeed on grounds other than those of the violation of public policy, for the parties' request to record the settlement agreement should be interpreted as a waiver of the grounds for refusing enforcement based on procedural irregularities that are covered by this provision.[698]

The scenario becomes much more confused if we turn to challenges of domestic awards (i.e., awards rendered in France that do not affect international trade). The starting point of our discussion is a relatively recent judgment rendered by the *Cour de cassation – M A c Société B-C* – according to which, consent awards are mere

---

692. Clay, *La Convention de New York*, *supra* n. 41, at 55.
693. CA Angers, 16 September 2008, No 07/01636.
694. Trib gr inst Paris, 6 February 2004, ordonnance d'exequatur.
695. Article 1514: 'Les sentences arbitrales sont reconnues ou exécutées en France si leur existence est établie par celui qui s'en prévaut et si cette reconnaissance ou cette exécution n'est pas manifestement contraire à l'ordre public international'.
696. CA Paris, 9 April 2009, No 07/17769.
697. Article 1520 of the French *Code of Civil Procedure*:

> Le recours en annulation n'est ouvert que si :
> 1° Le tribunal arbitral s'est déclaré à tort compétent ou incompétent ou
> 2° Le tribunal arbitral a été irrégulièrement constitué ou
> 3° Le tribunal arbitral a statué sans se conformer à la mission qui lui avait été confiée ou
> 4° Le principe de la contradiction n'a pas été respecté ou
> 5° La reconnaissance ou l'exécution de la sentence est contraire à l'ordre public international.

698. *See* the discussion with respect to English law, *supra* p. 185 ff. The same rationale applies in French and English law.

declaratory measures.[699] As such, they are not subject to enforcement as standard arbitral awards. A well-known arbitration scholar has referred to the judgment at hand as a death sentence for awards on agreed terms.[700] A few words on the nature of the dispute are necessary.

The dispute arose between two French lawyers who had constituted a limited liability partnership (LLP). One former partner brought suit against his colleague for alleged irregularities in the liquidation of his share of the partnership. The matter was brought before the *bâtonnier* of the Paris Bar, who was appointed as sole arbitrator. As the parties were able to reach an agreement during the course of the proceedings, the arbitrator recorded said agreement in an award. Later on, one of the parties refused to make payments under the terms of the agreed award on the basis of the *exceptio non adimpleti contractus* ('performance can be suspended if the other party remains idle').[701] The Versailles Court of Appeal found that an award on agreed terms was not subject to the *exceptio* because its adjudicative nature excluded the plethora of contractual remedies otherwise applicable to settlement agreements. By recording the settlement, the arbitrator would make the parties' agreement the arbitrator's own decision:

> [D]oit être qualifiée de sentence accord parties, acte juridictionnel ayant autorité de la chose jugée conformément à l'article 1476 du code de procédure civile, la sentence rendue le 16 mai 2002 qui entérine l'accord des parties intervenu en cours d'arbitrage, puisque l'arbitre fait sien l'accord des parties et que la transaction est incorporée dans la décision juridictionnelle.[702]

The *Cour de cassation* annulled the judgment of the lower court for an error of law (Article 1476 of the *Code of Civil Procedure*) since the act of recording a settlement, without the arbitrator providing reasons, could not amount to an adjudicative act:

> [L]'acte émanant de l'arbitre n'avait pas l'autorité de la chose jugée des sentences arbitrales et était au contraire concerné par l'article 2052 du code civil, consacré à l'autorité de la chose jugée de la transaction.[703]

The judgment rests on an assumption that awards on agreed terms are a creation of the parties, dressed up as awards. This disguise would prevent arbitrators from verifying the compliance of the agreement with the requirements of the *transaction* (reciprocal concessions, conformity with public policy).[704] The lack of reasons is, of course, an inevitable element of this peculiar type of award, because the parties, and not the arbitrators, have resolved the dispute. As a consequence, consent awards

---

699. Cass civ 1e, 14 November 2012, 1 Rev Arb 138 (2013) (note Jean Billemont).
700. Loquin, *L'arrêt de mort*, supra n. 98, at 476.
701. For an overview of the notion of the *exceptio*, see Philip O'Neill & Nawaf Salam, *Is the Exceptio Non Adimpleti Contractus Part of the New Lex Mercatoria* in Emmanuel Gaillard, *Transnational Rules in International Commercial Arbitration*, 147 (ICC Publishing 1993).
702. CA Versailles, 23 June 2011, No 09/08250.
703. Cass Civ, 14 November 2012, *supra* n. 700, at 138 ('La simple constatation, dans le dispositif de la décision, de l'accord des parties, sans aucun motif dans le corps de celle-ci, ne peut s'analyser en un acte juridictionnel').
704. *Ibid.* at 145.

rendered in France appear to have only contractual effects[705] and to be subject to the remedies applicable to the *contrat de transaction* (termination, rescission, resolution). Loquin further argues that only a special provision in the arbitration legislation, such as the one contained in the *Model Law*, could grant an adjudicative character to consent awards.[706]

While the Court of Appeal interpreted the award by consent as a *jugement d'expédient*, that is, an adjudicative act, the *Cour de cassation* opted to view it as a mere *jugement de donner acte*, which simply acknowledges the existence of a settlement. The *Cour de cassation* upheld a longstanding approach to consent awards. In *Guillet c Consorts Guillet*,[707] the parties had entered a settlement agreement before a sole arbitrator acting as *amiable compositeur*. While the document was entitled 'procès-verbal d'arbitrage et de transaction', the subtitled stated 'arbitral award' and was followed by the following statement:

> À l'instant même et sitôt connus les termes de l'arbitrage rendu par M. Philippe Burnel, toutes les parties composantes déclarent, par les présentes, qu'elles l'acceptent et le ratifient comme chose jugée entre elles, entendant qu'il ait aussi entre elles valeur de transaction entière, forfaitaire et définitive.

According to the *Cour de cassation*, the Paris Court of Appeal rightly qualified the act as a mere settlement due to the lack of an actual order (*condamnation*): this would exclude the possibility of the act having an adjudicative character, allowing the court to qualify it as a mere transaction.

[2] Alternatives in Light of the Lack of Enforcement of Domestic Consent Awards

With a bit of cynicism, one could say that the possibility that enforcement of a domestic award by consent will be refused is not the end of the world. The first and most obvious way to achieve an effect similar to enforcement would be to seize a court in order to request a decision declaring the existence of the *transaction* with a *jugement de donner acte*.[708] A second possibility, provided by Article 1567 of the *Code of Civil Procedure*, allows both parties to enforce the consent award as a mere settlement. However, it is rapidly apparent that this avenue will be subject to several inconveniences.[709] According to Article 1565, applicable in light of the reference made to it by Article 1567,[710] the

---

705. Loquin, *L'arrêt de mort*, supra n. 98, at 476.
706. *Ibid*.
707. Cass Civ 2e, 7 October 1981, No 80-11247, cited in Edouard Bertrand, *Sur le bon usage des sentences d'accord parties*, 24:1 ASA Bull 13, 13 (2006).
708. Deharo, *supra* n. 686, at para. 63.
709. The recent reform of this article has been met with a great deal of scepticism among French scholars. On the homologation of the settlement agreement and the incoherencies of the legislator, *see* Deharo, *supra* n. 686.
710. 'Les dispositions des articles 1565 et 1566 sont applicables à la transaction conclue sans qu'il ait été recouru à une médiation, une conciliation ou une procédure participative. Le juge est alors saisi par la partie la plus diligente ou l'ensemble des parties à la transaction'.

transaction will be *homologated* by the court that would otherwise have had jurisdiction to hear the dispute.[711]

This provision presents two difficulties. First, identifying the court that would have had jurisdiction may pose problems, especially when the *transaction* involves parties of different nationalities.[712] A different criterion could have been used instead, namely, the court where the settlement agreement was entered, in order to identify the appropriate court. In order to avoid any further complications, it would be advisable to include a forum selection clause identifying a court having jurisdiction, with precision, in the settlement agreement.

Second, it is far from clear what the standard of homologation refers to. In the specific context of settlement agreements, it should simply be understood as a decision declaring the *transaction* enforceable, provided that it violates neither public policy nor any kind of mandatory provisions (antitrust, tax, etc.). Article 1566(1) of the *Code of Civil Procedure* merely states that the court will decide upon the request for enforcement of the *transaction*, and that such a decision can be appealed according to the *procédure gracieuse* (Article 1566(3)). Therefore, it is not clear if this *procédure gracieuse* can be extended to the first decision on the homologation.

The doctrine defines *juridiction gracieuse* as the court's power to approve a private act: it consists of the application of an adjudicative power, that is, the power to tell what the law ought to be with respect to the *matière gracieuse*.[713] Understood in these terms, the provision contained in Article 1566(3) of the *Code of Civil Procedure* would suggest that the entire homologation should be governed by this procedure.

This interpretation is consistent with the legislator's attempt to introduce a form of review for settlement agreements. An interpretation to the contrary would nullify the provision at hand, for the role of the court would simply be one of registration, which is incompatible with the institution's function of verification and is usually reserved for other types of public officials.

Homologation would exclude a priori the existence of a dispute,[714] and this seems very reasonable if we consider the case of settlements. What seems difficult to reconcile with homologation, however, is the extent of the power of a court acting in a matter of *juridiction gracieuse*. In particular, the court would exercise two powers: the power to assess the legality of the act (i.e., its conformity with the law) and the power to verify the usefulness of entering such an act.[715]

---

711. 'L'accord auquel sont parvenues les parties à une médiation, une conciliation ou une procédure participative peut être soumis, aux fins de le rendre exécutoire, à l'homologation du juge compétent pour connaître du contentieux dans la matière considérée'.
712. If both parties are foreigners, it would seem that the *transaction* cannot be enforced at all: CA Versailles, 18 June 2003, *Miakassissa v République du Congo*, cited in Bertrand, *supra* n. 708, at 14 (while the text refers to Art. 1441 of the former legislation, we can assume that the same should be true for its successor, Art. 1567 of the current legislation, which has merely expanded the scope of the former provision): '[S]i les parties sont étrangères les juridictions françaises ne peuvent se reconnaître compétentes dès lors qu'aucun critère ordinaire de compétence territoriale n'est réalisé en France'.
713. Guinchard, *supra* n. 22, at 1311.
714. *Ibid.*
715. *Ibid.* at 1315.

While these powers, especially the second, seem particularly welcome in the usual cases falling within the *juridiction gracieuse* (essentially, family matters), problems arise with respect to the power to homologate a commercial settlement agreement. According to one author, the reference to this type of jurisdiction is simply an unfortunate mistake.[716] While the critiques do seem justified, it appears that the reference made by the *Code of Civil Procedure* to the *juridiction gracieuse* should be adapted to the circumstances of the case. We can thus come to the conclusion that the second power should not find application in cases dealing with the enforcement of settlement agreements.

The *Cour de cassation*'s holding with respect to former Article 1441-4 of the *Code of Civil Procedure* – which dealt with the enforcement of settlements prior to the 2012 reform of the code relating to out-of-court settlements, and as such can be regarded as the ancestor of Article 1567 of the same code – has addressed the proper extent of the court's powers of review: the review conducted by the court concerns only the nature of the agreement brought before it and its conformity with public policy.[717]

This confirms that, while the court's power of review is minimal, the enforcement of the settlement agreement cannot be granted as of right. The court will review the conformity of the agreement not only with public policy but also with respect to morals. Building on this consideration, some authors have suggested that the enforcement decision would not constitute an adjudicative act.[718] However, a more pragmatic interpretation should be preferred. Inasmuch as a court states what the law is – even with respect to a single *principle* (public policy), such as in the case at hand – the decision on the enforcement of the settlement agreement should be regarded as an adjudicative act.

This conclusion is in line with the 2012 reform of the *Code of Civil Procedure*, which further allows an appeal of a decision denying said enforcement (Article 1566(3)). At the same time, pursuant to Article 1566(1), this procedure may require the presence of both parties – we assume, whenever the settlement agreement does not appear, prima facie, to be in conformity with public policy and enforceable – reinforcing the interpretation of the court's order as an adjudicative act. Among the authoritative sources, this line of reasoning has achieved a consensus.[719]

This approach entails an essential corollary: if we agree upon the adjudicative nature of the decision on the enforcement of the settlement, we may provide the parties

---

716. Deharo, *supra* n. 686, at para. 65.
717. Cass civ 2e, 26 May 2011, No 06-19.527 [emphasis added].
718. *See* the authors cited by Guinchard, *supra* n. 22, at 1313.
719. *Ibid.* at 1313–1314; Frédérique Ferrand, *Matière contentieuse et matière gracieuse* in *Répertoire de droit civil*, para. 73 (2012); Cadiet & Jeuland, *supra* n. 669, at para. 99 ('[C]e qui caractérise l'acte juridictionnel, c'est davantage l'application, par le juge, d'une règle de droit à une situation de fait dont il est saisi. Or, cette confrontation du fait au droit, d'où découle la décision, n'est pas propre aux décisions contentieuses; le juge l'opère également dans son activité gracieuse. Dans les deux cas, le juge statue, se prononce [art. 25 et 28], et rend un jugement qui peut être frappé de voies de recours, ce qui n'a de sens qu'à la condition de lui reconnaître autorité de chose jugée. En vérité, cette égale nature juridictionnelle des décisions gracieuses et des décisions contentieuses tient à l'unité substantielle de l'activité judiciaire dans l'un et l'autre cas').

Chapter 6: Consent Awards §6.06

with the possibility of enforcing it abroad, under the applicable international conventions. This is of pivotal importance, since there are no international conventions allowing the enforcement of settlement agreements per se.[720] While the same could be said for foreign judgments, this latter form of decision has a greater rate of enforcement than settlements.[721]

[3]   Challenges to Domestic Consent Awards

Given the foregoing, the lack of recognition of domestic consent awards excludes, a priori, the applicability of provisions on challenges to arbitral awards (*recours en annulation*). As a result, a party interested in challenging a settlement agreement has two options. Pursuant to Article 1566 of the *Code of Civil Procedure*, the party can appeal the decision enforcing the settlement; alternatively, in cases where the other party has not requested enforcement, the only way to challenge the settlement is an ordinary suit whereby rescission or invalidity of the agreement may be invoked pursuant to Articles 2053 and following of the *Civil Code*.

Finally, in case of a breach of a settlement agreement, the innocent party can request the agreement's termination in accordance with the rules of contracts.

§6.06   CONCLUSION

As explained in the previous sections, significant divergences exist vis-à-vis the treatment of consent awards under international instruments and national arbitration acts. Arbitration instruments, such as the UNCITRAL *Model Law* and the *ICC Rules*, interested in facilitating the enforcement of settlement agreements, allow the arbitrators to record settlements in the form of consent awards. Once the parties' settlement has been scrutinized by the tribunal, it becomes an ordinary award. National legislators, however, struggle with the implementation of these objectives. While England endorses an approach that is favourable to these awards (facilitated by the existence of similar orders in national case law), it presents unsatisfactory and too wide-ranging grounds for challenging them. Conversely, in France, domestic consent awards are not (in light of the recent decision rendered by the *Cour de cassation*) considered to be awards but rather mere *transactions*.

It has been suggested that consent awards are a (useful) disguise for settlement agreements. As such, their contractual nature would exclude the existence of an

---

720. A notable exception may be found in the 1971 *Convention on the Recognition and Enforcement of Foreign Judgments in Civil and Commercial Matters* (1 February 1971, 1144 UNTS 249, Art. 19), which was, however, only ratified by five states and merely refers to in-court settlements, that is, settlements reached during normal proceedings in court.
721. A further notable exception may be found in Quebec's private international law (*see* Art. 3163 CCQ), which allows the enforcement of a foreign settlement provided that it is enforceable in its country of origin. On this particular point, *see* Gerald Goldstein, *La méthode de la reconnaissance: une nouvelle clé pour décoder les règles relatives à l'effet au Québec d'une transaction internationale*, 68 Rev Bar 279 (2009).

adjudicative act:⁷²² difficulties would arise with respect to the existing grounds for challenging an arbitral award.⁷²³ However, a different interpretation can be put forward: namely, consent awards can be regarded as *complex* decisions, in the sense that they are constituted by two distinct layers: first, the agreement of the parties; second, the arbitral tribunal's award.

The settlement of the parties is, beyond any question, the first layer and is a prerequisite of any consent award. As such, it presupposes the existence of a dispute: this means that a consent award cannot be issued where the parties have reached a settlement before the file has been transmitted to the tribunal.⁷²⁴ This is so because the claimant will usually be required to state its case in the request for arbitration, and an arbitral institution might decide not to move forward with the request if there is no dispute at all. Moreover, the need for an existing dispute is consistent with the supervisory task that the arbitrators are expected to exercise when reviewing a settlement that the parties wish to have recorded in the form of an award. To exercise such task, they must be aware of the facts of the case, and the respective claims of the parties. As far as the form of the settlement is concerned, it should be emphasized that there aren't any stringent requirements. Such an agreement may take multiple forms, including a written settlement agreement, a joint request directed to the tribunal, or an oral agreement reached before the tribunal. In all of these cases, the common denominator is the parties' will to cease contesting a given matter *before* the arbitrators. The agreement can touch upon single aspects of the dispute before the tribunal, such as the jurisdiction of the arbitrators, or can deal with the entire dispute. Accordingly, the tribunal will choose between rendering a partial award and a final award.

Once the parties have reached a settlement, the tribunal will add the second layer to the decision, in the form of their determination of whether to issue an award by consent. As noted it has been correctly noted, arbitral tribunals are never compelled to issue a consent award.⁷²⁵ As any other award, it remains an adjudicative decision rendered by the arbitrators and not merely an empty record of what the parties have agreed. Unlike a contentious award, where the arbitrators are required to resolve the dispute based on the parties' respective claims (monodimensional model), whenever the parties request an award by consent they are, de facto, replacing their previous claims with a new one: that is, the tribunal must decide whether the agreement is in compliance with public policy and the applicable mandatory rules of law. For the same

---

722. Tchakoua, *supra* n. 99, at 784.
723. *Ibid.* at 785.
724. In ICC arbitration, this situation would coincide with the entry into force of the terms of reference. For the same reasons, a settlement reached during mediation may prevent the appointment of an arbitrator and the subsequent rendering of a consent award. This is why some authors have suggested, as a matter of prudence, the appointment of an arbitrator prior to the beginning of the mediation, in order to leave open the possibility of recording a settlement agreement in the form of an award: Christopher Newmark & Richard Hill *Can a Mediated Settlement Become an Enforceable Arbitration Award?* 16:1 Arb Int 81, 85 (2000). This solution, however, seems not only unorthodox but also quite expensive, for the parties would need to deal with the fees of the arbitral institution and of the arbitral tribunal.
725. *See* Frédéric Bachand, *The Legal Nature of Arbitral Awards* in Andrea Bjorklund, Franco Ferrari & Stephan Kröll, *Cambridge Handbook of International Arbitration* (Cambridge University Press forthcoming in 2017).

reasons, the settlement should not exceed the scope of the dispute submitted to the arbitrators. While some elements reasonably connected to the original submissions may eventually become part of the settlement, the jurisdictional role of the arbitrators (i.e., assessing the conformity of the settlement with the applicable mandatory rules and public policy) can be exercised only with regard to the dispute before them.

As far as the nature of the power exercised by the arbitrators in this specific task, there is no doubt that in answering the parties' request, and by issuing a consent award, the tribunal is providing an *adjudicative* answer.[726] The term 'adjudicative' should here be interpreted liberally, as encompassing the existence of a binding decision rendered on the basis of a legal rule. In the case of a consent award, the arbitrators decide upon a claim (i.e., they scrutinize the settlement) on the basis of mandatory rules and public policy (thus also verifying whether they are in the presence of an actual, valid agreement). In support of this conclusion, it was shown that this type of adjudicative power is similar to the one granted to state courts in England and France (i.e., regarding consent orders and the homologation of settlements). Certainly, arbitral tribunals are private adjudicators, but this doesn't mean that we should arbitrarily limit their adjudicative powers, especially if the goal pursued by national legislators is that of providing a comprehensive alternative to state courts. The fact that UNCITRAL felt the need to develop an international instrument to foster the enforcement of settlements, which might end up covering settlement agreements reached in the course of an arbitration that are not recorded in the form of an award, and consent awards that are not enforceable under the law of the country where enforcement is sought,[727] should serve as 'food for thought' when considering dogmatic positions that attempt to restrict the adjudicative powers of the arbitrators.

It is worth adding some reflections on the argument against the adjudicative nature of consent awards. The formalistic argument according to which a consent order is not an adjudicative act because it lacks reasons and an order coming from the arbitrators has little weight in the context of international arbitration. First, as explained in Chapter 3, reasons are not always mandatory for contentious awards resolving the merits of the case. Even under French law, which adopts a strict position on this point, while the presence of reasons is important, their nature and length is usually irrelevant. Second, the real concern behind the lack of reasons is the need to protect weaker parties: if settlement agreements could be entered and could have the same force as an ordinary judgment without any type of constraint, the weaker party could be at risk of unjustly giving up its rights. Yet again, it is important to note that arbitral tribunals will grant consent awards only pursuant to a joint request from the parties. This alone seems to constitute a sufficient barrier against potential abuses. Furthermore, while the need to protect weaker parties may be a reality in the context of national litigation, where a great imbalance of resources between the parties may exist, the same is not true of international commercial arbitration, where there are fewer imbalances and higher levels of sophistication. Be that as it may, while it is true

---

726. Contrary to certain practices, this line of reasoning excludes the possibility of including an arbitration agreement in the consent award.
727. *Supra* §6.01.

that the various instruments analysed so far do not necessarily require the arbitrators to include reasons in a consent award,[728] in light of the consideration of the adjudicative nature of such an award, it would be advisable to include at least an embryonic form of reasoning in order to demonstrate that the tribunal has considered the conformity of the consent award with the applicable public policy and mandatory rules of law. This excludes, a priori, the formal issues raised by the possibility of enforcing awards without reasons.[729]

---

728. This is the case of the *ICC Rules*, the *Model Law*, and the English *Arbitration Act 1996*.
729. The lack of reasons in consent awards and its impact on enforcement are addressed by Gino Lörcher, *Enforceability of Agreed Awards in Foreign Jurisdictions*, 17:3 Arb Int 275 (2001).

CHAPTER 7
Awards *Ante Causam*

§7.01 INTRODUCTION

According to the prevailing sources, the common purpose of provisional measures in international commercial arbitration (also referred to as interim measures) is that of preserving a factual situation that risks being irremediably compromised.[731] Provisional measures therefore have a broad scope. Unsurprisingly the literature struggles to find a common denominator that may unite them under a single notion. Redfern and Hunter, a well-regarded authority, present them as follows:[732]

> During the course of an arbitration, it may become necessary for the arbitral tribunal or a national court to issue orders intended to preserve evidence, to protect assets, or in some other way to maintain the status quo pending the outcome of the arbitration proceedings themselves. Such orders take different forms and are known by different names.

Sébastien Besson, a leading arbitration expert on the topic, defines provisional measures as temporary measures, limited to the duration of the proceedings, and protecting the substantive rights of the requesting party or impeding the occurrence of acts that could compromise the continuation and effectiveness of the arbitration.[733] Similarly, according to Gary Born:

> [P]rovisional measures are awards or orders issued for the purpose of protecting one or both parties to a dispute from damage during the course of the arbitral

---

731. Catherine Kessedjian, *Définitions et conditions de l'octroi de mesures provisoires* in Jean-Michel Jacquet & Emmanuel Jolivet, *Les mesures provisoires dans l'arbitrage commercial international* 73, 73 (LexisNexis 2008).
732. Redfern, *supra* n. 1, at 320.
733. Sébastien Besson, *Les mesures provisoires et conservatoires dans la pratique arbitrale – Notion, types de mesures, conditions d'octroi et responsabilité en cas de mesures injustifiées* in *L'arbitrage international et l'urgence* 37, 39 (Bruylant 2014). *See also* Besson, *supra* n. 90, at 23 ff.

process ... [most often] intended to preserve a factual or legal situation so as to safeguard rights the recognition of which is sought from the tribunal having jurisdiction as to the substance of the case.[734]

Provisional measures are usually divided into two distinct categories: conservatory measures and provisional measures *strictu sensu*. While the former would consist in measures addressing the parties' respective positions during the course of the proceedings with a view to preserving the status quo, the latter would insure the effectiveness of the arbitrators' final award.[735] This classification, however, has not attained a consensus.[736] Gaillard and Savage, for instance, have stated that the term 'provisional measures' emphasizes the *nature* of the decision made – 'an interim or provisional order does not bind the court or arbitrator hearing the merits of the dispute'[737] – whereas 'conservatory measures' would indicate the *purpose* of the decision (preserving the rights of the requesting party, the status quo, or evidence).[738]

Without overemphasizing the importance of theoretical taxonomies, it is quite surprising to find such a significant disagreement. This situation calls therefore for a wider and clearer classification. Consistently, let us try to identify, first, a common denominator for provisional measures and, second, a taxonomy for categorizing such measures.

As dictated by the methodology implemented in this book, the analysis of the concept of provisional measures will be carried out with reference to both the Romano-canonical and the common law traditions (section §7.02). Consequently, I will examine the interplays between state courts and arbitrators (section §7.03). In particular, I will explain that the principle of complementarity dictates that state courts can provide provisional protection where the arbitral tribunal has not been constituted or is otherwise unable to act (*ante causam*). However, the rise of emergency arbitration proceedings puts into question the application of this principle (section §7.04). Emergency proceedings represent an attempt to allocate to an arbitral authority the ability to grant provisional protection *ante causam*. This situation calls for an analysis of the nature of emergency proceedings and of the decisions that result from them (section §7.05). Finally, I will conclude by arguing that emergency arbitration constitutes a type of arbitral adjudicative power. Emergency decisions are adjudicative: they constitute an attempt to anticipate the protection that would be provided by the arbitral tribunal after its constitution.

---

734. Born, *supra* n. 4, at 2426.
735. *See*, among others: Olivier Mignolet, *Les mesures provisoires et conservatoires prises par les arbitres* in Achille Saletti, *L'arbitre et le juge étatique* 165, 166 (Bruylant 2014); Didier Matray & Françoise Vidts, *Introduction générale* in *L'arbitrage international et l'urgence* 1, 21 (Bruylant 2014).
736. Thomas Clay, *Les mesures provisoires demandées à l'arbitre* in Jean-Michel Jacquet & Emmanuel Jolivet, *Les mesures provisoires dans l'arbitrage commercial international* 9, 13 (LexisNexis 2008).
737. Gaillard & Savage, *supra* n. 5, at 708.
738. *Ibid.*

§7.02 PROVISIONAL MEASURES IN THE ROMANO-CANONICAL AND COMMON LAW TRADITIONS

As far as the Romano-canonical tradition is concerned, it has been pointed out that the prerequisite for every interim measure amounts to the existence of an urgent situation.[739] Article 1449(2) of the French *Code of Civil Procedure* is particularly instructive on this point:[740]

> Sous réserve des dispositions régissant les saisies conservatoires et les sûretés judiciaires, la demande est portée devant le président du tribunal de grande instance ou de commerce, qui statue sur les mesures d'instruction dans les conditions prévues à l'article 145 et, en cas d'urgence, sur les mesures provisoires ou conservatoires sollicitées par les parties à la convention d'arbitrage.

With the exception of the definition provided by one author,[741] the definitions of provisional measures reviewed in the introduction completely overlook this quintessential requirement, in the absence of which no provisional measure could ever be granted. Such an urgent situation can be described using the Latin expression *periculum in mora* – 'the perils of waiting'.[742] Such a prerequisite constitutes an important guarantee against potential abuses. In other words, the restriction of a party's right to be heard, which is an inevitable consequence of this type of proceeding, is justified only in light of a truly urgent situation calling for immediate action.

The necessity of preserving the status quo, a concept often cited by the doctrine, shifts our attention away from the rationale behind provisional measures, that is, giving a prompt answer to an urgent situation. The qualities of the notion of *periculum in mora* are also those underlying the exceptional character of provisional measures. In other words, such measures are an exception to the final decisions rendered by arbitrators. It is worth noting that the same essential requirement – *periculum in mora* – is found in the common law tradition and, in particular, in the equitable remedy known as the *quia timet* injunction. Such a requirement is usually described in terms of an *imminent danger*.[743]

---

739. For an overview, *see* Mandrioli, *supra* n. 89, at 21 ff. *See also* Piero Calamandrei, *Introduzione allo studio sistematico dei provvedimenti cautelari* (Jovene 1936).
740. *See also* CA Caen, 10 October 2013, No 12/04006 ('Aux termes de l'article 1449 du code de procédure civile, *l'existence d'une convention d'arbitrage ne fait pas obstacle à ce qu'une partie saisisse, en cas d'urgence, le juge des référés aux fins de faire cesser un trouble manifestement illicite ou de prévenir un dommage imminent*, à la condition que le tribunal arbitral ne soit pas encore constitué, c'est à dire, selon l'article 1456 du même code, avant que le dernier arbitre désigné ait accepté sa mission').
741. Cécile Chainais, *Les mesures provisoires dans le nouveau droit français de l'arbitrage* in Achille Saletti, *L'arbitre et le juge étatique* 218, 282–282 (Bruylant 2014). *See also* Guinchard, *supra* n. 22, at 1332.
742. Calamandrei, *supra* n. 739, at 157.
743. The fact of articulating the *periculum in mora* requirement in terms of an imminent danger is not exclusive, however, to common law jurisdictions. On this point, cf. Art. 700 of the Italian *Code of Civil Procedure*.

In common law jurisdictions, the *periculum in mora* – or imminent danger – shall be accompanied by a further ingredient, the risk of irreparable damage.[744] As stated in *Fletcher v. Bealey*,[745] there are at least two necessary 'ingredients' for a *quia timet*:

> There must, if no actual damage is proved, be proof of imminent danger, and there must also be proof that the apprehended damage will, if it comes, be very substantial. I should almost say it must be proved that it will be irreparable, because, if the danger is not proved to be so imminent that no one can doubt that, if the remedy is delayed, the damage will be suffered, I think it must be shown that, if the damage does occur at any time, it will come in such a way and under such circumstances that it will be impossible for the Plaintiff to protect himself against it if relief is denied to him in a *quia timet* action.

The *periculum in mora* is sometimes accompanied by a further requirement, the *fumus boni iuris*,[746] that is, in the words of the 2006 UNCITRAL *Model Law on International Commercial Arbitration*, 'a reasonable possibility that the requesting party will succeed on the merits of the claim' (Article 17(A)(b)).[747]

Finally, as far as the categorization of interim measures is concerned, it seems useful to group them according to the moment at which they can be requested. Accordingly, such measures can be requested either before or after the appointment of the tribunal.

In the first scenario, the measures can be granted by an emergency arbitrator or a state court in support of the future arbitral proceedings. In the second scenario, they are always granted by an arbitral tribunal or a competent state court with a view to ensuring the continuation of the arbitration.

The present chapter will focus on arbitral provisional jurisdiction *ante causam*. This type of adjudicative power neither entails the existence of a dispute as a prerequisite for granting a provisional measure nor does it resolve a dispute. As such, it is problematic under the monodimensional model of arbitral adjudication.

§7.03 PROVISIONAL PROTECTION *ANTE CAUSAM* AND THE INTERPLAYS BETWEEN COURTS AND ARBITRATORS

[A] Courts' Jurisdiction on Provisional Measures Before the Constitution of the Tribunal

The lack of a permanent arbitral authority necessarily entails that parties to an arbitration agreement may resort to state courts in order to obtain necessary,

---

744. *See* Art. 700 of the Italian *Code of Civil Procedure*: an imminent and irreparable *prejudice*.
745. (1885), 28 Ch D 688. *See also Earl of Ripon v. Hobart* (1834) cited in Charles Purton Cooper, *Selected Cases Decided by Lord Brougham* (S. Sweet 1835) 333.
746. Mandrioli, *supra* n. 89, at 90.
747. Cf. *Blom ASA v. Pictometry International Corp*, 757 F. Supp. 2d 238 (2010) ('To obtain a preliminary injunction [pending arbitration], the moving party must establish (1) irreparable harm and (2) either (a) a *likelihood of success on the merits*, or (b) sufficiently serious questions going to the merits of its claims to make them fair ground for litigation, plus a balance of the hardships tipping decidedly in favor of the moving party') [emphasis added].

court-ordered interim measures if their arbitral tribunal has not yet been constituted. In theory, one could argue that the most appropriate course of action would be that of accelerating the constitution of the tribunal. Seeking the intervention of a state court in the presence of an arbitration agreement could, in fact, defeat the very purpose of having an arbitration. This is particularly true if the interim measure has an essential role, that is, if the mere fact of granting the measure will, de facto, resolve the dispute between the parties.

Imagine a case where the claimant entered into a contract, containing an arbitration clause, for the construction of a building. The respondent, a construction company, is an inch away from bankruptcy and refuses to stop operating a dangerous crane. If the claimant fails to obtain a provisional measure ordering the respondent not to operate such crane, it will be pointless to go to arbitration, as the respondent will not have sufficient funds to compensate the claimant for the damages caused by the crane.

The acceleration of the constitution of the arbitral tribunal, therefore, may not always be possible. In such a case, the interested party will be forced to request the intervention of state courts. This intervention is permitted by the so-called principle of complementarity (*principe de complémentarité*), which governs the interplay between state courts and arbitral tribunals in cases requiring interim measures.

[B] The Principle of Complementarity in French and English Arbitration Law

According to the principle of complementarity, a request for interim measures addressed to a state court is compatible with the existence of a binding arbitration agreement.[748] The principle thus creates an exception to the duty to resort to arbitration. Generally speaking, in fact, the arbitration agreement creates an exclusive forum for the resolution of the disputes covered by its scope. The parties have agreed to have their claims tried by arbitration.[749] To protect the exclusivity of the forum, the *New York Convention* prohibits the intervention of state courts in disputes covered by said agreement.[750]

As anticipated, however, state courts maintain nonetheless an ancillary jurisdiction for provisional measures. Not only is the principle of complementary enshrined in several jurisdictions but it is also clearly affirmed in the 2006 revision of the UNCITRAL

---

748. Chainais & Jarrosson, *supra* n. 90, at 65; Luis Enrique Graham, *Interim Measures: Ongoing Regulation and Practices (A View from the UNCITRAL Arbitration Regime)* in Albert Jan van den Berg, *50 Years of the New York Convention: ICCA International Arbitration Conference*, 561 (Kluwer Law 2009); Charles Price, *Conflict with State Courts* in Johan Billiet, *Interim Measures in International Commercial Arbitration*, 39 (Maklu 2007); Ali Yesilirmak, *Provisional Measures in International Commercial Arbitration*, 65 ff. (Kluwer Law 2005); Besson, *supra* n. 90, at 148.
749. These are known as the 'positive effects' of the arbitration agreement. *See* Gaillard & Savage, *supra* n. 5, at 381.
750. *Ibid.* at 402. A recognition of this principle is also found in several arbitration rules. *See* e.g., Art. 23 of the 2010 UNCITRAL *Rules*: 'The arbitral tribunal shall have the power to rule on objections that it has no jurisdiction, including any objection with reference to the existence or validity of the arbitration clause or of the separate arbitration agreement'.

Model Law on International Commercial Arbitration. In this regard, Article 17(J) provides:

> A court shall have the same power of issuing an interim measure in relation to arbitration proceedings, irrespective of whether their place is in the territory of this State, as it has in relation to proceedings in courts. The court shall exercise such power in accordance with its own procedures in consideration of the specific features of international arbitration.

A comparative overview of the French and English arbitration law (supplemented, when appropriate, by reference to other jurisdictions) demonstrates the wide support that this principle has encountered.

Let us start with an analysis of French arbitration legislation. Article 1449 of the French *Code of Civil Procedure* reads as follows:

> L'existence d'une convention d'arbitrage ne fait pas obstacle, tant que le tribunal arbitral n'est pas constitué, à ce qu'une partie saisisse une juridiction de l'État aux fins d'obtenir une mesure d'instruction ou une mesure provisoire ou conservatoire.

According to the above provision, a party to an arbitration agreement can apply to a state court for interim measures, provided that the arbitral tribunal has not yet been constituted.[751] The relevant time of constitution will have to be appreciated in light of the terms of the arbitration agreement and applicable arbitration rules.[752] At the same time, if the tribunal was constituted and an award was rendered, Article 1449 allows a party to seek further provisional relief from a state court, provided that the subject matter of the new dispute does not fall under the scope of the award.[753]

After the constitution of the tribunal, Article 1449 of the French *Code of Civil Procedure* creates an exclusive arbitral jurisdiction for interim measures. The provision encapsulates a principle that was affirmed on several occasions by the *Cour de*

---

751. *See* Chainais, *supra* n. 741, at 289. *See also*, for a recent application: CA Rouen, 27 February 2014, No 13/07021; CA Paris, 22 January 2013, No 12/11374.
752. CA Caen, 10 October 2013, No 12/04006 (the constitution requires, at a minimum, acceptance of the appointment as arbitrator: '[A]u jour où le juge des référés commerciaux a été saisi, par assignation du 19 octobre 2012, le tribunal arbitral n'était pas constitué puisque, selon les propres explications de la société Contextus, les deux arbitres désignés par chacune des parties n'ont désigné le président du tribunal arbitral que le 4 décembre 2012, lequel n'a accepté sa mission qu'ultérieurement').
753. CA Reims, 3 July 2012, No 11/01889 ('[L]'acte de mission soumettait aux arbitres la rupture du contrat d'exercice professionnel et ses conséquences et n'abordait pas, pas plus que la sentence rendue le 10 novembre 2011, la mesure d'ordre matériel sollicitée en référé par la société Clinique de Champagne...l'interdiction de connaître du litige visé par une convention d'arbitrage concerne le juge du fond mais pas le juge des référés, qu'ainsi, d'après l'article 1449 du code de procédure civile, l'existence d'une convention d'arbitrage ne fait pas obstacle, tant que le tribunal arbitral n'est pas constitué, ce qui est aujourd'hui le cas puisqu'il n'y a plus d'arbitre saisi, à ce qu'une partie saisisse une juridiction de l'Etat aux fins d'obtenir une mesure d'instruction ou une mesure provisoire ou conservatoire, que n'impliquant pas un examen au fond réservé à l'arbitre, les mesures sollicitées en référé n'empiètent pas sur la compétence des arbitres protégée par la clause d'arbitrage, dont l'efficacité n'est pas épuisée par la procédure qui a eu lieu').

Chapter 7: Awards *Ante Causam* §7.03[B]

cassation.[754] The consequences of the provision at hand – namely, the preclusion of an application for interim relief after the constitution of the tribunal – have been severely criticized. In particular, the provision would unreasonably limit the possibility of obtaining ex parte measures.[755]

The Paris Court of Appeal, aware of the risks inherent to a dogmatic reading of the provision, tried to reach a pragmatic compromise. The court clarified that the parties can nonetheless agree to leave the jurisdiction of state courts in place: even a mere reference to a set of arbitration rules will suffice to do so.[756] This exception will therefore cover a significant number of arbitration cases seated in France, especially if administered under the auspices of the *ICC Rules*, which provide, at Article 28(2) of the 2017 version, that:

> Before the file is transmitted to the arbitral tribunal, and in appropriate circumstances even thereafter, the parties may apply to any competent judicial authority for interim or conservatory measures. The application of a party to a judicial authority for such measures or for the implementation of any such measures ordered by an arbitral tribunal shall not be deemed to be an infringement or a waiver of the arbitration agreement and shall not affect the relevant powers reserved to the arbitral tribunal.

Another important clarification of the scope of application of Article 1449 of the French *Code of Civil Procedure* can be found in a decision rendered by the Caen Court of Appeal, according to which, in case of replacement of an arbitrator, the limit imposed by Article 1449 would become temporarily inapplicable until the new arbitrator accepts the appointment.[757]

The French position departs from a more classical approach, adopted by the Belgian *Code of Civil Procedure*, according to which parties can request interim

---

754. For an overview of the jurisdiction of French courts before the 2011 arbitration reform, *see* Alain Lacabarats, *Les mesures provisoires demandées au juge français en matière d'arbitrage international* in Jean-Michel Jacquet & Emmanuel Jolivet, *Les mesures provisoires dans l'arbitrage commercial international-Évolutions et innovations* 1, 3 (Litec 2008). *See also* Cass Civ 1e, 6 March 1990, 4 Rev Arb 633 (1990) ('en l'absence de volonté contraire des parties, recourant à un arbitrage international, l'existence d'une convention d'arbitrage, tant que le tribunal arbitral ad hoc n'est pas constitué et ne peut donc être effectivement saisi du litige, n'exclut pas, en cas d'urgence, laquelle avait été constatée en la cause, la compétence exceptionnelle du juge des référés pour accorder une provision lorsque la créance n'est pas sérieusement contestable'); Cass Civ 2e, 7 March 2002, No 00-11526 ('La clause compromissoire n'exclut pas, tant que le tribunal arbitral n'est pas constitué, la faculté de saisir le juge des référés aux fins de mesures provisoires ou conservatoires'); Cass Civ 1e, 6 December 2005, No 03-16572.
755. Chainais, *supra* n. 741, at 316.
756. CA Paris, 23 May 2013, No 12/14885 ('[L]es parties n'ont pas renoncé à la compétence du juge étatique, puisque l'article 28 du règlement d'arbitrage de la Chambre de commerce internationale, selon lequel, aux termes de l'article 22 précité, tout litige entre elles devra être tranché, prévoit que': Avant la remise du dossier au tribunal arbitral et même postérieurement si les circonstances s'y prêtent, les parties peuvent demander à toute autorité judiciaire des mesures provisoires ou conservatoires. La saisine d'une autorité judiciaire pour obtenir de telles mesures ou pour faire exécuter des mesures semblables prises par un tribunal arbitral ne contrevient pas à la convention d'arbitrage, ne constitue pas une renonciation à celle-ci, et ne préjudicie pas à la compétence du tribunal arbitral à ce titre').
757. CA Caen, 10 January 2013, No 12/03133.

measures from state courts either before or during the arbitration. Article 1683 of the Belgian *Code of Civil Procedure* reads:

> Une demande en justice, avant ou pendant la procédure arbitrale, en vue de l'obtention de mesures provisoires ou conservatoires et l'octroi de telles mesures ne sont pas incompatibles avec une convention d'arbitrage et n'impliquent pas renonciation à celle-ci.

Despite the apparent clarity of the provision at hand, the Belgian doctrine is divided as to its practical implications.[758] According to certain authors, Article 1683 would create a perfect interchangeability between state courts and arbitrators. The parties could thus seek provisional intervention from whomever they deem fit, be that a judge or an arbitrator.[759] According to a second group of authors,[760] if the arbitral tribunal is constituted, the provisional competence of state courts is to be excluded unless the arbitrators are, under the circumstances, incapable of providing an effective answer to the party's request.[761] Accordingly, the party wishing to seek the intervention of state courts should show the concrete circumstances that render the arbitral tribunal powerless vis-à-vis the request for interim measures.[762] Among such circumstances would be the need to issue a measure against third parties (to the arbitration agreement) and an ex parte request (i.e., a measure issued without hearing from the party against whom such measure is to be enforced).[763]

Finally, the parties could also waive their right to require state courts' intervention,[764] presumably in the arbitration agreement or a later accord.

---

758. For a thorough analysis, *see* Jean-François Van Drooghenbroeck, *Le juge, l'arbitre et le référé: nécessité fait loi* in Achille Saletti, *L'arbitre et le juge étatique*, 203 (Bruylant 2014).
759. Dirk De Meulemeester, *Voorlopige maatregelen in arbitrage* in Maud Piers, *De nieuwe arbitragewet 2013*, 71 (Intersentia 2014); Dirk De Meulemeester & Maud Piers, *The New Belgian Arbitration Law*, 3 ASA Bull 600 (2013).
760. This position was originally conceived by Jacques Van Compernolle, *Les mesures provisoires en droit Belge, Français et Italien, étude de droit comparé* (Bruylant 1998). *See also* Olivier Caprasse, *Les grands arrêts de la Cour de cassation belge en droit de l'arbitrage*, 1 B-Arbitra 145 (2013).
761. Van Drooghenbroeck, *supra* n. 758, at 215. In France, the position is supported by two authoritative commentators. *See* Jarrosson & Pellerin, *supra* n. 326, at 14.
762. Van Drooghenbroeck, *supra* n. 758, at 218.
763. Hakim Boularbah, *Le juge étatique 'bon samaritain' de l'arbitrage* in Michel Flamé & Philippe Lambrecht, *Hommage à Guy Keutgen*, 763 (Bruylant 2013). In order to facilitate the requirement of proving the arbitral tribunal's inability to act, Van Drooghenbroeck (*supra* n. 758, at 219) suggests that the arbitrator could state his or her ability (or inability) to provide an effective provisional measure. This mechanism could even be, according to the same author, specifically set out in the parties' arbitration agreement.
764. Tribunal Commercial de Hasselt, 16 February 2004, (2005) RDC 86. This decision is cited with approval by Caprasse, *supra* n. 742 at 145 ('Ni le fait que les parties ont prévu un arbitrage, ni le fait que les arbitres peuvent également organiser un référé, ni le fait que la demanderesse n'a pas mis l'arbitrage en route, empêche que le président du tribunal se prononce en cas d'urgence comme il est prévu à l'article 1679, si les parties ne l'ont pas exclu. L'affaire est également à considérer de facto comme urgente lorsqu'il faut admettre que cela prend du temps d'organiser l'arbitrage et qu'entre temps un préjudice difficile à réparer pourrait naître'). With reference to an analogous provision of the Italian *Code of Civil Procedure*, an Italian court has reached the opposite conclusion: the time required for the constitution of the arbitral tribunal cannot be considered, per se, as a relevant *periculum in mora*. *See* Tribunale di Nola Sez. II, 18 April 2013 (unpublished).

Chapter 7: Awards *Ante Causam* §7.03[B]

Now, the above jurisdictions raise delicate problems regarding the granting of interim measures in the phase preceding the beginning of the arbitration. While it is certainly desirable to preserve an effective recourse to state courts for provisional measures in the absence of a functioning arbitral tribunal, the risk of undermining the arbitration agreement is tangible. As correctly noted,[765] it would be advisable to require the courts to grant conditional interim measures, subordinating the effectiveness of such measures to the requirement to file a request for arbitration. A notable example of this choice can be found in Article 669-*octies*, section 3, of the Italian *Code of Civil Procedure*.

According to this provision, the party that has obtained the interim measure shall notify, within the time limit fixed by the court (which shall not exceed sixty days), the request for arbitration to the opposing party.[766] In the absence of such request, the opposing party can have the interim measure declared ineffective (Article 669-*novies*, section 2). It should be noted that this requirement operates vis-à-vis all interim measures issued by an Italian court, with the exception of a measure granted pursuant to Article 700 (*provvedimento d'urgenza*).[767] This implies that the requirement operates in cases of *sequestro* ('arrest'), which covers a large spectrum of interim measures. Article 700, in fact, only has a subsidiary function and can be applied only in cases where other interim measures are not capable of providing an effective answer.[768]

It seems that the same concern regarding the frustration of arbitration agreements is shared by English courts. In *Cetelem v. Roust Holdings*, it was held:[769]

> The whole purpose of giving the court power to make [provisional] orders is to assist the arbitral tribunal in cases of urgency or before there is an arbitration on foot. Otherwise, it is all too easy for a party who is bent on a policy of non-cooperation to frustrate the arbitral process. Of course, in any case where the court is called upon to exercise the power, it must take great care not to usurp the arbitral process and to ensure, by exacting appropriate undertakings from the claimant, that the substantive questions are reserved for the arbitrator.

This observation gives us the opportunity to discuss English law on provisional relief before the constitution of the arbitral tribunal. On this point, the relevant provision is found in section 44 of the English *Arbitration Act 1996*, which admits the possibility of requesting the intervention of state courts, 'to the extent that the arbitral tribunal, and any arbitral or other institution or person vested by the parties ... has no power or is unable for the time being to act effectively' (section 44(5)). The lack of a

---

765. Chainais & Jarrosson, *supra* n. 90, at 80.
766. *See* CA Genova I Sez, 16 May 2007 (unpublished) (the provision also requires the party to appoint an arbitrator – a circumstance that may be difficult to reconcile with certain institutional arbitration rules that proceeds with the appointment on behalf of the parties).
767. This exception is contemplated by Art. 669-*octies*, section 6, and extended to any kind of measure that may be able to anticipate the effects of a final decision. The exception also covers the cases addressed by Art. 688 (*damnun infectum* and *operis novi denuntiatio*). *See* Mandrioli, *supra* n. 89, Vol. IV, 262 ff.
768. *Ibid.* at 325. As a result, an Art. 700 measure is usually requested in situations akin to *quia timet* injunctions, that is, negative injunctions ordering the addressee to refrain from a certain conduct.
769. [2005] 1 WLR 3555 (CA) at para. 71. Excerpt cited in Sutton et al., *supra* n. 92, at 429–430.

constituted tribunal has been assimilated, by the literature, to a case of an inability to act effectively.[770] This position is supported by a well-known case.[771] In any event, it should be noted that the parties may validly decide to exclude the application of this provision (section 44(1)).[772] The exclusion, however, must be clear.[773]

Finally, interim relief before the constitution of the tribunal can only be sought in urgent cases,[774] since section 44(4) specifies that 'if the case is not one of urgency, the court shall act only on the application of a party to the arbitral proceedings ... made with the permission of the tribunal or the agreement in writing of the other parties'. However, if the arbitration rules chosen by the parties provide for an emergency arbitrator prior to constitution of the tribunal, this condition of inability to act effectively may not be met. In *Gerald Metals SA v. Timis*,[775] the High Court was seized with an application for a freezing injunction. The applicant had originally requested the appointment of an emergency arbitrator and/or the expedited formation of the arbitral tribunal under Article 9A and 9B of the *LCIA Rules*. The arbitral institution, however, rejected the request on grounds that the opposing party had given undertakings not to dispose of certain assets. In considering the application for the freezing injunction, Justice Leggatt first noted that the goal of Article 9A and 9B *LCIA Rules*, was that of reducing 'the need to invoke the assistance of the court in cases of urgency by enabling an arbitral tribunal to act quickly in an appropriate case'.[776] As such, only in cases where an emergency arbitrator, or a tribunal constituted under a set of expedited provisions, or an otherwise regularly constituted tribunal lack the sufficient powers will an application for a court-ordered interim measure under section 44 of the Act be successful.[777]

Another common law jurisdiction, the US, has moved in a similar direction. While the US *Federal Arbitration Act* (*FAA*) 'only grants federal courts the power to order provisional measures with regard to a narrow category of maritime disputes',[778] several *FAA* cases recognize the courts' power to issue interim measures 'to preserve

---

770. Merkin & Flannery, *supra* n. 96, at 177; Hakeem Seriki, *Injunctive Relief and International Arbitration*, 91 (Informa Law 2015); Sutton et al., *supra* n. 92, at 432; Kieron O'Callaghan & Jerome Finnis, *Support and Supervision by the Courts* in Julian D.M. et al., *Arbitration in England*, 430 (Kluwer Law 2013).
771. *Cetelem SA v. Roust Holdings Ltd* [2004] EWHC 3175 (QB).
772. This can be achieved in the arbitration clause or by a reference to a set of arbitration rules that are incompatible with the powers set out in section 44 of the English *Arbitration Act 1996*. *See Vertex Data Science v. Powergen Retail* [2006] 2 Lloyd's Rep. 591, cited in Sutton et al., *supra* n. 92, at 431.
773. O'Callaghan & Finnis, *supra* n. 770, at 430, citing *Re: Q's Estate* [1999] 1 Lloyd's Rep 931 and *SAB Miller v. East Africa Breweries* [2009] EWCA Civ 1564.
774. O'Callaghan & Finnis, *supra* n. 770, at 429. If the tribunal has not been constituted, urgency will be considered in re ipsa: *Econet Wireless Ltd v. Networks Ltd and Ors* [2006] EWHC 1568 (Comm).
775. [2016] EWHC 2327 (Ch).
776. *Ibid.* at para. 7.
777. *Ibid.* at para. 8. *See* Christina Schuetz, *Where to Seek Injunctive Relief Before the Constitution of the Arbitral Tribunal?* 1 ICC Bull 14, 15 (2017) ('The ruling ... shows that a party to an arbitration agreement seeking interim injunctive relief before the constitution of the tribunal may be expected to apply to the arbitral institution for the appointment of an emergency arbitrator').
778. Born, *supra* n. 4, at 2540.

the status quo and the meaningfulness of the arbitration process'[779] before the constitution of the arbitral tribunal. *Toyo Tire Holdings*[780] is particularly instructive. In this case, the claimant was appealing a district court decision rejecting a request for a preliminary injunction to prevent, among other things, the opposing party from terminating a partnership agreement. In this case, the parties were bound by the 1998 *ICC Rules*, and while a request for arbitration had been filed, the tribunal was not yet in place. The Court of Appeal took advantage of the case to clarify that 'the congressional desire to enforce arbitration agreements would frequently be frustrated if the courts were precluded from issuing preliminary injunctive relief to preserve status quo pending arbitration and, *ipso facto*, the meaningfulness of the arbitration process'.[781] Moreover, 'the selection of arbitrators and the constitution of the arbitral panel necessarily takes time. ... [P]arties would be without remedy when, as here, the delay associated with securing an arbitration panel's ruling on interim relief could defeat any ultimate award'.[782]

In conclusion, according to the principle of complementarity arbitrators are called upon to exercise a provisional form of adjudication, unless the arbitral tribunal is unable to act (or has not been constituted). In such a case, state courts can provide provisional relief. However, recent developments in administered arbitration will inevitably lead to questions about the application of such principle. As will be explained in the following part, emergency arbitration proceedings have now been implemented by the most important arbitration centres around the world, aiming to replace the provisional protection *ante causam* before state courts with an arbitral emergency procedure.

§7.04 THE EMERGENCE OF A PROVISIONAL ADJUDICATORY POWER *ANTE CAUSAM*

In recent years, arbitration users have become increasingly frustrated by the lack of a provisional form of arbitral protection before the constitution of the arbitral tribunal. As a consequence, a number of institutions began to offer a set of additional rules providing for an *emergency arbitrator*. Let us now consider how such proceedings are articulated in the arbitration rules of the most prominent arbitral institutions.

[A] The Precursor: The *International Arbitration Rules* of the ICDR

On 1 May 2006, the ICDR[783] was the first international arbitration institution to introduce an emergency arbitration procedure, from which the parties had to opt out in

---
779. *Blom ASA v. Pictometry International Corp*, 757 F. Supp. 2d 238 (2010).
780. *Toyo Tire Holdings of Ams Inc v. Cont'l Tire N. Am. Inc*, 609 F.3d 975 (2010).
781. *Ibid.* at para. 12.
782. *Ibid.* at paras 13-14.
783. The ICDR was established in 1996, and serves as the international branch of the American Arbitration Association (AAA). For more information, visit www.icdr.org.

order to exclude its application.[784] Article 37 ('Emergency Measures of Protection'), which was introduced with an amendment to the 2005 *International Arbitration Rules* (*ICDR Rules*), stated (section 2) that 'a party in need of emergency relief prior to the constitution of the tribunal shall notify the administrator and all other parties in writing of the nature of the relief sought and the reasons why such relief is required on an emergency basis'.

The provision is now incorporated in Article 6 of the 2014 *ICDR Rules*, according to which after an expedited appointment and the establishment of a schedule providing a reasonable opportunity for all parties to be heard (section 3), the emergency arbitrator becomes entitled to order or award any interim or conservancy measure deemed necessary (section 4). Unlike other institutions, the ICDR allows the arbitrator's decision to take the form of an award. This provision is of significant importance, for it takes a clear stand vis-à-vis the debate regarding the enforceability of decisions rendered by an emergency arbitrator. Moreover, according to Article 6 (section 5) of the *ICDR Rules*, the power to render a decision expires after the constitution of the tribunal, which will further become vested with the power to modify or vacate the interim award or order rendered by the emergency arbitrator.

Finally, according to Article 7, '[a] request for interim measures addressed by a party to a judicial authority shall not be deemed incompatible with Article 6 or with the agreement to arbitrate or a waiver of the right to arbitrate'. While this provision reaffirms the principle of complementarity[785] by clarifying that the emergency arbitrator procedure does not exclude, per se, the possibility of requesting a court-ordered interim measure (a circumstance that some arbitration acts seem to put into question),[786] it is unclear how a party will be able to justify the request for provisional protection before state courts. In such a case, in fact, the party will no longer be able to argue that the constitution of the tribunal would require an excessively long delay.

[B] The *Arbitration Rules* of the SCC: A Relief That Is Truly *Ante Causam*

In 2010, the Arbitration Institute of the SCC promulgated a new set of *Arbitration Rules* (*SCC Rules*) featuring a new emergency arbitrator.[787] The emergency arbitrator is now

---

784. Born, *supra* n. 4, at 2442. *See generally* Ben H. Sheppard & John M. Townsend, *Holding the Fort Until the Arbitrators Are Appointed: The New ICDR International Emergency Rules*, 2 Disp Res J 74 (2006); Joseph M. Tirado & Sarah Nelson Smith, *New ICDR International Emergency Measures Protection Rule*, 5 TDM 1 (2006); Guillaume Lemenez & Paul Quigley, *The ICDR's Emergency Arbitrator in Action- Part I: A Look at the Empirical Data*, 3 Disp Res J 60 (2008); Guillaume Lemenez & Paul Quigley, *The ICDR's Emergency Arbitrator in Action- Part II: Enforcing Emergency Arbitrator Decisions*, 4 Disp Res J 1 (2008); Mark Kantor, *Comparing Expedite Emergency Relief Under the AAA/ICDR, ICC and LCIA Arbitration Rules*, 24:8 CPR 136 (2006). *See also* Martin F. Gusy, James M. Hosking & Franz T. Schwarz, *A Guide to the ICDR International Arbitration Rules*, 299 ff. (Oxford University Press 2011).
785. *Supra* §7.07[B].
786. Compare section 44(5) of the *Arbitration Act 1996*, which subordinates court-ordered interim measures to the tribunal's inability to act.
787. For an overview of the *SCC Rules*, *see* Marie Öhrström, *SCC Rules* in Rolf A. Schütze, *Institutional Arbitration*, 815–862 (Verlag, Hart & Nomos, 2013). On the SCC emergency

regulated by the 2017 version of the *SCC Rules* (appendix II), which entered into force on 1 January 2017.

Article 1(1) of Appendix II states that '[a] party may apply for the appointment of an Emergency Arbitrator until the case has been referred to an Arbitral Tribunal pursuant to Article 22 of the Arbitration Rules'. As Article 9(4)(iii) of Appendix II suggests ('the emergency decision ceases to be binding if ... arbitration is not commenced within 30 days from the date of the decision'), any party can apply for such a measure even prior to the beginning of arbitration proceedings.[788]

Pursuant to Article 2 of Appendix II, the interested party shall file an application containing – *inter alia* – a summary of the dispute, a statement of the interim relief sought and the reasons for it, and a copy or *description* of the relevant arbitration agreement or clause. Appendix II neither cites nor reproduces the provision set out in Article 37(5) of the main text of the *SCC Rules*, according to which 'a request for interim measure made by a party to a judicial authority is not incompatible with the arbitration agreement or with these Rules'.

This regime raises an interesting question, namely, whether the SCC intended to foreclose pre-arbitration interim applications before state courts. The most likely answer is that the provision was not intended to forbid parties from seeking state courts' intervention but rather to discourage them from doing so.

After the appointment (which, pursuant to Article 4(1) of Appendix II, shall occur within twenty-four hours of the receipt of the application),[789] the emergency arbitrator is required to render a decision no later than five days from the date on which the application was referred to him or her (Article 8(1) of Appendix II). It is worth noting that the SCC board will not proceed with the appointment in cases of a manifest lack of jurisdiction over the dispute (Article 4(2) of Appendix II). This does not mean, however, that it will 'make *prima facie* jurisdictional decisions'.[790] On the contrary, the board will assess if the dispute *manifestly* falls outside the scope of the arbitration agreement (or clause), or is otherwise *manifestly* null, void, or ineffective, with the sole purpose of deciding if it should proceed with the appointment of the emergency arbitrator. The emergency arbitrator can be challenged 'within 24 hours from when the circumstances giving rise to the challenge ... became known to the party' bringing the challenge (Article 4(3) of Appendix II). While appendix II to the *SCC Rules* does not expressly require the emergency arbitrator to file a statement of independence, the institution indeed requires such a statement.[791]

---

arbitrator, *see* Patricia Shaughnessy, *Pre-arbitral Urgent Relief: The New SCC Emergency Arbitrator Rules*, 27:4 J Int'l Arb 337–360 (2010).

788. The terminology adopted in this provision is somewhat imprecise. The term 'party', in fact, usually presupposes the existence of proceedings. This could be avoided by specifying 'party to the arbitration agreement'.

789. Article 4(1) *SCC Rules*: 'The Board *shall seek to appoint* an Emergency Arbitrator *within 24 hours* of receipt of the application for the appointment of an Emergency Arbitrator' [emphasis added]. According to Shaughnessy, *supra* n. 787, at 340, the phrase 'seek to appoint' should provide flexibility for complex cases, allowing for a de facto extension of the 24-hour period.

790. Cf. Shaughnessy, *supra* n. 787, at 341.

791. Lotta Knapp, *SCC Practice–Emergency Arbitrator Decisions 2014* (online), http://www.sccinstitute.com/, at 2. Cf. Schedule 1, section 5 of the Singapore International Arbitration

Under the *SCC Rules*, the emergency arbitrator is required to conduct the procedure in an impartial manner, giving each party an equal and reasonable opportunity to present its case (Article of Appendix II), which refers to Article 23 of the *SCC Rules*). The same principles inspire the provision set out in Article 4(4) of Appendix II, according to which 'the emergency arbitrator cannot act as an arbitrator in any future arbitration relating to the dispute, unless otherwise agreed by the parties'.

The rules do not mention the requirements that the interested party must meet in order to obtain the requested interim measure. The matter will be left to the discretion of the arbitrator.[792] Moreover, it should be noted that the decision rendered by the emergency arbitrator can either take the form of an order or an award.[793] In any event, the decision shall be dated, signed, and state the reasons upon which it is based (Article 8(2)(ii) and (iii) of Appendix II).

Finally, it is worth discussing the effects of the emergency decision. The relevant provision is found in Article 9(3) of Appendix II – '[b]y agreeing to arbitration under the Arbitration Rules, the parties undertake to comply with any emergency decision without delay'.

This rule does not mean that the decision shall exclusively be treated as having a contractual nature. The *SCC Rules* simply acknowledge the fact that the decision is a temporary one. As stated by Article 9(2) of Appendix II, the decision can in fact be amended or revoked by the arbitral tribunal. Furthermore, the decision will cease to be binding if the arbitral tribunal makes a final award or the arbitration is not commenced[794] within thirty days from the date on which the emergency decision was issued (Article 9(4)(ii) and (iii) of Appendix II).[795]

[C]   The 2014 *Arbitration Rules* of the LCIA

Most recently, the LCIA has introduced a new set of rules providing for an emergency arbitrator.[796] According to Article 9B of the 2014 LCIA *Arbitration Rules* (*LCIA Rules*):

Centre (SIAC) 2016 *Arbitration Rules*: 'Prior to accepting appointment, a prospective Emergency Arbitrator shall disclose to the Registrar any circumstance that may give rise to justifiable doubts as to his impartiality or independence. Any challenge to the appointment of the Emergency Arbitrator must be made within one business day of the communication by the Registrar to the parties of the appointment of the Emergency Arbitrator and the circumstances disclosed'.

792. Shaughnessy, *supra* n. 787, at 343.
793. This conclusion is suggested by Art. 37(3) *SCC Rules*, which applies, pursuant to Art. 1(2) of Appendix II), also to emergency proceedings.
794. The arbitration is considered to be initiated on the date of the receipt of the request for arbitration. *See also* Öhrström, *supra* n. 787, at 820.
795. Article 9(4)(iv), Appendix II *SCC Rules* further states that the decision will cease to be binding if 'the case is not referred to an Arbitral Tribunal within 90 days from the date of the emergency decision'.
796. Dipen Sabharwal & Rebecca Zaman, *Vive la difference: Convergence and Conformity in the Rules Reforms of Arbitral Institutions: The Case of the LCIA Rules 2014*, 31:6 J Int'l Arb 700, 702 ff. (2014); Laurence Ponty, *Key Features of the LCIA Arbitration Rules*, 32:4 ASA Bull 757, 760–761 (2014).

Chapter 7: Awards *Ante Causam* §7.04[C]

in the case of emergency at any time prior to the formation or expedited formation of the Arbitral Tribunal (under Articles 5 or 9A), any party may apply to the LCIA Court for the immediate appointment of a temporary sole arbitrator to conduct emergency proceedings pending the formation or expedited formation of the Arbitral Tribunal (the 'Emergency Arbitrator').

The provision at hand presupposes that arbitration proceedings have to be already initiated by the claimant.[797] However, the filing of the respondent's answer is not necessary to proceed with an application for emergency arbitrator (Article 5.1).[798] The application, which can come from any party (Article 9.4 *LCIA Rules*), shall be delivered or notified to all other parties to the arbitration (Article 9.5 *LCIA Rules*). This excludes *ab initio* any ex parte proceedings.[799]

If we add the fact that the emergency arbitrator will be appointed by the LCIA court within three days of the receipt of the application[800] (if such an application is granted after a prima facie review)[801] and that he or she is required to render a decision no later than fourteen days following the appointment,[802] this may turn out to be a long timeframe, and as a result, the procedure may not always be able to cope with highly urgent situations.[803]

Furthermore, according to Article 9.5 of the *LCIA Rules*, the application shall set out: '(i) the specific grounds for requiring, as an emergency, the appointment of an Emergency Arbitrator; and (ii) the specific claim, with reasons, for emergency relief'. Such requirements raise the question of what test needs to be met by the interested party in order to obtain emergency relief.

---

797. Article 9.5 *LCIA Rules*.
798. Article 5.1 *LCIA Rules*: 'The formation of the Arbitral Tribunal by the LCIA Court shall not be impeded by any controversy between the parties relating to the sufficiency of the Request or the Response. The LCIA Court may also proceed with the arbitration notwithstanding that the Request is incomplete or the Response is missing, late or incomplete'.
799. Article 9.7 *LCIA Rules*: 'The Emergency Arbitrator may conduct the emergency proceedings in any manner determined by the Emergency Arbitrator to be appropriate in the circumstances, taking account of the nature of such emergency proceedings, the need to afford to each party, if possible, an opportunity to be consulted on the claim for emergency relief (whether or not it avails itself of such opportunity), the claim and reasons for emergency relief and the parties' further submissions (if any)'.
800. Pursuant to Art. 9.5 *LCIA Rules*, the emergency arbitrator can be challenged or revoked according to the rules set out in Art. 10 *LCIA Rules*. After the revocation, any party can apply for an expedited appointment of a replacement arbitrator.
801. Article 9.6 *LCIA Rules*. See Ponty, *supra* n. 796, at 761. This interpretation of Art. 9.5 *LCIA Rules* is suggested by an analogy with Art. 9 of the 1998 version of the Rules, under which *any party* could apply for the expedited formation of the tribunal. The LCIA court had – actually, *has*, since the provision was transposed in the 2014 version – to be persuaded of the prima facie existence of an 'exceptional urgency'. *See* Peter Turner & Reza Mohstashami, *A Guide to the LCIA Arbitration Rules*, 73 (Oxford University Press 2009). For an overview, *see* Sabina Konrad & Robert Hunter, *LCIA Rules* in Rolf A. Scütze, *Institutional Arbitration*, 445 ff. (Beck & Hart Publishing 2013).
802. Article 9.8 *LCIA Rules*.
803. In light of Art. 9.7 *LCIA Rules*, a helpful acceleration can nonetheless be obtained thanks to the lack of a mandatory hearing: ' … The Emergency Arbitrator is not required to hold any hearing with the parties (whether in person, by telephone or otherwise) and may decide the claim for emergency relief on available documentation'.

An author suggested that 'the LCIA Court will inter alia apply the usual test (sic!) as to whether the harm alleged by the applicant is likely to be repaired in a proper manner by subsequent monetary relief'.[804] However, as explained in the Introduction to this chapter, the *irreparable harm* test is far from generating a consensus.[805] Therefore, it would be advisable to develop an autonomous test, drawing on the peculiarities of international arbitration. The choice to avoid mentioning any specific test in Article 9.5 of the *LCIA Rules* was certainly not a coincidence.

Moreover, it should be noted that Article 9B on emergency relief ('Emergency') imposes, on its face, a strict requirement. In any case, we can assume that the emergency test of Article 9B of the *LCIA Rules* will be taken very seriously by the LCIA court, which, in the past, has proved to do likewise with the 'exceptional urgency' requirement for expedited formation under Article 9A of the *LCIA Rules*.[806]

In light of the above, the applicant is required to set out the reasons explaining why it is not possible to await the constitution of the tribunal. It should be noted, moreover, that since the assistance of the emergency arbitrator can also be sought in cases of expedited formation of the tribunal (Article 9A *LCIA Rules*), the *thema probandum* may have to vary accordingly.[807] That is, in cases involving expedited formation, which presupposes the existence of 'an exceptional urgency', the applicant will be required to explain why expedited formation alone would be insufficient and an emergency arbitrator is required.[808] This might turn out to be a cumbersome exercise. Furthermore this leads to an imbalance between a party requesting an expedited formation, and a party having opted for the regular constitution of the tribunal, for the first party will end up with a stricter test to meet. This raises the question of whether every party is expected to prove that expedited formation would not be sufficient. In light of the spirit of the applicable provisions, such an interpretation should be preferred. Article 9B would in fact imply a higher standard than the 'exceptional urgency' requirement set out in Article 9A.[809]

Turning now to the decision of the emergency arbitrator, Article 9.9 of the *LCIA Rules* states:

> An order of the Emergency Arbitrator shall be made in writing, with reasons. An award of the Emergency Arbitrator shall comply with Article 26.2 and, when made, take effect as an award under Article 26.8 (subject to Article 9.11). The Emergency Arbitrator shall be responsible for delivering any order or award to the Registrar, who shall transmit the same promptly to the parties by electronic means, in addition to paper form (if so requested by any party). In the event of any disparity between electronic and paper forms, the electronic form shall prevail.

---

804. Ponty, *supra* n. 796, at 761.
805. Cf. Yesilirmak, *supra* n. 748, at 3–4.
806. Several applications were in fact rejected under the 1998 rules (around 40%). *See* Turner & Mohstashami, *supra* n. 801, at 73.
807. Scherer et al., *supra* n. 453, at 163.
808. Cf. The London Court of International Arbitration, *Notes on Emergency Procedures* (online), http://www.lcia.org/adr-services/guidance-notes.aspx, at 2.
809. Scherer et al., *supra* n. 453, at 147.

Article 9.11 of the *LCIA Rules* further adds:

> Any order or award of the Emergency Arbitrator (apart from any order adjourning to the Arbitral Tribunal, when formed, any part of the claim for emergency relief) may be confirmed, varied, discharged or revoked, in whole or in part, by order or award made by the Arbitral Tribunal upon application by any party or upon its own initiative.

In light of the above provisions, the decision of the emergency arbitrator can either take the form of an order or of an award. In both cases, the arbitral tribunal has the power (even *sua sponte*) to modify or revoke such a decision. This situation raises the question not only of the nature of the emergency arbitrator's decision but also of its enforceability. These issues will be treated in section §7.05.

Finally, as anticipated, the principle of complementarity preserves the jurisdiction of state courts for interim relief. Consistently, the interaction between the emergency arbitrator and state courts is regulated by Article 9.12 of the *LCIA Rules* as follows:

> Article 9B [Emergency Arbitrator] shall not prejudice any party's right to apply to a state court or other legal authority for any interim or conservatory measures before the formation of the Arbitration Tribunal; and it shall not be treated as an alternative to or substitute for the exercise of such right. During the emergency proceedings, any application to and any order by such court or authority shall be communicated promptly in writing to the Emergency Arbitrator, the Registrar and all other parties.

Once again, given the sophisticated procedures set up for providing urgent relief, it will be difficult to justify the intervention of state courts.

[D] The *Arbitration Rules* of the International Court of Arbitration (ICC): A Missed Opportunity?

The current *Arbitration Rules* of the ICC entered into force on 1 March 2017.[810] They feature a set of provisions on emergency arbitration proceedings (namely, Article 29 *ICC Rules*, and appendix V *ICC Rules*, 'Emergency Arbitrator Rules'), which were originally introduced under the 2012 version of the *ICC Rules*.

---

810. For an overview of the previous 2012 version of the ICC Rules, which contain identical provisions on emergency arbitration, *see generally* Pierre Mayer & Eduardo Silva Romero, *Le nouveau règlement d'arbitrage de la Chambre de commerce internationale (CCI)*, 4 Rev Arb 897–922 (2011); Andreas Reiner & Christian Aschauer, *ICC Rules* in Rolf A. Schütze, *Institutional Arbitration*, 38 (Beck & Hart Publishing 2013); Karin Calvo Goller, *The 2012 ICC Rules of Arbitration–An Accelerated Procedure and Substantial Changes*, 29:3 J Int'l Arb 323–344 (2012); Elisabeth Leimbacher, *Efficiency Under the New ICC Rules of Arbitration of 2012: First Glimpse at the New Practice*, 31:2 ASA Bull 298–315 (2013).

[1] Exclusion of Emergency Arbitration

As a general rule, the provisions on emergency arbitration will apply unless the parties agree upon their exclusion or replacement with another pre-arbitral procedure for interim measures (Article 29(6)(b) and (c)), *ICC Rules*.[811] The scope of the second case of exclusion was subject to controversy. One commentator has suggested that the above provision would not lead to the exclusion of recourse to emergency proceedings, if the decision resulting from the pre-arbitral measure has a contractual nature.[812] This position was rejected by other authors,[813] on the ground that the exception was specifically introduced after the concerns voiced by the users of the International Federation of Consulting Engineers (FIDIC) model contracts,[814] which contain an ICC arbitration clause and provide for a form of pre-arbitral relief (i.e., a the decision rendered by the dispute board). Without going any further into the details of the matter, it is important to emphasize that the exception set out in Article 29(6)(c) of the *ICC Rules* excludes the possibility of resorting to ICC emergency arbitration only if the pre-arbitral procedure 'provides for the granting of conservatory, interim or similar measures'. The wording of the article will thus require a pragmatic analysis of the pre-arbitral mechanism chosen by the parties.

Article 29 of the *ICC Rules* provides for two other cases of exclusion: (i) 'the arbitration agreement under the Rules was concluded before 1 January 2012' (Article 29(6)(a) *ICC Rules*); and (ii) the parties are neither signatories of the arbitration agreement under the rules that is relied upon for the application nor successors to such signatories (Article 29(5) *ICC Rules*). While the first exception introduces a guarantee in favour of the parties that entered an arbitration clause or agreement before the original entry into force of the emergency arbitration provisions rules, the purpose of the second one would be that of reducing 'the potential for abuse of the procedure and to provide a prima facie jurisdictional test that is straightforward for the President'[815] of the International Court of Arbitration (who is responsible for the administration of emergency proceedings). As a result, Article 29(5) of the *ICC Rules* introduced a specific jurisdictional test,[816] whose principal purpose was excluding the application of

---

811. Fry, Greenberg & Mazza, *supra* n. 449, at para. 3-1101.
812. Nathalie Voser, *Overview of the Most Important Changes in the Revised ICC Arbitration Rules*, 29:4 ASA Bull 783, 814 (2011).
813. Fry, Greenberg & Mazza, *supra* n. 449, at para. 3-1102; Christopher Boog, *Commentary on the ICC Rules, Article 29 [Emergency arbitrator]* in Manuel Arroyo, *Arbitration in Switzerland: The Practitioners' Guide* 814, 818 (Kluwer Law 2013) 814 at 818 [Boog, *Article 29*].
814. *Ibid.* at 818.
815. Fry, Greenberg & Mazza, *supra* n. 449, at para. 3-1098.
816. Cf. Art. 6(3) and (4) *ICC Rules*. According to such provisions, objections related to the existence, validity, or scope of the arbitration agreement are to be decided by the arbitrators, unless the Secretary General decides to seize the International Court of Arbitration of the ICC (an independent body of the International Chamber of Commerce, which administers the resolution of disputes by arbitral tribunals). This decision will usually be taken in exceptional cases, either when there is no evidence of an arbitration agreement or when one of the claims in the request for arbitration refers to a non-signatory party.

emergency proceedings in treaty-based arbitrations[817] and rendering ineffective the group of companies and group of contracts doctrine (which may both allow for an extension of the scope of the arbitration agreement).[818]

Article 29(5) of the *ICC Rules* has an undeniable appeal and can be praised for its simplicity, which allows for an expedited procedure. It should be noted, however, that this provision alters the ordinary, subjective scope of an arbitration agreement. As a result, the jurisdiction of the emergency arbitrator will be more restricted if compared to that of the arbitral tribunal. Yet it seems difficult to justify why a non-signatory, which would otherwise be subject to the jurisdiction of the tribunal, should not have recourse to emergency proceedings. At the same time, the choice of the term 'signatory' will require a careful analysis in the assessment of the application.

[2] Emergency Arbitration Application and Proceedings

The application of emergency measures is regulated by Article 29(1) of the *ICC Rules*, and Article 1, appendix V, *ICC Rules*. The former provision states:

> A party that needs urgent interim or conservatory measures that cannot await the constitution of an arbitral tribunal ('Emergency Measures') may make an application for such measures pursuant to the Emergency Arbitrator Rules in Appendix V.[819] Any such application shall be accepted only if it is received by the Secretariat prior to the transmission of the file to the arbitral tribunal pursuant to Article 16 and irrespective of whether the party making the application has already submitted its 'Request for Arbitration'.

---

817. Nathalie Voser & Christopher Boog, *ICC Emergency Arbitrator Proceedings: An Overview*, para. 2.2.3 (ICC Publishing 2011); Fry, Greenberg & Mazza, *supra* n. 449, at para. 3-1098.
818. Christian Aschauer, *Use of the ICC Emergency Arbitrator to Protect the Arbitral Proceedings*, 23:2 ICC Bull 5, 8 (2012); Boog, *Article 29*, *supra* n. 813, at 815–816.
819. Article 1(3), Appendix V, *ICC Rules*:

> 'The Application shall contain the following information:
>
> a) the name in full, description, address and other contact details of each of the parties;
> b) the name in full, address and other contact details of any person(s) representing the applicant;
> c) a description of the circumstances giving rise to the Application and of the underlying dispute referred or to be referred to arbitration;
> d) a statement of the Emergency Measures sought;
> e) the reasons why the applicant needs urgent interim or conservatory measures that cannot await the constitution of an arbitral tribunal;
> f) any relevant agreements and, in particular, the arbitration agreement;
> g) any agreement as to the place of the arbitration, the applicable rules of law or the language of the arbitration;
> h) proof of payment of the amount referred to in Article 7(1) of this Appendix;
> i) any Request for Arbitration and any other submissions in connection with the underlying dispute, which have been filed with the Secretariat by any of the parties to the emergency arbitrator proceedings prior to the making of the Application.
> The Application may contain such other documents or information as the applicant considers appropriate or as may contribute to the efficient examination of the Application'.

In light of the above provision, a party can request the appropriate emergency measures only in case of urgent need for interim or conservatory measures 'that cannot await the constitution of the tribunal'. According to several authors, this would be the only substantive requirement set out by the *ICC Rules*.[820] This interpretation would ultimately encourage arbitrators to turn to the substantive conditions for interim measures enshrined in Article 17A of the UNCITRAL *Model Law on International Commercial Arbitration*.[821] Others have advocated the application of the general test contained in Article 28(1) of the *ICC Rules*[822] for applications for interim measures after the constitution of the arbitral tribunal.[823] In other words, the emergency arbitrator should be allowed to grant the 'appropriate' measures.[824]

In practice, emergency arbitrators have been shown to rely extensively on international standards, that is, 'whether there was a prima facie case for the measures requested and whether there was a risk of irreparable harm'.[825] Nevertheless, in one of the first ten cases under the *ICC Rules*, the applicant obtained interim relief 'despite the absence of such a risk, as the dispute would otherwise have worsened'.[826] Likewise, one commentator has suggested that a further requirement would be applicable, that is, the proportionality requirement.[827] This would mandate that the emergency measure could be granted only if the possible injury caused by the measure does not exceed the advantage obtained by the applicant.[828]

Moving on to the other procedural steps put forth by the *ICC Rules*, it is important to underline that according to Article 1(6), appendix V, *ICC Rules*, the president of the court will terminate the emergency arbitration proceedings 'if a Request for Arbitration has not been received by the Secretariat from the applicant within 10 days of the Secretariat's receipt of the Application, unless the emergency arbitrator determines that a longer period of time is necessary'. As shown above, the possibility of filing a request for emergency measures before submitting a request for arbitration is not only in line with the best practices of other arbitration institutions[829] but also a guarantee for an expedited procedure. This is a core tool for a truly *ante causam* protection. At the same

---

820. Voser & Boog, *supra* n. 817, at para. 3.3; Boog, *Article 29*, *supra* n. 813, at 819; Aschauer, *supra* n. 818, at 8; Eliseo Castineira, *The Emergency Arbitrator in the 2012 ICC Rules of Arbitration*, 4 Cah Arb 67 (2012); W. Laurence Craig & Laurent Jaeger, *The 2012 ICC Rules: Important Changes and Issues for Future Resolutions*, 4 Cah Arb 15, 18 (2012); Andrea Carlevaris & José Ricardo Feris, *Running in the ICC Emergency Arbitrator Rules: The First Ten Cases*, 23:1 ICC Bull 25, 36 (2014).
821. *Ibid*.
822. Article 28(1) *ICC Rules*: 'Unless the parties have otherwise agreed, as soon as the file has been transmitted to it, the arbitral tribunal may, at the request of a party, order any interim or conservatory measure it deems appropriate. The arbitral tribunal may make the granting of any such measure subject to appropriate security being furnished by the requesting party. Any such measure shall take the form of an order, giving reasons, or of an award, as the arbitral tribunal considers appropriate'.
823. Fry, Greenberg & Mazza, *supra* n. 449, at para. 3-1059; Boog, *Article 29*, *supra* n. 813, at 819.
824. Carlevaris & Feris, *supra* n. 820, at 36.
825. *Ibid*.
826. *Ibid*.
827. Aschauer, *supra* n. 818, at 10.
828. *Ibid*.
829. In particular, see *SCC Rules*, *supra* p. 223 ff.

time, the ten-day period for filing the request for arbitration constitutes a barrier against potential abuses, especially where the applicant intends to use the emergency proceedings to put pressure on the opposing party.[830]

After receipt of the application and a positive decision by the president of the court to move ahead with the emergency proceedings, the Secretariat will transmit a copy of the application and the documents attached thereto to the responding party (Article 1(5), appendix V, *ICC Rules*). In the meantime (i.e., 'normally within two days from the Secretariat's receipt of the Application'),[831] the president will appoint an emergency arbitrator (Article 2(1), appendix V, *ICC Rules*), unless the file has already been transmitted to the arbitral tribunal (Article 2(2), appendix V, *ICC Rules*). As one commentator notes, the Secretariat will normally advise the President 'as to suitable candidates to act as emergency arbitrators'.[832]

Under the *ICC Rules*, the emergency arbitrator is considered for all intents and purposes an *arbitrator*. This role implies that he or she shall be and remain impartial and independent vis-à-vis the parties involved in the dispute (Article 2(4), appendix V, *ICC Rules*), and will be required – before being appointed – to sign a statement of acceptance, availability, impartiality, and independence (Article 2(5), appendix V, *ICC Rules*).[833] Consequently, each party will have the opportunity to challenge the arbitrator within three days of the receipt of the notification of his or her appointment, or from the later date 'when that party was informed of the facts and circumstances on which the challenge is based' (Article 3(1), appendix V, *ICC Rules*). The challenge will be decided by the ICC court, giving the arbitrator and the parties an opportunity to provide comments in writing (Article 3(2), appendix V, *ICC Rules*).[834] It should be noted that such a challenge does not have a suspensive effect on the emergency proceedings.[835] In any event, the emergency arbitrator will not be allowed to act 'in any arbitration relating to the dispute that gave rise to the application' (Article 2(6), appendix V, *ICC Rules*).

If, under the *ICC Rules*, the emergency arbitrator is considered to be an arbitrator, then the emergency proceedings – *mutatis mutandi* – shall be considered arbitration proceedings. Confirmation of this line of reasoning can be found in at least two

---

830. Christopher Boog, *Commentary on the ICC Rules, Appendix V [Emergency arbitrator rules]* in Manuel Arroyo, *Arbitration in Switzerland* 826, 829 (Kluwer Law 2013) [Boog, *Appendix V*].
831. Article 2(1) Appendix V ICC Rules.
832. Boog, *Appendix V*, *supra* n. 830, at 830. This practice is confirmed by Carlevaris & Feris (*supra* n. 820, at 29), according to whom 'the appointments made [so far] were made by the President following discussions with the Secretariat's management and the relevant case management team on the qualities required for the matter. Immediately upon receipt of the Application a shortlist of potential candidates was drawn up by the President in collaboration with the Secretariat'.
833. According to the prevailing opinion, such a statement will have to satisfy the general requirement set out in Art. 11(2) *ICC Rules*: 'The prospective arbitrator shall disclose in writing to the Secretariat any facts or circumstances which might be of such a nature as to call into question the arbitrator's independence in the eyes of the parties, as well as any circumstances that could give rise to reasonable doubts as to the arbitrator's impartiality'. *See* Voser & Boog, *supra* n. 817, at 89; Boog, *Appendix V*, *supra* n. 830, at 831.
834. According to Fry, Greenberg & Mazza (*supra* n. 449, at para. 3-1056), the Secretariat will usually assign a three-day period for gathering such comments.
835. Boog, *Appendix V*, *supra* n. 830, at 833.

provisions of the *ICC Rules*, namely, Articles 4(1) and 5(2) (appendix V *ICC Rules*). The former provision reads:

> If the parties have agreed upon the place of arbitration, such place shall be the place of the emergency proceedings. In the absence of such agreement, the President shall fix the place of the emergency arbitrator proceedings, without prejudice to the determination of the place of the arbitration pursuant to Article 18(1) of the Rules.

In light of the above, it is clear that the need for fixing a place for the proceedings can only be explained by identifying an analogy between arbitration and emergency proceedings.[836] In this context, the place of arbitration becomes a gravitational force that regulates the interactions between state courts and arbitrators in a significant number of cases.[837]

A further confirmation of the fact that emergency proceedings are to be considered as arbitration proceedings is found in Article 5(2), appendix V of the *ICC Rules*, pursuant to which '[t]he emergency arbitrator shall conduct the proceedings in the manner which the emergency arbitrator considers to be appropriate, taking into account the nature and the urgency of the Application. In all cases, the emergency arbitrator shall act fairly and impartially and ensure that each party has a reasonable opportunity to present its case'. As will be explained in the following part, the compliance with these rules of 'natural justice' can in fact only be explained by an attempt to put in place a judicial-like procedure.

On a more practical level, it should be noted that the emergency arbitrator must establish a procedural timetable for the proceedings 'within as short a time as possible, normally within two days from the receipt of the file'[838] (Article 5(1), appendix V, *ICC Rules*), in order to guarantee a prompt response to the urgent situation invoked by the applicant. As correctly noted, this leaves the question of ex parte measures open for discussion.[839] In fact, while it is clear that the application for emergency measures shall be notified to the other party,[840] the emergency arbitrator could still order an ex parte

---

836. Fabio Santacroce, *The Emergency Arbitrator: A Full-Fledged Arbitrator Rendering an Enforceable Decision?* 31:2 Arb Int 282, 296 (2015).
837. For an overview, *see* Born, *supra* n. 4, at 1575 ff. In a nutshell, the place of arbitration – also known as arbitral seat – can influence '(a) the national arbitration legislation applicable to the arbitration; (b) the law applicable to the "external" relationship between the arbitration and national law and courts (including annulment of awards and selection and removal of arbitrators); (c) the law applicable to the "internal" procedures of the arbitration (including requirements for equality of treatment and due process); and (d) the law presumptively applicable to the substantive validity of the arbitration agreement. In addition, the law of the arbitral seat can indirectly affect a number of other aspects of the arbitral process, which again can be of substantial importance. These include (e) where the award is "made" for purposes of the New York Convention; (f) in some cases, the likely nationality and other characteristics of the arbitrators; and (g) in some cases, the likely approach to the arbitral procedure'. *Ibid.* at 2052.
838. That is, usually within two days of the Secretariat's transmission of the file to the emergency arbitrator (Art. 2(3), Appendix V, *ICC Rules*).
839. Boog, *Appendix V, supra* n. 830, at 836.
840. Article 1(5), Appendix V, *ICC Rules*.

interim measure prior to the hearing with both parties.[841] These comments lead us to the decision rendered by the emergency arbitrator under the *ICC Rules*, to which we shall now turn.

[3] The Emergency Arbitration Decision

Pursuant to Article 29(2) of the *ICC Rules* and Article 6(1), Appendix V, *ICC Rules*, the emergency arbitrator's decision shall take the form of an order. Such an order shall determine whether the application is admissible 'and whether the emergency arbitrator has jurisdiction to order Emergency Measures' (Article 6(2), appendix V, *ICC Rules*).[842] Furthermore, the order shall be made in writing 'no later than 15 days from the date on which the file was transmitted to the emergency arbitrator' (Article 6(4), appendix V, *ICC Rules*), unless the president of the court agrees to extend such a limit 'pursuant to a reasoned request from the emergency arbitrator or on the President's own initiative' (Article 6(4), appendix V, *ICC Rules*).[843] It shall also state the reasons upon which it is based, and be dated and signed by the emergency arbitrator (Article 6(3), appendix V, *ICC Rules*).

The above provisions raise several questions. The first one concerns the form of the decision rendered by the emergency arbitrator, which, pursuant to Article 29(2) of the *ICC Rules*, shall take the form of an order. In this regard, several commentators have explained that the choice of the term 'order' was preferred over 'award' mainly to exclude the scrutiny of the ICC court (Article 33 *ICC Rules*).[844] The Secretariat would take over a similar role – albeit with more rapidity and flexibility – by conducting an informal review[845] and providing the emergency arbitrator with a checklist 'to ensure that their orders satisfy minimum formal requirements and contain all necessary information'.[846] This would not negate the adjudicative power of emergency arbitrators.[847]

Without getting any further into the debate regarding the real nature of emergency measures, which will be discussed in section §7.06, it is worth underscoring the evident weakness of the argument according to which the decision of the emergency arbitrator was termed an 'order' just to avoid the scrutiny of the ICC court. Had that been the real concern, an exception to the general rule set out in Article 33 of the *ICC Rules* could have been easily introduced in the body of provisions governing emergency proceedings, as has been done for the case of the jurisdictional test carried out by the president of the court pursuant to Article 1(5), appendix V, *ICC Rules*. The choice

---

841. Cf. Voser & Boog, *supra* n. 817, at 87; Baruch Baigel, *The Emergency Arbitrator Procedure under the 2012 ICC Rules: A Juridical Analysis*, 31:1 J Int'l Arb 1, 2 (2014).
842. It should be noted that the emergency arbitrator is also required to directly notify the order to the parties and the Secretariat (Art. 6(5), Appendix V, *ICC Rules*).
843. Two commentators have observed that the same result can be reached through a joint request of the parties. *See* Voser & Boog, *supra* n. 817, at 91.
844. Voser & Boog, *supra* n. 817, at 86; Boog, *Article 29*, *supra* n. 813, at 819.
845. Fry, Greenberg & Mazza, *supra* n. 449, at para. 3-1081.
846. Carlevaris & Feris, *supra* n. 820, at 14.
847. Voser & Boog, *supra* n. 817, at 86; Boog, *Article 29*, *supra* n. 813, at 820. Cf. Baigel, *supra* n. 841, at 17.

of the term 'order' might be an indicator of the attempt to limit the effectiveness of the emergency measures to the contractual level, which, however, might prevent their enforcement as arbitral awards. It might also have been intended to leave the question to the evolution of national laws and international practices.

The second question raised by the provisions on the decision rendered by the emergency arbitrator revolves around Article 6(2), appendix V, *ICC Rules*. In light of this provision, the emergency arbitrator is, in fact, required to decide whether the application is admissible pursuant to Article 29(1) of the *ICC Rules* 'and whether [he or she] has jurisdiction to order Emergency Measures'.

This implies a decision on: (i) the prerequisites set out in Article 29(5) and (6) of the *ICC Rules*; (ii) the substantive requirement of Article 29(1) of the *ICC Rules* (i.e., an urgent situation that cannot await the constitution of the tribunal) and any other substantive requirement applicable under the circumstances of the case (e.g., *fumus boni iuris* and irreparable harm); and (iii) whether there is a prima facie valid arbitration agreement.[848] This last requirement is particularly problematic.

It is not entirely clear, in fact, why the standard of review of the validity of the arbitration clause should be a prima facie one. It appears that the decision at hand may in reality constitute a final jurisdictional determination.

[4] The Effects of the Emergency Arbitration Decision on the Arbitration Proceedings

The effects of the emergency arbitrator's order on the arbitration proceedings are regulated by Article 29(3) and (4) of the *ICC Rules*, which reads:

> (3) The emergency arbitrator's order shall not bind the arbitral tribunal with respect to any question, issue or dispute determined in the order. The arbitral tribunal may modify, terminate or annul the order or any modification thereto made by the emergency arbitrator.
> (4) The arbitral tribunal shall decide upon any party's requests or claims related to the emergency arbitrator proceedings, including the reallocation of the costs of such proceedings and any claims arising out of or in connection with the compliance or noncompliance with the order.

In light of the above provision, the arbitral tribunal can modify, terminate, or annul the order in question.[849] In this regard, it has been noted that the arbitral tribunal would 'fulfil a quasi-appellate role. ... In practice, however, the arbitral tribunal will be reluctant to overturn an order unless the objecting party can show that [the surrounding] circumstances have changed'.[850] The emergency arbitrator's decision is therefore destined to be a temporary one, both with respect to the parties and to the proceedings. This is so not only because the arbitral tribunal can modify the emergency order but also because the emergency arbitrator himself or herself can do so (Article 6(8),

---

848. Voser & Boog, *supra* n. 817, at 91; Boog, *Appendix V*, *supra* n. 830, at 840.
849. Fry, Greenberg & Mazza, *supra* n. 449, at para. 3-1090. On the possibility of an appeal or setting aside of the order, *see* Boog, *Article 29*, *supra* n. 830, at 821.
850. Voser & Boog, *supra* n. 817, at 87.

appendix V, *ICC Rules*).[851] Moreover, the temporary character of the emergency decision is easily identifiable in cases where the arbitral tribunal was never constituted or proceedings were otherwise terminated. In fact, as stated by Article 6(6), appendix V, *ICC Rules*, the order shall cease to be binding upon:

> (a) the President's termination of the emergency arbitrator proceedings pursuant to Article 1(6) of this Appendix [failure to file a request for arbitration within the applicable time limit];
> ...
> (d) the withdrawal of all claims or the termination of the arbitration before the rendering of a final award.

[5] The Interplays with State Courts

Finally, Article 29(7) of the *ICC Rules* adopts the principle of complementarity, according to which the jurisdiction of state courts in provisional matters remains intact, even in presence of a provisional arbitral power. The article at hand states:

> The Emergency Arbitrator Provisions are not intended to prevent any party from seeking urgent interim or conservatory measures from a competent judicial authority at any time prior to making an application for such measures, and in appropriate circumstances even thereafter, pursuant to the Rules. Any application for such measures from a competent judicial authority shall not be deemed to be an infringement or a waiver of the arbitration agreement. Any such application and any measures taken by the judicial authority must be notified without delay to the Secretariat.

Having examined the provisions on emergency arbitration of the most influential arbitration rules, we must now broaden our discussion of emergency arbitration proceedings. In particular, the questions that need to be tackled are those of the status of the emergency arbitrator and the nature of the decision that he or she renders. These topics are treated in section §7.05, below.

§7.05 THE NATURE AND ENFORCEMENT OF EMERGENCY DECISIONS: THE 2006 AMENDMENTS TO THE UNCITRAL *MODEL LAW*

In Chapter 3, I explained that Romano-canonical and common law jurisdictions endorse two different ways of assessing whether a dispute resolution mechanism can amount to arbitration. The French doctrine of *acte juridictionnel* holds that if a third party renders a decision similar to a judgment, then he or she must be an arbitrator; English authorities, on the contrary, hold that if the procedure administered by a third party has a judicial-like nature, then one must be in presence of an arbitration.

In light of the above, considering an emergency arbitrator as an actual arbitrator is highly problematic in French arbitration law. The only way to conclude that the emergency arbitrator is a real arbitrator would be to assume – by relying on a

---

851. Only upon a reasoned request from the Parties. *Ibid.* at 91.

hypothetical will of the parties – that the arbitration agreement intended to confer the *iuris dictio* to the emergency arbitrator.[852] Conversely, English law provides a definition of arbitration that is much more flexible. To conclude that the emergency arbitrator is truly an arbitrator, it is sufficient to show that emergency arbitration proceedings have a judicial-like nature. This nature is fairly easy to demonstrate, for this type of procedure clearly aims to anticipate the provisional measures granted by state courts before the constitution of the arbitral tribunal. This alone would suffice to prove that these proceedings have a judicial-like character. Yet there are several other reasons supporting this conclusion.

In this respect, an author has observed that emergency arbitrators: (i) make judicial determinations to establish whether they can consider the application for emergency measures and (ii) must remain impartial and independent.[853] Moreover, the decisions rendered are similar to those granted by an arbitral tribunal after its constitution.

The above suggests that emergency arbitration proceedings are indeed a form of arbitration.[854] This raises the following question: what is the nature of emergency decisions? Their provisional and reversible character has led many authors to conclude that these decisions have the same nature as provisional measures granted by an arbitral tribunal during the course of an arbitration.[855] Yet uncertainties remain as to which form such emergency decisions can take. In this respect, it is worth emphasizing that the arbitration rules analysed in this chapter have taken very different stands on this issue: while the *ICDR Rules*,[856] *SCC Rules*,[857] and *LCIA Rules*[858] allow the emergency arbitrator to choose between an order and an award as the form of an emergency decision, the *ICC Rules* dictate that emergency decisions can only take the form of an order.[859] Obviously, this question of form bears important consequences for the enforceability of emergency decisions. While, under English law, provisional measures can be enforced as awards, the same is controversial under French law. In this regard, Jacques Pellerin emphasized that the definition of arbitral award adopted by the is unsatisfactory: finality cannot be a decisive attribute of awards, especially given the

---

852. Cf. Santacroce, *supra* n. 836, at 292.
853. *Ibid.* at 299.
854. *See*, most recently, *International Steel Services Inc v. Dynatec Madagascar SA* (2016 ONSC 2810). In this recent Ontario case, the applicant had attempted to initiate ICC emergency proceedings. However, the opposing party objected. This objection constituted an obstacle because the parties' arbitration agreement was concluded before the entry into force of the 2012 *ICC Rules* (cf. Art. 29(6), 2012 *ICC Rules*). The applicant opted to file a request for an interim injunction before the Ontario Superior Court, which found that the 'issue of interim relief should have been dealt with before an arbitrator under the ICC emergency arbitration rules as requested by [the applicant]'. The court took into consideration the opposing party's refusal to participate in emergency arbitration as an indicator supporting the granting of the injunction. The case, therefore, implicitly suggests that emergency arbitration can be regarded as a type of arbitration, whose goal is to provide measures that are similar to court-ordered injunctions.
855. Boog, *Article 29*, *supra* n. 813, at 820; Fry, Greeberg & Mazza, *supra* n. 449, at para. 3-1086.
856. Article 6(5) 2014 ICDR *International Arbitration Rules*.
857. Article 1(2), Appendix II, 2017 *SCC Rules*.
858. Article 9.9 2014 *LCIA Rules*.
859. Article 6(1), Appendix V, 2017 *ICC Rules*.

Chapter 7: Awards *Ante Causam* §7.05

importance that provisional measures play in international commercial arbitration.[860] He proposed that, given the absence of a legislative definition of award, the parties be allowed (with the consent of the tribunal) to agree that a provisional measure will take the form of an award. Such a proposal is based on the consideration that the will of the parties is a foundational element of arbitration.[861]

It is worth noting that the issue regarding the form of provisional measures has been tackled by the 2006 amendments of the UNCITRAL *Model Law*.[862] The same alternative regarding form (award or order) found in the arbitration rules analysed in the preceding section is also present in this soft law instrument.[863] More specifically, Article 17(2) states:[864]

> An interim measure is any temporary measure, *whether in the form of an award or in another form*, by which, at any time prior to the issuance of the award by which the dispute is finally decided, the arbitral tribunal orders a party to:
> (a) Maintain or restore the status quo pending determination of the dispute;
> (b) Take action that would prevent, or refrain from taking action that is likely to cause, current or imminent harm or prejudice to the arbitral process itself;
> (c) Provide a means of preserving assets out of which a subsequent award may be satisfied; or
> (d) Preserve evidence that may be relevant and material to the resolution of the dispute
> [emphasis added].

---

860. Pellerin, *supra* n. 3, at 682. *See also* Cécile Chainais, *Note – 29 novembre 2007, Cour d'appel de Paris (1re Ch. C), 17 juin 2009, Cour de cassation (1re Ch. Civ.), 3 juillet 2008, Cour d'appel de Paris (1re Ch. C), 25 septembre 2008, Cour d'appel de Paris (1re Ch.)*, 4 Rev Arb 748, 757 (2009).
861. Pellerin, *supra* n. 860, at 686 ('La question est alors de savoir si la volonté des parties peut être considérée comme un élément de la qualification ou, dit autrement, si, en plus de l'élément objectif, l'acte juridictionnel, l'élément subjectif peut être retenu. Or, la considération de la volonté est au fondement de l'arbitrage: le pouvoir juridictionnel est confié par les parties aux arbitres, qui l'ont accepté. Dès lors, que les parties puissent disposer du droit de fixer les formes des décisions arbitrales ne contrarie pas la liberté des arbitres, qui pourront choisir la forme qui leur paraît la plus adaptée et la plus juste').
862. *See generally* Fabien Gélinas, *From Harmonized Legislation to Harmonized Law: Hurdles and Tools, Judicial and Arbitral Perspectives* in Frédéric Bachand & Fabien Gélinas, *The UNCITRAL Model Law After 25 Years: Global Perspectives on International Commercial Arbitration* 261, 262–263 (JurisNet 2013) (commenting on the difficulties surrounding the preparation and implementation of harmonized legislation).
863. Cf. Alain Prujiner, *Éléments d'une Loi Type reformée* in Frédéric Bachand & Fabien Gélinas, *D'une réforme à une autre, Regards croisés sur l'arbitrage au Québec* 221, 232 (Éditions Yvon Blais 2013) ('Le [nouvel] article 17 réitère le pouvoir d'ordonner des mesures provisoires d'un tribunal arbitral. Il précise que la mesure provisoire est une mesure temporaire qu'elle prenne la forme d'une sentence ou une autre forme. L'objectif de cette mesure doit être de préserver ou rétablir le statu quo, d'empêcher la survenance d'un préjudice, d'assurer la sauvegarde de biens nécessaires à l'exécution de la sentence ou la sauvegarde d'éléments de preuve'). The amendments, however, were criticized for failing to specifically consider the introduction of emergency arbitral proceedings. *See also* Dana Renée Bucy, *The Future of Interim Relief in International Commercial Arbitration under the Amended UNCITRAL Model Law*, 25:3 Am Un Int'l L Rev 579, 606 (2010).
864. For a commentary, *see* Peter Binders, *International Commercial Arbitaration and Conciliation in UNCITRAL Model Law Jurisdictions*, 242–243 (Sweet & Maxwell 2010).

The most interesting element of Article 17(2) is that this provision does not indicate a preference as to the form of provisional measures, which can be either awards or orders.[865] This removes the ambiguity regarding requirements of form, contained in the 1985 *Model Law*, which did not mention the issue of form at all.[866] An *excursus* on the *travaux préparatoires* of Article 17(2) of the 2006 UNCITRAL *Model Law* will allow us to emphasize that the decision not to impose a specific form in this provision resulted from the need to ensure flexibility, so as to guarantee that provisional measures would be enforced in the vast majority of jurisdictions.

At the outset, it should be observed that the 2006 amendments to the *Model Law* gave rise to a great deal of criticism, especially during the period of the *travaux préparatoires* (which lasted nearly six years).[867] Echoes of these controversies can be found in the declarations of the United Kingdom (UK) and French delegations, which cast some doubts as to UNCITRAL's ability to truly reach a consensus that could eventually lead to the harmonization of national arbitration laws.[868]

Turning now to the merits of the debate on the form of provisional measures, authoritative commentators have aptly summarized the compromise reached during the *travaux préparatoires*:[869]

---

865. Or any decision rendered in 'any other form' (cf. Art. 17(2)).
866. Article 17, 1985 UNCITRAL *Model Law* ('Unless otherwise agreed by the parties, the arbitral tribunal may, at the request of a party, order any party to take such interim measure of protection as the arbitral tribunal may consider necessary in respect of the subject-matter of the dispute ... ').
867. The possibility of granting ex parte measures has been the most controversial point. However, since emergency arbitral proceedings generally cannot be conducted ex parte (although this is not always the case), the present section will not deal with the discussions on this issue. *See*, for an overview, Carole Malinvaud, *The Amendment to the UNCITRAL Model Law on Interim Measures: A Compromise on Ex Parte Measures* in *The UNCITRAL Model Law on International Commercial Arbitration: 25 Years* 99, 103-105 (Maklu 2010) (clarifying that these measures are subject to an 'opt-in' mechanism).
868. UNCITRAL, *Comments Received from Member States and International Organizations–United Kingdom*, UN Doc A/CN.9/609/Add.4 (18 May 2006) at para. 2.5 ('[T]he United Kingdom has mixed feelings about the completion of this project. On the one hand, we are of course happy that the Working Group has finally arrived at an agreed draft ... leaving the way clear, at last, for new projects. On the other hand, however, it is the nature of this process itself that gives rise to serious concerns ... '); UNCITRAL, *Comments Received from Member States and International Organizations–France*, UN Doc A/CN.9/609/Add.5 (30 May 2006) at paras 1, 2 ('The French delegation notes with regret that the Working Group's method of functioning did not fully meet its expectations. It felt that, on numerous occasions, every effort had not been made to reach truly consensus solutions. ... The reports of the Working Group are sometimes elliptical on these matters and do not sufficiently make the point that a compromise could be achieved only under particularly difficult conditions. As to the substance, the French delegation gives a mixed appraisal of the work of the Working Group'). *See also* Ali Yesilirmak, *Provisional Measures* in Julian D.M. Lew, *Pervasive Problems in International Arbitration* 185, 200 (Kluwer Law 2006) ('[the] author believes that the amendment to the *Model Law* in respect of the enforcement of arbitral provisional measures is not sufficient to reach harmonization as there has already been and is likely to be disharmony in existing/future laws').
869. Howard Holtzmann, Joseph Neuhaus et al., *A Guide to the 2006 Amendments to the UNCITRAL Model Law on International Commercial Arbitration: Legislative History and Commentary*, 168-169 (Kluwer Law 2015).

The Working Group chose to address the form of an interim measure in the amended Article 17 (which was not addressed in the 1985 Law), in acknowledgement of the requirement in some legal systems that an interim measure be in the form of an award in order for the measure to be recognized or enforced. Instead of requiring that interim measures take the form of an award, however, the Working Group preferred the broad formulation of an interim measure as 'any temporary measure, whether in the form of an award or in another form.' The prevailing view within the Working Group was that it would be undesirable for the *Model Law* to be overly prescriptive in respect of the form of an interim measure.

Since the beginning of the discussions, during the thirty-second session of the Working Group on Arbitration, it was noted that 'interim measures [are] in practice issued in different forms and under different labels, which [include] ... interim awards, and that the form in which the interim measure of protection [is] ... issued should not influence' its enforcement, an idea that could be based on Articles 35 and 36 of the 1985 *Model Law*.[870] Moreover, it was pointed out that 'sometimes the purpose of designating a decision as an order (as distinguished from an award) was to prevent it being challenged in court, whereas the purpose of designating it as an award was to allow it to be treated as an award'.[871] It was also emphasized that, while provisional measures generally have a temporary nature, which allows the arbitrators to review and alter them in case of supervening circumstances, they may also have 'final and significant consequences that cannot be reversed even if the measure is later modified or turns out to be unnecessary'[872] – hence the importance of implementing effective tools for the enforcement and annulment of such measures.

Eventually, a pragmatic approach emerged: the possibility of enforcing provisional measures was essential because they often constituted a strong guarantee

---

870. UNCITRAL, *Report of the Working Group on Arbitration on the Work of its Thirty-Second Session*, UN Doc A/CN.9/468 (20–31 March 2000) at para. 72. *See also* 2012 UNCITRAL Digest on the Model Law on International Commercial Arbitration, 86 (United Nations 2012) ('An important innovation of the revision lies in the establishment ... of a regime for the recognition and enforcement of interim measures, which was modeled, as appropriate, on the regime for the recognition and enforcement of arbitral awards under articles 35 and 36 of the *Model Law*').
871. UNCITRAL, *Report of the Working Group on Arbitration–Possible Uniform Rules on Certain Issues Concerning Settlement of Commercial Disputes: Conciliation, Interim Measures of Protection, Written Form for Arbitration Agreement*, UN Doc A/CN.9/485 (20 November – 1 December 2000), para. 83.
872. UNCITRAL, *Report of the Working Group on Arbitration – Possible Uniform Rules on Certain Issues Concerning Settlement of Commercial Disputes: Conciliation, Interim Measures of Protection, Written Form for Arbitration Agreement*, UN Doc A/CN.9/WG.II/WP.108 (14 January 2000) para. 66. *See also* para. 100 ('The measures of protection discussed here are interim or temporary in relation to the final award. They do not represent the final resolution of the dispute in that they might be modified by the arbitral tribunal as matters evolve during the arbitral proceedings, and that they should be taken into account and merged in the arbitral tribunal's final adjudication of the dispute'). *See also* Gerold Herman, *Does the World Need Additional Uniform Legislation on Arbitration?* in Julian D.M. Lew, *Arbitration Insights: Twenty Years of the Annual Lecture of the School of International Arbitration* 223, 246 (Kluwer Law 2007) ('in my view an interim measure is not only "binding" (on the parties) but also "final" in the sense of "definite" according to its terms, which typically include a time limitation or a revision possibility'); Born, *supra* n. 4, at 2514.

against the potential frustration of the entire arbitration.[873] Therefore, the working group's main objective became that of ensuring that provisional measures could be enforced 'in a similar fashion as arbitral awards', keeping in mind that the content of these arbitral decisions differed in several respects.[874]

For the sake of clarity, it should be recalled that the working group did consider removing the phrase 'whether in the form of an award or in another form' from its draft of Article 17(2).[875] However, the proposal to do so was rejected since 'the phrase in question substantially added to the draft paragraph by clarifying that, depending on the circumstances and on the jurisdiction, interim measures might be issued in a variety of forms'.[876]

Proposals were also made to qualify, with specific terminology, provisional measures adopted in the form of awards:[877]

> One suggestion was that the words 'arbitral award' should be replaced by the words 'partial or interim award'. In support of that proposal it was stated that the words 'arbitral award' were often understood as referring to the final award in the arbitration proceedings, whereas an order of interim measures, even if issued in the form of an award, was typically an interlocutory decision. Some support was expressed for that proposal, although most speakers objected to the use of the words 'partial award', since those words typically referred to a final award that disposed of part of the dispute, but would not appropriately describe an interim measure. Doubts were expressed as to whether the words 'interlocutory award' would adequately cover the various types of interim measures that might be issued in the form of an award. *After discussion, the preference within the Working Group was for simply deleting the word 'arbitral' without further qualifying the nature of the award.*

Despite the numerous discussions, the decision to adopt language that would provide provisional measures with the greatest possibility of enforcement prevailed.[878]

---

873. *Report of the Working Group* (14 January 2000), *supra* n. 872, at paras 73–74 ('The need for enforceability is usually supported by arguments such as that the final award may be of little value to the successful party if actions of the recalcitrant party have rendered the outcome of the proceedings largely useless (e.g., by dissipating assets or removing them from the jurisdiction); or that preventable loss or damage should not be allowed to happen (e.g., if a party refuses to take precautionary measures at the construction site or it fails to continue construction works while the dispute is being resolved). Thus, it is argued, in some cases an interim order may in practice be as important as the award. In connection with arguments in favour of enforceability of interim measures of protection, it has been pointed out that international arbitrations are often held in places where neither party has assets or commercial operations (so called "neutral" places). This often means that the action to be taken pursuant to an interim measure ordered by the arbitral tribunal is to be taken outside of the jurisdiction where the arbitration takes place. Therefore, to the extent it is possible to establish a regime for court assistance in enforcing interim measures, there should be a possibility for enforcement by courts in both the State of arbitration as well as outside that State'). *See also Ibid.* at para. 81.
874. *Ibid.* at para. 82.
875. UNCITRAL, *Report of the Working Group on Arbitration on the Work of its Thirty-Sixth Session*, UN Doc A/CN.9/508 (12 April 2002) para. 65.
876. *Ibid.*
877. *Ibid.* at para. 66 [emphasis added].
878. UNCITRAL, *Working Group on Arbitration, Forty-First Session*, UN Doc A/CN.9WG.II/WP.131 (26 July 2004) para. 46 (Moreover, in order to avoid potential controversy, the working group felt the need to specify that 'the explanatory material to be prepared at a later stage ... should

Finally, as Article 17(H) of the 2006 UNCITRAL *Model Law* makes clear, the enforcement of provisional measures under that provision is not conditional on form, which is left to Article 17(2).[879] The same provision further adds that such measures will be enforced 'irrespective of the country in which [they] were issued'. This reinforces the flexibility found in the 2006 amendments to the *Model Law*, which, essentially, are geared toward guaranteeing the maximum degree of enforcement of provisional measures, indicating that the form of these arbitral decisions will not harm their effectiveness.

A recent example of the implementation of these mechanisms can be found in the new *Code of Civil Procedure* of Quebec.[880] The current version of Article 638 reads as follows:

> The arbitrator may, on a party's request, take any provisional measure or any measure to safeguard the parties' rights for the time and subject to the conditions the arbitrator determines and, if necessary, require that a suretyship be provided to cover costs and the reparation of any prejudice that may result from such a measure. Such a decision is binding on the parties but one of them may, if necessary, ask the court to homologate the decision to give it the same force and effect as a judgment of the court.

Since the end of the 1980s and early 1990s, international commercial arbitration in Canada has been modernized thanks to the implementation of the 1985 UNCITRAL *Model Law*,[881] as well as the adoption of the *New York Convention*. In this country,

---

make it clear that the wording adopted regarding the form in which an interim measure might be issued should not be misinterpreted as taking a stand in respect of the controversial issue as to whether or not an interim measure issued in the form of an award would qualify for enforcement under the New York Convention').

879. See Holtzmann & Neuhaus, *supra* n. 869, at 181–182. *See also* Art. 17(H) (Recognition and Enforcement):

> (1) An interim measure issued by an arbitral tribunal shall be recognized as binding and, unless otherwise provided by the arbitral tribunal, enforced upon application to the competent court, irrespective of the country in which it was issued, subject to the provisions of Art. 17 I.
> (2) The party who is seeking or has obtained recognition or enforcement of an interim measure shall promptly inform the court of any termination, suspension or modification of that interim measure.
> (3) The court of the State where recognition and enforcement is sought may, if it considers it proper, order the requesting party to provide appropriate security if the arbitral tribunal has not already made a determination with respect to security or where such a decision is necessary to protect the rights of third parties.

880. *See generally Commentaires de la Ministre de la Justice, Code de procédure civile* (Ch. C-25 01) (Wilson & Lafleur 2015); Denis Ferland & Benoît Emery, *Précis de Procedure Civile du Québéc* (Éditions Yvon Blais 2015). For an overview, *see* Frédéric Bachand, *Les principes généraux de la justice civile et le nouveau Code de procédure civile*, 60:2 MLJ 447 (2015).

881. This is true whether at the provincial, federal, or territorial level. *See* Marc Lalonde & Lex Alexeev, *National Report for Canada (2012)* in Jan Paulsson & Lise Bosman, *ICCA International Handbook on Commercial Arbitration* 1, 1–2 (Kluwer Law 2012). For an overview, *see* Alain Prujiner & Nabil Antaki, *Proceedings of the First International Commercial Arbitration Conference* (Wilson & Lafleur 1986); Henri Alvarez, *La nouvelle législation canadienne sur l'arbitrage commercial international*, 4 Rev Arb 529, 534–538 (1986) (focusing on British Columbia's *International Commercial Arbitration Act*); Alain Prujiner, *Les nouvelles règles de l'arbitrage au*

commercial arbitration is a matter falling under provincial regulation.[882] Federal regulation will only apply 'in relation to matters where at least one of the parties to the arbitration is Her Majesty in right of Canada, a departmental corporation or a Crown corporation or in relation to maritime or admiralty matters'.[883]

In Quebec, this soft law instrument was adopted and incorporated into the *Code of Civil Procedure* in 1986.[884] Recently, the new Quebec *Code of Civil Procedure*, which entered into force in 2015, aimed to update the previous code's provisions so as to reflect the 2006 amendments of the *Model Law*.[885] In this respect, it was pointed out that the former articles dealing with provisional relief were unsatisfactory, since, for instance, arbitral tribunals could only grant provisional measures if the parties had so agreed.[886] Stricter limits also existed as to the types of measures that could be granted by the arbitrators.[887] It is apparent that the provisions contained in Articles 638 and following are based on the 2006 amendments of Article 17 of the *Model Law*.[888] In particular, Article 638 now refers to Article 645 (homologation) for the enforcement of provisional measures, creating a unified regime for the enforcement of both arbitral awards and provisional measures.[889] It is worth noting that such enforcement is not

---

Québec, 4 Rev Arb 425, 425–427 (1987) (describing the importance of the *Model Law* and the implementation of the *New York Convention*); Claude R. Thomson & Annie Finn, *International Commercial Arbitration: A Canadian Perspective*, 18:2 Arb Int 205 (2002). The work of the Uniform Law Conference of Canada played a key role in the modernization process of international arbitration in Canada. *See* ULCC, *Report of the Working Group on International Arbitration*, para. 1 (2012) ('In 1986 the Conference developed the Uniform International Commercial Arbitration Act (Uniform ICAA). The Uniform ICAA subsequently was implemented, with relatively minor amendments in some cases, through provincial legislation in all provinces and territories other than British Columbia and Québec. While British Columbia was an active participant in the work of the Conference, it enacted its own forms of International Commercial Arbitration Act and Foreign Arbitral Awards Act before the Conference had completed its work. The BC statute was similar in substance to the Uniform ICAA, but different in form. In Québec, many of the concepts set out in the Uniform ICAA were incorporated into the Civil Code and the Code of Civil Procedure').

882. Thomson & Finn, *supra* n. 881, at 206; Cf. sections 92(13) and 92(14) of the *Constitution Act, 1867*.
883. Section 5(2) of the (federal) *Arbitration Act*.
884. Nabil Antaki, *Regard intimiste sur l'état de l'arbitrage au Québec il y a 25 ans* in Bachand & Gélinas, *supra* n. 863, 17–18; Bachand, *L'intervention du juge*, *supra* n. 467, at para. 405.
885. *Commentaires de la Ministre*, *supra* n. 880, at 461 ff. This decision is in line with the policy recommendations expressed by ULCC, in its 2012 *Working Report* (*supra* n. 881, at para. 15, n. 2): 'The New Uniform ICAA should continue to give effect to Canada's ratification of the New York Convention and should be based on the *Model Law* and the 2006 Amendments, refined as necessary to reflect Canadian law, practice or public policy or to further the objective of keeping Canada at the forefront in the field of international commercial arbitration law'. *See also* ULCC, *Final Report and Commentary of the Working Group on New Uniform Arbitration Legislation*, para. 58 (2014) (recommending the adoption of the 1006 amendments, and explaining that 'Article 17H makes orders or awards for interim measures enforceable in a similar manner to other awards').
886. Frédéric Bachand, *Vers une nouvelle réforme du droit québécois de l'arbitrage conventionnel* in Bachand & Gélinas, *supra* n. 863, 237 at 253.
887. *Ibid*.
888. *Commentaires de la Ministre*, *supra* n. 880, at 461–462.
889. David Ferland, *L'arbitrage* in Denis Ferland & Benoît Emery, *Précis de procédure civile du Québec* 709, 751 (Éditions Yvon Blais 2014). While Art. 638 refers to provisional measures rendered by arbitral tribunals seated in Quebec, Art. 652 makes clear that provisional measures

conditional on the form of the decision. This is consistent with the legislative history of the 2006 amendments of the *Model Law*,[890] which indicates that arbitral tribunals have a great deal of flexibility and that form is, ultimately, secondary.[891]

In conclusion, the 2006 amendments to the *Model Law* and the legislative reform in Quebec provide a new approach to emergency measures: they show the attempt, although essentially confined to provisional measures, to move beyond the dogma according to which 'only awards will be enforced before state courts'. At the same time, as explained at the beginning of this section, these changes have been controversial and, to date, have not found uniform recognition in national arbitration laws. Most importantly, the above shows that the use of awards as pragmatic tools for the enforcement of various types of decisions is still persistent.

§7.06 CONCLUSION

Emergency arbitration proceedings constitute an expansion of the adjudicative powers of the arbitrators. This means that although they are not, technically speaking, part of the proceedings on the merits of the case, they qualify as a type of judicial-like procedure. It follows that unlike French law, under English law the decisions rendered by emergency arbitrators have the same adjudicative nature of those rendered by ordinary arbitral tribunals. Obviously, it is pointless to compare emergency decisions – especially for enforcement purposes – to contentious awards on the merits, for these two types of decisions are expressions of different adjudicative powers. If the latter type of decision responds to a claim of the parties on the merits, the former provisionally manages their legal entitlements, with a view to supporting the ensuing arbitration proceedings.

---

issued by arbitrators outside Quebec can also be enforced ('La sentence arbitrale rendue hors du Québec, qu'elle ait été ou non confirmée par une autorité compétente, peut être reconnue et déclarée exécutoire comme un jugement du tribunal si l'objet du différend est susceptible d'être réglé par arbitrage au Québec et si sa reconnaissance et son exécution ne sont pas contraires à l'ordre public. Il en est de même à l'égard d'une mesure provisionnelle ou de sauvegarde').

890. As far as international arbitration is concerned, the *Code of Civil Procedure* specifies that 'Lorsqu'un arbitrage met en cause des intérêts de commerce international y compris de commerce interprovincial, le présent titre s'interprète, s'il y a lieu, en tenant compte de la Loi type sur l'arbitrage commercial international adoptée le 21 juin 1985 par la Commission des Nations Unies pour le droit commercial international, de même que ses modifications' (Art. 649(1)).

891. It should be noted, nonetheless, that other Canadian provinces have taken a different route, in order to guarantee the enforcement of provisional measures. The *Ontario International Arbitration Act* constitutes a notable example. In particular, section 9 of said act, which adopts the 1985 UNCITRAL *Model Law*, states that '[a]n order of the arbitral tribunal under Article 17 of the *Model Law* for an interim measure of protection and the provision of security in connection with it is subject to the provisions of the *Model Law* as if it were an award'. *See* Brian Casey, *Arbitration Law of Canada: Practice and Procedure*, 309 (JurisNet 2011) ('Ontario has modified the *Model Law* by s. 9 of the Ontario International Act to deem interim measures "awards". This then triggers the enforcement provisions of the *Model Law* found in article 35, giving the Ontario court power to enforce interim measures granted by an arbitral tribunal as it would an award').

Despite their peculiar nature, a significant number of arbitral institutions (and of jurisdictions belonging to the common law tradition) suggest that emergency decisions can take the form of an award. Surely, the choice of the form is most certainly related to the desire to guarantee the enforcement of emergency decisions before state courts.[892] This need to guarantee enforcement shows a further inconsistency of the conception according to which only contentious decisions on the merits deserve to be qualified as awards: emergency decisions and contentious decisions on the merits are simply the expression of different adjudicative powers. Recent reforms, featuring provisions on the enforceability of emergency decisions, also support this conclusion.[893]

---

892. Cf. Robert Sills, *The Continuing Role of the Courts in the Era of the Emergency Arbitrator* in Albert van den Berg, *Legitimacy: Myths, Realities and Challenges* 278, 283 (Kluwer Law 2015).
893. *See* e.g., Ch. 609 *Arbitration Ordinance* (Hong Kong) of 1 June 2011, as amended in 2014 (section 22A and 22B). *See also* Michelle Grando, *The Coming of Age of Interim Relief in International Arbitration: A Report from the 28th Annual ITA Workshop* (online), http://kluwerarbitrationblog.com/2016/07/20/the-coming-of-age-of-interim-relief-in-international-arbitration-a-report-from-the-28th-annual-ita-workshop/.

CHAPTER 8
Conclusion: The Need for a Non-unitary Notion of Award

At the outset of the book, I explained that the difficulties relating to the notion of arbitral award result from: (i) an excessive emphasis on the contractual dimension of arbitration (the so-called contractual theory) and (ii) the reliance on an out-dated conception of adjudication used to define arbitration (the so-called adjudicative theory, which conceives the role of arbitrators as being limited to providing a final resolution of a dispute between the parties – the 'contentious' function).

I have explained that these two approaches are incompatible with the current practice of international commercial arbitration, for: (i) the institutional setting has brought about a conception of arbitration that relies on the image of a comprehensive adjudicative institution, far removed from the original contractual model and (ii) the adjudicative theory – based on a definition of adjudication as the final resolution of disputes by speaking the law – albeit while trying to emancipate arbitration from the contractual model, relies on a conception of adjudication that is now outdated. Nowadays, in fact, adjudication has moved beyond the mere rendering of judgments finally resolving a dispute by speaking the law. This evolution is noticeable in both state litigation and international commercial arbitration.[894] With respect to the latter, I have underlined that a variegated set of adjudicative powers can now be observed in arbitral practice. This diversification resulted from the effort made by the institutions operating in the field of international commercial arbitration to provide adjudicative powers that are similar to the evolving powers of state courts. Since the effectiveness of such powers depends on the possibility of enforcing them, one can observe a tendency to place the label of award on heterogeneous types of decisions with a view to ensuring their enforcement. The notion of award has thus been invoked in the context of different arbitral decision-making areas. As a result, in an attempt to move

---

894. The latest, 2016 version of the Quebec *Code of Civil Procedure*, is an eloquent example of the transformation of state litigation and a clear shift away from the purely monodimensional adjudicative model.

beyond the unitary notion of award, four different types of awards can be observed: (i) contentious awards, (ii) jurisdictional awards, (iii) awards by consent, and (iv) awards *ante causam*. These awards respond to different needs, being the expression of different adjudicative powers. Qualifying these arbitral decisions as awards hasn't necessarily made consensus; however, it is uncontroversial that there is a clear tendency in favour of using the notion of award to guarantee that these decisions be enforced.

While contentious awards are final, law-speaking decisions on one or more substantive claims filed by the parties, jurisdictional awards are decisions regarding the tribunal's competence, based on the jurisdictional boundaries defined by the arbitration agreement.[895] Consent awards are decisions recognizing a settlement reached by the parties during the course of an arbitration. Awards *ante causam* (though the same is true for provisional awards rendered by an arbitral tribunal appointed to hear the merits of the case) are provisional decisions granting a temporary response to urgent situations.

Whatever their form may be, these decisions are the expression of different types of adjudicative powers. The contentious power is the most important one and aims to provide a comprehensive answer to the parties' demand for arbitral justice. It presupposes the existence of a dispute between the parties and will result in a final, law-speaking decision on how to manage the legal entitlements that are vindicated by each party. The final character of the status quo established by the contentious decision will be sanctioned by the res judicata doctrine.

The jurisdictional power, by contrast, responds to another basic function: determining the boundaries of arbitral justice in a given case. Much like in the context of state litigation, this power ensures the proper allocation of the contentious power among the competing fora. It defines the conditions for accessing arbitral justice as well as the interplays between this type of justice and state justice. True, this adjudicative power also presupposes a dispute, yet not because the ensuing decision will resolve one but rather because, in its absence, the parties will not need to seek arbitral justice. Most importantly, the jurisdictional power exists independently from the contentious one. The sole fact of having competing fora requires precise rules on the allocation of the contentious power, so that each of them can establish under which conditions it will hear a given dispute. Here, the label of award is used with respect to jurisdictional decisions to guarantee their enforcement, allowing for a clear allocation of jurisdiction between courts and arbitrators.

The power to record settlements is a non-contentious power allowing for the homologation of a private act representing the will of the parties (i.e. the settlement agreement). This type of adjudicative power aims to assess whether the act is a genuine one, respecting the applicable mandatory rules and public policy. It presupposes the convergence of the interests of parties to a dispute who were able to resolve their differences in a non-contentious way. The label of award is once again used with

---

895. Interestingly enough, this power is independent from the agreement itself, since the arbitrators can render an enforceable jurisdictional decision even in the absence of a valid arbitration agreement (i.e., the so-called negative ruling).

Chapter 8: Conclusion: The Need for a Non-unitary Notion of Award

respect to these decisions to answer a pragmatic concern: ensuring that the convergence of the parties' interests shall have the same effect as a contentious decision, thus sanctioning the status quo designed by the parties to the settlement.

The provisional power, which was examined in the context of emergency arbitration proceedings, is a type of power that allows for responses dealing with urgent situations. Its function is that of providing a temporary answer, so that a party's decision to seek arbitral justice (and the time required to obtain a contentious award) will not result in harm. The emergency (or provisional) power presupposes the existence of a present (or future) dispute. It results in an urgent decision (i.e., an award *ante causam*), based on an appearance of legal entitlements. Again, the label of award is sometimes used with regard to this type of decision for purely pragmatic reasons, in order to ensure the effectiveness of the emergency decision. While arbitration rules require that the request for emergency measures be followed by a request for arbitration, it is not impossible to imagine that the decision rendered by the emergency arbitrator will suffice to prevent claims from being brought. It may, in fact, encourage both of the parties to settle, perhaps after the constitution of the arbitral tribunal, and to request an award by consent. If this were to become a frequent outcome in practice, arbitration centres could probably reconsider the requirement of filing a request for arbitration at the same time as the request for emergency proceedings, so that the temporary decision is not subordinated to the proceedings on the merits. In fact, if both parties are satisfied with the decision of the emergency arbitrator, then the award *ante causam* could be granted a final character, in the sense that it could obtain res judicata effects.

I should indulge on an important point. The above description of the arbitral decisions that are increasingly deserving to be qualified as 'awards', should not be taken for an attempt to sketch a theoretical taxonomy of arbitral awards. It merely results from the observation of the current state of affairs in the field. As a consequence, it is possible that the notion of award will no longer be invoked in the future for some of the above arbitral decisions, and that, on the other hand, other decisions that are not mentioned in this book will undergo the attempt of being qualified as awards. Despite this, the central point of the analysis should maintain its strength: whenever faced with key arbitral decisions rendered in the context of arbitral proceedings, it is likely that arbitration users and constituents will attempt to impose the characterization of 'award' with a view to guaranteeing their enforcement. At the same time, the existence of different types of awards and variegated forms of adjudicative power indicates that arbitral justice must now be described as multidimensional. The multiple dimensions of adjudicative power correspond to different needs of arbitration users. This is the essence of the multidimensional model of arbitration, which underlines that the administration of justice is a complex endeavour. While the contentious adjudicative power retains a central role, other adjudicative powers, ancillary to the general goal of resolving a dispute between the parties, are now commonly used by arbitrators.

From the above considerations, it seems that the multidimensional model is now more descriptively accurate than the monodimensional model embraced by the adjudicative theory of arbitration (i.e., arbitrators resolve in a final manner a dispute on the merits). If this proposition is true, then one has to accept the fact that there cannot be a unitary notion of arbitral award, but rather that there must be a non-unitary one: each function of arbitral justice (or, in other words, each type of adjudicative power) will entail a different type of award. This is so because, contrarily to the decisions rendered by state courts whose enforcement can be guaranteed regardless of the form that they take (at least at the domestic level, given that private international law rules may affect their enforcement in foreign jurisdictions), arbitral decisions will in most cases be enforced by states only if they amount to awards. Yet this situation should not be seen as an inconsistency – it is a natural evolution stimulated by the development of arbitral justice and is in conformity with the *New York Convention*, which has preserved the conception according to which only arbitral awards can be enforced by state courts. True, future conventions could probably go beyond this, allowing for the enforcement of arbitral decisions that are not awards. This course of action should be favoured, with a view to also ensuring the uniformity of international commercial arbitration.[896]

The same cannot be said with regard to uniform legislation, such as the UNCITRAL *Model Law*. As explained in the previous chapters, and particularly in the portions of the book dealing with the jurisdictional awards and the provisional awards, UNCITRAL may have embarked on a dangerous course. In particular, attempts have been made to marginalize the notion of award, by creating specific procedural mechanisms that allow the interested parties to obtain the recognition and enforcement of quintessential arbitral decisions, even if taken in the form of an order. This is extremely problematic, since: (i) these procedural mechanisms are not enacted with an international convention, so that the necessary uniformity is something that cannot be taken for granted, and (ii) the multiplication of special procedural mechanisms is per se problematic because it complicates the intervention of state courts in the arbitral process, something which is at odds with the framework shaped by the *New York Convention*. Moreover, (iii) while allowing for the enforcement of decisions taken in the form of an order, the *Model Law* still accepts that the same decisions can take the form of awards, which entails a potential juxtaposition of enforcement mechanisms. The same decision can thus be subject to different mechanisms depending on the form that the arbitrators decide to use. Most importantly, in times of dire competition among several jurisdictions across the world to attract an increasing number of international arbitral proceedings, it may be questioned whether the soft law philosophy behind the *Model Law* will be able to guarantee uniformity.

As far as arbitration laws are concerned, I have shown that we are still in a phase of transition. The notion of award is either presented in a unitary or non-unitary way, so as to restrict or expand the number of enforceable decisions. The unitary notion of award is championed by French arbitration law. While the French *Code of Civil*

---

896. Uniformity is threatened if national legislators are allowed to each take a different approach, by passing laws ensuring the enforcement of decisions other than awards. A recent example can be found in Hong Kong's arbitration ordinance, section 22A and 22B, which treats emergency arbitrators and arbitral tribunals as the same, with a view to guaranteeing the enforcement of emergency orders.

Chapter 8: Conclusion: The Need for a Non-unitary Notion of Award

Procedure fails to provide an explicit definition, French courts have constantly held – mainly in the context of annulment proceedings – that an award is 'a final decision, resolving in full or in part the dispute submitted to the arbitrators, concerning either the merits, the competence of the tribunal, or another preliminary objection putting the proceedings to an end'.[897] In this regard, Loquin has underlined that the position endorsed by French courts since 1994, has replaced a prior series of cases adopting a broader definition of arbitral awards, encompassing all decisions *resolving a dispute between the parties*, including procedural orders.[898] It is extremely important to understand that this position is only apparently in contrast with the theories developed by Gaillard on international commercial arbitration as a transnational legal order: the reduction of state courts' intervention, resulting from a narrow definition of award, leads to a true autonomous character of arbitration. The absence of review by state courts guarantees the discretion of arbitral tribunals, preventing any type of interference.

In light of the above, the unitary notion of arbitral award can be defined as follows:[899]

> An award is the arbitral tribunal's final decision resolving the dispute between the parties by speaking the law.

The non-unitary conception, on the other hand, supported by the Westphalian conception of international commercial arbitration,[900] does not perceive as a negative occurrence that state courts may step in to support the arbitral process. At odds with French law, English arbitration law endorses a non-unitary notion of arbitral award. A potential explanation for this can be found in the criterion used to distinguish arbitration from similar dispute resolution mechanisms such as expert determination. Several cases indicate that, unlike French law, which gives pivotal importance to the *acte juridictionnel* doctrine, the *conditio sine qua non* for arbitration in England is not the nature of the decision rendered by the third party (the arbitrator) but rather the

---

897. Cass Civ 1e, 12 October 2011, No 09-72.439; CA Paris, 29 October 2009, No 08-18544. These decisions are based on a 1994 case rendered by the Paris Court of Appeal (Sardi sud). *See* CA Paris, 25 March 1994, 2 Rev Arb 391 (1994) (Annotation Charles Jarrosson).
898. Loquin, *Arbitrage International*, *supra* n. 78, at 369–370 ('Ces décisions utilisaient la définition de l'acte juridictionnel proposée par H. Motulsky, lequel existe dès l'instant qu'un tiers tranche sur les prétentions antagonistes des parties'). *See* CA Paris, 9 July 1992, 2 Rev Arb 303 (1993) (Annotation Charles Jarrosson), which allowed a *recours en annullation* against an order issued by the arbitral tribunal regulating the conduct of the proceedings (' … ces ordonnances ont ainsi tranché des questions de procédure litigieuses entre les parties, et constituent des décisions de nature juridictionnelle exprimant le pouvoir reconnu aux arbitres pour décider de leur propre compétence et régler de manière autonome la procédure arbitrale').
899. The term 'dispute', used in this definition, includes a dispute on jurisdiction.
900. The Westphalian conception holds that the international arbitration is anchored to the legal order of the seat chosen for a given arbitration. *See* Emmanuel Gaillard, *Legal Theory of International Arbitration*, 28 ff. (Brill 2010). As a result, according to the tenants of this model, the intervention and supervision throughout the arbitral process is a normal and perhaps even desirable occurrence. Cf. Frédéric Bachand, *Do transnational Rules Matter?* in Albert van den Berg, *ICCA Congress–The Coming of a New Age?* 389, 391 (Kluwer Law 2013).

nature of the procedure that led to that decision. In other words, the distinctive feature of arbitration is that its procedure has 'something in the nature of a judicial inquiry'.[901]

The above explains the flexibility of the English *Arbitration Act 1996*, which specifies (section 47) that 'the tribunal may make more than one award at different times on different aspects of the matters to be determined', which include 'a part only of the claims or cross-claims' (section 47(b)). Most importantly, the non-unitary definition allows for the accommodation of provisional decisions under the umbrella of the notion of arbitral award (section 49), including orders for the payment of money or the disposition of property as between the parties (section 49(2)(a)). These decisions are treated as awards, despite the fact that their effectiveness has an expiration date.[902] At the same time, these decisions are not final, for the tribunal will be able to reconsider the matter in the final award dealing with the merits of the dispute (section 47(3)).[903]

The non-unitary notion of arbitral award further allows for the inclusion of other important decisions rendered by arbitral tribunals, such as awards by consent (section 51), which record a settlement reached by the parties.[904] Much like provisional awards, consent awards have not found uniform recognition in France.

In light of the above, the non-unitary notion of arbitral award can be summarized as follows:

> An award is a decision rendered following a judicial-like procedure, which either establishes the jurisdictional boundaries of the tribunal, or leads to a resolution of a dispute or prevents the frustration of the arbitral proceedings.

As explained earlier, this definition presupposes that awards do not have a unique function. Every decision regulating important junctures of the proceedings, such as in the case of a provisional measure or an award by consent, is susceptible to being defined as an arbitral award, provided that it can lead to a direct or indirect resolution of the dispute.

Is the existence of two different notions of arbitral award problematic?

The main difficulty with the unitary notion of arbitral award is that of being based on a narrow definition of *acte juridictionnel*, and, as a result, on a narrow understanding of the role of adjudication, limited to the final resolution of a dispute, which is now at odds with the role of international commercial arbitration today (i.e., that of providing an effective and comprehensive alternative to state courts).

In light of the above, one may wonder if a non-unitary notion of award should be preferred. Based on the traditional common law understanding of adjudication – which is not limited to the role of resolving disputes by speaking the law[905] – such a definition of award has the advantage of covering important decisions such as

---

901. *Wilky Property House Holdings Plc v. London & Surrey Investments Ltd* [2011] EWHC 2226 at para. 27. *See also Jivraj v. Hashwani* [2011] UKSC 40 at para. 41; *David Wilson Homes Ltd v. Survey Services Ltd* [2001] 1 EWCA Civ 34 at paras 13–14.
902. *See Konkola Copper* Mines, *supra* n. 95, at paras 88–97. Cf. Art. 17, *2006 UNCITRAL Model Law*.
903. Cf. Merkin & Flannery, *supra* n. 96, at 156.
904. Section 51(3) of the *Arbitration Act 1996*: 'An agreed award shall state that it is an award of the tribunal and shall have the same status and effect as any other award on the merits of the case' [emphasis added]; *See also* Art. 30, 2006 UNCITRAL *Model Law*.
905. Glenn, *supra* n. 40, at 239–241.

Chapter 8: Conclusion: The Need for a Non-unitary Notion of Award

jurisdictional awards, consent awards, provisional measures, and the decisions rendered by emergency arbitrators.

True, the non-unitary notion of award also has a problematic aspect, that is, an inherent weakness to counter a potential exponential multiplication of enforceable arbitral decisions, including decisions with minor relevance. While the concern may be founded in theory, it shouldn't be a great cause for concern in practice. The institutional setting of international commercial arbitration – that is, the very source stimulating the development of a multidimensional arbitral adjudication – is incompatible with a wild and uncontrolled development of types of arbitral awards. In other words, it is in the best interest of this institutional setting to aim only for the enforcement of indispensable decisions and, hence, to use the label of award only when it is really necessary. As a matter of fact, the review of an award remains a form of intrusion and submission to an external element, that is, state courts, and may result in a fragmentation of arbitral proceedings. It is thus very unlikely that the label of award would be placed on decisions that have little relevance, with the sole purpose of opening them up to review by state courts. This occurrence would be inconsistent with the main goal of developing a comprehensive alternative to state courts, since it would eventually lead to an ineffective form of arbitral adjudication.

From the above, I hope to have succeeded in showing that international commercial arbitration, in light of the various types of adjudicative powers it involves, would benefit from the general acceptance of a non-unitary notion of award. The definition of the notion of arbitral award bears important consequences for both arbitral and state justice: the notion regulates the interplays between them, so that if its definition is narrower, the corresponding adjudicative power of the arbitrators will also be narrower. Conversely, if the notion is wider, then the adjudicative power shall also be wider. Assuming that international commercial arbitration and state litigation in civil matters can be regarded as similar institutions, then the non-unitary notion aligns with (and perhaps can even be regarded as a consequence of) the trend toward the reduction of states' efforts in civil justice. The more state justice shrinks, the more arbitral justice expands, assuming functions that were once an exclusive prerogative of state courts. As a consequence, the non-unitary definition leads to a reduction of state courts' direct role in the administration of justice concerning international commercial dealings, essentially limiting it to a form of supervision of arbitral justice (and of private methods of dispute resolution).

What does the adoption of the non-unitary notion of award entail? The recognition of broad adjudicative powers entails that arbitrators will be subject to greater control: the more arbitral justice expands, the more it will need to justify itself in the eyes of the public. This will require, sooner rather than later, greater efforts in terms of legitimization. The days in which arbitrators would merely affect the rights of the parties to the disputes before them are long gone. They are now dispensers of justice, and their decisions can have an impact on the public at large.

The international arbitration community is fully aware of this.[906] The title of the 2014 gathering of the International Council for Commercial Arbitration ('Legitimacy: Myths, Realities, Challenges') is eloquent.[907] Only through greater efforts to justify the legitimacy of arbitral justice will arbitrators and arbitral institutions be able to maintain (and perhaps increase their) social acceptance.[908] These gains can be achieved by insisting on two different points.

First, a strict adherence to the common constitutional principles that define civil justice is necessary. This constitutional exercise is not problematic and should already be guaranteed by the grounds for refusal of enforcement found in the *New York Convention*.[909]

Second, legitimization must also be built in a non-legal sense. The goal here is to show that international commercial arbitration is open and transparent. This latter facet is certainly one requiring a great deal of work and which can be best achieved through absolute transparency about the functioning of arbitral institutions. Systematic publication of sanitized versions of awards[910] and divulgation of central information regarding the process of selection of arbitrators (coupled with an increase in terms of their diversity) seem to be simple and effective tools in this regard.[911]

In this non-strictly legal context, the most important goal in order to obtain and maintain legitimization, is underlining that arbitral tribunals seek justice. The most important element of civil justice, in fact, is to show that justice has been done. This goal quickly translates into showing that justice appears to be done. This is a central principle: a decision is just if it has followed the applicable rules (both procedural and substantive). Consistently, key information pertaining to how arbitral tribunals and arbitral institutions appear to do justice should thus be divulged to the public. A failure to do so may entail severe costs and lead to an adjudicative institution inept at replacing state courts.

As the complexity of the adjudicative power of arbitrators increases and the types of decisions that they render diversify, a dogmatic refusal to move beyond the monodimensional adjudicative model based on contentious awards – that is, a final,

---

906. See generally Jean-Baptiste Racine, *Sur l'idéologie de la transparence en droit de l'arbitrage* in *Mélanges Mayer* 727 (Lextenso 2015).
907. See generally Albert van den Berg, *Legitimacy: Myths, Realities, Challenges-ICCA Congress Series no. 18* (Kluwer Law 2015).
908. Cf. Madsen, *supra* n. 128, at 409–410.
909. Stephan W. Schill, *Developing a Framework for the Legitimacy of International Arbitration* in van den Berg, *supra* n. 906, 789 at 814.
910. In order to foster a form of *persuasive* precedent of arbitral awards. See Alexis Mourre, *Precedent and Confidentiality in International Commercial Arbitration* in Yas Banifatemi, *Precedent in International Arbitration* 39, 50 ff. (Juris Publishing 2007); François Perret, *Is There a Need for Consistency in International Commercial Arbitration* in Ibid. 25 at 33; Pierre Mayer, *La liberté de l'arbitre*, 2 Rev Arb 339, 359 (2013); Jean-Michel Jacquet, *Avons-nous besoin d'une jurisprudence arbitrale?* 3 Rev Arb 445, 456 (2010). For an empirical study on the use of precedent in international arbitration, *see* Gabrielle Kaufmann-Kohler, *Arbitral Precedent: Dream, Necessity or Excuse?* 23:3 Arb Int 357 (2007).
911. Christophe Seraglini, *Who Are the Arbitrators? Myths, Reality, and Challenges* in van den Berg, *supra* n. 906, at 602–605.Cf. Article 11(4) 2017 *ICC Rules*. The newest version of the ICC Rules no longer contains 'the prohibition on communicating reasons for the Court's decisions relating to the constitution of the arbitral tribunal'. See Feris, *supra* n. 246 at 64.

Chapter 8: Conclusion: The Need for a Non-unitary Notion of Award

law-speaking decision resolving the dispute between the parties – may bear negative consequences, condemning arbitration to a static method of adjudication unable to match the challenges that it has to face. To respond to these challenges, international commercial arbitration must accept, to the fullest extent, its actual role in the administration of justice, which, in turn, means accepting its new public dimension and deploying greater efforts in doing what every adjudicative institution does: showing that it is legitimate and genuinely interested in pursuing the interests of justice.

Bibliography

Articles and Book Chapters

Henri Alvarez, *La nouvelle législation canadienne sur l'arbitrage commercial international*, 4 Rev Arb 529 (1986).

Jean-Pierre Ancel, *L'arbitre juge*, 4 Rev Arb 717 (2012).

Neil Andrews, *Civil Procedure* in Andrew Burrows, *English Private Law* 1320 (Oxford University Press 2013).

Nabil Antaki, *Regard intimiste sur l'état de l'arbitrage au Québec il y a 25 ans* in Frédéric Bachand & Fabien Gélinas, *D'une réforme à une autre, Regards croisés sur l'arbitrage au Québec* 9 (Éditions Yvon Blais 2013).

Christian Aschauer, *The Use of ICC Emergency Proceedings to Protect Arbitral Proceedings*, 23:2 ICC Bull 5 (2012).

Frédéric Bachand, *Les principes généraux de la justice civile et le nouveau Code de procédure civile*, 60:2 447 (2015).

Frédéric Bachand, *Vers une nouvelle réforme du droit québécois de l'arbitrage conventionnel* in Frédéric Bachand & Fabien Gélinas, *D'une réforme à une autre, Regards croisés sur l'arbitrage au Québec* 237 (Éditions Yvon Blais 2013).

Frédéric Bachand, *Court Intervention in International Arbitration: The Case for Compulsory Judicial Internationalism*, 1:6 J Disp Res 83 (2012).

Frédéric Bachand, *Kompetenz-Kompetenz, Canadian-Style*, 25:3 Arb Int 431 (2009).

Frédéric Bachand, *Does Article 8 of the Model Law Call for a Prima Facie Review of Arbitral Tribunals' Jurisdiction?* 22:3 Arb Int 463 (2006).

Baruch Baigel, *The Emergency Arbitrator Procedure Under the 2012 ICC Rules: A Juridical Analysis*, 31:1 J Int'l Arb 1 (2014).

Paul Beaumont, *Hague Choice of Court Agreements Convention 2005: Background, Negotiations, Analysis, Current Status*, 5:1 J Priv Int'l L 125 (2009).

Edouard Bertrand, *Sur le bon usage des sentences d'accord-parties*, 21:4 ASA Bull 13 (2006).

Sébastien Besson, *Les mesures provisoires et conservatoires dans la pratique arbitrale – Notion, types de mesures, conditions de l'octroi et responsabilité en cas de mesures injustifiées* in Guy Keutgen, *L'arbitrage international et l'urgence* 37 (Bruylant 2014).

Francisco Blavi, *Bifurcation of ICC Arbitral Proceedings – A Selection of Recent Procedural Orders*, 1 ICC Bull 46 (2017).

Mathieu de Boisséson & José Pinto, *Le nouveau droit français de l'arbitrage*, 32 Rev Br Arb 7 (2011).

Richard Boivin & Nicola Mariani, *International Arbitration in Canada*, 20:5 J Int'l Arb 508 (2003).

Laurence Boo, *Ruling on Jurisdiction – Is That an Award?* 3:2 A Int'l Arb J 125 (2007).

Christopher Boog, *Commentary on the ICC Rules, Article 29 [Emergency Arbitrator]* in Manuel Arroyo, *Arbitration in Switzerland: The Practitioner's Guide* 814 (Kluwer Law 2013).

Gary Born, *A New Generation of International Adjudication*, 4 DLJ 775 (2012).

Hakim Boularbah, *Le juge étatique 'bon samaritain' de l'arbitrage* in Michel Flamé & Philippe Lambrecht, *Hommage à Guy Keutgen* 763 (Bruylant 2013).

Pierre Bourdieu, *The Force of Law*, 38 Hast L J 805 (1987).

Andreas Bucher, *Court Intervention in Arbitration* in Richard B. Lillich & Charles Brower, *International Arbitration in the 21st Century: Towards 'Judicialization' and Uniformity?* 29 (Transnational Publishers 1994).

Dana Renée Bucy, *The Future of Interim Relief in International Commercial Arbitration Under the Amended UNCITRAL Model Law*, 25:3 Am U Int'l L Rev 579 (2010).

Michael Bühler & Pierre Heitzmann, *The 2017 ICC Expedited Rules: From Softball to Hardball?* 34:2 JOIA 121 (2017).

Loïc Cadiet, *Sources and Destiny of French Civil Procedure in a Globalized World* in Cloin Picker & Guy Seidman, *The Dynamism of Civil Procedure–Global Trends and Developments* 63 (Springer 2016).

Karin Calvo Goller, *The 2012 ICC Rules of Arbitration – An Accelerated Procedure and Substantial Changes*, 29:3 J Int'l Arb 323 (2012).

Thomas Carbonneau, *National Law and the Judicialization of Arbitration: Manifest Destiny, Manifest Disregard, or Manifest Error?* In Richard Lillich & Charles Brower, *International Arbitration in the 21st Century: Towards 'Judicialization' and Uniformity?* 115 (Transnational Publishers 1994).

Guido Carducci, *Remarques sur la nature juridique de l'arbitrage en droit italien et français à partir de l'arrêt Corte di Cassazione, 8 octobre 2013*, 1 Rev Arb 139 (2015).

Andrea Carlevaris & José Ricardo Feris, *Running the ICC Emergency Arbitrator Rules: The First Ten Cases*, 23:1 ICC Bull 25 (2014).

Eliseo Castineira, *The Emergency Arbitrator in the 2012 ICC Rules of Arbitration*, 4 Cah Arb 67 (2012).

Cécile Chainais, *Les mesures provisoires dans le nouveau droit français de l'arbitrage* in Achille Saletti, *L'arbitre et le juge étatique* 128 (Bruylant 2014).

Cécile Chainais & Charles Jarrosson, *L'urgence avant la constitution du tribunal arbitral* in *L'arbitrage international et l'urgence* 61 (Bruylant 2014).

Thomas Clay, *La Convention de New York vue par la doctrine française* 27:1 ASA Bull 50 (2009).

Thomas Clay, *Les mesures provisoires demandées à l'arbitre* in Jean-Michel Jacquet & Emmanuel Jolivet, *Les mesures provisoires dans l'arbitrage commercial international* 9 (LexisNexis 2008).

Laurence Craig & Laurent Jaeger, *The 2012 ICC Rules: Important Changes and Issues for Future Resolutions*, 4 Cah Arb 15 (2012).

Sophie Crépin, *Le contrôle des sentences arbitrales par la Cour d'appel de Paris depuis les réformes de 1980 et 1981*, 4 Rev Arb 521 (1991).

Roger Cotterrell, *From Living Law to the Death of Social-Sociology in Legal Theory* in Michael Freeman, *Law and Sociology* 16 (Oxford University Press 2006).

René David, *Arbitrage du XIXème et arbitrage du XXème siècle* in *Mélanges offerts à René Savatier* 219 (Dalloz 1965).

Hedge Dedek, *From Norms to Facts: The Realization of Rights in Common and Civil Private Law*, 56:1 MLJ 77 (2010).

Yes Dezalay & Mikael Rask Madsen, *The Force of Law and Lawyers: Pierre Bourdieu and the Reflexive Sociology of Law*, 8 An Rev L & Soc Sci 433 (2012).

Jean-François van Drooghenbroeck, *Le juge, l'arbitre et le référé: nécessité fait loi* in Achille Saletti et al., *L'arbitre et le juge étatique* 203 (Bruylant 2014).

Clotilde Druelle-Korn, *De la pensée à l'action économique: Étienne Clémentel, un ministre visionnaire*, 16:1 Hist-Pol 1 (2012).

Harry Edwards, *Alternative Dispute Resolution: Panacea or Anathema?* 99:3 H L Rev 668.

José Ricardo Feris, *The 2017 ICC Rules of Arbitration and the New ICC Expedited Procedure Provisions – A View from Inside the* Institution, 1 ICC Bull 63 (2017).

David Ferland, *L'arbitrage* in Denis Ferland & Benoît Emery, *Précis de procédure civile du Québec* 709 (Éditions Yvon Blais 2014).

Louis Flannery, *The English Statutory Framework* in Julian D.M. Lew et al., *Arbitration in England with Chapters on Scotland and Ireland* 210 (Kluwer Law 2013).

Yves Fortier & Annie Lespérance, *La contribution des Nations Unies au développement de l'arbitrage international*, 1 MJDR 56 (2014).

Philippe Fouchard, *Les institutions permanentes d'arbitrage devant le juge étatique*, 3 Rev Arb 225 (1987).

Philippe Fouchard, *Où va l'arbitrage international?* 34:2 MLJ 435 (1989).

Philippe Fouchard, *Typologie des institutions d'arbitrage*, 2 Rev Arb 281 (1990).

Phillipe Fouchard, *Une initiative contestable de la CNUDCI*, 12:3 ASA Bull 369 (1994).

Michael Freeman, *Law and Sociology* in Michael Freeman, *Law and Sociology* 1 (Oxford University Press 2006).

Emmanuel Gaillard, *Sociology of International Arbitration*, 31:1 Arb Int (2015).

Emmanuel Gaillard & Yas Banifatemi, *The Negative Effects of Competence-Competence: The Rule of Priority in Favor of the Arbitrators* in Emmanuel Gaillard & Domenico Di Pietro, *Enforcement of Arbitration Agreements and Arbitral Awards* 257 (Cameron May 2008).

Marc Galanter, *The Travails of Total Justice* in Robert Gordon & Morton Horwitz, *Law, Society, and History* 103 (Cambridge University Press 2011).

Nora Gallagher, *Parallel Proceedings, Res Judicata, Lis Pendens: Problems and Possible Solutions* in Loukas A. Mistelis & Julian D.M. Lew, *Pervasive Problems in International Arbitration* 329 (Kluwer Law 2006).

Fabien Gélinas, *From Harmonized Legislation to Harmonized Law: Hurdles and Tools, Judicial and Arbitral Perspectives* in Frédéric Bachand & Fabien Gélinas, *The UNCITRAL Model Law After 25 Years: Global Perspectives on International Commercial Arbitration* 261 (JurisNet 2013).

Rémy Gerbay, *Is the End Nigh Again? An Empirical Assessment of the Judicialization of International Arbitration*, 25 Am Rev Int'l Arb 223 (2014).

Varun N. Ghosh, *An Uncertain Shield – Res Judicata in Arbitration*, 31:4 Arb Int 661 (2015).

Gerald Goldstein, *La méthode de la reconnaissance: une nouvelle clé pour décoder les règles relatives à l'effet au Québec d'une transaction internationale*, 68 Rev Bar 279 (2009).

Louis Enrique Graham, *Interim Measures: Ongoing Regulation and Practices* in Albert van den Berg, *50 Years of the New York Convention* 561 (Kluwer Law 2009).

William Graham, *International Commercial Arbitration: The Developing Canadian Profile* in Robert Paterson & Bonita Thompson, *UNCITRAL Arbitration Model in Canada* 77 (Carswell 1987).

Florian Grisel, *Droit et non-droit dans les sentences arbitrales CCI: une perspective historique*, 25:2 ICC Bull 13 (2014).

Bernard Hanotiau, *The Res Judicata Effect of Arbitral Awards*, Supp ICC Bull 43 (2003).

Jill Harries, *Creating Legal Space: Settling Disputes in the Roman Empire* in Catherine Hezser, *Rabbinic Law in its Roman and Near Eastern Context* 63 (Tübingen 2003).

Dominique Hascher, *Les perspectives françaises sur le contrôle de la sentence internationale ou étrangère*, 1:2 MJDR 12 (2015).

Dominique Hascher, *The Review of International Awards in France* in Emmanuel Gaillard, *The Review of International Arbitral Awards in France* 97 (JurisNet 2008).

Dominique Hascher, *L'autorité de la chose jugée des sentences arbitrales* in *Travaux du comité français de DIP* 17 (Pédone 2004).

Jean Hilaire, *L'arbitrage dans la période moderne*, 2 Rev Arb 187 (2000).

Michel Humbert & Bruno de Loynes de Fumichon, *L'arbitrage à Rome*, 2 Rev Arb 285 (2003).

Gunther J. Horvath, *The Judicialization of International Arbitration* in Stphan Kröll et al., *Liber Amicorum Eirc Bergsten* 251 (Kluwer Law 2011).

Jean-Michel Jacquet, *Avons-nous besoin d'une jurisprudence arbitrale?* 3 Rev Arb 445 (2010).

Carine Jallamion, *Arbitrage et pouvoir politique en France du XVIIème au XIXème siècle*, 1 Rev Arb 2 (2005).

Charles Jarrosson & Jacques Pellerin, *Le droit français de l'arbitrage après le décret du 13 janvier 2011*, 1 Rev Arb 5 (2011).

Bibliography

Sigward Jarvin, *La Cour d'arbitrage de la CCI pendant la deuxième guerre mondiale* in Laurent Lévy & Yves Derains, *Liber Amicorum en l'honneur de Serge Lazareff* 311 (Pédone 2011).

Yves Jeanclos, *La pratique de l'arbitrage au XIIème et XVème siècle*, 3 Rev Arb 417 (1999).

Emmanuel Jolivet, Giacomo Marchisio & Fabien Gélinas, *Trade Usages in ICC Arbitration* in Fabien Gélinas, *Trade Usages and Implied Terms in the Age of Arbitration* 211 (Oxford University Press 2016).

Herbert Felix Jolowicz, *The Judex and the Arbitral Principle*, 2 RIDA 477 (1949).

Gabrielle Kaufmann-Kohler, *Arbitral Precedent: Dream, Necessity or Excuse?* 3 Arb Int 357 (2007).

Dominic Kelly, *The International Chamber of Commerce*, 10:2 N Pol Eco 259 (2005).

Catherine Kessedjian, *Définitions et conditions de l'octroi de mesures provisoires* in Jean-Michel Jacquet & Emmanuel Jolivet, *Les mesures provisoires dans l'arbitrage commercial international* 73 (LexisNexis 2008).

Jennifer Kirby, *What Is an Award, Anyway?* 31:4 J Int'l Arb 475 (2014).

Richard Kreindler, *Settlement Agreements and Arbitration in the Context of the ICC Rules*, 9:2 ICC Bull 22 (1998).

Stephan Kröll, *Recourse Against Negative Decisions on Jurisdiction*, 20:1 Arb Int 55 (2004).

Alain Lacabarats, *Les mesures provisoires demandées au juge français en matière d'arbitrage international* in Jean-Michel Jacquet & Emmanuel Jolivet, *Les mesures provisoires dans l'arbitrage commercial international-Évolutions et innovations* 3 (Litec 2008).

Pierre Lalive, *De la fureur réglementaire*, 12:2 ASA Bull 213 (1994).

Marc Lalonde & Lex Alexeev, *National Report for Canada (2012)* in Jan Paulsson & Lise Bosman, *ICCA International Handbook on Commercial Arbitration* 1 (Kluwer Law 2012).

Elisabeth Leimbacher, *Efficiency Under the New ICC Rules of Arbitration of 2012: First Glimpse at the New Practice*, 31:2 ASA Bull 783 (2013).

Guillaume Lemenez & Paul Quigley, *The ICDR's Emergency Arbitrator in Action Part I: A Look at Empirical Data*, 3 Disp Res J 60 (2008).

Guillaume Lemenez & Paul Quigley, *The ICDR's Emergency Arbitrator in Action Part II: Enforcing Emergency Arbitrator Decisions*, 4 Dis Res J 1 (2008).

Julian D.M. Lew, *Achieving the Dream: Autonomous Arbitration* in Julian D.M. Lew & Loukas A. Mistelis, *Arbitration Insights* 455 (Kluwer Law 2007).

Éric Loquin, *L'arrêt de mort des sentences d'accord-parties*, 2 RTD Comm 476 (2013).

Gino Lörcher, *Enforceability of Agreed Awards in Foreign Jurisdictions* (2001) 17:3 Arbitration International 275.

Mikael Rask Madsen, *Sociological Approaches to International Courts* in Cesare Romano et al., *Oxford Handbook of International Adjudication* 388 (Oxford University Press 2013).

Carole Malinvaud, *The Amendment to the UNCITRAL Model Law on Interim Measures: A Compromise on Ex Parte Measures* in *The UNCITRAL Model Law on International Commercial Arbitration: 25 Years* 99 (Maklu 2010).

Jonathan Mance, *The Review of Arbitral Awards in England* in Emmanuel Gaillard, *The Review of International Arbitral Awards* 119 (JurisNet 2008).

Giacomo Marchisio, *Jurisdictional Matters in International Commercial Arbitration: Why Arbitrators Stand on an Equal Footing with State Courts*, 31:4 J Int'l Arb 455 (2014).

Giacomo Marchisio, *Recent Solutions to Old Problems: A Look at the Expedited Procedure Under the Newly Revised ICC Rules of Arbitration*, 1 ICC Bull 76 (2017).

Louis Marquis, *La notion d'arbitrage commercial international en droit québécois*, 37 MLJ 448 (1992).

Mario Matteucci, *The History of Unidroit and the Methods of Unification*, 66 L Lib J 286 (1973).

Pierre Mayer, *La liberté de l'arbitre*, 2 Rev Arb 339 (2013).

Pierre Mayer, *L'arbitre et la loi* in *Études offertes à Pierre Catala* 225 (Litec 2001).

Pierre Mayer & Eduardo Silva Romero, *Le nouveau règlement d'arbitrage de la Chambre de Commerce Internationale (CCI)*, 4 Rev Arb 897 (2011).

Ewan McKendrick, *Discharge by Agreement* in *Chitty on Contracts* 1607 (Sweet & Maxwell 2012).

Ernest Metzger, *An Outline of Civil Procedure*, 9 R Leg Trad 1 (2013).

Dirk de Meulemeester & Maud Piers, *The New Belgian Arbitration Law*, 3 ASA Bull 600 (2013).

Olivier Mignolet, *Les mesures provisoires et conservatoires prises par les arbitres* in Achille Saletti, *L'arbitre et le juge étatique* 165 (Bruylant 2014).

Alexis Mourre, *Precedent and Confidentiality in International Commercial Arbitration* in Yas Banifatemi, *Precedent in International Arbitration* 39 (Juris Publishing 2007).

Alexis Mourre, *Is there Life After an Award?* in Pierre Tercier, *Post Award Issues* 1 (JurisNet 2011).

Simon Nesbitt & Michael Darowski, *LCIA Arbitration Rules – Article 26* in Loukas A. Mistelis, *Concise International Arbitration* 546 (Kluwer Law 2015).

Christopher Newmark & Richard Hill, *Can a Mediated Settlement Become an Enforceable Arbitration Award?* 16:1 Arb Int 81 (2000).

Hans Peter Müller, *Durkheim's Political Sociology* in Stephen P. Turner, *Emile Durkheim: Sociologist and Moralist* 93 (Routledge 1993).

Karin Oellers-Frahm, *Expanding the Competence to Issue Provisional Measures–Strengthening the International Adjudicative Function* in Armin Von Bogdandy & Ingo Venzke, *International Judicial Law Making* 389 (Springer 2011).

Mark Oliver Saville, *Departmental Advisory Committee on Arbitration Law, Report of February 1996*, 13:3 Arb Int 311 (1997).

Kieran O'Callaghan & Jerome Finnis, *Support and Supervision by the Courts* in Julian D.M. Lew et al., *Arbitration in England with Chapters on Ireland and Scotland* 430 (Kluwer Law 2013).

Philip O'Neill & Nawaf Salam, *Is the Exceptio Non Adimpleti Contractus Part of the New Lex Mercatoria?* in Emmanuel Gaillard, *Transnational Rules in International Commercial Arbitration* 147 (ICC Publishing 1993).

William Park, *Determining Arbitral Jurisdiction: Allocation of Tasks between Courts and Arbitrators*, 8 Am Rev Int'l Arb 133 (1997).
Jan Paulsson, *Arbitration in Three Dimensions*, 7 TDM 1 (2010).
Jacques Pellerin, *La sentence arbitrale: incertitudes et propositions* in Mélanges Mayer 679 (LGDJ 2015).
Philipp Peters & Christian Koller, *The Award and the Courts – The Notion of Arbitral Award: An Attempt to Overcome a Babylonian Confusion* in Christian Klausegger, Peter Klein et al., *Austrian Yearbook on International Arbitration* 137 (Manz'sche Verlags 2010).
Mark A. Pollack, *Political Science and International Adjudication* in Cesare Romano et al., *Oxford Handbook of International Adjudication* 357 (Oxford University Press 2013).
Laurence Ponty, *Key Features of the LCIA Arbitration Rules*, 32:4 ASA Bull 757 (2014).
Alain Prujiner, *L'arbitre et le droit*, 1:1 MJDR 33 (2014).
Alain Prujiner, *Éléments d'une Loi Type reformée* in Frédéric Bachand & Fabien Gélinas, *D'une réforme à une autre, Regards croisés sur l'arbitrage au Québec* 221 (Éditions Yvon Blais 2013).
Alain Prujiner, *Les nouvelles règles de l'arbitrage au Québec*, 4 Rev Arb 425 (1987).
Jean-Baptiste Racine, *La sentence d'incompétence*, 4 Rev Arb 730 (2010).
Jean-Baptiste Racine, *Sur l'idéologie de la transparence en droit de l'arbitrage* in *Mélanges en l'honneur du Professeur Pierre Mayer* 727 (Lextenso 2015).
Luca Radicati di Brozolo, *Res Judicata* in Pierre Tercier, *Post Awards Issues* 127 (JurisNet 2011).
Cesare Romano, *The Shadow Zones of International Adjudication* in Cesare Romano et al., *The Oxford Handbook of International Adjudication* 90 (Oxford University Press 2013).
Cesare Romano, Karen Alter & Yuval Shany, *Mapping International Adjudicative Bodies, The Issues, The Players* in Cesare Romano et al., *The Oxford Handbook of International Adjudication* 3 (Oxford University Press 2013).
Ripen Sabharwal & Rebecca Zaman, *Vive la différence: Convergence and Conformity in the Rules Reforms of Arbitral Institutions–The Case of the LCIA 2014 Rules*, 31:6 J Int'l Arb 700 (2014).
Fabio Santacroce, *The Emergency Arbitrator: A Full-Fledged Arbitrator Rendering an Enforceable Decision?* 31:2 Arb Int 282 (2015).
Yves Sassier, *Réfléxion autour du sens d'instituere, institutio, instituta* in Jean-Philippe Bras, *L'Institution* 19 (L'Harmanattan 2008).
Christophe Seraglini & Denis Mouralis, *L'arbitrage commercial international* in Jacques Beguin & Michel Menjucq, *Traité du droit du commerce international* 2 (LexisNexis 2011).
Richard Scott, *Approaching Adulthood: The Maturing of Institutional Theory*, 37:5 Theory & Soc 427 (2008).
Patricia Shaughnessy, *Pre-Arbitral Urgent Relief: The New SCC Emergency Arbitrator Rules*, 27:4 J Int'l Arb 337 (2010).

Bibliography

Robert Sills, *The Continuing Role of the Courts in the Era of the Emergency Arbitrator* in Albert van den Berg, *Legitimacy: Myths, Realities and Challenges* 278 (Kluwer Law 2015).

Audrey Sheppard, *The Scope and Res Judicata Effects of Arbitral Awards* in Guy Keutgen, *Arbitral Procedure at the Dawn of the New Millenium* 263 (Bruylant 2005).

Ben Sheppard & John Townsend, *Holding the Fort Until the Arbitrators Are Appointed: The New ICDR International Emergency Rules*, 2 Disp Res J 74 (2006).

John Sorabji, *English Civil Justice After the Woolf and Jackson Reforms* (Cambridge University Press 2014).

Sven Steinmo, *Historical Institutionalism* in Donatella Della Porta & Michael Keating, *Approaches and Methodologies in Social Sciences* 118 (Cambridge University Press 2008).

Alec Stone Sweet, *Judicialization and the Construction of Governance* in Martin Shapiro & Alec Stone Sweet, *On Law, Politics, and Judicialization* 55 (Oxford University Press 2002).

Alec Stone Sweet & Florian Grisel, *The Evolution of International Arbitration: Delegation, Judicialization, Governance* in Walter Matti & Thomas Dietz, *International Arbitration and Global Governance: Contending Theories and Evidence* 22 (Oxford University Press 2014).

David Stevenson, *The First World War and European Integration*, 34:4 Int'l H Rev 841 (2012).

Roy Suddaby, William Foster & Albert Mills, *Historical Institutionalism* in Marcelo Bucheli & Daniel Wadhwani, *Organisations in Time* 100 (Oxford University Press 2014).

Neal C. Tale, *Why the Expansion of Judicial Power?* in Neal C. Tale & Torbjörn Vallinder, *The Global Expansion of Judicial Power* 26 (New York University Press 1995).

Jean-Marie Tchakoua, *Le statut de la sentence d'accord-parties: les limites d'un déguisement bien utile*, 7 Int'l Buss L J 775 (2002).

Joseph Tirado & Sarah Nelson Smith, *The New ICDR International Emergency Measures Rules*, 5 TDM 1 (2006).

Claude R. Thomson & Annie Finn, *International Commercial Arbitration: A Canadian Perspective*, 18:2 Arb Int 205 (2002).

Marc Trachtenberg, *A New Economic Order: Étienne Clémentel and the French Economic Diplomacy during the First World War*, 10:2 Fre hist'l Stud 315 (1977).

Louise Ellen Teitz, *The Hague Choice of Court Convention: Validating Party Autonomy and Providing an Alternative to Arbitration*, 53:3 Am J Comp L 543 (2005).

Pierre Tercier, *La légitimité de l'arbitrage*, 4 Rev Arb 653 (2011).

Craig Tevendale & Andrew Cannon, *Enforcement of Awards* in Julian D.M. Lew et al., *Arbitration in England with Chapters on Scotland and Ireland* 563 (Kluwer Law 2013).

Natalie Voser, *An Overview of the Most Important Changes in the Revised ICC Arbitration Rules*, 29:4 ASA Bull 783 (2011).

David Wolfson & Susanna Charlwood, *Challenges to Arbitration Awards* in Julian D.M. Lew et al., *Arbitration in England with Chapters on Scotland and Ireland* 526 (Kluwer Law 2013).
Ali Yesilirmak, *Provisional Measures* in Julian D.M. Lew, *Pervasive Problems in International Arbitration* 185 (Kluwer Law 2006).
Adrian Zuckerman, *Justice in Crisis: Comparative Dimensions of Civil Procedure* in Adrian Zuckerman, *Civil Justice in Crisis* 3 (Oxford University Press 1999).

Books

Craig Anderson, *Roman Law* (Dundee University Press 2009).
David Armstrong, Theo Farrel & Hélène Lambert, *International Law and International Relations* (Cambridge University Press 2012).
Vincenzo Arangio Ruiz, *Istituzioni di diritto romano* (Jovene 1927).
Paul-Henri Antonmattei & Jacques Raynard, *Droit civil: contrats spéciaux* (LexisNexis 2013).
Frédéric Bachand, *L'intervention du juge canadien avant et durant un arbitrage commercial international* (Éditions Yvon Blais 2005).
Samuel Barkin, *International Organization: Theories and Institutions* (Macmillan 2006).
Babak Barin & Marie-Claude Rigaud, *L'arbitrage consensuel au Québec – Receuil de jurisprudence* (Éditions Yvon Blais 2012).
Silvia Barona & Carlos Esplugues, *Global Perspectives on ADR* (Intersentia 2014).
William Beick, *Absolutism in France* (Cambridge University Press 1985).
Alain Bénabent, *Droit des contrats spéciaux civils et commerciaux* (LGDJ 2013).
Klaus Peter Berger, *International Economic Arbitration* (Kluwer Law 1993).
Laure Bernheim – Van de Casteele, *Les principes fondamentaux de l'arbitrage* (Bruylant 2012).
Sébastien Besson, *Arbitrage international et mesures provisoires* (Schulthess 1998).
Louis Boyer, *La notion de transaction* (Sirey 1947).
Sylvain Bollée, *Les méthodes du droit international privé à l'épreuve des sentences arbitrales* (Economica 2004).
Gary Born, *International Commercial Arbitration* (Kluwer Law 2014).
Ronald A. Brand & Paul M. Herrup, *The Hague Convention on Choice of Court Agreements* (Cambridge University Press 2008).
Loïc Cadiet & Emmanuel Jeuland, *Droit judiciaire privé* (LexisNexis 2013).
Loïc Cadiet, Jacques Normand & Soraya Amrani Mekki, *Théorie générale du procès* (Presses Universitaires de France 2013).
Ernest Caparros, Hélène Thériault & Jean Thorn, *Code of Canon Law Annotated* (Wilson & Lafleur 2004).
Mauro Cappelletti, *The Judicial Process in a Comparative Perspective* (Clarendon Press 1989).
Jean Carbonnier, *Sociologie juridique* (Presses Universitaires de France 1994).
Brian Casey, *Arbitration Law of Canada: Practice and Procedure* (JurisNet 2011).

Bibliography

Cécile Chainais, *La protection juridictionnelle provisoire dans le procès civil en droit français et italien* (Dalloz 2007).
Giuseppe Chiovenda, *Istituzioni di diritto processuale civile* (Jovene 1936).
Thomas Clay, *L'arbitre* (Dalloz 2001).
Thomas Clay, *Le nouveau droit français de l'arbitrage* (Lextenso 2011).
Jacques van Compernolle, *Les mesures provisoires en droit Belge, Français et Italien* (Bruylant 1998).
Roger Cotterrell, *Emile Durkheim in a Moral Domain* (Stanford University Press 1999).
Roger Cotterrell, *Sociology of Law* (Butterworths 1984).
Laurence Craig et al., *International Chamber of Commerce Arbitration* (ICC Publishing 1990).
Laurence Craig, William Park & Jan Paulsson, *International Chamber of Commerce Arbitration* (Oceana Publishing 2000).
Clyde Croft, Christopher Kee et al., *A Guide to the UNCITRAL Arbitration Rules* (Cambridge University Press 2013).
René David, *L'arbitrage dans le commerce international* (Economica 1982).
Yves Dezalay & Brian Garth, *Dealing in Virtue* (Chicago University Press 1996).
Yves Derains & Eric Scwartz, *A Guide to ICC Rules of Arbitration* (Kluwer Law 2005).
Trevor Farrow, *Civil Justice, Privatization, and Democracy* (University of Toronto Press 2014).
Denis Ferland & Benoît Emery, *Précis de Procedure Civile du Québéc* (Éditions Yvon Blais 2015).
David Foskett, *The Law and Practice of the Compromise* (Sweet & Maxwell 2010).
Philippe Fouchard, *L'arbitrage commercial international* (Dalloz 1965).
Jason Fry, Simon Greenberg & Francesca Mazza, *The Secretariat's Guide to ICC Arbitration* (ICC Publishing 2012).
Emmanuel Gaillard & John Savage, *Fouchard Gaillard Goldman on International Commercial Arbitration* (Kluwer Law 1999).
Emmanuel Gaillard, *Legal Theory of International Arbitration* (Martinus Nijhoff 2010).
Fabien Gélinas et al., *Foundations of Civil Justice* (Springer 2015).
Rémy Gerbay, *The Functions of Arbitral Institutions* (Kluwer Law 2016).
René Girard, *Des choses cachées depuis la fondation du monde* (Bernard Grasset 1978).
Paul Frédéric Girard, *Manuel élémentaire de droit romain* (Dalloz 2003).
Patrick Glenn, *Legal Traditions of the World* (Oxford University Press 2014).
Stephen Goldberg, *Dispute Resolution* (Kluwer Law 2012).
Jacob Grierson & Annet van Hooft, *Arbitrating Under the 2012 ICC Rules* (Kluwer Law 2012).
Florian Grisel, *L'arbitrage international ou le droit contre l'ordre juridique* (LGDJ 2011).
Serge Guinchard et al., *Procédure civile* (Dalloz 2014).
Martin Gusy, James Hosking & Franz Schwar, *A Guide to the ICDR International Arbitration Rules* (Oxford University Press 2011).
Albert Hamscher, *The Parliament of Paris After the Fronde* (Pittsburgh University Press 2009).
Bernard Hanotiau, *Complex Arbitrations* (Kluwer Law 2006).
Jacques Héron & Thierry Le Bars, *Droit judiciaire privé* (Lextenso 2012).

Howard Holtzmann, Joseph Neuhaus et al., *A Guide to the 2006 Amendments to the UNCITRAL Model Law on International Commercial Arbitration: Legislative History and Commentary* (Kluwer Law 2015).
Charles Jarrosson, *La notion d'arbitrage* (LGDJ 1985).
John Jolowicz, *On Civil Procedure* (Oxford University Press 2000).
Herbert Felix Jolowicz & Barry Nicholas, *Historical Introduction to the Study of Roman Law* (Cambridge University Press 1972).
David Johnston, *Roman Law in Context* (Cambridge University Press 1999).
Joshua Karton, *The Culture of Arbitration* (Oxford University Press 2013).
Antoine Kassis, *Problèmes de base de l'arbitrage* (LGDJ 1987).
Antoine Kassis, *Réfexions sur le règlement d'arbitrage de la Chambre de Commerce Internationale* (LGDJ 1988).
John Kendall, *Expert Determination* (Sweet & Maxwell 2001).
Herbert Kronke, Patricia Nacimiento et al., *Recognition and Enforcement of Foreign Arbitral Awards: A Global Commentary on the New York Convention* (Kluwer Law 2010).
Martine Lachance, *Le contrat de transaction* (Éditions Yvon Blais 2005).
Claire Lemercy & Jérôme Sgard, *Arbitrage privé international et globalisation(s)* (CNRS 2015).
Daniel Levy, *Les abus de l'arbitrage commercial international* (L'Harmanattan 2015).
Dean Lewis, *The Interpretation and Uniformity of the Uncitral Model Law on International Commercial Arbitration* (Kluwer Law 2016).
Christopher Liebscher, *The Healthy Award* (Kluwer Law 2003).
Éric Loquin, *L'arbitrage du commerce international* (Lextenso 2015).
Nicklaus Luhman, *A Sociological Theory of Law* (Routledge 1985).
Louis Marquis, *Droit de la prévention et du règlement des différends* (Éditions Revue de droit 2015).
Crisanto Mandrioli, *Corso di diritto processuale civile* (Giappichelli 2009).
Pierre Mayer & Vincent Heuzé, *Droit international privé* (Montchrestien 2007).
Pierre Mayer & Vincent Heuzé, *Droit international privé* (LGDJ 2014).
Robert Merkin & Louis Flannery, *Arbitration Act 1996* (Routledge 2014).
Henri Motulsky, *Écrits – études et notes sur l'arbitrage* (Dalloz 1976).
Peter Murray & Rolf Stürner, *German Civil Justice System* (Carolina Academic Press 2004).
Bruno Oppetit, *Théorie de l'arbitrage* (Dalloz 1998).
François Ost, *Dire le droit, faire justice* (Bruylant 2007).
Jan Paulsson, *The Idea of Arbitration* (Oxford University Press 2013).
Silvio Perrozzi, *Istituzioni di diritto romano* (Vallardi 1928).
Brainard Guy Peters, *Institutional Theory in Political Science* (Continuum International Publishing 2012).
Jean-François Poudret & Sébastien Besson, *Comparative Law of International Arbitration* (Sweet & Maxwell 2007).
Laurent Poulet, *Transaction et protection des parties* (LGDJ 2013).
Alain Prujiner & Nabil Antaki, *Proceedings of the First International Commercial Arbitration Conference* (Wilson & Lafleur 1986).

Bibliography

Attila Ràcz, *Courts and Tribunals* (Akadémia Kiadó 1980).
Alan Redfern & Martin Hunter, *Redfern & Hunter on International Commercial Arbitration* (Oxford University Press 2015).
George Ridgeway, *The Merchants of the Peace* (Columbia University Press 1938).
Leonard Riskin, *Dispute Resolution and Lawyers* (West Academic Publishing 2014).
Jean Robert, *L'arbitrage* (Dalloz 1993).
Derek Roebuck & Bruno de Loynes de Fumichon, *Roman Arbitration* (Oxford University Press 2004).
Pieter Sanders, *Quo Vadis Arbitration?* (Kluwer Law 1999).
Maxi Scherer, Lisa Richman & Rémy Gerbay, *Arbitrating under the 2014 LCIA Rules* (Kluwer Law 2015).
Christopher Schreuer et al., *The ICSID Convention: A Commentary* (Cambridge University Press 2009).
Rold Schütze, *Institutional Arbitration* (Hart Publishing 2013).
Yuval Shany, *Assessing the Effectiveness of International Courts* (Oxford University Press 2014).
Stuart Sime, *Civil Procedure* (Oxford University Press 2010).
David St John Sutton, Judith Gill & Matthew Gearing, *Russel on Arbitration* (Sweet & Maxwell 2007).
Alec Sweet Stone & Martin Shapiro, *On Law, Politics, and Judicialization* (Oxford University Press 2002).
Mario Talamanca, *Istituzioni di diritto romano* (Giuffre 1990).
Sabine Thuilleaux, *L'arbitrage commercial au Québec* (Éditions Yvon Blais 1991).
Peter Turner & Reza Mohstashami, *A Guide to the LCIA Arbitration Rules* (Oxford University Press 2009).
Alan Uzelac & CH van Rhee, *Public and Private Justice* (Intersentia 2007).
Albert van den Berg, *Legitimacy: Myths, Realities, Challenges–ICCA Congress Series no. 18* (Kluwer Law 2015).
Albert van den Berg, *The New York Convention of 1958* (Kluwer Law 1981).
Steven Vago, *Law and Society* (Pearson 2008).
Dominique Vidal, *Droit français de l'arbitrage interne et international* (Lextenso 2012).
Natalie Voser & Christopher Boog, *ICC Emergency Arbitrator Proceedings: An Overview* (ICC Publishing 2011).
Max Weber, *Economy and Society* (University of California Press 1978).
Thomas Webster & Michael Bühler, *Handbook of ICC Arbitration* (Sweet & Maxwell 2014).
Leopold Wenger, *Institutes of the Roman Law of Civil Procedure* (Liberal Arts Press 1986).
Reinmar Wolff, ed, *The New York Convention* (Hart Publishing 2012).
Ali Yesilirmak, *Provisional Measures in International Commercial Arbitration* (Kluwer Law 2005).
Adrian Zuckerman, *On Civil Procedure* (Sweet & Maxwell 2013).

Table of Cases

United Kingdom

House of Lords (HL)

Fiona Trust & Holding Corp v. Privalov, [2008] 1 Lloyd's Rep 254 (House of Lords), 93
Sirius International Insurance Co v. FAI General Insurance Ltd [2004] UKHL 54, 119, 120
Sutcliffe v. Thackrah [1974] 1 All ER 859 at 870 (House of Lords), 73
Scott v. Avery [1856] 5 HL Cas 811 (House of Lords), 30

Privy Council (UKPC)

Texan Management Ltd & Ors v. Pacific Electric Wire & Cable Company [2009] UKPC 46, 98
Associated Electric & Gas Insurance Services v. European Reinsurance Company of Zurich [2003] UKPC 11, 80

Supreme Court of the United Kingdom (UKSC)

Jivraj v. Hashwani [2011] UKSC 40, 19, 75, 180
Dallah Real Estate v. Ministry of Religious Affairs [2010] UKSC 46, 92

Court of Appeal of England and Wales (EWCA)

Trust Risk Group SPA v. Amrust Europe Ltd [2015] EWCA Civ 437, 92
Joint Stock Company 'Aeroflot Airlines' v. Berezovsky & Ors [2013] EWCA Civ 784, 93
Zurich Insurance Company Plc v. Hayward [2011] EWCA Civ 641, 121
SAB Miller v. East Africa Breweries [2009] EWCA Civ 1564, 150
Albon v. Naza Motor Trading Bhd [2007] EWCA Civ 1124, 92
Hoddinott & Ors v. Persimmon Homes (Wessex) Ltd [2007] EWCA Civ 1203, 98
Al-Naimi v. Islamic Press Agency [2000] 1 Lloyd's Rep 522 (CA), 92

Table of Cases

High Court of England and Wales (EWHC)

Gerald Metals SA v. Timis [2016] EWHC 2327 (CH), 150
C v. D1, D2, and D3 [2015] EWHC 2126, 100
Konkola Copper Mines v. U&M Mining Zambia Ltd [2014] EWHC 2374, 19, 79
OMV Petrom SA v. Glencore International AG [2014] EWHC 242, 81
Navios International Inc v. Sangamon Transportation Group [2012] EWHC 166, 72
Nestor Maritime SA v. Sea Anchor Shipping Co Ltd [2012] EWHC 996, 125
West Tankers Inc v. Allianz SPA & Assicurazione Generali SPA [2012] EWHC 854, 94
Terna Bahrain Holding Company v. Ali Marzook Al Bin Kamil Al Shamsi and Ors [2012] EWHC 3283, 72, 124
Hudson v. New Media Holding Company LLC [2011] EWHC 3068, 120
JSC BTA Bank v. Ablyyazov & Ors [2011] 2 Lloyd's Rep 129, 93
Wilky Property Holdings Plc v. London & Surrey Investments Ltd [2011] EWHC 2226, 74
Community Care North East v. Durham County Council [2010] EWHC 959, 119
Dawes v. Treasure and Son Ltd [2010] EWHC 3218, 122
British Telecommunications Plc v. SAE Group Inc [2009] EWHC 252, 93
Elektrim SA v. Vivendi Universal SA [2007] EWHC 11, 125
Halifax Life Ltd v. Equitable Life Assurance Society [2007] EWHC 503, 73
A v. B [2006] EWHC 2006, 93
Eco et Wireless Ltd v. Networks Ltd & Ors [2006] EWHC 1568, 150
Halpern v. Halpern [2006] EWHC 603, 126
Halpern v. Halpern [2006] EWHC 1728, 127
Law Debenture Trust Corp Plc v. Elektrim Finance BV [2005] EWHC 1412, 93
Sawyer v. Atatri Interactive Inc [2005] EWHC 2351, 98
Bernard Schulte GmbH & Co Kg & Ors v. Nile Holdings Ltd [2004] EWHC 977, 19
Cetelem SA v. Roust Holdings Ltd [2004] EWHC 3175, 150
Agrimex Ltd v. Tradigrain SA [2003] EWHC 1656, 73
Hussmann (Europe) Ltd v. Al Ameen Development & Trade Co [2000] EWHC 210, 19, 74

Canada

Supreme Court

Dell Computer Corp v. Union des Consommateurs, [2007] SCC 34, 94
Lac D'Amiante du Québec Ltée v. Québec Inc, [2001] 2 RSC 743, 56
Sport Maska Inc v. Zittrer, [1988] 1 SCR 564, 75
Zodiak International Productions Inc v. The Polish People's Republic, [1983] 1 SCR 529, 30

Lower Courts

International Steel Services Inc v. Dynatec Madagascar SA [2016] ONSC 2810, 166

United States

T.co Metals LLC v. Dempsey Pipe & Supply Inc, 592 F Supp 329 (2010), 80 (Found as 592)
Boom ASA v. Pictometry International Corp, 757 F Supp 238 (2010), 144, 151
Toyo Tire Holdings of Ams Inc v. Continental Tire Inc, 609 F Supp 975 (2010), 151
Trade & Trasp. Inc v. Natural Petroleum Charterers Inc, 931 F Supp 191 (2d Cir 1991), 80

Singapore

Tomolugen Holdings Ltd v. Silica Investors Ltd & ors [2015] SGCA 57, 94
BLC and others v. BLB and another [2014] SGCA 40, 8
The Titan Unity [2013] SGHCR 28, 94

France

Cour de Cassation (Cass Civ)

Cass Civ 1^e, 8 July 2015, No 13-25.846, 65
Cass Civ 1^e, 18 March 2015, No 14-13.336, 104
Cass Civ 1^e, 2 April 2014, No 11-14.692, 130
Cass Civ 1^e, 5 March 2014, No 12-29.112, 68
Cass Civ 2^e, 3 October 2013, (2014) Revue de l'arbitrage 643 (Annotation Vincent Chantebout), 65
Cass Civ 1^e, 14 November 2012, (2013) Revue de l'arbitrage 138 (Annotation Jean Billemont), 133
Cass Civ 2^e, 26 May 2011, No 06-19.527, 136
Cass Civ 1^e, 12 April 2011, No 11-14.123, 68
Cass Civ 2^e, 3 March 2011, No 10-15.505, 131
Cass Civ 1^e, 6 October 2010, (2010) Revue de l'arbitrage 813 (Annotation François-Xavier Train), 104
Cass Civ 1^e, 28 May 2008, No 07-13.266, 68
Cass Civ 1^e, 9 January 2008, (2008) Yearbook of Commercial Arbitration 478, 91
Cass Civ 1^e, 29 June 2007, (2007) Revue de l'arbitrage 507 (Annotation Emmanuel Gaillard), 65
Cass Civ 1^e, 3 October 2006, (2008) Revue de l'arbitrage 85 (Annotation Charles Jarrosson), 64
Cass Civ 1^e, 7 June 2006, (2006) Revue de l'arbitrage 945 (Annotation Christophe Seraglini), 91
Cass Civ 3^e, 6 December 2005, No 03-16.572, 147
Cass Civ 2^e, 7 March 2002, No 00-11.526, 147
Cass Civ 1^e, 14 June 2000, (2001) 4 Revue de l'arbitrage 729, 63
Cass Civ 1^e, 10 May 1995, (1995) Revue de l'arbitrage 617 (Annotation Emmanuel Gaillard), 90

Cass Civ 1ᵉ, 6 March 1990, (1990) Revue de l'arbitrage 633, 147
Cass Civ 3ᵉ, 10 July 1991, No 90-11.847, 131

Cour d'Appel de Paris (CA Paris)

CA Paris, 25 February 2014, No 13/07021, 146
CA Paris, 17 December 2013, (2014) Revue de l'arbitrage 948 (Annotation Daniel Cohen), 101
CA Paris, 23 May 2013, No 12/14885, 147
CA Paris, 22 January 2013, No 12/11374, 146
CA Paris, 20 November 2012, No 11/12192, 65, 69
CA Paris, 27 October 2011, No 10/12982, 65
CA Paris, 29 September 2011, No 11/06269, 64
CA Paris, 21 January 2010, (2010) Revue de l'arbitrage 339, 130
CA Paris, 9 April 2009, No 07/17769, 132
CA Paris, 5 November 2008, No 06/22858, 131
CA Paris, 7 October 2004, (2005) Revue de l'arbitrage 737, 70
CA, Paris, 8 October 1998, (2000) Revue de l'arbitrage 128, 69
CA Paris, 17 June 1997, (1997) Revue de l'arbitrage 584 (Annotation Dominique Bureau), 63
CA Paris, 21 November 1991, (1992) Revue de l'arbitrage 494 (Annotation Marie-Claire Rivier), 64
CA Paris, 27 October 1988, (1990) Revue de l'arbitrage 908 (Annotation Bertrand Moreau), 64
CA Paris, 16 June 1988, (1989) Revue de l'arbitrage 309 (Annotation Charles Jarrosson), 104
CA Paris, 4 March 1986, (1987) Revue de l'arbitrage 167, 130

International Tribunals and Arbitral Tribunals

European Court of Human Rights (ECHR)

Regent Company v. Ukraine, ECHR, 3 April 2008, 16, 47
Klausecker v. Germany, ECHR, 6 January 2015, 47

Arbitral Awards and Procedural Orders

ICC Procedural Order No. 18864/2013, 96
ICC Procedural Order No. 14338/2008, 96
ICC Final Award No. 17020/2011, 40 YB Comm Arb 294, 89
ICC Final Award No. 16426/2011, unpublished, 113
ICC Final Award No. 14667/2011, 40 YB Comm Arb 51, 94
ICC Final Award No. 12656/2006, unpublished, 113
ICC Final Award No. 12226/2004, in Jean-Jacques Arnaldez, *Collection of ICC Awards 2001–2007* (Kluwer Law 2009) 667, 84
ICC Final Award No. 9800/2000, in Jean-Jacques Arnaldez, *Collection of ICC Awards 2001–2007* (Kluwer Law 2009) 659, 84
ICC Final Award No. 6233/1992, in Jean-Jacques Arnaldez, *Collection of ICC Awards 2001–2007* (Kluwer Law 2009) 332, 84
ICC Final Award No. 3267/1989, in Sigvard Jarvin, Yves Derains & Jean-Jacques Arnaldez, *Collection of ICC Awards 1986–1990* (Kluwer Law 1994) 43, 84
ICC Final Award No. 3540/1980, in Sigvard Jarvin & Yves Derains, *Collection of ICC Awards 1947–1985* (Kluwer Law 1994) 105, 84
A v Z, Order No. 5 (2002), 21:4 ASA Bulletin 810 (Ad Hoc Arbitration), 84

Conventions

Convention of 30 June 2005 on Choice of Court Agreements, entered into force on 1 October 2015, 44 ILM 1291, 2

Convention on the Law Applicable to Contractual Obligations, 19 June 1980, 1605 UNTS 28023, OJ 1980 L 266, 126

Convention on the Recognition and Enforcement of Foreign Judgments in Civil and Commercial Matters, 1 February 1971, 1144 UNTS 249, 137

Convention on the Settlement of Disputes between States and Nationals of Other States, 18 March 1965, 757 UNTS 159, 17 UST 1270, 115

Convention on the Recognition and Enforcement of Foreign Arbitral Awards, 10 June 1958, 330 UNTS 38, 21 UST 2571, 127

Geneva Convention on the Execution of Foreign Awards of 1927, 92 League of Nations Treaty Series (1929) 302, 34

Protocol on Arbitration Clauses in Commercial Matters of 1923, 27 League of Nations Treaty Series (1924) 158, 34

Index

A

Acte juridictionnel doctrine, 17, 70, 73, 85, 165
Alternative dispute resolution (ADR), 44
2006 Amendments to the UNCITRAL Model Law
  interim measure
    Article 17(2), 167
  provisional measures, 168-169
    Article 17(H), 171
    awards, adopted in forms of, 170
    enforcement of, 169-170
    language adoption, 170
    Quebec Code of Civil Procedure, 171-173
  travaux préparatoires, 168
Arbitral awards
  acte juridictionnel, 3
  defined, 16, 77
  Gaillard and Savage's definition, 1
  neglect of
    adjudicative theory, 3
    contractual theory, 2
  Redfern and Hunter's definition, 1-2
Arbitral institutions' influence on international commercial arbitration
  notion of contentious award in arbitral practice (*See* Arbitral practice, notion of contentious award in)
  notion of contentious award in national arbitration acts

awards, scope of enquiry on, 61
  English Arbitration Act 1996 (*See* Arbitration Act 1996)
  French Code of Civil Procedure (*See* French Code of Civil Procedure)
  notion of contentious judgment in Western law (*See* Notion of contentious judgment in Western law)
Arbitral practice, notion of contentious award in
  arbitration rules description on contentious award, 84
  Article 26 of LCIA Arbitration Rules (2014), 83
  ICC Rules, 82
Arbitration
  classical Roman law, under, 15-16
  definition, 13
    Charles Jarrosson, by, 17
    Henri Motulsky, by, 17
    Lord Campbell, description by, 30
  monodimensional model: arbitrator resolves dispute
    acte juridictionnel, 17
    award defined, 16
    classical Roman law, Arbitration under, 15-16
    element, definition by, 16
    finality, 16
    fonction juridictionnelle, 17
    goal, 15

Index

multidimensional model: arbitrator renders justice, 17
adjudicative powers types, 18
conditio sine qua non for arbitration in England, 19
international arbitration, 18–19
New York Convention
  arbitral award definition, 20
  fragmentation of international law, 22
  harmonization rule, 22–23
  notion of award, 20
  UNCITRAL Model Law, and, 20–21
  Vienna Convention, 21
nineteenth century, in, 28–30
Arbitration Act 1996
  consent awards
    arbitrators role, 121–122
    challenges, 122–127
    enforcement, 127
    section 68(2), challenges under, 124–125
    section 73(1), challenges under, 122–123
  formal requirements
    French law *vs.*, 72–73
    Section 52, 71–72
  jurisdictional awards
    null and void or inoperative arbitration agreement, 93
    section 9(1), 92
    section 30(1), 92
  non-unitary notion of award, 180
  requirements, 81
    formal (*See* subhead formal requirements)
    substantive (*See* subhead substantive requirements)
  substantive requirements
    arbitration *vs.* expert determination, 76
    award described, 73
    awards and orders, distinction between, 77
    contractual clause, 75–76
    dispute resolution clause, 74
    expert status and function, 75
    procedural criterion, 73–74
    provisional awards, 78–79
    res judicata, 80
    section 39, 78
    section 47, 77
Arbitration Institute of the Stockholm Chamber of Commerce (SCC), 42
Arbitrators
  consent awards under Arbitration Act 1996, role in
    issue of validity of compromise (section 30), 122
    putative arbitrators, 122
    section 51, 122
    settlement agreements, 121–122
Awards ante causam
  emergence of provisional adjudicatory power (*See* Emergence of provisional adjudicatory power *ante causam*)
  provisional measures (*See* Provisional measures)
  provisional protection and interplays between courts and arbitrators
  courts' jurisdiction before constitution of tribunal, 144–145
  principle of complementarity (*See* Principle of complementarity in French and English Arbitration Law)

C

CAM. *See* Milan Chamber of Arbitration (CAM)
China International Economic and Trade Arbitration Commission (CIETAC), 42
CIETAC. *See* China International Economic and Trade Arbitration Commission (CIETAC)

206

Index

Cognitio extra ordinaria, 55
Competence-competence principle, 91
Compromise
  consent judgments and orders, 119
  defined, 118
  element of, 119
  Tomlin order, 119
    Community Care North East v. Dashwood, 120
    Sirius International Insurance Co v. FAI General Insurance Ltd, 119–120
Consent awards
  adjudicative nature of, 139–140
  Arbitration Act 1996
    arbitrators' role, 121–122
    challenges, 122–127
    enforcement, 127
    section 68(2), challenges under, 124–125
    section 73(1), challenges under, 122–123
  England, in
    Arbitration Act 1996 (*See* subhead: Arbitration Act 1996)
    national framework (*See* subhead: national framework: England)
  France, in
    French arbitration law (*See* French arbitration law)
    French Code of Civil Procedure: consent awards (*See* French Code of Civil Procedure)
  French Code of Civil Procedure
    contrat de transaction, 128–130
    jugement sur accord des parties, 130–131
  ICC arbitration
    forms of consent awards, 113–114
    settlement agreements (Article 20), 111–112
    statistics on consent awards, 112–113
  UNCITRAL's instrument, 114
  national framework: England
    compromise (*See* Compromise)
    consent order, 120
    estoppels, 121
    Model Law and section 51 of Arbitration Act 1996
      relationship between, 118
    Section 51 of Arbitration Act 1996, 118
  UNCITRAL Model Law on International Commercial Arbitration
    Article 30(1), 114, 116–117
    drafting of, 116
    request for an award by consent, 117
    revised draft of UNCITRAL Arbitration Rules, 117
    travaux préparatoires, 114–115
    unilateral request, 117
Consent judgments, 59
Consent orders, 120
Contentious awards
  notion
    arbitral practice, in (*See* Arbitral practice, notion of contentious award in)
    national arbitration acts, in (*See* National arbitration acts, notion of contentious award in)
Contentious judgments, 59
Contractualization
  description, 4–5
  of public justice *vs.* judicialization of private justice, 4–5
Convention on the Execution of Foreign Arbitral Awards (1927), 34–35

D

Declaratory judgments, 59
DIS. *See* German Institute of Arbitration (DIS)

Index

E

ECHR. *See* European Court of Human Rights (ECHR)
Emergence of provisional adjudicatory power *ante causam*
  ICC arbitration rules
    application and proceedings, 159–163
    decision, 163–164
    emergency arbitration decision, effects on proceedings, 164–165
    exclusion of emergency arbitration, 158–159
    State Courts, interplays with, 165
  ICDR Rules
    Article 6 of 2014 ICDR Rules, 152
    Emergency Measures of Protection (Article 37), 152
    request for interim measures (Article 7), 152
  LCIA Arbitration Rules
    application for emergency arbitrator, 155
    appointment of emergency arbitrator, 155
    Article 9.5, 155
    Article 9.9, 156
    autonomous test, 156
    emergency arbitrator and state courts, interactions between (Article 9.12), 157
    emergency relief: Article 9B, 154–155
    thema probandum, 156
  SCC Arbitration Rules, 152–154
Emergency arbitrator
  appointment of, 150
  arbitral institutions for (*See* Emergence of provisional adjudicatory power *ante causam*)
Estoppels, 121

European Court of Human Rights (ECHR)
  arbitral tribunal and state court, 47

F

Final award
  defined, 77, 78
Finality, 16
  Cour de cassation, description by, 68–70
  res judicata *vs.*, 68
Final judgements, 55
Fiona test, 94
French arbitration law
  alternatives to lack of enforcement of domestic consent awards
    Article 1441-4 of Code of Civil Procedure, 136–137
    Article 1567 of Code of Civil Procedure, 134–135
    court, identification of, 135
    homologation, 135
    juridiction gracieuse, 135–136
    procédure gracieuse, 135
    transaction with *jugement de donner acte*, 134
  challenges to domestic consent awards, 137
  international or foreign consent awards enforced, 131–132
  challenges of domestic awards, 132–133
  dispute, nature of, 133
  general rules, 132
  'procès-verbal d'arbitrage et de transaction' document, 134
French Code of Civil Procedure
  consent awards
    contrat de transaction, 128–130
    jugement sur accord des parties, 130–131
  contrat de transaction
    Article 1567, 130
    definition by Article 2044, 128

elements of, 129
divergences
  existence of award, 84–85
  validity of award, 85
formal requirements
  claims and arguments of parties (Article 1482), 63
  domestic arbitration (Article 1483), 63
  mistake or omission (Article 1485(2)), 64
  nullity of award, 63–64
  partial nullity, 64–65
  provisions for domestic arbitration (Article 1506), 63
  signing of awards (Article 1513), 62
jugement sur accord des parties
  jugement de donner acte, 130–131
  jugement d'expédient, 130
jurisdictional awards
  Article 1448(1), 91
  competence-competence principle, 91
non-unitary notion of award, 178–179
substantive requirements
  acte juridictionnel, 66
  annulment proceedings, 65–66
  functus officio doctrine, 66–67
  notion of international arbitral award, 65
  res judicata effect, 66–67
Functus officio doctrine, 66–67

G

Geneva Convention on the Execution of Foreign Arbitral Awards of 1927, 34–35
Geneva Protocol on Arbitration Clauses, 34
German Institute of Arbitration (DIS), 42

H

Harmonization rules (New York Convention), 22–23
Hong Kong International Arbitration Centre (HKIAC), 42

I

ICC Arbitration Rules
  application and proceedings, 159–163
  decision, 163–164
  emergency arbitration decision, effects on proceedings, 164–165
    Article 29(3) and (4), 164
    Article 6(6), appendix V, 165
  exclusion of emergency arbitration as arbitration proceedings (Article 5(2), appendix V), 162
  Article 29(5), 158–159
  Article 29(6)(a), 158
  Article 1, appendix V, 159–160
  challenge, 161
  FIDIC model contracts, 158
  pre-arbitral procedure, 158
  procedural timetable, 162–163
  termination of proceedings (Article 1(6), appendix V), 160–161
  State Courts, interplays with, 165
ICC Vienna Congress, 35
ICDR. *See* International Centre for Dispute Resolution (ICDR)
Institutions on international commercial arbitration
arbitration
  beginning of twenty-first century, 41–46
  Lord Campbell, description by, 30
  nineteenth century, in, 28–30
  second half of twentieth century, 38–41
  twentieth century, in first half of, 30–38

Index

consecration of institutions
  actors contributing to institutionalization, 41–43
  ADR (*See* Alternative dispute resolution (ADR))
consequences of institutional roots
  bureaucratization, 46
  empirical works, 48
  ICC procedure, 46–47
  international adjudicative bodies, 47
  judicialization of arbitration, 48
  paradigmatic shift, 48
ICC (*See* International Chamber of Commerce (ICC))
institutionalism
  ICC, 28
  political sciences, in, 26
  sociological studies, in, 26
privatization of justice
  ADR, 44
  crisis of civil justice, 44–45
  judges, 45–46
Interlocutory judgements, 55
International Centre for Dispute Resolution (ICDR), 42
International Centre for Dispute Resolution (ICDR) Rules
  Article 6 of 2014 ICDR Rules, 152
  Emergency Measures of Protection (Article 37), 152
  request for interim measures (Article 7), 152
International Centre for the Settlement of Investment Disputes (ICSID) Arbitration Rules, 114–115
International Chamber of Commerce (ICC), 6
  consent awards, 110–114
  contentious award, 82
  Convention on the Execution of Foreign Arbitral Awards (1927), 34–35
  draft awards, review of, 46
  Geneva Convention on the Execution of Foreign Arbitral Awards of 1927, 34–35
  Geneva Protocol on Arbitration Clauses, 34
  historical overview of International Court of Arbitration, 33
  ICC Arbitration Rules (*See* ICC Arbitration Rules)
  impetus in favour of arbitration
    Convention on the Execution of Foreign Arbitral Awards (1927), 34–35
    Geneva Convention on the Execution of Foreign Arbitral Awards of 1927, 34–35
    Geneva Protocol on Arbitration Clauses, 34
  institutionalism, 30
  international cases, 42–43
  international commercial arbitration, difficulties implementing
    ICC Vienna Congress, 35
    UNIDROIT, 35–38
  international regime, 38–41
  terms of reference, 46
  UNIDROIT, 35–38
  Vienna Congress, 35
International commercial arbitration, arbitral institutions influence on. *See* Arbitral institutions' influence on international commercial arbitration
International Federation of Consulting Engineers (FIDIC) model contracts, 158
Irreparable harm test, 156

J

Judgment
  common law tradition, defined under, 57
  consent, 59

contentious, 59
declaratory, 59
final, 55
interlocutory, 55
order *vs.*, 58
Romano-canonical tradition, defined under, 57
Zuckerman definition of, 57
Judicialization
administration of civil justice, 5
Alec Stone Sweet's definition of, 4
description, 4
of private justice *vs.* contractualization of public justice, 4–5
private matters, in, 4–5
Jugement de donner acte, 134
Juridiction gracieuse
defined, 135
Jurisdictional awards
arbitral tribunals, jurisdictional decisions by, 88–89
Article 16(3) of 2006 UNCITRAL Model Law, 105
bifurcation, issue of, 94–96
common law perspective, 98–99
monodimensional model, 88–89
negative jurisdictional ruling
applicable test for review, 104–105
challenges against, admissibility of, 103–104
Germany, 102
recours en annulation, admissibility of, 104
section 1059 ZPO (German Code of Civil Procedure), 102
UNCITRAL Model Law, 102
peculiarities of recourse under Article 16(3) of Model Law
Articles 34 and 36 of Model Law, 106–107
two-step challenge procedure, 105–106
positive jurisdictional rulings, 99–101
role of state courts in pre-award phase
bifurcation, issue of, 94–96

England and other jurisdictions, 92–94
France, 90–92
Romano-canonical perspective, 97
UNCITRAL Model Law
Article 16(1), 105–106
Article 16(3), 106–107

L

London Court of International Arbitration (LCIA) Arbitration Rules
application for emergency arbitrator, 155
appointment of emergency arbitrator, 155
Article 9.5, 155
Article 9.9, 156
autonomous test, 156
emergency arbitrator and state courts, interactions between (Article 9.12), 157
emergency relief: Article 9B, 154–155
thema probandum, 156

M

Milan Chamber of Arbitration (CAM), 42
Monodimensional adjudicative model: arbitrator resolves dispute
acte juridictionnel, 17
award defined, 16
classical Roman law, Arbitration under, 15–16
element, definition by, 16
finality, 16
fonction juridictionnelle, 17
goal of, 15
Multidimensional model: arbitrator renders justice
adjudicative powers, types, 18
conditio sine qua non for arbitration in England, 19
international arbitration, 18

211

Index

N

National arbitration acts, notion of contentious award in
  description of awards, 61–62
  English Arbitration Act 1996 (*See* Arbitration Act 1996)
  French Code of Civil Procedure (*See* French Code of Civil Procedure)
  scope of enquiry on awards, 61
New York Convention, 14, 109
  arbitral award definition, 20
  arbitration agreement, presumptive validity of, 40
  Article VII(1), 127
  benefits to ICC and its institutional model of administered arbitration, 40–41
  enforcement of awards, 40
  fragmentation of international law, 22
  harmonization rules, 22–23
  notion of award, 20
  UNCITRAL Model Law, and, 20–21
  Vienna Convention, 21
Non-unitary notion of award
  adoption of, 181
  awards *ante causam*, 176
  consent awards, 176
  definition, 180–181
  emergency awards (Changed to awards *ante causam* in text in page 176)
  English Arbitration Act 1996, 180
  French Code of Civil Procedure, 178–179
  international commercial arbitration, 175–176
  jurisdictional power, 176
  legitimization, 182–183
  multidimensional mode, 177–178
  notion of arbitral award defined, 179
  power to record settlements, 176–177
  problematic aspect in, 181
  provisional power in emergency arbitration proceedings, 177
  UNCITRAL Model Law, 178
Notion of awards
  arbitral award defined, 179
  contentious award (*See* Notion of contentious award)
  international commercial arbitration, in
    arbitral award, uncertainties regarding definition of, 1–4
    scope and limitations, 8–9
    theory and methodology, 4–8
  non-unitary notion of award (*See* Non-unitary notion of award)
Notion of contentious award
  in arbitral practice
    arbitration rules description on contentious award, 84
    Article 26 of LCIA Arbitration Rules (2014), 83
    ICC Rules, 82
  national arbitration acts, in
    description of awards, 61–62
    English Arbitration Act 1996 (*See* Arbitration Act 1996)
    French Code of Civil Procedure (*See* French Code of Civil Procedure)
    scope of enquiry on awards, 61
Notion of contentious judgment in Western law
  classic Roman procedure and absence of *ius dicere*
    apud iudicem phase, 54
    in iure phase, 54
    ius civile, 53–54
    litis contestatio agreement, 54
    ordo iudiciorum, 53
  contemporary epiphanies
    action and claim, 58
    consent judgments, 59
    contentious judgments, 59
    declaratory judgments, 59
    judgment *vs.* order, 58

Romano-canonical and common law traditions, 56
extra cognitio and emergence of *ius dicere*, 55–56
final judgements, 55
interlocutory judgements, 55
in iure and *apud iudicem* phases distinction between, 55
partial judgements, 55
historical inceptions, 52
   classic Roman procedure and absence of *ius dicere*, 53–55
   extra cognitio and emergence of *ius dicere*, 55–56
   ius dicere
      absence of, 53–55
      emergence of, 55–56
   judgments, effects of, 59–60
Nullity of award, 63–64

O

Order
   judgment vs., 58
Ordinance
   Romano-canonical tradition, defined under, 57

P

Partial awards, 77
Partial judgements, 55
Partial nullity of awards, 64–65
Patrick Glenn's theory of legal traditions, 7
Pound Conference, 44
Prima facie test, 91, 94
Principle of complementarity in French and English Arbitration Law
   arbitration agreement binding, 145
   Article 9A and 9B LCIA Rules, 150
   Article 28(2) ICC Rules, 147
   Article 17(J) Model law, 146
   Article 1449 of French Code of Civil Procedure, 146

emergency arbitrator, appointment of, 150
frustration of arbitration agreements, 149
interim measures, 149
provisional relief: section 44 of English Arbitration Act 1996, 149–150
US Federal Arbitration Act (FAA), 150–151
Provisional measures
   categories, 142
   Gaillard and Savage, description on, 142
   Gary Born, definition, 141–142
   Redfern and Hunter, presentation, 141
   Romano-Canonical and Common Law Traditions
      Article 1449(2) of the French Code of Civil Procedure, 142
      fumus boni iuris, 144
      imminent danger, 144
      periculum in mora, 143
      quia timet, ingredients for, 144
   Sébastien Besson, definition on, 141
Putative arbitrators, 122

Q

Quebec Code of Civil Procedure, 171–173
   Article 638, 171–172

R

Res dubia, 128
Res judicata
   defined, 60
   English Arbitration Act 1996
      cause of action estoppel, 80–81
      functus officio, 80
   French Code of Civil Procedure
      arbitral appeal, 70
      concentration des moyens principle, 67–68

Index

conception négative, 67
conception positive, 67
finality vs. res judicata, 68
functus officio doctrine, 66–67
International Law Association definition of, 60
Res litigiosa, 128

S

Settlement agreement, 137–138
 enforcement of, 115
 recording of, 115
 revised draft of UNCITRAL Arbitration Rules, 117
Singapore International Arbitration Centre (SIAC), 42
Stockholm Chamber of Commerce (SCC) Arbitration Rules, 152–154

T

Tomlin order, 118–121

U

UNCITRAL Draft Uniform Instrument on the Enforcement of International Commercial Settlement Agreements, 114
UNCITRAL Model Law, 19
international commercial arbitration: consent awards
 Article 30(1), 114, 116–117
 drafting of, 116
 request for an award by consent, 117
 revised draft of UNCITRAL Arbitration Rules, 117
 travaux préparatoires, 114–115
 unilateral request, 117
New York Convention and, 20–21
non-unitary notion of award, 178
UNIDROIT, 35–38
US Federal Arbitration Act (FAA), 150–151

V

Vienna Convention, 21, 22

W

Westphalian conception of international commercial arbitration, 179–180
Woolf Report of 1996, 44

214

INTERNATIONAL ARBITRATION LAW LIBRARY

1. Moshe Hirsch, *The Arbitration Mechanism of the International Center for the Settlement of Investment Disputes*, 1993 (ISBN 07-923-1993-1).
2. Aida B. Avanessian, *Iran-United States Claims Tribunal in Action*, 1993 (ISBN 18-533-3902-4).
3. Isaak I. Dore, *The UNCITRAL Framework for Arbitration in Contemporary Perspective*, 1993 (ISBN 18-533-3573-8).
4. Vesna Lazić, *Insolvency Proceedings and Commercial Arbitration*, 1998 (ISBN 90-411-1115-8).
5. Joachim Frick, *Arbitration in Complex International Contracts*, 2001 (ISBN 90-411-1662-1).
6. Katherine Lynch, *The Forces of Economic Globalization: Challenges to the Regime of International Commercial Arbitration*, 2003 (ISBN 90-411-1994-9).
7. Christoph Liebscher, *The Healthy Award: Challenge in International Commercial Arbitration*, 2003 (ISBN 90-411-2011-4).
8. Hamid G. Gharavi, *The International Effectiveness of the Annulment of an Arbitral Award*, 2003 (ISBN 90-411-1717-2).
9. Abdulhay Sayed, *Corruption in International Trade and Commercial Arbitration*, 2004 (ISBN 90-411-2236-2).
10. Gabrielle Kaufmann-Kohler & Thomas Schultz, *Online Dispute Resolution: Challenges for Contemporary Justice*, 2004 (ISBN 90-411-2318-0).
11. Christopher R. Drahozal & Richard W. Naimark (eds), *Towards a Science of International Arbitration: Collected Empirical Research*, 2005 (ISBN 90-411-2322-9).
12. Ali Yeşilirmak, *Provisional Measures in International Commercial Arbitration*, 2005 (ISBN 90-411-2353-9).
13. Christian Bühring-Uhle, *Arbitration and Mediation in International Business*, second revised edition, 2006 (ISBN 978-9-041-12256-8).
14. Bernard Hanotiau, *Complex Arbitrations: Multiparty, Multicontract, Multiissue and Class Actions*, 2006 (ISBN 978-9-041-12442-5).
15. Loukas A. Mistelis & Julian D.M. Lew (eds), *Pervasive Problems in International Arbitration*, 2006 (ISBN 978-9-041-12450-0).
16. Julian D.M. Lew & Loukas A. Mistelis (eds), *Arbitration Insights – Twenty Years of the Annual Lecture of the School of International Arbitration, Sponsored by Freshfields Bruckhaus Deringer*, 2006 (ISBN 978-9-041-12606-1).
17. Mark Kantor, *Valuation for Arbitration: Compensation Standards, Valuation Methods and Expert Evidence*, 2008 (ISBN 978-9-041-12735-8).
18. Christoph Brunner, *Force Majeure and Hardship under General Contract Principles: Exemption for Non-Performance in International Arbitration*, 2009 (ISBN 978-90-411-2792-1).

19. Loukas A. Mistelis & Stavros L. Brekoulakis (eds), *Arbitrability: International & Comparative Perspectives*, 2009 (ISBN 978-90-411-2730-3).
20. Sam Luttrell, *Bias Challenges in International Commercial Arbitration: The Need for a 'Real Danger' Test*, 2009 (ISBN 978-90-411-3191-1).
21. Monique Sasson, *Substantive Law in Investment Treaty Arbitration: The Unsettled Relationship between International Law and Municipal Law*, 2010 (ISBN 978-90-411-3223-9).
22. Ileana M. Smeureanu, *Confidentiality in International Commercial Arbitration*, 2011 (ISBN 978-90-411-3226-0).
23. Won Kidane, *China-Africa Dispute Settlement: The Law, Economics and Culture of Arbitration*, 2011 (ISBN 978-90-411-3674-9).
24. Karel Daele, *Challenge and Disqualification of Arbitrators in International Arbitration*, 2012 (ISBN 978-90-411-3799-9).
25. Crina Baltag, *The Energy Charter Treaty: The Notion of Investor*, 2012 (ISBN 978-90-411-3428-8).
26. Alexandra Diehl, *The Core Standard of International Investment Protection: Fair and Equitable Treatment*, 2012 (ISBN 978-90-411-3869-9).
27. Manuel Indlekofer, *International Arbitration and the Permanent Court of Arbitration*, 2013 (ISBN 978-90-411-4766-0).
28. Günther J. Horvath & Stephan Wilske (eds), *Guerrilla Tactics in International Arbitration*, 2013 (ISBN 978-90-411-4002-9).
29. Albert Badia, *Piercing the Veil of State Enterprises in International Arbitration*, 2014 (ISBN 978-90-411-5162-9).
30. Nadja Erk, *Parallel Proceedings in International Arbitration: A Comparative European Perspective*, 2014 (ISBN 978-90-411-5264-0).
31. Simon Vorburger, *International Arbitration and Cross-Border Insolvency: Comparative Perspectives*, 2014 (ISBN 978-90-411-5419-4).
32. Ahmad Ali Ghouri, *Interaction and Conflict of Treaties in Investment Arbitration*, 2015 (ISBN 978-90-411-5417-0).
33. Reto Marghitola, *Document Production in International Arbitration*, 2015 (ISBN 978-90-411-5159-9).
34. Alfonso Gómez-Acebo, *Party-Appointed Arbitrators in International Commercial Arbitration*, 2016 (ISBN 978-90-411-6671-5).
35. Jonas von Goeler, *Third-Party Funding in International Arbitration and Its Impact on Procedure*, 2016 (ISBN 978-90-411-5015-8).
36. Dean Lewis, *The Interpretation and Uniformity of the UNCITRAL Model Law on International Commercial Arbitration: Focusing on Australia, Hong Kong and Singapore*, 2016 (ISBN 978-90-411-6700-2).
37. Stavros Brekoulakis, Julian D.M. Lew & Loukas Mistelis (eds), *The Evolution and Future of International Arbitration*, 2016 (ISBN 978-90-411-7004-0).
38. Rémy Gerbay, *The Functions of Arbitral Institutions*, 2016 (ISBN 978-90-411-6217-5).

39. Maximilian Clasmeier, *Arbitral Awards as Investments: Treaty Interpretation and the Dynamics of International Investment Law*, 2017 (ISBN 978-90-411-8357-6).
40. Tony Cole (ed.), *The Roles of Psychology in International Arbitration*, 2017 (ISBN 978-90-411-5921-2).
41. Pietro Ferrario, *The Adaptation of Long-Term Gas Sale Agreements by Arbitrators*, 2017 (ISBN 978-90-411-8232-6).
42. Jacob B. van de Velden, *Finality in Litigation The Law and Practice of Preclusion: Res Judicata (Merger and Estoppel), Abuse of Process and Recognition of Foreign Judgments*, 2017 (ISBN 978-90-411-8342-2).
43. Dolores Bentolila, *Arbitrators as Lawmakers*, 2017 (ISBN 978-90-411-8354-5).
44. Giacomo Marchisio, *The Notion of Award in International Commercial Arbitration: A Comparative Analysis of French Law, English Law, and the UNCITRAL Model Law*, 2017 (ISBN 978-90-411-8391-0).